The Politics of Dissolution

The Quest
for a National
Identity & the
American
Civil War

The Politics
of Dissolution

Marshall L
DeRosa

EDITOR

Transaction Publishers
New Brunswick (U.S.A.) and London (U.K.)

Copyright © 1998 by Transaction Publishers, New Brunswick, New Jersey 08903.

All rights reserved under International and Pan-American Copyright Conventions. No part of this book may be reproduced or transmitted in any form or by any means, electronic or mechanical, including photocopy, recording, or any information storage and retrieval system, without prior permission in writing from the publisher. All inquiries should be addressed to Transaction Publishers, Rutgers—The State University, New Brunswick, New Jersey 08903.

This book is printed on acid-free paper that meets the American National Standard for Permanence of Paper for Printed Library Materials.

Library of Congress Catalog Number: 97-29445
ISBN: 1-56000-349-9
Printed in the United States of America

Library of Congress Cataloging-in-Publication Data

DeRosa, Marshall L., 1955–
    The politics of dissolution : the quest for a national identity and the American Civil War / Marshall L. DeRosa, editor.
        p. cm.
    ISBN: 1-56000-349-9
    1. United States—History—Civil War, 1861–1965—Causes—Sources. 2. United States—Politics and government—1857–1861—Sources. 3. United States—Politics and government—1861–1865—Sources. 4. Secession—Southern States—Sources. 5. Rhetoric—Political aspects—United States—History—19th century. I. DeRosa, Marshall L., 1955–   .
E459.D37   1997
937.7'11—dc21   97-29445
                                                                       CIP

When a sieve is shaken, the husks appear;

so do a man's faults when he speaks.

As the test of what the potter molds is in the furnace,

so in his conversation is the test of a man.

The fruit of a tree shows the care it has had;

so too does a man's speech disclose the bent of his mind.

Praise no man before he speaks,

for it is then that men are tested.

(Sirach, 27: 4-7)

ACKNOWLEDGMENTS

Several colleagues stand out as facilitating the final product you have before you. Political Scientist Ross M. Lence (University of Houston) and historians Clyde Wilson (University of South Carolina), Stephen D. Engel (Florida Atlantic University), and Richard Gamble (Palm Beach Atlantic College).

My wife Mary and our three children Elijah, Isabella, and Abigail, also deserve credit for patiently yielding to me the time and support requisite to what proved to be a six year project. My earnest thanks to them.

Contents

Preface

I

Several factors have led to the compilation of the following antebellum U. S. Senate speeches. They include: First, an appreciation that the union of States organized under the Articles of Confederation was incompletely supplanted in 1789 with the adoption of the Constitution; specifically, the extent to which the U.S. Constitution altered national and state relations was significantly ambiguous. As the union matured much of the ambiguity attendant on the drafting and ratification processes was incrementally addressed, but time also exacerbated the difficulties attendant on two governments exercising concurrent jurisdiction within the same territorial limits.[1] The late antebellum period marks the nexus where substantive disagreements over the extent of national and state governmental powers collided, resulting in unprecedented damage to the ties that had held the Union together for the previous seventy-one years. As the speeches of the thirty-sixth Congress make clear, House and Senate members were essentially attempting to discern the substance of the Union regarding states' rights and national supremacy within the context of American federalism—notably the fundamental point of contention during the drafting and ratifying conventions from 1787-1791.[2] As was the case during the Founding, underlying the partisan debates in the thirty-sixth Congress was the issue of liberty, which can be pointedly defined as the absence of unjustifiable coercion;[3] and, in this particular instance, the use of national coercion as a means to maintaining the Union vis-à-vis a State's liberty to exercise the right of self-determination.

Second, the assertion that the southern states stumbled headlong into secession with such rapidity and passion that they knew not what they were doing is simply wrong. Many Senators in the South and North were very much concerned with the intensity and duration of an impending civil war between the States; nevertheless, the exit of southern States from the Union was deliberative and, from the southern perspective, constitutional. Regardless, conventional scholarship portrays a distorted account of events. For example, in a chapter titled "The Counterrevolution of 1861," Professor James McPherson cites eighty-six sources, mostly from antebellum newspapers and recent studies. Of the eighty-six citations there is only one substantive reference to speeches made in the thirty-sixth Congress. Certainly one should expect a wide range of opinions and motives coming to the fore at such a momentous constitutional and political crisis, especially in openly partisan publications such as newspapers and pamphlets; but characterizations such as "the enmity of the Southerner for the Northerner surpassed that of the Greek for the Turk" or that the southern view was that "a Lady's thimble will hold all the blood that will be shed"[4] are distortions. Eminent contemporary scholars should be wary of placing undue emphasis on the views of antebellum writers who had little or no accountability to an electoral base, as was not the case with Senators from the southern States. The speeches delivered on the floor of the Senate manifest a very different mood than that of enmity, as would be expected when intelligent and patriotic men, North, South, and West, accountable to their constituencies—their respective States and political parties—embarked on uncharted political waters. Moreover, this collection of U.S. Senate speeches raises, at a minimum, substantial objections to claims that the secession movement was non-deliberative, irrational, and unconstitutional. Secession was not only extensively analyzed, but also considered by many Senators as a necessary step towards peaceful reconstruction of the Union.

Third, because these pre-Seventeenth Amendment Senators were accountable to the prevailing political sentiments of their respective state constituencies through their respective state legislatures—a political reality reiterated time and again in the course of their speeches—my editorial decision to include in this collection only Senate speeches, without House speeches, was made. This does not mean that the speeches made in the U.S. House of Representatives were neither insightful nor influential. Neither is it meant to imply that the Senate speeches excluded lacked those two qualities. What it does mean is that the speeches included are representative of official policies and public sentiments, without being redundant.

Fourth, the superb oratory of the period needs to be recovered and made readily available. The speeches are both eloquent and learned, not to mention high political drama. These speeches are not standard special interest advocacy; rather, they emanated from an appreciation of history—classical and contemporary—and civic republicanism to such an extent that they are informative about the fundamental principles of American constitutionalism. This too was intentional as the Senators engaged in determined efforts to explicate the foundations of the American republican regime for their contemporaries and posterity.

Fifth, the history lessons that emanate from these speeches are significant. The issues of the late antebellum period were not new to American politics, somewhat incrementally heightened yes, but not new. Senators orated about the historical challenges to the Union—such as the Virginia and Kentucky Resolutions, the Hartford Convention of 1814, nullification crises of the 1820s and 1830s, the various territorial disputes, and the Douglas-Lincoln debates—in attempts to legitimatize their respective policies towards secession. These historical events were significant in the intellectual development of antebellum political mindsets, and because 1860-1861 rationalizations for and against secession recapitulate those events from historical perspectives, we are treated to insightful lessons in American political theory and history. As Senators built evidence for their respective positions regarding the necessity and constitutionality of secession and the application of national coercion, they re-articulated theoretical and historical arguments of previous events and controversies; thus, even though the "Political Bands which connected" North and South began to snap well before the secession winter of 1860-1861,[5] focusing attention on Senate debates from the late antebellum period will include historical accounts, albeit distorted at times, of those earlier events. But even the historical distortions are in and of themselves significantly informative. They indicate that all sides were fervently committed to their varying interpretations of American republicanism, with the varying interpretations grounded in what the respective adherents believed to be constitutional and/or justifiable.

And sixth, these speeches are relevant to contemporary inquiries into democratic theory. As contemporary political, economic, and technological developments rapidly shift power from the traditional

American federal arrangement to governmental, non-governmental, and corporate transnational organizations, Americans ignore at their own peril significant debates addressing territorial republicanism and its relationship to the "extended republic."[6] As was the issue in 1776, 1787, and 1861, liberty versus coercion is fundamental to understanding and developing American constitutionalism and its concomitant the rule of law; and the proximity of the government to the governed—the heart of the extended republic debates in the Philadelphia 1787 and Montgomery 1861 conventions—is a key element.

II

The politics of dissolution that eventually culminated in the American Civil War resulted from an accumulation of sectionally divisive political, economical, and cultural events. These events spanned a period of some thirty to forty years. The crux of national debate during the secession winter of 1860-1861 centered on the nature of the American republican experiment, and the speeches that follow constitute the official statements of the public men—South, North, and West—as they struggled with policy questions that led them to the assessment of the national identity.[7] Southerners were particularly conscious of what they perceived to be a train of events that justified their political separation from the United States in order to preserve the republican experiment. And it was a political separation; they realized that business and cultural ties would in many cases continue unabated and perhaps even multiply. The southern secessionists were cognizant that important ties that bound the sections together transcended the U.S. Constitution, and peaceful secession—in contradistinction to southern secession met with national coercion—was integral to leaving those ties intact.

On the other hand, many northern unionists were fearful that southern political independence jeopardized northern commercial interests. Consequently, these unionists were not about to let the South secede in peace. For example, losing access to the Gulf of Mexico via the Mississippi River was a major concern. Hence, an increasingly consolidated Union was rationalized on the grounds that it was necessitated by economic interests. Accordingly, the Northern commitment to commercial freedom for northern States—on the scale of empire—justified the use of national coercion to keep the southern States within the expanding commercial orbit of the Union. This justification is particularly evident in Republican Senators' policy towards the right of secession for States organized from territories either purchased from European colonial powers or acquired as war spoils. These States, Louisiana, Florida, Texas, etc., were considered to be provincial outposts and the property of the empire, lacking certain prerogatives of the original thirteen States if those prerogatives were to be exercised to the detriment of the empire. Republican Senators viewed the admission of States into the Union as an investment in the empire, in contradistinction to a commitment to the spread of democratic principles. Accordingly, the secession of those States was viewed by Republicans as a divestment of the empire, democratic principles notwithstanding, a divestment they were unwilling to incur.

Moderates were hopeful that the 1789 model could be held together by a series of amendments and goodwill, more or less maintaining the status quo. But, as is often the case with highly controversial policy issues, passionately held positions often tend to dominate the terms and tone of the debate, and thereby the course of events. The partisan and sectional alignments which had become deeply engrained by the late antebellum period were manifest in the speaking records of individual Senators. The profound regime question over the substance of the Union increasingly dominated the politics of the late antebellum Congress. A senator's speech addressing a State's right to self-determination vis-à-vis national economic interests not only trumped all viable attempts at compromise, but hardened northern Republicans and southern Democrats in their respective positions. In other words, at this stage compromise was not a viable option as long as each side held fast to their respective positions and intended to act accordingly.

III

The rhetoric of the Congressmen who took to the floors of the House and Senate as the Union was unraveling and the Confederacy was taking shape, emanated from what can descriptively be denoted as an imaginative constitutionalism. The adjective "imaginative" is an important qualifier, insofar as it depicts subjective visions of the way things ought to be, and at this stage of American constitutional development rhetoric was utilized as an instrument to articulate and actualize the respective visions.

Obviously *imagination* is an important qualifier in the case of secession, due to the fact that successfully executed constitutional secession lacked precedent[8] and during this critical period of American constitutional development there were two mutually exclusive positions regarding a State's constitutional right to secede. It was becoming increasingly evident in the minds of the Congressmen that the 1789 model was being stretched to its governing limits. Many northerners imagined an indissoluble nation; a nation committed and competent to establish a commercial empire consisting of States, but certainly not subordinate to the States. Lincoln manifested this view when he disparagingly posited and reiterated during the crisis that a State was essentially a "district of country with inhabitants . . . If a State, in one instance, and a county in another, should be equal in the number of people, wherein is that State any better than the county."[9] Southerners, however, envisioned a confederation of sovereign States consenting to the establishment of a national government competent to the achievement of constitutionally sanctioned tasks, without coercively subjecting the States to constitutionally suspect national policies. Their battle cry of freedom was states' rights, in contradistinction to a coercive unitary union. Within the context of these two polarized views, the late antebellum congressional rhetoric was dialectical to the extent that it constituted inquiries about which model was the most legitimate and achievable. Having settled on a model, Senators proceeded to articulate to their constituents, their partisan rivals, the international community, and posterity, that their respective positions were not only constitutional, but also morally and pragmatically justified.

Significantly, these men were addressing the most profound of all regime issues—the nature and basis of the American political community—while simultaneously coping with constitutional, political, and military crises. The speeches consist of two distinct elements, dialectical positions and rhetorical pleas,[10] as the theoretical and practical necessities of the moment converged and reciprocally influenced one another. In other words, both the northern and southern leadership had the arduous task of attempting to make their respective imaginative constitutionalisms conform to the realities of practical politics and, conversely, the practical realities conform to their respective imaginative constitutional models. The culmination of the North's success in realizing this arduous task is manifested in the election of Lincoln and his administration's response to secession. The South's success is manifested in the procedurally systematic implementation of secession and the drafting and ratification of the C.S.A. Constitution.

IV

The origins of constitutionalism, which later took form in the C.S.A. Constitution, are complex. Nevertheless, certain ideas about those origins can be readily dismissed through analysis of congressional debates and the actual—in contradistinction to the presumed—constitution Southerners debated, ratified, and enforced through four years of war. Moreover, presumptions that firebrand political opportunists created the Southern constitutionalism circa 1861 and subsequently brought practical politics in tow are oversimplifications. Regional distinctiveness was recognized as a component of the constitutional arrangement ratified in 1789, and therein are to be found the distinctive origins of the southern and northern imaginative constitutionalisms; and as the course of events incrementally exacerbated certain aspects of regional diversity, the dissolution of the Union correspondingly gained momentum. The recognition by Southerners, Northerners, and later Westerners, that there existed significant regional differences intensified as the nation developed. Intensification took on a hostile tone which became increasingly obvious in national politics. As Donald Davidson instructs us, these regional differences are "best described politically, for it is in politics that the pressures that divide or unite a people finally take shape."[11] The passage of the Alien and Sedition Acts, the election of Jefferson, the War of 1812, the Missouri Compromise, the tariff controversies, the Mexican War, bleeding Kansas, John Brown, and the rise of the Republican Party, substantiate Davidson's hypothesis on a sliding scale of intensification.

Consider a typical commentary that misreads the relevance of regionalism in the sectional conflict: "Thus from the first days of southern independence there existed a widespread and self-conscious effort to create an ideology of Confederate nationalism to unite and inspire the new nation. In many particulars, this endeavor built upon antebellum attempts to encourage southern distinctiveness. . . . The creation of Confederate nationalism . . . was a prerequisite to Confederate survival,"[12] and the collateral claim that Southern nationalism was a ruse by a slaveocracy; that Southern "nationhood was itself a creation of this interest—of the dominant class's effort to protect its cherished way of life from the challenge of American national control."[13] Such conclusions are misleading oversimplifications, maintaining that elitist conspirators were uniquely behind the creation and subsequent political organization of Southern distinctiveness. Obviously, the movement towards Southern secession had an identifiable leadership, many of whom were slaveowners, but these leaders, as is the case generally for leaders in a republican political process, were constrained by the interests of those they represented, the overwhelming majority of whom were not slaveowners.[14] But the political reality of republican constraints was not unique to the South, and is certainly not convincing evidence that the peculiar institution was the essence of the C.S.A. If a slaveocracy was the mastermind behind C.S.A. secession, then how does one explain that the C.S.A. Constitution prohibited the importation of slaves, did not mandate slavery, left the issue to the States (i.e., popular sovereignty within a State, in contrast to a territory which was the common property of all the States), and was open to the admission of free States?[15] Moreover, to claim that "the realities of power distribution in the South dictated that Confederate ideology be at once elitist in purpose yet popular in appeal, a condition that became increasingly difficult to meet" may prove too much. For example, the fact that Confederate ideology had to be popular in appeal may be evidence that the elites were accountable to popular control, to the same extent that their northern counterparts were, if not more so.[16]

V

Enough has been said by way of introduction. The purpose of this collection of Senate speeches[17] is not to rehash the voluminous commentary of secondary literature on the causes of and rationalizations for secession and its aftermath. To the contrary; this collection is designed to present the rhetorical landscape of the late antebellum period as events were unfolding. Towards that end it is time to revisit the climactic senatorial orations of the secession winter of 1860-1861.

By that time the impending crisis had, indeed, arrived. As the constitutional case for a states' rights-centered federal union was being made by southern Senators in contradistinction to the Republican Party's nationalistic model, events in-doors and out-of-doors were heightening the urgency of the political circumstances to which Senators had to respond. For example the events in South Carolina—secession on December 20, the transfer of U.S. troops from Fort Moultrie to Fort Sumter, and the failure of various legislative compromise initiatives—with all the attendant economic and social developments commingled with political crises, intensified the impetus towards national dissolution. Nevertheless, in the midst of all the commotion, one should not lose sight of the fundamental issue underlying the Senate speeches included in this collection: The right of self-government within the context of the rule of law. In the final analysis, the basic balance sheet of the conflict was not the death of slavery, secession, and six hundred thousand men,[18] but rather the successes and failures of the American experiment in republican self-government.

[1] As tensions occasionally intensified and the boundaries between state and national powers needed to be explicated, the U.S. Supreme Court established nationalistic precedent with cases such as *McCulloch* v. *Maryland* [17 U.S. (4 Wheat.) 316 (1819)]—national commercial supremacy—and *Cohens* v. *Virginia* [19 U.S. (6 Wheat.) 264 (1821)]—national judicial supremacy; nevertheless, the undercurrent of states' rights continued to flow unabated.

[2] As is reflected in Publius' criticism of the Antifederalists' adherence to States' rights, such as the reference to their blind devotion to the "political monster of an *imperium in imperio*" (*The Federalist Papers*, No. 15).

[3] Liberty in this sense "does not mean all good things or the absence of all evil. It is true to be free may mean freedom to starve, to make costly mistakes, or to run mortal risks. . . . But if liberty may therefore not always seem preferable to other goods, it is a distinctive good that needs a distinctive name. . . . it describes the absence of a particular obstacle—coercion by other men. . . . It does not assure us of any particular opportunities, but leaves it to us to decide what we shall make of the circumstances in which we find ourselves"(F. A. Hayek, *The Constitution of Liberty*, [Chicago, 1960], 18-19; cited in M. Stanton Evans, *The Theme Is Freedom: Religion, Politics, And The American Tradition* [Washington, DC: Regnery Publishing, Inc., 1994], 23).

[4] James M. McPherson, *Battle Cry Of Freedom: The Civil War Era* (New York: Oxford University Press, 1988), 234, 238.

[5] See David M. Potter's *The Impending Crisis: 1848-1861* (New York: Harper Torchbooks, 1976) for a concise historical account of events.

[6] See the Antifederalists' concerns about the centralization of economic and political power in *The Complete Anti-Federalist*, Herbert J. Storing, ed., (Chicago, 1981), Madison's understanding of the extended republic in *The Federalist* #10, and for a more recent view Robert A. Dahl, "A Democratic Dilemma: System Effectiveness versus Citizen Participation," *Political Science Quarterly*, vol. 109, no. 1, Spring 1994, pp. 23-34.

[7] See M. E. Bradford, "A Long Farewell To Union," in *Against The Barbarians and Other Reflections on Familiar Themes* (Columbia: University of Missouri Press, 1992), 216.

[8] The American Revolution excepted; see Bradford, "All To Do Over: The Revolutionary Precedent and the Secession of 1861" in *A Better Guide Than Reason: Federalists & Anti-Federalists* (New Brunswick, NJ: Transaction Publishers, 1994), 153-167. Most senators, Republicans and Democrats, acknowledged the right to secede, but for the Republicans it was a revolutionary right in contradistiction to a constitutional right.

[9] Potter, 561.

[10] I am indebted to Richard Weaver's *The Ethics of Rhetoric* (Davis, CA: Hermagoras Press, 1985) for this distinction.

[11] Donald Davidson, *Regionalism And Nationalism In The United States: The Attack on Leviathan* (New Brunswick, NJ: Transaction Publishers, 1991), 22.

[12] Drew Gilpin Faust, *The Creation of Confederate Nationalism* (Baton Rouge: LSU Press, 1988), 14.

[13] Ibid., 15.

[14] See Ludwell H. Johnson, *North Against South: The American Iliad, 1848-1877* (Columbia, SC: The Foundation for American Education, 1993), 1.

[15] See my *The Confederate Constitution of 1861: An Inquiry Into American Constitutionalism* (University of Missouri Press, 1991).

[16] Many view Southern nationalism through anti-southern spectacles. A case in point is the notion pertaining to southern millenarianism. As if the southern leadership, in a disingenuous and unholy

way, attempted to draft the Almighty into its ranks as a means to obscure nefarious political/economic objectives. For example, Professor Faust maintains that Southerners " . . . rendered religion and nationalism inseparable. Such an ideology transformed God himself into a nationalist and made war for political independence into a crusade" (Faust, 28). The Northern leadership's tendency of cloaking political objectives with religious zealotry is manifested in the symbolic battle hymn that dwarfs Southerners invoking the blessings of Divine Providence; it begins, *Mine eyes have seen the glory of the Coming of the Lord; He is trampling out the vintage where the grapes of wrath are stored; He hath loosed the fateful lightning of his terrible swift sword; His truth is marching on.* Another example is Lincoln's second inaugural. Within the context of the American tradition, it was not that the South recruited God to their cause; rather, the South sought divine vindication in its struggle for Southern independence. Initially, however, the paramount emphasis was constitutional/political and not theological, as the antebellum Senate speeches make clear.

[17] In way of disclaimer, permit me to reiterate that many pertinent speeches from the House and Senate by necessity could not be included in this collection for length and readability reasons. The speeches included (from the *Congressional Globe*, 36th Congress, second session) are, however, representative without being redundant.

[18] *The Impending Crisis* concludes: "Exactly four years after the surrender—that is, on April 14, 1865—Robert Anderson returned to raise the flag over Fort Sumter. By then, the sounds of battle had given way to the stillness at Appomattox and the issues that inflamed the antebellum years had been settled. Slavery was dead; secession was dead; and six hundred thousand men were dead. That was the basic balance sheet of the sectional conflict"(Potter, 583).

1

Party Platforms for the Election of 1860

Constitutional Union Party Platform[1]

Whereas, Experience has demonstrated that Platforms adopted by the partisan conventions of the country have had the effect to mislead and deceive the people, and at the same time to widen the political divisions of the country, by the creation and encouragement of geographical and sectional parties; therefore

Resolved, that it is both the part of patriotism and duty to *recognize* no political principle other than THE CONSTITUTION OF THE COUNTRY, THE UNION OF THE STATES, AND THE ENFORCEMENT OF THE LAWS, and that, as representatives of the Constitutional Union men of the country, in National Convention assembled, we hereby pledge ourselves to maintain, protect, and defend, separately and unitedly, these great principles of public liberty and national safety, against all enemies, at home and abroad; believing that thereby peace may once more be restored to the country; the rights of the People of the States reestablished, and the Government again placed in

---

[1] John Bell of Tennessee and Edward Everett of Massachusetts were the party's presidential and vice-presidential nominees. They carried Virginia, Kentucky, and Tennessee, with approximately 600,000 popular votes and 39 electoral college votes. [The *National Party Platforms, 1840-1956*, Kirk H. Porter and Donald Bruce Johnson, eds. (The University of Illinois Press, 1956), 30-33, is the source of the information in chapter one.]

that condition of justice, fraternity and equality, which, under the example and Constitution of our fathers, has solemnly bound every citizen of the United States to maintain a more perfect union, establish justice, insure domestic tranquillity, provide for the common defense, promote the general welfare, and secure the blessings of liberty to ourselves and our posterity.

Democratic Party (Northern Faction) Platform[2]

1. *Resolved*, That we, the Democracy of the Union in Convention assembled, hereby declare our affirmance of the resolutions unanimously adopted and declared as a platform of principles by the Democratic Convention at Cincinnati, in the year 1856, believing that Democratic principles are unchangeable in their nature, when applied to the same subject matters; and we recommend, as the only further resolutions, the following;[3]

[. . . 1. That the Federal Government is one of limited power, derived solely from the Constitution; and the grants of power made therein ought to be strictly construed by all the departments and agents of the government; and that it is inexpedient and dangerous to exercise doubtful constitutional powers.

2. That the Constitution does not confer upon the General Government the power to commence and carry on a general system of internal improvements.

3. That the Constitution does not confer authority upon the Federal Government, directly or indirectly, to assume the debts of the several States, contracted for local and internal improvements, or other State purposes; nor would such assumption be just or expedient.

4. That justice and sound policy forbid the Federal Government to foster one branch of industry to the detriment of any other, or to cherish the interests of one portion to the injury of another portion of our common country; that every citizen and every section of the country has a right to demand and insist upon an equality of rights and privileges, and to complete and ample protection of persons and property from domestic

---

[2] Stephen A. Douglas of Illinois and Herschel V. Johnson of Georgia were the party's presidential and vice-presidential nominees. They carried one state, Missouri, and approximately 1,400,000 popular and 12 electoral college votes.

[3] Within the brackets are the pertinent planks from the 1856 Cincinnati Democratic Platform (ibid., 24, 25); both the Douglas and Breckinridge factions incorporated the 1856 Platform into their respective 1860 party platforms.

violence or foreign aggression.

5. That it is the duty of every branch of Government to enforce and practice the most rigid economy in conducting our public affairs, and that not more revenue ought to be raised than is required to defray the necessary expenses of the Government, and for the gradual but certain extinction of the public debt.

6. That the proceeds of the public lands ought to be sacredly applied to the national objects specified in the Constitution; and that we are opposed to any law for the distribution of such proceeds among the States, as alike inexpedient in policy and repugnant to the Constitution.

7. That Congress has no power to charter a national bank; that we believe such an institution one of deadly hostility to the best interest of the country, dangerous to our republican institutions and the liberties of the people, and calculated to place the business of the country within the control of a concentrated money power, and above the laws and the will of the people; and that the results of Democratic legislation in this and in all other financial measures upon which issues have been made between the two political parties of the country, have demonstrated to candid and practical men of all parties, their soundness, safety, and utility, in all business pursuits.

8. That the separation of the moneys of the Government from banking institutions is indispensable for the safety of the funds of the Government and the rights of the people. . . .

Resolved, That we reiterate with renewed energy of purpose the well considered declarations of former Conventions upon the sectional issue of Domestic slavery, and concerning the reserved rights of the States.

1. That Congress has no power under the Constitution, to interfere with or control the domestic institutions of the several States, and that such States are the sole and proper judges of everything appertaining to their own affairs, not prohibited by the Constitution; that all efforts of the abolitionists, or others, made to induce Congress to interfere with questions of slavery, or to take incipient steps in relation thereto, are calculated to lead to the most alarming and dangerous consequences; and that all such efforts have an inevitable tendency to diminish the happiness of the people and endanger the stability and permanency of the Union, and ought not to be countenanced by any friend of our political institutions.

2. That the foregoing proposition covers, and was intended to embrace the whole subject of slavery agitation in Congress; and therefore, the Democratic party [sic] of the Union, standing on this national platform,

will abide by and adhere to a faithful execution of the acts known as the compromise measures, settled by the Congress of 1850; "the act for reclaiming fugitives from service or labor," included; which act being designed to carry out an express provision of the Constitution, cannot, with fidelity thereto, be repealed, or so changed as to destroy or impair its efficiency.

3. The Congress will resist all attempts at renewing, in Congress or out of it, the agitation of the slavery question under whatever shape or color the attempt may be made.

4. That the Democratic party will faithfully abide by and uphold, the principles laid down in the Kentucky and Virginia resolutions of 1798, and in the report of Mr. Madison to the Virginia Legislature in 1799; that it adopts those principles as constituting one of the main foundations of its political creed, and is resolved to carry them out in their obvious meaning and import.

And that we may more distinctly meet the issue on which a sectional party, subsisting exclusively on the slavery agitation, now relies to test the fidelity of the people, North and South, to the Constitution and the Union—

1. *Resolved*, That claiming fellowship with, and desiring the cooperation of all who regard the preservation of the Union under the Constitution as the paramount issue—and repudiating all sectional parties and platforms concerning domestic slavery, which seek to embroil the States and incite to treason and armed resistance to law in the Territories; and whose avowed purposes, if consummated, must end in civil war and disunion, the American Democracy recognize and adopt the principles contained in the organic laws establishing the Territories of Kansas and Nebraska as embodying the only sound and safe solution of the "slavery question" upon which the great national idea of the people of this whole country can repose in its determined conservatism of the Union— NONINTERFERENCE BY CONGRESS WITH SLAVERY IN STATE AND TERRITORY, OR IN THE DISTRICT OF COLUMBIA.

2. That this was the basis of the compromises of 1850—confirmed by both the Democratic and Whig parties in national Conventions— ratified by the people in the election of 1852, and rightly applied to the organization of Territories in 1854.

3. That by the uniform application of this Democratic principle to the organization of territories, and to the admission of new States, with or without domestic slavery, as they may elect—the equal rights, of all the States will be preserved intact—the original compacts of the

Constitution maintained inviolate—and the perpetuity and expansion of this Union insured to its utmost capacity of embracing, in peace and harmony, every future American State that may be constituted or annexed, with a republican form of government. . . .]

2. Inasmuch as difference of opinion exists in the Democratic party as to the nature and extent of the powers of a Territorial Legislature, and as to the duties and powers of Congress, under the Constitution of the United States, over the institution of slavery within the Territories,

Resolved, That the Democratic party will abide by the decision of the Supreme Court of the United States upon these questions of Constitutional law.

3. *Resolved*, That it is the duty of the United States to afford ample and complete protection to all its citizens, whether at home or abroad, and whether native or foreign born.

4. *Resolved*, That one of the necessities of the age, in a military, commercial, and postal point of view, is speedy communication between the Atlantic and Pacific States; and the Democratic party pledge such Constitutional Government aid as will insure the construction of a Railroad to the pacific coast, at the earliest practical period.

5. *Resolved*, That the Democratic party are [sic] in favor of the acquisition of the Island of Cuba on such terms as shall be honorable to ourselves and just to Spain.

6. *Resolved*, That the enactments of the State Legislatures to defeat the faithful execution of the Fugitive Slave Law, are hostile in character, subversive of the Constitution, and revolutionary in their effect.

7. *Resolved*, That it is in accordance with their interpretation of the Cincinnati platform, that during the existence of the Territorial Governments the measure of restriction, whatever it may be, imposed by the Federal Constitution on the power of the Territorial Legislature over the subject of the domestic relations, as the same has been, or shall hereafter be finally determined by the Supreme Court of the United States, should be respected by all good citizens, and enforced with promptness and fidelity by every branch of the general government.

Democratic Party (Southern Faction) Platform[4]

Resolved, That the platform adopted by the Democratic party at Cincinnati (*supra*) be affirmed, with the following explanatory resolutions:

1. That the Government of a Territory organized by an act of Congress is provisional and temporary, and during its existence all citizens of the United States have an equal right to settle with their property in the Territory, without their rights, either of person or property, being destroyed or impaired by Congressional or Territorial legislation.

2. That it is the duty of the Federal Government, in all its departments, to protect, when necessary, the rights of persons and property in the Territories, and wherever else its constitutional authority extends.

3. That when the settlers in a Territory, having an adequate population, form a State Constitution, the right of sovereignty commences, and being consummated by admission into the Union, they stand on an equal footing with the people of other States, and the State thus organized ought to be admitted into the Federal Union, whether its Constitution prohibits or recognizes the institution of slavery.

Resolved, That the Democratic party are in favor of the acquisition of the Island of Cuba, on such terms as shall be honorable to ourselves and just to Spain, at the earliest practical moment.

Resolved, That the enactments of the State Legislatures to defeat the faithful execution of the Fugitive Slave Law are hostile in character, subversive of the Constitution, and revolutionary in their effect.

Resolved, That the Democracy of the Union of the United States recognize it as the imperative duty of this Government to protect the naturalized citizen in all his rights, whether at home or in foreign lands, to the same extent as its native-born citizens.

WHEREAS, One of the greatest necessities of the age, in a political, commercial, postal and military point of view, is a speedy communication between the Pacific and Atlantic coasts. Therefore, be it

Resolved, That the National Democratic party do hereby pledge themselves to use every means in their power to secure the passage of

---

[4] John C. Breckinridge of Kentucky and Joseph Lane of Oregon were the party's presidential and vice-presidential nominees. They carried Delaware, southern New Jersey which was not a winner take-all state, Maryland, North Carolina, South Carolina, Georgia, Florida, Alabama, Mississippi, Arkansas, Louisiana, and Texas, with a total of approximately 848,000 popular and 72 electoral college votes.

some bill, to the extent of the constitutional authority of Congress, for the construction of a Pacific Railroad from the Mississippi River to the Pacific Ocean, at the earliest practical moment.

Republican Party Platform[5]

Resolved, That we, the delegated representatives of the Republican electors of the United States, in Convention assembled, in discharge of the duty we owe to our constituents and our country, unite in the following declarations:

1. That the history of the nation during the last four years, has fully established the propriety and necessity of the organization and perpetuation of the Republican party, and that the causes which called it into existence are permanent in their nature, and now, more than ever before, demand its peaceful and constitutional triumph.

2. That the maintenance of the principles promulgated in the Declaration of Independence and embodied in the Federal Constitution, "That all men are created equal; that they are endowed by their Creator with certain inalienable [sic] rights; that among these are life, liberty and the pursuit of happiness; that to secure these rights, governments are instituted among men, deriving their just powers from the consent of the governed," is essential to the preservation of our Republican institutions; and that the Federal Constitution, the Rights of the States, and the Union of the States must and shall be preserved.

3. That to the Union of the States this nation owes its unprecedented increase in population, its surprising development of material resources, its rapid augmentation of wealth, its happiness at home and its honor abroad; and we hold in abhorrence all schemes for disunion, come from whatever source they may. And we congratulate the country that no Republican member of Congress has uttered or countenanced the threats of disunion so often made by Democratic members, without rebuke and with applause from their political associates; and we denounce those threats of disunion, in case of a popular overthrow of their ascendancy as denying the vital principles of a free government, and as an avowal of

---

[5] Abraham Lincoln of Illinois and Hannibal Hamlin of Maine were the presidential and vice-presidential nominees. They carried Maine, Vermont, New Hampshire, Massachusetts, Rhode Island, Connecticut, northern New Jersey, New York, Pennsylvania, Ohio, Indiana, Michigan, Wisconsin, Iowa, Minnesota, Oregon, and California, with a total of approximately 1,866,000 popular and 180 electoral college votes.

contemplated treason, which it is the imperative duty of an indignant people sternly to rebuke and forever silence.

4. That the maintenance inviolate of the rights of the states, and especially the right of each state to order and control its own domestic institutions according to its own judgment exclusively, is essential to that balance of powers on which the perfection and endurance of our political fabric depends; and we denounce the lawless invasion by armed force of the soil of any state or territory, no matter under what pretext, as among the gravest of crimes.

5. That the present Democratic Administration has far exceeded our worst apprehensions, in its measureless subserviency to the exactions of sectional interest, as especially evinced in its desperate exertions to force the infamous Lecompton Constitution upon the protesting people of Kansas; in construing the personal relations between master and servant to involve an unqualified property in persons; in its attempted enforcement everywhere, on land and sea, through the intervention of Congress and of the Federal Courts of the extreme pretensions of a purely local interest; and in its general and unvarying abuse of the power intrusted [sic] to it by a confiding people.

6. That the people justly view with alarm the reckless extravagance which pervades every department of the Federal Government; that a return to rigid economy and accountability is indispensable to arrest the systematic plunder of the public treasury favored by partisans; while the recent startling developments of frauds and corruptions at the Federal metropolis, show that an entire change of administration is imperatively demanded.

7. That the new dogma that the Constitution, of its own force, carries slavery into any or all of the territories of the United States, is a dangerous political heresy, at variance with the explicit provisions of that instrument, with contemporaneous exposition, and with legislative and judicial precedent; is revolutionary in its tendency, and subversive of the peace and harmony of the country.

8. That the normal condition of all the territory of the United States is that of freedom; That, as our Republican fathers, when they had abolished slavery in all our national territory, ordained that "no persons should be deprived of life, liberty or property without due process of law," it becomes our duty, by legislation, whenever such legislation is necessary, to maintain this provision of the Constitution against all attempts to violate it; and we deny the authority of Congress, of a territorial legislature, or of any individuals, to give legal existence to slavery in

any territory of the United States.

9. That we brand the recent reopening of the African slave trade, under cover of our national flag, aided by perversions of judicial power, as a crime against humanity and a burning shame to our country and age; and we call upon Congress to take prompt and efficient measures for the total and final suppression of that execrable traffic.

10. That in the recent vetoes, by their Federal Governors, of the acts of the legislatures of Kansas and Nebraska, prohibiting slavery in those territories, we find a practical illustration of the boasted Democratic principle of Non-Intervention and Popular Sovereignty, embodied in the Kansas-Nebraska Bill, and a demonstration of the deception and fraud involved therein.

11. That Kansas should, of right, be immediately admitted as a state under the Constitution recently formed and adopted by her people, and accepted by the House of Representatives.

12. That, while providing revenue for the support of the general government by duties upon imports, sound policy requires such an adjustment of these imports as to encourage the development of the industrial interest of the whole country; and we commend that policy of national exchanges, which secures to the workingmen liberal wages, to agriculture remunerative prices, to mechanics and manufacturers an adequate reward for their skill, labor, and enterprise, and to the nation commercial prosperity and independence.

13. That we protest against any sale or alienation to others of the public lands held by actual settlers, and against any view of the free-homestead policy which regards the settlers as paupers or suppliants for public bounty; and we demand the passage by Congress of the complete and satisfactory homestead measure which has already passed the House.

14. That the Republican party is opposed to any change in our naturalization laws or any state legislation by which the rights of citizens hitherto accorded to immigrants from foreign lands shall be abridged or impaired; in favor of giving a full and efficient protection to the rights of all classes of citizens, whether native or naturalized, both at home and abroad.

15. That the appropriations by Congress for river and harbor improvements of a national character, required for the accommodation and security of existing commerce, are authorized by the Constitution, and justified by the obligation of Government to protect the lives and property of its citizens.

16. That a railroad to the Pacific Ocean is imperatively demanded by

the interests of the whole country; that the federal government ought to render immediate and efficient aid in its construction; and that, as preliminary thereto, a daily overland mail should be promptly established.

17. Finally, having thus set forth our distinctive principles and views, we invite the cooperation of all citizens, however differing on other questions, who substantially agree with us in their affirmance and support.

2

This Modern Revolution

Senator Benjamin F. Wade, Ohio
December 17, 1860

Benjamin Wade (1800-1878) was born in Massachusetts and moved to Ohio with his parents in 1821. He was a teacher and studied medicine in Albany, New York, from 1823-1825, when he returned to Ohio to study law. From 1835-1837 he was the prosecuting attorney for Ashtabula County, Ohio. He served in the Ohio senate in 1837 and 1838 and also as a judge in the third judicial court from 1847-1851. He was elected as a Whig to the U.S. Senate, commencing his term on March 4, 1851; he was reelected as a Republican in 1856 and 1863, but was an unsuccessful candidate for renomination to the U.S. Senate and for vice president in the Republican National Convention in 1868. In 1871 he was appointed as a U.S. Government director of the Pacific Railroad and a member of the Santo Domingo Commission; the former exercised oversight on $60,000,000 and 45,000,000 acres of land transferred to railroad companies, while the latter was charged by President Grant to pave the way for the annexation of the Dominican Republic. The following speech articulated the Republican Party's policy towards secession and was used by Southern and Northern Democrats as evidence of the Republican Party's determination to avoid a compromised settlement of sectional *hostilities on terms amicable to Southern "rights" and interests. Southern Democrats were especially convinced that Senator Wade represented the Republican Party's indubitable policy to subdue the South by forcible means. Senator Wade dismissed Southern concerns as lacking substance and fueled by treasonous opportunistic agitators, i.e., northern and southern Democrats. Senator Wade maintained that the U.S. Government is not only justified, but required to utilize all necessary force to keep the Union intact.*

Mr. WADE. Mr. President, at a time like this, when there seems to be a wild and unreasonable excitement in many parts of the country, I certainly have very little faith in the efficacy of any argument that may be made; but at the same time, I must say, when I hear it stated by many Senators in this Chamber, where we all raised our hands to Heaven, and took a solemn oath to support the Constitution of the United States, that we are on the eve of a dissolution of this Union, and that the Constitution is to be trampled under foot—silence under such circumstances seems to me akin to treason itself.

I have listened to the complaints on the other side patiently, and with an ardent desire to ascertain what was the particular difficulty under which they were laboring. Many of those who have supposed themselves aggrieved have spoken; but I confess that I am now totally unable to understand precisely what it is of which they complain. Why, sir, the party which lately elected their President, and are prospectively to come into power, have never held an executive office under the General Government, nor has any individual of them. It is most manifest, therefore, that the party to which I belong has as yet committed no act of which anybody can complain. If they have fears as to the course that we may hereafter pursue, they are mere apprehensions—a bare suspicion; arising, I fear, out of their unwarrantable prejudices, and nothing else.

I wish to ascertain at the outset whether we are right; for I tell gentlemen that, if they can convince me that I am holding any political principle that is not warranted by the Constitution under which we live, or that trenches upon their rights, they need not ask me to compromise it. I will be ever ready to grant redress, and to right myself whenever I am wrong. No man need approach me with a threat that the Government under which I live is to be destroyed; because I hope I have now, and ever shall have, such a sense of justice that, when any man shows me that I am wrong, I shall be ready to right it without price or compromise.

Now, sir, what is it of which gentlemen complain? When I left my home in the West to come to this place, all was calm, cheerful, and contented. I heard no discontent. I apprehended that there was nothing to interrupt the harmonious course of our legislation. I did not learn that, since we adjourned from this place at the end of the last session, there had been any new fact intervening that should at all disturb the public mind. I do not know that there has been any encroachment upon the rights of any section of the country since that time; I came here, therefore, expecting to have a very harmonious session. It is very true, sir, that the great Republican party which has been organized ever since you repealed the Missouri compromise, and who gave you, four years ago, full warning that their growing strength would probably result as it has resulted, have carried the late election; but I did not suppose that would disturb the equanimity of this body. I did suppose that every man who was observant of the signs of the times might well see that things would result precisely as they have resulted. Nor do I understand now that anything growing out of that election is the cause of the present excitement that pervades the country.

Why, Mr. President, this is a most singular state of things. Who is it that is complaining? They that have been in a minority? They that have been the subjects of an oppressive and aggressive Government? No, sir. Let us suppose that when the leaders of the old glorious Revolution met at Philadelphia eighty-four years ago to draw up a bill of indictment against a wicked King and his ministers, they had been at a loss what they should set forth as the causes of their complaint. They had no difficulty in setting them forth so that the great article of impeachment will go down to all posterity as a full justification of all the acts they did. But let us suppose that, instead of its being these old patriots who had met there to dissolve their connection with the British Government, and to trample their flag under foot, it had been the ministers of the Crown, the leading members of the British Parliament, of the dominant party that had ruled Great Britain for thirty years previous: who would not have branded every man of them as a traitor? It would be said: "You who have had the Government in your own hands; you who have been the ministers of the Crown, advising everything that has been done, set up here that you have been oppressed and aggrieved by the action of that very Government which you have directed yourselves." Instead of a sublime revolution, the uprising of an oppressed people, ready to battle against unequal power for their rights, it would have been an act of treason.

How is it with the leaders of this modern revolution? Are they in a position to complain of the action of this Government for years past?

Why, sir, they have had more than two thirds of the Senate for many years past, and until very recently, and almost have that now. You—who complain, I ought to say—represent but a little more than one fourth of the free people of these United States, and yet your counsels prevailed all along for at least ten years past. In the Cabinet, in the Senate of the United States, in the Supreme Court, in every department of the Government, your officers, or those devoted to you, have been in the majority, and have dictated all the policies of this Government. Is it not strange, sir, that they who now occupy these positions should come here and complain that their rights are stricken down by the action of the Government?

But what has caused this great excitement that undoubtedly prevails in a portion of our country? If the newspapers are to be credited, there is a reign of terror in all the cities and large towns in the southern portion of this community that looks very much like the reign of terror in Paris during the French revolution. There are acts of violence that we read of almost every day, wherein the rights of northern men are stricken down, where they are sent back with indignities, where they are scourged, tarred, feathered, and murdered, and no inquiry made as to the cause. I do not suppose that the regular Government, in times of excitement like these, is really responsible for such acts. I know that these outbreaks of passion, these terrible excitements that sometimes pervade a community, are entirely irrepressible by the law of the country. I suppose that is the case now; because if these outrages against northern citizens were really authorized by the State authorities there, were they a foreign Government, everybody knows, if it were the strongest Government on earth, we should declare war upon her in one day.

But what has caused this great excitement? Sir, I will tell you what I suppose it is. I do not (and I say it frankly) so much blame the people of the South; because they believe, and they are led to believe by all the information that ever comes before them, that we, the dominant party to-day, who have just seized upon the reigns of this Government, are their mortal enemies, and stand ready to trample their institutions under foot. They have been told so by our enemies at the North. Their misfortune, or their fault, is that they have lent a too easy ear to the insinuations of those who are our mortal enemies, while they would not hear us.

Now I wish to inquire, in the first place, honestly, candidly, and fairly, whether the southern gentlemen on the other side of the Chamber, that complain so much, have any reasonable grounds for that complaint—I mean when they are really informed as to our position.

Northern Democrats have sometimes said that we had personal liberty bills in some few of the States of the North, which somehow trenched upon the rights of the South under the fugitive bill to recapture their runaway slaves; a position that in not more than two or three cases, so far as I can see, has the slightest foundation in fact; and even of those where it is most complained of, if the provisions of their law are really repugnant to that of the United States, they are utterly void, and the courts would declare them so the moment you brought them up. Thus it is that I am glad to hear the candor of those gentlemen on the other side, that they do not complain of these laws. The Senator from Georgia [Mr. IVERSON] himself told us that they have never suffered any injury, to his knowledge and belief, from those bills, and they cared nothing about them. The Senator from Virginia [Mr. MASON] said the same thing; and I believe the Senator from Mississippi, [Mr. BROWN.] You all, then, have given up this bone of contention, this matter of complaint which northern men have set forth as a grievance more than anybody else.

Mr. MASON. Will the Senator indulge me one moment?

Mr. WADE. Certainly.

Mr. MASON. I know he does not intend to misrepresent me or other gentlemen here. What I said was, that the repeal of those laws would furnish no cause of satisfaction to the southern States. Our opinions of those laws we gave freely. We said the repeal of those laws would give no satisfaction.

Mr. WADE. Mr. President, I do not intend to misrepresent anything. I understood those gentlemen to suppose that they had not been injured by them. I understood the gentleman from Virginia to believe that they were enacted in a spirit of hostility to the institutions of the South, and to object to them not because the acts themselves had done them any hurt, but because they were really a stamp of degradation upon southern men, or something like that—I do not quote his words. The other Senators that referred to it probably intended to be understood in the same way; but they did acquit these laws of having done them injury to their knowledge or belief.

I do not believe that these laws were, as the Senator supposed, enacted with a view to exasperate the South, or to put them in a position of degradation. Why, sir, these laws against kidnapping are as old as the common law itself, as that Senator well knows. To take a freeman and forcibly carry him out of the jurisdiction of the State, has ever been, by all civilized countries, adjudged to be a great crime; and in most of them, wherever I have understood anything about it, they have penal laws to punish such an offense. I believe the State of Virginia has one to-day as stringent in all its provisions as almost any other of which you complain. I have not looked over the statute-books of the South; but I do not doubt that there will be found this species of legislation upon all your statute-books.

Here let me say, because the subject occurs to me right here, the Senator from Virginia seemed not so much to point out any specific acts that northern people had done injurious to your property, as what he took to be a dishonor and a degradation. I think I feel as sensitive upon that subject as any other man. I know myself, I am the last man that would be the advocate of any law or any act that would humiliate or dishonor any section of this country, or any individual in it; and, on the other hand, let me tell these gentlemen I am exceedingly sensitive upon that same point, whatever they may think about it. I would rather sustain an injury than an insult or dishonor; and I would be as willing to inflict it upon others as I would be to submit to it myself. I never will do either the one or the other if I know it.

I have already said that these gentlemen who make these complaints have for a long series of years had this Government in their own keeping. They belong to the dominant majority. I may say that these same gentlemen who rise up on this floor and draw their bill of indictment against us, have been the leaders of that dominant party for many years past. Therefore, if there is anything in the legislation of the Federal Government that is not right, you, and not we, are responsible for it; for we never have been invested with the power to modify or control the legislation of the country for an hour. I know that charges have been made and rung in our ears, and reiterated over and over again, that we have been unfaithful in the execution of your fugitive bill. Sir, that law is exceedingly odious to any free people. It deprives us of all the old guarantees of liberty that the Anglo-Saxon race everywhere have considered sacred—more sacred than anything else.

Mr. GREEN (Missouri). Will the Senator from Ohio allow me to say a word?

Mr. WADE. Certainly.

Mr. GREEN. It is simply this: It has been said that the practical operation of the so-called liberty bills of the North has not affected anybody; but they do act as evidence of a public sentiment adverse to the execution of the Federal law to reclaim our slaves under the Constitution; and a repeal of those laws would not be worth one single straw while the sentiment remains. I know from practical observation that in nine cases out of ten you cannot catch a fugitive slave; and I know more than that; you forfeit your life whenever you make the attempt.

One word more: when it is said that this fugitive slave law is obnoxious to the North, and runs counter to these old guarantees concerning personal liberty, I say that the recovery of fugitives from justice is, under the Constitution and under the law, just as summary without trial by jury, and must of necessity be so. Why is not the same complaint made about forgers, and murderers, and scoundrels that steal? Not a word of liberty bills in their behalf; but all for the negro. [Applause in the galleries.]

The PRESIDING OFFICER, (Mr. FOSTER [Connecticut] in the chair.) The Chair will feel called upon to enforce the order to clear the galleries if any disturbance occurs hereafter.

Mr. WADE. Never mind, Mr. President; let them cheer the fugitive slave law if they please. I have no objection to it.

Mr. MASON. I ask the Senator to allow me one instant. I wish to say that if this disorder again occurs—if this indignity is again offered to the Senate—I shall deem it my duty to insist that the rules of the Senate be enforced, and the galleries cleared.

Mr. HALE (New Hampshire). Suppose we consider that threat made for every day during the rest of the session. It has been made every day heretofore, and has never been enforced, and probably never will be. [Laughter.]

The PRESIDING OFFICER. The Chair will repeat that he will feel himself bound by the rules of the Senate to order the galleries to be cleared if a disturbance is made, without a motion from any member of the Senate, considering that the Chair is bound to enforce the rules. The Senator from Ohio will proceed.

Mr. WADE. Mr. President, the gentleman says, if I understood him, that these fugitives might be turned over to the authorities of the State from whence they came. That would be a very poor remedy for a free man in humble circumstances who was taken under the provisions of this bill in a summary way, to be carried—where? Where he came from? There is no law that requires that he should be carried there. Sir, if he is a free man he may be carried into the market place anywhere in a slave State; and what chance has he, a poor, ignorant individual, and a stranger, of asserting any rights there, even if there were no prejudices or partialities against him? That would be a mere mockery of justice and nothing else, and the Senator well knows it. Sir, I know that from the stringent, summary provisions of this bill, free men have been kidnapped and carried into captivity and sold into everlasting slavery. Will any man who has a regard to the sovereign rights of the State rise here and complain that a State shall not make a law tō protect her own people against kidnapping and violent seizures from abroad? Of all men, I believe those who have made most of these complaints should be the last to rise and deny the power of a sovereign State to protect her own citizens against any Federal legislation whatever. These liberty bills, in my judgment, have been passed, not with a view of degrading the South, but with an honest purpose of guarding the rights of their own citizens from unlawful seizures and abductions. I was exceedingly glad to hear that the Senators on the other side had risen in their places and had said that the repeal of those laws would not relieve the case from the difficulties under which they now labor.

How is it with the execution of your fugitive bill? Sir, I have heard it here, I have read it in the papers, I have met it everywhere, that the people of the free States, and especially the great Republican party, were unfaithful on this subject, and did not properly execute this law. It has been said, with such a tone and under such circumstances here, that, although I was sure that in the State from which I come these insinuations had no foundation in truth, I could not rise here and repel them in the face of those that say, We will not believe a single word you say [sic]. I never did, and I never would, until our enemies, those who have ever opposed us and who have censured us upon this subject, had arisen here in their places, and at length, with a magnanimity that I commend, have said that this was not so. My colleague, with a magnanimity for which I give him my thanks, has stood forth here to testify that in the State which I in part represent, the Republican courts and the Republican juries have fulfilled this repulsive duty with perfect faithfulness. So said the Senator from Illinois, [Mr. DOUGLAS]; and if I understood him, so also said the Senator from Indiana, [Mr. FITCH.] Therefore, sir, this calumny upon us is removed so far as the statement of our political enemies can make the averment good. I know that our courts, when a case is brought before them—I do not care what their politics may be—feel bound to administer the law just as they find it; and let me say to gentlemen from the South upon the other side, where you have lost one slave from the unfaithfulness of our legislative or judicial tribunals, we have had ten men murdered by your mobs, frequently under circumstances of the most savage character.

Why, sir, I can hardly take up a paper—and I rely, too, upon southern papers—which does not give an account of the cruel treatment of some man who is traveling for pleasure or for business in your quarter; and the lightest thing you do is to visit him with a vigilance committee, and compel him to return: "We give you so long to make your way out of our coast." "What is the accusation?" "Why, sir, you are from Ohio." They do not even inquire what party he belongs to, or what standard he has followed. I say this is the case, if I may rely on the statements of your own papers; and many of these outrages occur under circumstances of cruelty that would disgrace a savage; and we have no security now in traveling in nearly one half of the Union, and especially the gulf States of this Confederacy. I care not what a man's character may be; he may be perfectly innocent of every charge; he may be a man who has never violated any law under heaven; and yet if he goes down into those States, and it is ascertained that he is from the North, and especially if he differs from them in the exercise of his political rights, if he has voted for Lincoln instead of for somebody else, it is a mortal offense, punishable by indignity, by tar and feathers, by stripes, and even by death; and yet you, whose constituents are guilty of all these things, can stand forth and accuse us of being unfaithful to the Constitution of the United States! Gentlemen had better look at home.

Gentlemen, it will be very well for us all to take a view of all the phases of this controversy before we come to such conclusions as seem to have been arrived at in some quarters. I make the assertion here that I do not believe, in the history of the world, there ever was a nation on earth or a people where a law repugnant to the general feeling was ever executed with the same faithfulness as has been by your most savage and atrocious fugitive bill in the North. You yourselves can scarcely point out any case that has come before any northern tribunal in which the law has not been enforced to the very letter. You ought to know these facts, and you do know them. You all know that when a law is passed anywhere to bind any people, who feel, in conscience, or for any other reason, opposed to its execution, it is not in human nature to enforce it with the same certainty as a law that meets with the approbation of the great mass of the citizens. Every rational man understands this, and every candid man will admit it. Therefore it is that I do not violently impeach you for your unfaithfulness in the execution of many of your laws. You have in South Carolina a law by which you take free citizens of Massachusetts or any other maritime State, who visit the city of Charleston, and lock them up in jail under the penalty, if they cannot pay the jail fees, of eternal slavery staring them in the face—a monstrous law, revolting to the best feelings of humanity and violently in conflict with the Constitution of the United States. I do not say this in way of recrimination; for the excitement pervading the country is now so great that I do not wish to add a single coal to the flame; but nevertheless I wish the whole truth to appear.

Then, sir, what is it of which complaint is made? You have had the legislative power of the country and you have had the Executive of the country, as I have already said. You own the Cabinet, you own the Senate, and, I may add, you own the President of the United States as much as you own the servant upon your own plantation. [Laughter.] I cannot see, then, very clearly, why it is that southern men can rise here and complain of the action of this Government. I have already shown that it is perfectly impossible for you now to point out any act of which the Republican party can possibly be guilty, of which you complain; because at no period yet have they had the power of making any rule or regulation or law that could, by possibility, affect you; and, therefore, I understand that when Senators rise up here to justify the overthrow of this Government, to break it up, to resolve it into its original elements, they do so upon the mere suspicion that the Republican party may somehow affect their rights or violate the Constitution.

Sir, what doctrines do we hold detrimental to you? is [sic] the next inquiry that I wish to make. Are we the setters forth of any new doctrines under the Constitution of the United States? I tell you nay. There is no principle held to-day by this great Republican party that has not had the sanction of your Government in every department for more than seventy years. You have changed your opinions. We stand where we used to stand. That is the only difference. Upon the slavery question, the only doctrine you can find touching it in our platform or our action, the only position we occupy in regard to it, is that formerly occupied by the most revered statesmen of this nation. Sir, we stand where Washington stood, where Jefferson stood, where Madison stood, where Monroe stood. We stand where Adams and Jackson, and even Polk, stood. That revered statesman, Henry Clay, of blessed memory, with his divine breath asserted the doctrine that we hold to-day. Why, then, are we held up before the community as violators of your rights? You have come in late in the day to accuse us of harboring these opinions.

I ask, then, what doctrines do we hold of which you can rightfully complain? You have pointed out none. You do not complain of the execution of the fugitive slave bill; you do not complain of the liberty bills; you do not complain that Mr. Lincoln is a violent man, who will probably do you any injury. The Senator from Georgia told us that he had no apprehensions that Mr. Lincoln, in his administration, would do any act in violation of your rights, or in violation of the Constitution of the United States.

Mr. IVERSON. Will the Senator allow me to ask him when I said that?

Mr. WADE. I do not quote the Senator's words, but I believe I have them here.

Mr. IVERSON. The Senator is mistaken. I made no such remark.

Mr. WADE. Then I would thank the Senator to repeat what his remark was on that point; for I understood him as I have stated.

Mr. IVERSON. I refer the Senator to the record of my speech.

Mr. WADE. I think it is there. I understood the Senator expressly to say what I have stated—I will look up the sentence—that he had not any apprehension that Mr. Lincoln would do anything in violation of the Constitution of the United States; but the Senator's grievance, as I understood it, was, that a hostile chief magistrate might, within the power of the Constitution, so administer the Government as to do away with slavery in ten years. That is what I understood him to say.

Mr. IVERSON. I did say, in substance, that the Republican party having the power of the Government, without any palpable violation of the Constitution, might so operate upon the institution of slavery as to affect it, and probably extinguish it; but I did not say that I did not apprehend from Mr. Lincoln any violation of the Constitution of the United States. I do apprehend that he will violate the Constitution whenever he can with impunity; wherever he can affect the institution of slavery by such violation.

Mr. WADE. It is of no great consequence what the Senator said on that subject. I will only say that from Mr. Lincoln's character and conduct, from his youth up, you have no right to draw any inference that he will trespass upon the rights of any man; and if you harbor any such suspicion, it is in consequence of an unwarranted prejudice, and nothing else.

Now, sir, I should like to have the Senators on the other side tell me when ever [sic] a Republican has violated, or ever proposed to violate, a right of theirs. I have listened to your arguments here for about a week. They are all in very general terms. They are very loosely drawn indictments, and I do not know where to meet you at all. Is there anything in our platform detrimental to your rights, unless in modern times you have set up a construction of the Constitution of the United States differing from ours?—we following the old beaten track of every department of the Government for more than seventy years, and you switching off, as it were, upon another track, and setting up yours as orthodox—that is all. [Laughter.] You say that we must follow you. We choose to follow the old landmarks. That is the complaint against us.

Mr. POWELL (Kentucky). The Senator from Ohio will allow me. He seems to assert that we have made no specific charge against any Republican. Why, sir, in the very few remarks which I made in the running debate a few days ago, I called the Senator's attention to the act of the present Governor Dennison, of Ohio, who refused to deliver up a fugitive from justice from the State of Kentucky, charged with the offense of negro stealing. I wish to know from the Senator, whether or not he justifies or approves of the action of Governor Dennison in that case? That is a specific and direct charge upon the record. I have the record before me. I have the opinion of the attorney general and Governor of Ohio setting forth distinctly that they refused to deliver that fugitive from justice, because he was not charged with an offense that was a crime under the laws of Ohio, or the common law. I wish to know distinctly from the Senator whether he justifies his Governor in that act?

Mr. WADE. The Senator has asked me a question that is a little difficult: it is a subject on which lawyers and judges may differ. It is a question that I have investigated a little since it was up incidentally before. I know that the practice of the different States has been variant upon it; but Mr. Stanberr, now a citizen of the Senator's own State, and, I believe, one of the first lawyers in it, gave an opinion precisely like that of Mr. Dennison, upon which the present attorney general of Ohio founded his; and he says he got it from a decision in Kentucky upon the same subject. I do not know how that is; I have not resorted to all these old records; but I believe, from all I know, that he was following the precedent set by your own Governor; but whether he was or not, there has always been a difficulty upon that subject. I know very well that when States have created crimes of acts which are not *mala in se*, when they have passed laws barely prohibitory of some act which is not deemed immoral, many of the States have refused to surrender fugitives under any such circumstances; and I am far from saying that they are not right. However, it is a question of law about which I leave legal gentlemen to their own opinion. Certainly, you can draw no inference against the Governor of Ohio for following precedents that had been set, if I am rightly informed, by your own Governor, and especially when one of the most conservative men that I know, now a resident of your own State, and one of the best lawyers, I presume, either in that State or Ohio, laid down the rule as a precedent on which Governor Dennison went. All this is entirely aside from the issue; it is a question affecting the return of fugitives from justice, of which I heard no complaint until the other day.

Mr. POWELL. The Senator will allow me to say that I do not think he has answered my question. I wish to know whether the Senator justifies and approves the act of his Governor? So far as the precedent of the Governor of Kentucky is concerned, I should be obliged to the Senator if he would produce it; but I do not believe that any such precedent exists. I wish the gentleman to say directly whether or not he approves the act of his Governor in this case.

Mr. WADE. I do not care to be catechized on a question of law arising incidentally here; and the reason is, because I should want to go more deeply into the precedents and history of that kind of adjudication than I am now prepared for. I certainly cannot condemn the Governor of Ohio for acting in accordance with that which everybody may well see might exist everywhere. I would like to answer as a judge would on the bench, when inquired of as to what is the law. That determines it. I would not be governed by any prejudice growing out of the peculiar nature of the case; but I should inquire what is the law. I am for administering the law as it is; and if anybody can tell me precisely what it is in this respect, I am for it without any regard to the subject-matter upon which it operates.

Mr. POWELL. I despair of getting an answer from the Senator on that subject. I have brought a case, and put it distinctly to him, and he refuses either to justify or condemn. I have brought forward a case in which the Republican Governor of his own State has put the laws and Constitution of his country under his feet, and, in my judgment, as I said the other day, acted in disregard of his oath. The Senator does not meet the question. He speaks in eulogy of the Republicans, as having executed the fugitive slave law. I would ask that honorable Senator if he himself is in favor of the rigid execution of the fugitive slave law. It is unnecessary to be dealing in this kind of generalities [sic]. I wish to know from the honorable Senator himself, as one of the leaders of his party, if he stands here to proclaim to the Senate and to the country that he is in favor of executing the fugitive slave law; and I wish further to ask the Senator if the Republican Legislature of the State of Ohio has not passed a statute backing up Governor Dennison in the decision to which I have referred, and whether or not he approves of that legislation?

Mr. WADE. Mr. President, I do not know that I am a witness in this case, and certainly not to answer all the law questions in the world. [Laughter.] I have told the Senator all that I think I ought to tell him. I am for the execution of any law that is a law; but I am not here *argu-eulo*, on the spur of the occasion, to attempt to decide what that law is on a disputed question. I will never do that. [Mr. POWELL rose.] I would rather not be interrupted, because nothing can come of these questions. I do not ask the Senator any questions, and I do not like to be questioned in this way, because it leads me off from the train of my argument.

Mr. POWELL. The Senator speaks of offenses that are *mala in se*. I ask him whether he regards stealing a slave an offense of that kind?

Mr. WADE. Mr. President, I do not choose to be catechized on these subjects—

Mr. POWELL. I presume not.

The PRESIDING OFFICER, (Mr. Foster in the chair.) The Senator from Ohio has the floor, unless he chooses to yield it.

Mr. WADE. I think I have made all the answer to the Senator that I ought to make under the circumstances.

Mr. POWELL. If the Senator will allow me, I will say that I have a resolution—

The PRESIDING OFFICER. Does the Senator from Ohio give way?

Mr. POWELL. A resolution passed by the Republican State convention of his State in June last—

The PRESIDING OFFICER. Does the Senator from Ohio give way to the Senator from Kentucky?

Mr. WADE. I would rather continue my argument.

Mr. POWELL. Will the Senator allow me to catechize him on that resolution?

Mr. WADE. No, sir; I will not be catechized any further.

Mr. POWELL. I suppose not. I would then say to the honorable Senator that he should not ask for special cases unless he is willing to be catechized and face the music on them.

Mr. WADE. I will not be catechized upon the Levitical law, or any other law, under these circumstances. It is very easy to ask a great many questions that a man is not prepared to answer, especially a lawyer or a judge. I do not think there is any great difficulty involved in the questions that the gentleman puts; but they are out of place; they are entirely disconnected with the course of argument that I am pursuing.

Mr. POWELL. If the Senator will allow me, I will remind him that he called upon Senators on this side of the Chamber to specify.

Mr. WADE. I called upon them to specify what they complained of in regard to the fugitive slave bill, and the gentleman has got up a case where he says the Governor of Ohio refused to issue his warrant to deliver up a fugitive from justice; and then he catechizes me as to whether I am in favor of the decision or against it, or the legislation founded upon it. I do not know anything about either, more than I have stated.

Now, Mr. President, I have shown, I think, that the dominant majority here have nothing to complain of in the legislation of Congress, or in the legislation of any of the States, or in the practice of the people of the North, under the fugitive slave bill, except so far as they say certain State legislation furnishes some evidence of hostility to their institutions. And here, sir, I beg to make an observation. I tell the Senator, and I tell the Senators, that the Republican party of the northern States, so far as I know, and of my own State in particular, hold the same opinions with regard to this peculiar institution of yours that are held by all the civilized nations of the world. We do not differ from the public sentiment of England, of France, of Germany, of Italy, and every other civilized nation on God's earth; and I tell you frankly that you never found, and you never will find, a free community that are in love with your peculiar institution. The Senator from Texas [Mr. WIGFALL] told us the other day that cotton was king, and that by its influence it would govern all creation. He did not say so in words, but that was the substance of his remark; that cotton was king, and that it had its subjects in Europe who dared not rebel against it. Here let me say to that Senator, in passing, that it turns out that they are very rebellious subjects, and they are talking very disrespectfully at present of that king that he spoke of. They defy you to exercise your power over them. They tell you that they sympathize in this controversy with what you call the black Republicans. Therefore I hope that, so far as Europe is concerned at least, we shall hear no more of this boast that cotton is king; and that he is going to rule all the civilized nations of the world, and bring them to his footstool. Sir, it will never be done.

But, sir, I wish to inquire whether the southern people are injured by, or have any right to complain of, that platform of principles that we put out, and on which we have elected a President and Vice President. I have no concealments to make, and I shall talk to you, my southern friends, precisely as I would talk upon the stump on the subject. I tell you that in that platform we did lay it down that we would, if we had the power, prohibit slavery from another inch of free territory under this Government. I stand on that position to-day. I have argued it probably to half a million people. They stand there, and have commissioned and enjoined me to stand there forever; and, so help me God, I will. I say to you frankly, gentlemen, that while we hold this doctrine, there is no Republican, there is no convention of Republicans, there is no paper that speaks for them, there is no orator that sets forth their doctrines, who ever pretends that they have any right in your States to interfere with your peculiar institution; but, on the other hand, our authoritative platform repudiates the idea that we have any right or any intention ever to invade your peculiar institution in your own States.

Now, what do you complain of? You are going to break up this Government; you are going to involve us in war and blood, from a mere suspicion that we shall justify that which we stand everywhere pledged not to do. Would you be justified in the eyes of the civilized world in taking so monstrous a position, and predicating it on a bare, groundless suspicion? We do not love slavery. Did you know that before to-day? before [sic] this session commenced? Have you not a perfect confidence that the civilized world are against you on this subject of loving slavery or believing that it is the best institution in the world? Why, sir, everything remains precisely as it was a year ago. No great catastrophe has occurred. There is no recent occasion to accuse us of anything. But all at once, when we meet here, a kind of gloom pervades the whole community and the Senate Chamber. Gentlemen rise and tell us that they are on the eve of breaking up this Government, that seven or eight States are going to break off their connection with the Government, retire from the Union, and set up a hostile Government of their own, and they look imploringly over to us, and say to us "you can prevent it; we can do nothing to prevent; but it all lies with you." Well, sir, what can we do to prevent it? You have not even condescended to tell us what you want; but I think I see through the speeches that I have heard from gentlemen on the other side. If we give up the verdict of the people, and take your platform, I do not know but you would be satisfied with it. I think the Senator from Texas rather intimated, and I think the Senator from Georgia more than intimated, that if we would take what is exactly the Charleston platform on which Mr. Breckinridge was placed, and give up on that which we won our victory, you would grumblingly and hesitatingly be satisfied.

Mr. IVERSON. I would prefer that the Senator would look over my remarks before quoting them so confidently. I made no such statement as that. I did not say that I would be satisfied with any such thing. I would not be satisfied with it.

Mr. WADE. I did not say that the Senator said so; but by construction I gathered that from his speech. I do not know that I was right in it.

Mr. IVERSON. The Senator is altogether wrong in his construction.

Mr. WADE. Well, sir, I have now found what the Senator said on the other point to which he called my attention a little while ago. Here it is:

Nor do we suppose that there will be any overt acts upon the part of Mr. Lincoln. For one, I do not dread these overt acts. I do not propose to wait for them. Why, sir, the power of this Federal Government could be so exercised against the institution of slavery in the southern States, as that, without an overt act, the institution would not last ten years. We know that, sir; and seeing the storm which is approaching, although it may be seemingly in the distance, we are determined to seek our own safety and security before it shall burst upon us and overwhelm us with its fury, when we are not in a situation to defend ourselves.

That is what the Senator said.

Mr. IVERSON. Yes; that is what I said.

Mr. WADE. Well, then, you did not expect that Mr. Lincoln would commit any overt act against the Constitution—that was not it—you were not going to wait for that, but were going to proceed on your supposition that probably he might; and that is the sense of what I said before.

Well, Mr. President, I have disavowed all intention on the part of the Republican party to harm a hair of your heads anywhere. We hold to no doctrine that can possibly work you an inconvenience. We have been faithful to the execution of all the laws in which you have any interest, as stands confessed on this floor by your own party, and as is known to me without their confessions. Is it not, then, that Mr. Lincoln is expected to do any overt act by which you may be injured; you will not wait for any; but anticipating that the Government may work an injury, you say you will put an end to it, which means simply, that you intend either to rule or ruin this Government. That is what your complaint comes to; nothing else. We do not like your institution, you say. Well, we never liked it any better than we do now. You might as well have dissolved the Union at any other period as now, on that account, for we stand in relation to it precisely as we have ever stood: that is, repudiating it among ourselves as a matter of policy and morals, but nevertheless admitting that where it is out of our jurisdiction, we have no hold upon it, and no designs upon it.

Then, sir, as there is nothing in the platform on which Mr. Lincoln was elected of which you complain, I ask, is there anything in the character of the President elect [sic] of which you ought to complain? Has he not lived a blameless life? Did he ever transgress any law? Has he ever committed any violation of duty of which the most scrupulous can complain? Why, then, your suspicion that he will? I have shown that you have had the Government all the time until, by some misfortune or maladministration, you brought it to the very verge of destruction, and the wisdom of the people had discovered that it was high time that the scepter should depart from you, and be placed in more competent hands;

I say that this being so, you have no constitutional right to complain; especially when we disavow any intention so to make use of the victory we have won as to injure you at all.

This brings me, sir, to the question of compromises. On the first day of this session, a Senator rose in his place and offered a resolution for the appointment of a committee to inquire into the evils that exist between the different sections, and to ascertain what can be done to settle this great difficulty! That is the proposition, substantially. I tell the Senator that I know of no difficulty; and as to compromises, I had supposed that we were all agreed that the day of compromises was at an end. The most solemn compromises we have ever made have been violated without a whereas. Since I have had a seat in this body, one of considerable antiquity, that had stood for more than thirty years, was swept away from your statute-books. When I stood here in the minority arguing against it; when I asked you to withhold your hand; when I told you it was a sacred compromise between the sections, and that when it was removed we should be brought face to face with all that sectional bitterness that has intervened; when I told you that it was a sacred compromise which no man should touch with his finger, what was your reply? That it was a mere act of Congress—nothing more, nothing less—and that it could be swept away by the same majority that passed it. That was true in point of fact, and true in point of law; but it showed the weakness of compromises. Now, sir, I only speak for myself; and I say that, in view of the manner in which other compromises have been heretofore treated, I should hardly think any two of the Democratic party would look each other in the face and say "compromise" without a smile. [Laughter.] A compromise to be brought about by act of Congress, after the experience we have had, is absolutely ridiculous.

But what have we to compromise? Sir, I am one of those who went forth with zeal to maintain the principles of the great Republican party. In a constitutional way we met, as you met. We nominated our candidates for President and Vice President, and you did the same for yourselves. The issue was made up; and we went to the people upon it. Although we have been usually in the minority; although we have been generally beaten, yet, this time, the justice of our principles, and the maladministration of the Government in your hands, convinced the people that a change ought to be wrought; and after you had tried your utmost, and we had tried our utmost, we beat you; and we beat you upon the plainest and most palpable issue that was ever presented to the American people, and one that they understood the best. There is no mistaking it;

and now, when we come to the Capitol, I tell you that our President and our Vice President must be inaugurated, and administer the Government as all their predecessors have done. Sir, it would be humiliating and dishonorable to us if we were to listen to a compromise by which he who has the verdict of the people in his pocket, should make his way to the presidential chair. When it comes to that, you have no Government; anarchy intervenes; civil war may follow it; all the evils that come to the human imagination may be consequent upon such a course as that. The moment the American people cut loose from the sheet anchor of free government and liberty—that is, whenever it is denied in this Government that a majority fairly given shall rule—the people are unworthy of free government. Sir, I know not what others may do; but I tell you that, with the verdict of the people given in favor of the platform upon which our candidates have been elected, so far as I am concerned, I would suffer anything to come before I would compromise that away. I regard it as a case where I have no right to extend comity or generosity. A right, an absolute right, the most sacred that a free people can ever bestow on any man, is their undisguised, fair verdict, that gives him a title to the office that he is chosen to fill; and he is recreant to the principle of free government who will ask a question beyond the fact whether a man has the verdict of the people, or if he will entertain for a moment a proposition in addition to that. It is all I want. If we cannot stand there, we cannot stand anywhere. Any other principle than that would be as fatal to you, my friends, as to us. On any other principle, anarchy must immediately ensue.

You say that he comes from a particular section of the country. What of that? If he is an honest man, bound by his constitutional duties, has he not as good a right to come from one side as the other? Here, gentlemen, we ought to understand each other's duties a little. I appeal to every candid man upon the other side, and I put this question: if you had elected your candidate, Mr. Breckinridge, although we should have been a good deal disheartened, as everybody is that looses his choice in such a matter as this; although it would have been an overthrow that we should have deplored very much, as we have had occasion almost always to deplore the result of national elections, still do you believe that we would have raised a hand against the Constitution of our country because we were fairly beaten in an election? Sir, I do not believe there is a man on the other side who will not do us more credit than to suppose that if the case were reversed, there would be any complaint on our side. There never has been any from us under similar circumstances, and there would not be now. Sir, I think we have patriotism enough to overcome the pride and the prejudice of the canvass, and submit gracefully to the unmistakable verdict of the people; and as I have shown that you have nothing else to complain of, I take it that this is your complaint. Some of you have said that the election of Mr. Lincoln showed a hostility to you and your institution. Sir, it is the common fate of parties to differ, and one does not intend to follow exactly the course of policy of the other; but when you talk of constitutional rights and duties, honest men will observe them alike, no matter to what party they belong.

I say, then, that so far as I am concerned, I will yield to no compromise. I do not come here begging, either. It would be an indignity to the people I represent if I were to stand here parleying as to the rights of the party to which I belong. We have won our right to the Chief Magistracy of this nation in the way that you have always won your predominance; and if you are willing to do justice to others as to exact it from them, you would never raise an inquiry as to a committee for compromise. Here I beg, barely for myself, to say one thing more. Many of you stand in an attitude hostile to this Government; that is to say, you occupy an attitude where you threaten that, unless we do so and so, you will go out of this Union and destroy the Government. I say to you, for myself, that, in my private capacity, I never yielded to anything by way of threat, and in my public capacity I have no right to yield to any such thing; and therefore I would not entertain a proposition for any compromise; for, in my judgment, this long, chronic controversy that has existed between us must be met, and met upon the principles of the Constitution and laws, and met now. I hope it may be adjusted to the satisfaction of all; and I know no other way to adjust it, except that way which is laid down by the Constitution of the United States. Whenever we go astray from that, we are sure to plunge ourselves into difficulties. The old Constitution of the United States, although commonly and frequently in direct opposition to what I could wish, nevertheless, in my judgment, is the wisest and best Constitution that ever yet organized a free Government; and by its provisions I am willing, and intend, to stand or fall. Like the Senator from Mississippi, I ask nothing more. I ask no engrafting upon it. I ask nothing to be taken away from it. Under its provisions a nation has grown faster than any other in the history of the world ever did before in prosperity, in power, and in all that makes a nation great and glorious. It has ministered to the advantages of this people; and now I am unwilling to add or to take away anything till I can see much clearer than I can now that it wants either any addition or lopping off.

There is one other subject about which I ought to say something. On that side of the Chamber, you claim the constitutional right, if I understand you, to secede from the Government at pleasure, and set up an adverse Government of your own; that one State, or any number of States, have a perfect constitutional right to do it. Sir, I can find no warrant in the Constitution for any doctrine like that. In my judgment, it would be subversive of all constitutional obligation. If this is so, we really have not now, and never have had, a Government; for that certainly is no Government of which a State can do just as it pleases, any more than it would be of an individual. How can a man be said to be governed by law, if he will obey the law or not just as he sees fit? It puts you out of the pale of Government, and reduces this Union of ours, of which we have all boasted so much, to a mere conglomeration of States, to be held at the will of any capricious member of it. As to South Carolina, I will say that she is a small State; and probably, if she were sunk by an earthquake to-day, we would hardly ever find out, except by the unwonted harmony that might prevail in this Chamber. [Laughter.] But I think she is unwise. I would be willing that she should go her own gait, provided we could do it without an example fatal to all government; but standing here in the highest council of the nation, my own wishes, if I had any, must be under the control of my constitutional duty.

I do not see how any man can contend that a State can go out of this Union at pleasure, though I do not propose now to argue that question, because that has been done by men infinitely more able to argue it than I am. When it was raised some thirty years ago, and challenged the investigation of the best minds of this nation of all parties, it received a verdict that I supposed had put it at rest forever. General Jackson, with all the eminent men that surrounded him in his Cabinet, and in the councils of the nation, with hardly any exception, except Mr. Calhoun, held that the doctrine was a delusion, not to be found in the Constitution of the United States; and not only so, but utterly destructive of all Governments. Mr. Calhoun held the contrary. Mr. Webster, in his great controversy with Mr. Hayne upon that subject, was supposed to have overthrown him, even upon nullification, so utterly, that it was believed at the time that the doctrine could never arise or sprout up again. But here it is to-day in full bloom and glory; a State has a right to secede. Mr. Calhoun did not hold so. He held that a State had the right to nullify a law of Congress that they [sic] believed to be unconstitutional. He took that distinction between the power of a State to nullify a law of Congress and secession. Grounding herself upon the resolutions of 1789-99, he held that a State, in her sovereign capacity, judging in the last resort as to whether a law was warranted by the Constitution or not, must be the sole judge of the infraction of the Constitution by the enactment of a law, and also of the mode of remedy. In that, he hardly had a second at that period. But when you come to the doctrine of secession, he himself says that that is not a constitutional remedy. He did not treat it as such. Nay, sir, he goes much further than the President of the United States has gone in his message, in which he declares that the United States has no power to make war upon a seceding State. Mr. Calhoun says we undoubtedly have that power. One remedy he calls peaceable and constitutional, and the other not. I have not the book with me; I intended to have brought it, but forgot it; but you will find this doctrine laid down in his famous letter to Governor Hamilton, taking and working out the distinction between peaceable nullification and secession, that puts an end to all the relationship between the General Government and the State, and enables the General Government, if they see fit, to declare war upon such a State. Therefore I take it that a State has no constitutional right to go out of this Government.

I acknowledge to the fullest extent, the right of revolution, if you may call it a right, and the destruction of the Government under which we live, if we are discontented with it, and on its ruins to erect another more in accordance with our wishes. I believe nobody at this day denies the right; but they that undertake it, undertake it with this hazard: if they are successful, then all is right, and they are heroes; if they are defeated, they are rebels. That is the character of all revolution: if successful, of course it is well; if unsuccessful, then the Government from which they have rebelled treats them as traitors.

I do not say this because I apprehend that any party intends to make war upon a seceding State. I only assert their right from the nature of the act, if they see fit to do so; but I would not advise nor counsel it. I should be very tender of the rights of the people, if I had full power over them, who are about to destroy a Government which they deliberately come to the conclusion they cannot live under; but I am persuaded that the necessities of our position compel us to take a more austere ground, and hold that if a State secedes, although we will not make war upon her, we cannot recognize her right to be out of the Union, and she is not out until she gains the consent of the Union itself; and that the Chief Magistrate of the nation, be he who he may, will find under the Constitution of the United States that it is his sworn duty to execute the law in every part and parcel of this Government; that he cannot be released from that obligation; for there is nothing in the Constitution of the United States that would warrant him in saying that a single star has fallen from this galaxy of stars in the Confederacy. He is sworn not to know that a State has seceded, or pay the least respect to their resolutions that claim they have. What follows? Not that we would make war upon her, but we should have to exercise every Federal right over her if we had the power; and the most important of these would be the collection of the revenues. There are many rights that the Federal Government exercises over the States for the peculiar benefit of the people there, which, if they did not want, they could dispense with. If they did not want the mails carried there, the President might abolish the offices, and cease to carry their mails. They might forego any such duty peculiarly for the benefit of the people. They might not elect their officers and send them here. It is a privilege they have; but we cannot force them to do it. They have the right under the Constitution to be represented upon equal terms with any other State; but if they see fit to forego that right, and do not claim it, it is not incumbent upon the President to endeavor to force them to do an act of that kind.

But when you come to those duties which impose obligations upon them, in common with the other members of the Confederacy, he cannot be released from his duty. Therefore, it will be incumbent on the Chief Magistrate to proceed to collect the revenue of ships entering their ports, precisely in the same way and to the same extent that he does now in every other State of the Union. We cannot release him from that obligation. The Constitution, in thunder tonce [sic], demands that he shall do it alike in the ports of every State. What follows? Why, sir, if he shuts up the ports of entry so that a ship cannot discharge her cargo there or get papers for another voyage, then ships will cease to trade; or, if he undertakes to blockade her, and thus to collect it, she has not gained her independence by secession. What must she do? If she is contented to live in this equivocal state all would be well, perhaps; but she could not live there. No people in the world could live in that condition. What will they do? They must take the initiative and declare war upon the United States; and the moment that they levy war force must be met with force; and they must, therefore, hew out their independence by violence and war. There is no other way under the Constitution, that I know of, whereby a Chief Magistrate of any politics could be released from this duty. If this State, though seceding, should declare war against the United States, I do not suppose there is a lawyer in this body but what would say that the act of levying war is treason against the United States. That is where it results. We might just as well look the matter right in the face.

The Senator from Texas says—it is not exactly his language—we will force you to an ignominious treaty up in Faneuil Hall. Well, sir, you may. We know you are brave; we understand your prowess; we want no fight with you; but, nevertheless, if you drive us to that necessity, we must use all the powers of this Government to maintain it intact in its integrity. If we are overthrown, we but share the fate of a thousand other Governments that have been subverted. If you are the weakest, then you must go to the wall; and that is all there is about it. That is the condition in which we stand, provided a State sets herself up in opposition to the General Government.

I say that is the way it seems to me, as a lawyer. I see no power in the Constitution to release a Senator from this position. Sir, if there was any other, if there was an absolute right of secession in the Constitution of the United States when we stepped up there to take our oath of office, why was there not an exception in that oath? Why did it not run "that we would support the Constitution of the United States unless our State shall secede before our term was out?" Sir, there is no such immunity. There is no way by which this can be done that I can conceive of, except it is standing upon the Constitution of the United States, demanding equal justice for all, and vindicating the old flag of the Union. We must maintain it, unless we are cloven down by superior force.

Well, sir, it may happen that you can make your way out of the Union, and that, by levying war upon the Government, you may vindicate your right to independence. If you should do so, I have a policy in mind. No man would regret more than myself that any portion of the people of these United States should think themselves impelled, by grievance or anything else, to depart out of this Union, and raise a foreign flag and a hand against the General Government. If there was any just cause on God's earth that I could see that was within my reach, of honorable release from any such pretended grievance, they should have it; but they set forth none; I can see none. It is all a matter of prejudice, superinduced unfortunately, I believe, as I intimated before, more because you have listened to the enemies of the Republican party and what they said of us, while, from your intolerance, you have shut out all light as to what our real principles are. We have been called and branded in the North and in the South and everywhere else, as John Brown men, as men hostile to your institutions, as mediating an attack upon your own States—a thing that no Republican ever dreamed of or ever thought of, but has protested against as often as the question has been up; but your people believe it.

No doubt they believe it because of the terrible excitement and reign of terror that prevails there. No doubt they think so, but it arises from false information, or the want of information—that is all. Their prejudices have been appealed to until they have become uncontrolled and uncontrollable.

Well, sir, if it shall be so; if that "glorious Union," as we call it, under which the Government has so long lived and prospered, is now about to come to a final end, as perhaps it may, I have been looking around to see what policy we should adopt; and through that gloom which has been mentioned on the other side, if you will have it so, I still see a glorious future for those who stand by the old flag of the nation. There lie the fair fields of Mexico all before us. The people there are prejudiced against you. They fear you intend to overrun and enslave them. You are a slavery propaganda, and you are fillibusters [sic]. That has raised a violent antagonism between you and them. But, sir, if we were once released from all obligation to this institution, in six months they would invite us to take a protectorate over them. They owe England a large debt, and she has been coaxing and inviting us to take the protectorate of that nation. They will aid us in it; and I say to the commercial men of the North, if you go along with me, and adopt this policy, if we must come to this, you will be seven-fold indemnified by the trade and commerce of that country for what you lose by the secession. Talk about eating ice and granite in the North! Why, sir, Great Britain now carries on a commerce with Mexico to the amount of nearly a hundred million dollars. How much of it do we get? Only about eight million. Why so? Because, by our treatment of Mexico, we have led them to fear and to hate us; and they have been compelled, by our illiberal policy, to place themselves under the shadow of a stronger nation for their own protection.

The Senator from Illinois [Mr. DOUGLAS] and my colleague [Mr. PUGH] have said that we Black Republicans were advocates of negro equality, and that we wanted to build up a black government. Sir, it will be one of the most blessed ideas of the times, if it shall come to this, that we will make inducements for every free black among us to find his home in a more congenial climate in Central America or in Lower Mexico, and we will be divested of every one of them; and then, endowed with the splendid domain that we shall get, we will adopt a homestead policy, and we will invite the poor, the destitute, industrious white man from every clime under heaven, to come in there and make his fortune. So, sir, we will build up a nation, renovated by this process, of white laboring men. You may build yours up on compulsory servile labor, and the two will flourish side by side; and we shall very soon see whether your principles, or that state of society, or ours, is the most prosperous or vigorous. I might say, sir, that, divested of this institution, who doubts that the provinces of Canada would knock at our doors in a day? Therefore, my friends, we have all the elements for building up an empire—a Republic, founded on the great principles of the Declaration of Independence, that shall be more magnificent, more powerful, and more just than this world has ever seen at any other period. I do not know that I should have a single second for this policy; but it is a policy that occurs to me, and it reconciles me in some measure to the threatened loss or secession of these States.

But, sir, I am for maintaining the Union of these States. I will sacrifice everything but honor to maintain it. That glorious flag of ours, by any act of mine, shall never cease to wave over the integrity of this Union as it is. But if they will not have it so, in this new, renovated Government of which I have spoken, the 4th of July, with all its glorious memories, will never be repealed. The old flag of 1776 will be in our hands, and shall float over this nation forever; and this Capitol, that some gentlemen said would be reserved for the southern republic, shall still be the Capitol. It was laid out by Washington; it was consecrated by him; and the old flag that he vindicated in the Revolution shall still float from the Capitol. [Applause in the galleries.]

The PRESIDING OFFICER. The Sergeant-at-Arms will take proper measures to preserve order in the gallery or clear it.

Mr. WADE. I say, sir, I stand by the Union of these States. Washington and his compatriots fought for that good old flag. It shall never be hauled down, but shall be the glory of the Government to which I belong, as long as my life shall continue. To maintain it, Washington and his compatriots fought for liberty and the rights of man. And here I will add that my own father, although but a humble soldier, fought in the same great cause, and went through hardships and privations sevenfold worse than death, in order to bequeath it to his children. It is my inheritance. It was my protector in infancy, and the pride and glory of my riper years; and, Mr. President, although it may be assailed by traitors on every side, by the grace of God, under its shadow I will die.

3

Constitutional Compromise

Senator John J. Crittenden, Kentucky
December 18, 1860

John Jordan Crittenden (1787-1863) completed his preparatory studies in Kentucky; he went on to Washington College (now Washington and Lee University) and William and Mary College in Virginia; he studied law and was admitted to the bar and commenced practice in Kentucky. In 1809 and 1810 he served as attorney general for the Illinois Territory and as an aide in the War of 1812, after which he returned to Kentucky to practice law and was elected to the Kentucky legislature. He was first elected to the U.S. Senate in 1817 and resigned in 1819. He was appointed U.S. district attorney in 1827 and removed from office in 1829 by President Jackson. In 1828 he was nominated by President Adams to be an associate justice to the U.S. Supreme Court, but was not confirmed by the Senate. He was elected again to the U.S. Senate and served from March 1835 to March 1841, when he was appointed U.S. Attorney General by President Harrison and served from March 5 to September 13, 1841. He was then appointed and subsequently elected to fill the vacancy resulting from the resignation of Senator Henry Clay and served from March 1842 to June 1848 when he resigned and was elected Governor of Kentucky, serving from 1848-1850 when he resigned from the governorship to serve as President Fillmore's U.S. Attorney General from 1850-1853. In 1855 he was again elected to the U.S. Senate and served until 1861. From 1861 to 1863 he served in the U.S. House of Representatives as a Unionist. In this speech Senator Crittenden is critical of the party politics that have produced the crisis and offers several amendments designed to curtail the effects of partisan ambitions and thereby diffuse sectional tensions; otherwise, "disunion, revolution, war, havoc and anarchy will follow, and the great Republic will fall prostrate and in ruins."

Mr. CRITTENDEN. I am gratified, Mr. President, to see in the various propositions which have been made, such a universal anxiety to save the country from the dangerous dissensions which now prevail; and I have, under a very serious view and without the least ambitious feeling whatever connected with it, prepared a series of constitutional amendments, which I desire to offer to the Senate, hoping that they may form, in part at least, some basis for measures that may settle the controverted questions which now so much agitate our country. Certainly, sir, I do not propose now any elaborate discussion of the subject. Before presenting these resolutions, however, to the Senate, I desire to make a few remarks explanatory of them, that the Senate may understand their general scope.

The questions of an alarming character are those which have grown out of the controversy between the northern and southern sections of our country in relation to the rights of the slaveholding States in the Territories of the United States, and in relation to the rights of the citizens of the latter in their slaves. I have endeavored by these resolutions to meet all these questions and causes of discontent, and by the amendments to the Constitution of the United States, so that the settlement, if we can happily agree on any, may be permanent, and leave no cause for future controversy. These resolutions propose, then, in the first place, in substance, the restoration of the Missouri compromise [sic], extending the line throughout the Territories of the United States to the eastern border of California, recognizing slavery in all the territory south of it; with a provision, however, that when any of those Territories, north or south, are formed into States, they shall then be at liberty to exclude or admit slavery as they please; and that, in the one case or the other, it shall be no objection to their admission into the Union. In this way, sir, I propose to settle the question, both as to territory and slavery, so far as it regards the Territories of the United States.

I propose, sir, also, that the Constitution shall be so amended as to declare that Congress shall have no power to abolish slavery in the District of Columbia so long as slavery exists in the States of Maryland and Virginia; and that they shall have no power to abolish slavery in any of the places under their special jurisdiction within the southern States.

These are the constitutional amendments I propose, and embrace the whole of them in regard to the questions of territory and slavery. There are propositions in relation to grievances, and in relation to controversies, which I suppose are within the jurisdiction of Congress. I propose, in regard to legislative action, that the fugitive slave law, as it is commonly called, shall be declared by the Senate to be a constitutional act, in strict pursuance of the Constitution. I propose to declare, that it has been decided by the Supreme Court of the United States to be constitutional, and that the southern States are entitled to a faithful and complete execution of that law, and that no amendment shall be made hereafter to it which will impair its efficiency. But, thinking that it would not impair its efficiency, I have proposed amendments to it in two particulars. I have understood from gentlemen of the North that there is an objection to the provision giving a different fee where the commissioner decides to deliver the slave to the claimant, from that which is given where he decides to discharge the alleged slave; the law declares that in the latter he shall have but five dollars, while in the other he shall have ten dollars—twice the amount in one case than in the other. The reason for this is very obvious. In case he delivers the servant to his claimant, he is required to draw out a lengthy certificate, stating the principal and substantial grounds on which his decision rests, and return him either to the marshal or to the claimant to remove him to the State from which he escaped. It was for that reason that a larger fee was given to the commissioner, where he had the largest service to perform. But, sir, the act being viewed unfavorably and with great prejudice, in a certain portion of our country, this was regarded as very obnoxious, because it seemed to give an inducement to the commissioner to return the slave to the master, as he thereby obtained the larger fee of ten dollars instead of the smaller one of five dollars. I have said, let the fee be the same in both cases.

I have understood, furthermore, sir, that inasmuch as the fifth section of that law was worded somewhat vaguely, its general terms had admitted of the construction in the northern States that all the citizens were required, upon the summons of the marshal, to go with him to hunt up, as they express it, and arrest the slave; and this is regarded as obnoxious. They have said, "in the southern States you make no such requisition on the citizen;" nor do we, sir. The section, construed according to the intention of the framers of it, I suppose, only intended that the marshal should have the same right in the execution of the process for the arrest of a slave that he has in all other cases of process that he is required to execute—to call on the *posse comitatus* for assistance where he is resisted in the execution of his duty, or where, having executed his duty by the arrest, an attempt is made to rescue the slave. I propose such an amendment as will obviate this difficulty and limit the right of the master and the duty of the citizen to cases where, as in regard to all other process, persons may be called upon to assist in resisting opposition to the execution of the laws.

I have provided further, sir, that the amendments to the Constitution which I here propose, and certain other provisions of the Constitution itself, shall be unalterable, thereby forming a permanent and unchangeable basis for peace and tranquillity among the people. Among the provisions in the present Constitution, which I have by amendment proposed to render as unalterable, is that provision of the first article of the Constitution which provides the rule for representation, including in the computation three fifths of the slaves. That is to be rendered unchangeable. Another is the provision for the delivery of fugitive slaves. That is to be rendered unchangeable.

And with these provisions, Mr. President, it seems to me we have a solid foundation upon which we may rest our hopes for the restoration of peace and good-will among all the States of this Union, and all the people. I propose, sir, to enter into no particular discussion. I have explained the general scope and object of my proposition. I have provided, further, which I ought to mention, that, there having been some difficulties experienced in the courts of the United States in the South in carrying into execution the laws prohibiting the African slave trade, all additions and amendments which may be necessary to those laws to render them effectual should be immediately adopted by Congress, and especially the provisions of those laws which prohibit the importation of African slaves into the United States. I have further provided it as a recommendation to all the States of this Union, that whereas laws have been passed of an unconstitutional character, (and all laws are of that character which either conflict with the constitutional acts of Congress, or which in their operation hinder or delay the proper execution of the acts of Congress,) which laws are null and void, and yet, though null and void, they have been the source of mischief and discontent in the country, under the extraordinary circumstances in which we are placed; I have supposed that it would not be improper or unbecoming in Congress to recommend to the States, both North and South, the repeal of all such acts of theirs as were intended to control, or intended to obstruct the operation of the acts of Congress, or which in their operation and in their application have been made use of for the purpose of such hindrance and opposition, and that they will repeal these laws or make such explanations or corrections of them as to prevent their being used for any such mischievous purpose.

I have endeavored to look with impartiality from one end of our country to the other; I have endeavored to search up what appeared to me to be the causes of discontent pervading the land; and, as far as I am capable of doing so, I have endeavored to propose a remedy for them. I am far from believing that, in the shape in which I present these measures, they will meet with the acceptance of the Senate. It will be sufficiently gratifying if, with all the amendments that the superior knowledge of the Senate may make to them, they shall, to any effectual extent, quiet the country.

Mr. President, great dangers surround us. The Union of these States is dear to the people of the United States. The long experience of its blessings, the mighty hopes of the future, have made it dear to the hearts of the American people. Whatever politicians may say; whatever of dissension may, in the heat of party politics, be created among our people, when you come down to the question of the existence of the Constitution, that is a question beyond all party politics; that is a question of life and death. The Constitution and the Union are the life of this great people— yes, sir, the life of life. We all desire to preserve them, North and South; that is the universal desire. But some of the southern States, smarting under what they conceive to be aggressions of their northern brethren and of the northern States, are not contented to continue this Union, and are taking steps, towards a dissolution of the Union, and towards the anarchy and the bloodshed, I fear, that are to follow. I say, sir, we are in the presence of great events. We must elevate ourselves to the level of the great occasion. No party warfare about mere party questions or party measures ought now to engage our attention. They are left behind; they are as dust in the balance. The life, the existence of our country, of our Union, is the mighty question; and we must elevate ourselves to all those considerations which belong to this high subject.

I hope, therefore, gentlemen will be disposed to bring the sincerest spirit of conciliation, the sincerest spirit and desire to adjust all these difficulties, and to think nothing of any little concessions of opinions that they may make, if thereby the Constitution and the country can be preserved.

The great difficulty here, sir—I know it; I recognize it as the difficult question, particularly with the gentlemen from the North—is the admission of this line of division for the territory, and the recognition of slavery on the one side, and the prohibition of it on the other. The recognition of slavery on the southern side of that line is the great difficulty, the question with them. Now, I beseech them to think, and you Mr. President, and all, to think whether, for such a comparative trifle as that, the Union of this country is to be sacrificed. Have we realized to ourselves the momentous consequences of such an event? When has the world seen such an event? This is a mighty empire. Its existence spreads its influence throughout the civilized world. Its overthrow will be the greatest shock that civilization and free government have received; more extensive in its consequences; more fatal to mankind and the great principles upon which the liberty of mankind depends, than the French revolution with all its blood, and with all its war and violence. And all for what? Upon questions concerning this line of division between slavery and freedom? Why, Mr. President, suppose this day all the southern States, being refused this right; being refused this partition; being denied this privilege, were to separate from the northern States, and do it peacefully, and then were to come to you peacefully and say, "let there be no war between us; let us divide fairly the Territories of the United States:" could the northern section of the country refuse so just a demand? What would you then give them? What would be the fair proportion? If you allowed them their fair relative proportion, would you not give them as much as is now proposed to be assigned on the southern side of that line, and would they not be at liberty to carry their slaves there, if they pleased? You would give them the whole of that; and then what would be its fate?

Is it upon the general principle of humanity, then, that you [addressing Republican Senators] wish to put an end to slavery, or is it to be urged by you as a mere topic and point of party controversy to sustain party power? Surely I give you credit for looking at it upon broader and more generous principles. Then, in the worst event, after you have encountered disunion, that greatest of all political calamities to the people of this country, and the disunionists come, the separating States come, and demand or take their portion of the Territories, they can take, and will be entitled to take, all that will now lie on the southern side of the line which I have proposed. Then they will have a right to permit slavery to exist in it; and what do you gain for the cause of anti-slavery? Nothing whatever. Suppose you should refuse their demand, and claim the whole for yourselves: that would be a flagrant injustice which you would not be willing that I should suppose would occur. But if you did, what would be the consequence? A State north and a State south, and all the States, north and south, would be attempting to grasp at and seize this territory, and to get all of it that they could. That would be the struggle, and you would have war; and not only disunion, but all these fatal consequences would follow from your refusal now to permit slavery to exist, to recognize it as existing, on the southern side of the proposed line, while you give to the people there the right to exclude it when they come to form a State government, if such would be their will and pleasure.

Now, gentlemen, in view of this subject, in view of the mighty consequences, in view of the great events which are present before you, and of the mighty consequences which are just now to take effect, is it not better to settle the question by a division upon the line of the Missouri compromise? For thirty years we lived quietly and peacefully under it. Our people, North and South, were accustomed to look at it as a proper and just line. Can we not do so again? We did it then to preserve the peace of the country. Now you see this Union in the most imminent danger. I declare to you that it is my solemn conviction that unless something be done, and something equivalent to this proposition, we shall be a separated and divided people in six months from this time. That is my firm conviction. There is no man here who deplores it more than I do; but it is my sad and melancholy conviction that that will be the consequence. I wish you to realize fully the danger. I wish you to realize fully the consequences which are to follow. You can give increased stability to the Union; you can give it an existence, a glorious existence, for great and glorious centuries to come, by now setting it upon a permanent basis, recognizing what the South considers as its rights; and this is the greatest of them all: It is that you should divide the territory by this line and allow the people south of it to have slavery when they are admitted into the Union as States, and to have it during the existence of the territorial government. That is all. Is it not the cheapest price at which such a blessing as this Union was ever purchased? You think, perhaps, or some of you, that there is no danger, that it will but thunder and pass away. Do not entertain such a fatal delusion. I tell you it is not so. I tell you that as sure as we stand here disunion will progress. I fear it may swallow up even old Kentucky in its vortex—as true a State to the Union as yet exists in the whole Confederacy—unless something be done; but that you will have disunion, that anarchy and war will follow it, that all this will take place within six months, I believe as confidently as I believe in your presence. I want to satisfy you of the fact.

Mr. President, I rise to suggest another consideration. I have been surprised to find, upon a little examination, that when the peace of 1783 was made, which recognized the independence of this country by Great Britain, the States north of Mason and Dixon's line had but a territory of one hundred and sixty-four thousand square miles, while the States south of Mason and Dixon's line had more than six hundred thousand square miles. It was so divided. Virginia shortly afterwards ceded to the United States all that noble territory northwest of the Ohio river, and excluded slavery from it. That changed the relative proportion of territory. After that, the North had four hundred and twenty-five thousand square miles, and the South three hundred and eighty-five thousand. Thus, at once, by the concession of Virginia, the North, from one hundred and sixty-four thousand, rose to four hundred and twenty-five thousand square miles, and the South fell from six hundred thousand to three hundred and eighty-five thousand square miles. By that cession the South became smaller in extent than the North. Well, let us look beyond. I intend to take up as little time as possible, and to avoid details; but take all your subsequent acquisitions of Florida, of Louisiana, of Oregon; of Texas, and the acquisitions made from Mexico. They have been so divided and so disposed of that the North has now two millions, two hundred thousand square miles of territory, and the South has less than one million.

Under these circumstances, when you have been so greatly magnified—I do not complain of it, I am stating facts—when your section has been made so mighty by these great acquisitions, and to a great extent with the perfect consent of the South, ought you to hesitate now upon adopting this line which will leave to you on the north side of it nine hundred and odd thousand square miles, and leave to the South only two hundred and eighty-five thousand? It will give you three times as much as it will give her. There is three times as much land in your portion as in hers. The South has already occupied some of it, and it is in States; but altogether the South gets by this division two hundred and eighty-five thousand square miles, and the North nine hundred thousand. The result of the whole of it is, that the North has two million two hundred thousand square miles and the South only one million.

I mention this as no reproach, as no upbraiding, as no complaint—none at all. I do not speak in that spirit; I do not address you in that temper. But these are the facts, and they ought, it seems to me, to have some weight; and when we come to make a peace-offering, are we to count it, are we to measure it nicely in golden scales? You get a price, and the dearest price, for all the concession asked to be made—you have the firmer establishment of your Union; you have the restoration of peace and tranquillity, and the hopes of a mighty future, all secured by this concession. How dearly must one individual, or two individuals, or many individuals, value their private opinions if they think them more important to the world than this mighty interest of the Union and the Government of the United States!

Sir, it is a cheap sacrifice. It is a glorious sacrifice. This Union cost a great deal to establish it; it cost the yielding of much of public opinion and much of policy, besides the direct or indirect cost of it in all the war to establish the independency of this country. When it was done, General Washington himself said, Providence has helped us, or we could not have accomplished this thing. And this gift of our wisest men; this great work of their hands; this work in the foundation and the structure of which Providence himself, with his benignant [sic] hand, helped—are we to give it all up for such small considerations? The present exasperation; the present feeling of disunion, is the result of a long-continued controversy on the subject of slavery and of territory. I shall not attempt to trace that controversy; it is unnecessary to the occasion, and might be harmful. In relation to such controversies, I will say, though, that all the wrong is never on one side, or all the right on the other. Right and wrong, in this world, and in all such controversies, are mingled together. I forebear now any discussion or any reference to the right or wrong of the controversy, the mere party controversy; but in the progress of party, we now come to a point where party ceases to deserve consideration, and the preservation of the Union demands our highest and our greatest exertions. To preserve the Constitution of the country is the highest duty of the Senate, the highest duty of Congress—to preserve it and to perpetuate it, that we may hand down the glories which we have received to our children and to our posterity, and to generations far beyond us. We are, Senators, in positions where history is to take notice of the course we pursue.

History is to record us. Is it to record that when the destruction of the Union was imminent; when we saw it tottering to its fall; when we saw brothers arming their hands for hostility with one another, we stood quarreling about points of party politics; about questions which we attempted to sanctify and to consecrate by appealing to our conscience as the source of them? Are we to allow such fearful catastrophics to occur while we stand trifling away our time? While we stand pious, showing our inferiority to the great and mighty dead, showing our inferiority to the high positions which we occupy, the country may be destroyed and ruined; and to the amazement of all the world, the great Republic may fall prostrate and in ruins, carrying with it the very hope of that liberty with it, in place of the peace we have enjoyed, nothing but revolution and havoc and anarchy. Shall it be said that we have allowed all these evils to come upon our country, while we were engaged in the petty and small disputes and debates to which I have referred? Can it be that our name is to rest in history with this everlasting stigma and blot upon it?

Sir, I wish to God, it was in my power to preserve this Union by renouncing or agreeing to give up every conscientious and other opinion. I might not be able to discard it from my mind; I am under no obligation to do that. I may retain the opinion, but if I could do so great a good as to preserve my country and give it peace, and its institutions and its Union stability, I will forego any action upon my opinions. Well now my friends, [addressing the Republican Senators,] that is all that is asked of you. Consider it well, and do not distrust the result. As to the rest of this body, gentlemen from the South, I would say to them, can you ask more than this? Are you bent on revolution and disunion? God forbid it. I cannot believe that such madness possesses the American people. This gives reasonable satisfaction. I can speak with confidence only of my own State. Old Kentucky will be satisfied with it, and she will stand by the Union and die by the Union if this satisfaction be given. Nothing shall seduce her. The clamor of no revolution, the seductions and temptations of no revolution, will tempt her to move one step. She has stood always by the side of the Constitution; she has always been devoted to it, and is this day. Give her this satisfaction, and I believe all the States of the South that are not desirous of disunion as a better thing than the Union and the Constitution, will be satisfied and will adhere to the Union, and shall go on again in our great career of national prosperity and national glory.

But, sir, it is not necessary for me to speak to you of the consequences that will follow disunion. Who of us is not proud of the greatness we have achieved? Disunion and separation destroy that greatness. Once disunited, we are no longer great. The nations of the earth who have looked upon you as a formidable Power, a mighty Power, and rising to untold and immeasurable greatness in the future, will scoff at you. Your flag, that now claims the respect of the world, protects American property in every port and harbor of the world, that protects the rights of your citizens everywhere, what will become of it? What becomes of its glorious influence? It is gone; and with it the protection of American citizens and property. To say nothing of the national honor which it displayed to all the world, the protection of your rights, the protection of your property abroad is gone with that national flag, and we are hereafter to conjure and contrive different flags for our different republics according to the feverish fancies of revolutionary patriots and disturbers of the peace of the world. No, sir; I want to follow no such flag. I want to preserve the union of my country. We have it in our power to do so, and we are responsible if we do not do it.

I do not despair of the Republic. When I see before me Senators of so much intelligence and so much patriotism, who have been so honored by their country, sent here as the guardians of that very union which is now in question, sent here as the guardians of our national rights, and as guardians of our national flag, I cannot despair; I cannot despond. I cannot but believe that they will find some means of reconciling and adjusting the rights of all parties, by concessions, if necessary, so as to preserve and give more stability to the country and to its institutions.

4

Preserve the Union

Senator Andrew Johnson, Tennessee
December 18 and 19, 1860

Andrew Johnson (1808-1875) was born in North Carolina, apprenticed as a tailor at the age of ten, and worked as a tailor in the Carolinas and Tennessee, after moving there in 1825. In 1828 he organized a workingman's political party and served as its leader. From 1828 onward Johnson steadily advanced from a labor political activist to local, state, and national political prominence. He first served in the U.S. Senate as a Democrat from 1857 to 1862, when he resigned in order to be appointed by President Lincoln as Military Governor of Tennessee with the rank of Brigadier General of Volunteers. He was nominated as a War Democrat and elected to the vice presidency in 1864. On April 15, 1865, he became President of the United States as a result of Lincoln's assassination. On May 16, 1868, he barely escaped the two-thirds vote in the Senate for impeachment; the vote was thirty-five for conviction and nineteen for acquittal. In 1869 and 1872 he lost elections for Senate and House seats respectively, but was successful in his 1874 election to the U.S. Senate. In this speech Johnson conceded the right to revolution, but denied a State's constitutional right to secede. He also conceded that the "great law of self-preservation" dictates that the national government do whatever is necessary to keep the Union intact. From a

*practical viewpoint, he reprimanded both sections, North and South, for
pursuing policies detrimental to their respective long-term interests.*

Mr. JOHNSON. Mr. President, by the joint resolution now before
the Senate, three amendments to the Constitution of the United States
are proposed. One proposes to change the mode of election of President
and Vice President of the United States from the electoral college to a
vote substantially and directly by the people. The second proposes that
the Senators of the United States shall be elected by the people, once in
six years, instead of by the Legislatures of the respective States. The
third provides that the Supreme Court shall be divided into three classes:
the term of the first class is to expire in four years from the time that the
classification is made; of the second class in eight years; and of the third
class in twelve years; and as the vacancies occur they are to be filled by
persons chosen one half from the slave States, and the other half from
the non-slaveholding States, thereby taking the judges of the Supreme
Court, so far as their selection goes, from the respective divisions of the
country. This proposition, in substance, was offered many years ago, in
the House of Representatives; it has been somewhat changed, and is now
offered again for the consideration of the Senate.

Mr. President, if these amendments had been made, or the
Constitution had been in the shape now proposed, I think the difficulties
that are now upon the country would have been obviated. It would have
been required that either the President or the Vice President should be
taken from the South. That would have destroyed, to some extent, the
sectional character of our recent election. The next provision of the
amendment would require the votes cast for President and Vice President
to be cast by districts; and if we are to take as an indication the returns to
the House of Representatives of a majority of twenty-seven against the
incoming Administration, it is pretty conclusive that a President differing
in politics and sentiments from the one who has been recently elected
would have been chosen. Each district would have voted directly for the
President and Vice President of the United States. The individual having
a majority of the votes in that district would be considered as receiving
one electoral vote, just as we count the votes for one member of Congress.
Hence, if all the votes in the respective districts had been cast on the
same principle, we should now have a majority of twenty-seven in
opposition to the incoming Administration; they would have given us a
majority in the electoral colleges. It seems to me, if these propositions
were adopted and made a part of the Constitution, that, to a very great

extent, the difficulty and complaint that is now manifested in different portions of the country would be obviated, and especially so with some improvement or modification of the law which provides for the restoration of fugitives from labor.

It is not my purpose, sir, to discuss these propositions to amend the Constitution in detail today, and I shall say but little more in reference to them and to their practical operation; but, as we are now, as it were, involved in revolution, (for there is a revolution, in fact, upon the country,) I think it behooves every man, and especially every one occupying a public place, to indicate, in some manner, his opinions and sentiments in reference to the questions that agitate and distract the public mind. I shall be frank on this occasion in giving my views and taking my positions, as I have always been upon questions that involve the public interest. I believe it is the imperative duty of Congress to make some effort to save the country from impending dissolution; and he that is unwilling to make an effort to preserve the Union, or, in other words, to preserve the Constitution, and the Union as an incident resulting from the preservation of the Constitution, I think is unworthy of public confidence, and the respect and gratitude of the American people. I say it devolves upon every one who can contribute in the slightest degree to this result to come forward and make some effort, reasonable in its character, to preserve the Union of these States by a preservation of the Constitution.

In most that I shall say on this occasion, I shall not differ very essentially from my southern friends. The difference will consist, as I think, from what I have heard and what I see published in the various periodicals of the day, in the mode and manner by which this great end is to be accomplished. Some of our southern friends think that secession is the mode by which these ends can be accomplished; that if the Union cannot be preserved in its spirit, by secession they will get those rights secured and perpetuated that they have failed to obtain within the Union. I am opposed to secession. I believe it is no remedy for the evils complained of. Instead of acting with that division of my southern friends who take ground for secession, I shall take other grounds while I try to accomplish the same end.

I think that this battle ought to be fought not outside, but inside of the Union, and upon the battlements of the Constitution itself. I am unwilling, of my own volition, to walk outside of the Union which has been the result of a Constitution made by the patriots of the Revolution. They formed the Constitution; and this Union that is so much spoken of, and which all of us are so desirous to preserve, grows out of the

Constitution; and I repeat, I am not willing to walk out of the Union growing out of the Constitution, that was formed by the patriots and, I may say, the soldiers of the Revolution. So far as I am concerned, and I believe I may speak with some degree of confidence for the people of my State, we intend to fight that battle inside and not outside of the Union; and if anybody must go out of the Union, it must be those who violate it. We do not intend to go out. It is our Constitution; it is our Union, growing out of the Constitution; and we do not intend to be driven from it or out of the Union. Those who have violated the Constitution either in the passage of what are denominated personal liberty bills, or by their refusal to execute the fugitive slave law—they having violated the instrument that binds us together—must go out and not we. I do not think we can go before the country with the same force of position demanding of the North a compliance with the Constitution and all its guarantees, if we violate the Constitution by going out ourselves, that we shall if we stand inside of the Constitution, and demand a compliance with its provisions and guarantees; or if need be, as I think it is, to demand additional securities. We should make that demand inside of the Constitution, and in the manner and mode pointed out by the instrument itself. Then we keep ourselves in the right; we put our adversary in the wrong; and though it may take a little longer to accomplish the end, we take the right means to accomplish an end that is right in itself.

I know that sometimes we talk about compromises. I am not a compromiser, nor a conservative, in the usual acceptation of those terms. I have been generally considered radical, and I do not come forward to-day in anything that I shall say or propose, asking anything to be done upon the principle of compromise. If we ask for anything, it should be for that which is right and reasonable in itself. It being right, those of whom we ask it, upon the great principle of right, are bound to grant it. Compromise! I know in the common acceptance of the term it is to agree upon certain propositions in which some things are conceded on one side and others conceded on the other. I shall go for enactments by Congress or for amendments to the Constitution, upon the principle that they are right and upon no other ground. I am not for compromising right with wrong. If we have no right, we ought not to demand it. If we are in the wrong, they should not grant us what we ask. I approach this momentous subject on the great principles of right, asking nothing and demanding nothing but what is right in itself and which every right-minded man and a right-minded community and a right minded-people, who wish the preservation of this Government, will be disposed to grant.

In fighting this battle, I shall do it upon the basis laid down by a portion of the people of my own State, in a large and very intelligent meeting. A committee of the most intelligent men in the country reported, in the shape of resolutions, to this meeting the basis upon which I intend to fight this great battle for our rights. They reported this resolution:

Resolved, That we deeply sympathize with our sister southern States, and freely admit that there is good cause for dissatisfaction and complaint on their part, on account of the recent election of sectional candidates to the Presidency and Vice Presidency of the United States; yet we, as a portion of the people of a slaveholding community, are not for seceding or breaking up the union of these States until every fair and honorable means has been exhausted in trying to obtain, on the part of the non-slaveholding States, a compliance with the spirit and letter of the Constitution and all its guarantees; and when this shall have been done, and the States now in open rebellion against the laws of the United States, in refusing to execute the fugitive slave law, shall persist in their present unconstitutional course, and the Federal Government shall fail or refuse to execute the laws in good faith, it (the Government) will not have accomplished the great design of its creation, and will therefore, in fact, be a practical dissolution, and all the States, as parties, be released from the compact which formed the Union.

The people of Tennessee, irrespective of party, go on and declare further:

That in the opinion of this meeting no State has the constitutional right to secede from the Union without the consent of the other States which ratified the compact. The compact, when ratified, formed the Union without making any provision whatever for its dissolution. It (the compact) was adopted by the States *in toto and forever, 'without reservation or condition;'* hence a secession of one or more States from the Union, without the consent of the others ratifying the compact, would be revolution, leading in the end to civil, and perhaps servile war. While we deny the right of a State, constitutionally, to secede from the Union, we admit the great and inherent right of revolution, abiding and remaining with every people, but a right which should not be exercised, except in extreme cases, and in the last resort, when grievances are without redress, and oppression has become intolerable.

They declare further:

That in our opinion, we can more successfully resist the aggression of Black Republicanism by remaining within the Union, than we can by going out of it; and more especially so, while there is a majority of both branches in the National Legislature opposed to it, and the Supreme Court of the United States is on the side of law and the Constitution.

They go on, and declare further:

That we are not willing to abandon our northern friends who have stood by

the Constitution of the United States, and in standing by it have vindicated
our rights, and in their vindication have been struck down; and now, in
their extremity, we cannot and will not desert them by seceding, or otherwise
breaking up the Union.

This is the basis upon which a portion of the people of Tennessee,
irrespective of party, propose to fight this battle. We believe that our true
position is inside of the Union. We deny the doctrine of secession; we
deny that a State has the power, of its own volition, to withdraw from the
Confederacy. We are not willing to do an unconstitutional act, to induce
or to coerce others to comply with the Constitution of the United States.
We prefer complying with the Constitution and fighting our battle, and
making our demand inside of the Union.

I know, Mr. President, that there are some who believe—and we see
that some of the States are acting on that principle—that a State has the
right to secede; that, of its own will, it has a right to withdraw from the
Confederacy. I am inclined to think, and I know it is so in fact, that in
many portions of the country this opinion has resulted from the resolutions
of your own State, sir, [Mr. Mason in the chair,] of 1798 and 1799. I
propose to-day to examine that subject, for I know from the examination
of it that there has been a false impression made upon my own mind in
reference to those resolutions, and the power proposed to be exercised
by a State seceding upon its own will. When we come to examine those
resolutions, we find that the third reads as follows:

> That this Assembly doth explicitly and peremptorily declare that it views
> the powers of the Federal Government, as resulting from the compact, to
> which the States are parties, as limited by the plain sense and intention of
> the instrument constituting that compact, as no further valid than they are
> authorized by the grants enumerated in that compact; and that in case of a
> deliberate, palpable, and dangerous exercise of other powers not granted
> by the said compact, the States who are parties thereto have the right, and
> are in duty bound, to interpose for arresting the progress of the evil, and for
> maintaining within their respective limits, the authorities, rights, and liberties
> appertaining to them.

The phraseology of the Kentucky resolutions [sic] is somewhat
broader and more extensive than that a State, of its own will, has the
right to secede or withdraw from the Union. The Kentucky resolution
goes on to declare that a State has the right to judge of the infraction of
the Constitution, as well as the mode and measure of redress. This is
what is declared by that resolution which is repeated by so many in
speeches and publications made through the country. Now, let Mr.
Madison speak for himself as to what he meant by that resolution. Mr.

Madison, in his report upon those resolutions, goes on and states expressly that in the resolution the word "States" is used, notwithstanding the word "respective" is used. Mr. Madison says:

It appears to your committee to be a plain principle, founded in common sense, illustrated by common practice, and essential to the nature of compacts, that, where resort can be had to no tribunal superior to the authority of parties, the parties themselves must be the rightful judges, in the last resort, whether the bargain made has been pursued or violated. The Constitution of the United States was formed by the sanction of the States, given by each in its sovereign capacity. It adds to the stability and dignity, as well as to the authority of the Constitution, that it rests on this legitimate and solid foundation. The States, then, being the parties to the constitutional compact, and in their sovereign capacity, it follows of necessity, that there can be no tribunal above their authority, to decide, in the last resort, whether the compact made by them be violated; and, consequently, that, as the parties to it, they must themselves [that is the States] decide, in the last resort, such questions as may be of sufficient magnitude to require their interposition.

"The States" is the idea that is kept up through the report. He further remarks:

But the resolution has done more than guard against misconstruction, by expressly referring to cases of a *deliberate, palpable,* and *dangerous* nature. It specifies the object of the interposition, which it contemplates to be solely that of the progress of the *evil* of usurpation, and of maintaining the authorities, rights, and liberties appertaining to the States, as parties to the Constitution.

Now we find, by the examination of this subject, that Mr. Madison, in his report, explains it, and repudiates the idea that a State, as a member of the compact, has a right to judge of an infraction of the Constitution or any other grievance, and, upon its own volition, withdraw from the Confederacy. I will here read a letter of Mr. Madison to Nicholas P. Trist, in explanation of this very proposition:

MONTPELIER, *December* 23, 1832.

DEAR SIR: I have received yours of the 19th, inclosing [sic] some South Carolina papers. There are in one of them some interesting views of the doctrine of secession, among which one that had occurred to me, and which for the first time I have seen in print, namely: that if one State can at will withdraw from the others, the others can withdraw from her, and turn her, *nolentem volentem,* out of the Union.

Until of late there is not a State that would have abhorred such a doctrine more than South Carolina, or more dreaded an application of it to herself. The same may be said of the doctrine of nullification, which she now preaches as the only doctrine by which the Union can be saved.

I partake of the wonder that the men you name should view secession in the light mentioned. The essential difference between a free Government and a Government not free is, that the former is founded in compact, the parties to which are mutually and equally bound by it. Neither of them, therefore, can have a greater right to break off from the bargain than the others have to hold him to it; and certainly there is nothing in the Virginia resolutions of 1798 adverse to this principle, which is that of common sense and common justice.

The fallacy which draws a different conclusion from them lies in confounding a single party with the parties to the constitutional compact of the United States. The latter, having made the compact, may do what they will with it. The former, as one of the parties, owes fidelity to it till released by consent or absolved by an intolerable abuse of the power created. In the Virginia resolutions and report the plural number (States) is in every instance used whenever reference is made to the authority which presided over the Government.

He says the plural is used; that "States" is the word that is used; and when we turn to the resolution we find it just as Mr. Madison states, thereby excluding the idea that a State can separately and alone determine the question, and have the right to secede from the Union.

As I am now known to have drawn those documents. I may say, as I do with a distinct recollection, that it was intentional. It was in fact required by the course of reasoning employed on the occasion. The Kentucky resolutions, being less guarded, have been more easily perverted. The pretext for the liberty taken with those of Virginia is the word 'respective' prefixed to the 'rights, &c.' to be secured within the States. Could the abuse of the expression have been foreseen or suspected, the form of it would doubtless have been varied. But what can be more consistent with common sense than that all having the rights, &c., should unite in contending for the security of them to each?

It is remarkable how closely the nullifiers, who make the name of Mr. Jefferson the pedestal for their colossal heresy, shut their eyes and lips whenever his authority is ever so clearly and emphatically against them. You have noticed what he says in his letters to Monroe and Carrington (pp. 43 and 203, vol. 2) with respect to the power of the old Congress to coerce delinquent States: and his reason for preferring for the purpose a naval to a military force; and, moreover, his remarks that it was not necessary to find a right to coerce in the Federal articles, that being inherent in the nature of a compact. It is high time that the claim to secede at will should be put down by the public opinion, and I am glad to see the task commenced by one who understands the subject.

I know nothing of what is passing at Richmond more than what is seen in the newspapers. You were right in your foresight of the effect of passages in the late proclamation. They have proven a leaven for much fermentation there, and created an alarm against the danger of consolidation balancing that of disunion.

With cordial salutations,

JAMES MADISON,

Nicholas P. Trist.

I have another letter of Mr. Madison, written in 1833, sustaining and carrying out the same interpretation of the resolutions of 1798 and 1799. I desire to read some extracts from that letter. Mr. Madison says:

> Much use has been made of the term 'respective' in the third resolution of Virginia, which asserts the right of the *States*, in case of sufficient magnitude, to interpose 'for maintaining within their *respective* limits the authorities, &c., appertaining to them; the term 'respective' being construed to mean a constitutional right in *each State, separately*, to decide on and resist by force encroachments within its limits. A foresight and apprehension of the misconstruction might easily have guarded against it. But, to say nothing of the distinction between ordinary and extreme cases, it is observable that in this, as in other instances throughout the resolutions, the plural number (*States*) is used in referring to them; that a concurrence and cooperation of all might well be contemplated in interpositions for effecting the objects within reach; and that the language of the closing resolution corresponds with this view of the third. The course of reasoning in the report on the resolutions required the distinction between a *State* and *the States*.
>
> It surely does not follow, from the fact of the States, or rather the people embodied in them having, as parties to the constitutional compact, no tribunal above them, that in controverted meanings of the compact, a minority of the parties can rightfully decide against the majority, still less that a single party can decide against the rest and as little that it can at will withdraw itself altogether from its compact with the rest.
>
> The characteristic distinction between free governments and governments not free, is that the former are founded on compact, not between the government and those for whom it acts, but among the parties creating the government. Each of these being equal, neither can have more right to say that the compact has been violated and dissolved than every other has to deny the fact, and to insist on the execution of the bargain. An inference from the doctrine that a single State has a right to secede at will from the rest, is that the rest would have an equal right to secede from it; in other words, to turn it, against its will, out of its union with them. Such a doctrine would not, till of late, have been palatable anywhere, and nowhere less so than where it is now most contended for.

When these letters are put together they are clear and conclusive. Take the resolutions; take the report; take Mr. Madison's expositions of them in 1832 and 1833; his letter to Mr. Trist; his letter to Mr. Webster; his letter to Mr. Rives; and when all are summed up, this doctrine of a State, either assuming her highest political attitude or otherwise, having the right of her own will to dissolve all connection with this Confederacy, is an absurdity, and contrary to the plain intent and meaning of the Constitution of the United

States. I hold that the Constitution of the United States makes no provision, as said by the President of the United States, for its own destruction. It makes no provision for breaking up the Government, and no State has the constitutional right to secede and withdraw from the Union.

In July, 1788, when the Constitution of the United States was before the convention of New York for Ratification, Mr. Madison was in the city of New York. Mr. Hamilton, who was in the convention, wrote a letter to Mr. Madison to know if New York could be admitted into the Union with certain reservations or conditions. One of these reservations or conditions was, as Mr. Hamilton says in his letter, that they should have the privilege of receding within five or seven years if certain alterations and amendments were not made to the Constitution of the United States. Mr. Madison, in reply to that letter, makes use of the following emphatic language, which still further corroborates and carries out the idea that the Constitution makes no provision for breaking up the government, and that no State has a right to secede. Mr. Madison says:

New York, *Saturday evening.*

My Dear Sir: Yours of yesterday is this instant come to hand; and I have but a few minutes to answer it. I am sorry that your situation obliges you to listen to propositions of the nature you describe. My opinion is, that a reservation of a right to withdraw if amendments be not decided on under the form of the Constitution within a certain time, is a *conditional* ratification; that it does not make New York a member of the new Union, and consequently that she could not be received on that plan. Compacts must be reciprocal—this principle would not in such a case be preserved. The Constitution requires an adoption *in toto* and *forever.*

This is the language of Mr. Madison.

It has been so adopted by the other States. An adoption for a limited time would be as defective as an adoption of some of the articles only. In short, any *condition* whatever must vitiate the ratification. What the new Congress, by virtue of the power to admit new States, may be *able* and disposed to do in such case, I do not inquire, as I suppose that is not the material point at present. I have not a moment to add more my fervent wishes for your success and happiness. The idea of reserving a right to withdraw was started at Richmond, and considered as a conditional ratification, which was itself abandoned as worse than a rejection.JAMES MADISON, Jr.

I know it is claimed, and I see it stated in some of the newspapers, that Virginia and some of the other States made a reservation, upon ratification of the Constitution, that certain conditions were annexed; that they came in upon certain conditions, and therefore had a right, in consequence of those conditions, to do this or the other thing. When we examine the journal of the convention, we find that no mention is made of any reservation on the ratification of the Constitution by the State of Virginia. We find that Mr. Madison says, in his letter to Mr. Hamilton, that this idea was first mooted at Richmond, and was abandoned as worse than a rejection. His letter was written after the ratification of the Constitution of the United States by the State of Virginia. Hence he spoke with a knowledge of the fact that existed, that no reservation was made; and even if it had been made by one of the parties, and not sanctioned by the other parties to the compact, what would it have amounted to? Then we see that Mr. Madison repudiates the doctrine that a State has the right to secede. We see that his resolutions admit of no such construction. We see that Mr. Madison, in his letter to Mr. Hamilton, puts the interpretation that this Constitution was adopted *in toto* and forever, without reservation and without condition.

I know that the inquiry may be made, how is a State, then, to have redress? There is but one way, and that is expressed by the people of Tennessee. You have entered into this compact; it was mutual; it was reciprocal; and of your own volition have no right to withdraw and break the compact, without the consent of the other parties. What remedy, then, has the State? It has a remedy that remains and abides with every people upon the face of the earth—when grievances are without a remedy, or without redress, when oppression becomes intolerable, they have the great inherent right of revolution, and that is all there is of it.

Sir, if the doctrine of secession is to be carried out upon the mere whim of a State, this Government is at an end. I am as much opposed to a strong, or what may be called by some a consolidated Government, as it is possible for a man to be; but while I am greatly opposed to that, I want a Government strong enough to preserve its own existence; that will not fall to pieces by its own weight or whenever a little dissatisfaction takes place in one of its members. If the States have the right to secede at will and pleasure, for real or imaginary evils or oppressions, I repeat again, this Government is at an end; it is not stronger than a rope of sand; its own weight will tumble it to pieces and it cannot exist. Notwithstanding this doctrine may suit some who are engaged in this perilous and impending crisis that is now upon us, duty to my country, duty to my State, and duty to my kind, require me to avow a doctrine that I believe will result in the preservation of the Government, and to repudiate one that I believe will result in its overthrow, and the consequent disasters to the people of the United States.

If a State can secede at will and pleasure, and this doctrine is maintained, why, I ask, on the other hand, and as Mr. Madison argues in one of his letters, cannot a majority of the States combine and reject a State out of the Confederacy? Have a majority of these States, under the compact they have made with each other, the right to combine and reject any one of the States from the Confederacy? They have no such right; the compact is reciprocal. It was ratified without reservation or condition, and it was ratified "*in toto* and forever;" such is the language of James Madison; and there is but one way to get out of it without the consent of the parties, and that is, by revolution.

I know that some touch on the subject with trembling and fear. They say, here is a State that, perhaps by this time, has seceded, or if not, she is on the road to secession, and we must touch this subject very delicately; and that if the State secedes, conceding the power of the Constitution to her to secede, you must talk very delicately upon the subject of coercion. I do not believe the Federal Government has the power to coerce a State; for by the eleventh amendment of the Constitution of the United States it is expressly provided that you cannot even put one of the States of this Confederacy before one of the courts of the country as a party. As a State, the Federal Government has no power to coerce it; but it is a member of the compact to which it agreed in common with the other States, and this Government has the right to pass laws, and to enforce those laws upon individuals within the limits of each State. While the one proposition is clear, the other is equally so. This Government can, by the Constitution of the country and by the laws enacted in conformity with the Constitution, operate upon individuals, and has the right and the power, not to coerce a State, but to enforce and execute the law upon individuals within the limits of a State.

I know the term, "to coerce a State," is used in an *ad captandum* manner. It is a sovereignty that is to be crushed! How is a State in the Union? What is her connection with it? All the connection she has with the other States is that which is agreed upon in the compact between the States. I do not know whether you may consider it in the Union or out of the Union, or whether you simply consider it a connection or a disconnection with the other States; but to the extent that a State nullifies or sets aside any law or any provision of the Constitution, to that extent it has dissolved its connection, and no more. I think the States that have passed their personal liberty bills, in violation of the Constitution of the United States, coming in conflict with the fugitive slave law, to that extent have dissolved their connection, and to that extent it is revolution. But because some of the free States have passed laws violative of the Constitution; because they have, to some extent, dissolved their connection with this Government, does that justify us of the South in following that bad example? Because they have passed personal liberty bills, and have, to that extent, violated the compact which is reciprocal, shall we turn around, on the other hand, and violate the Constitution by coercing them to a compliance with it? Will we do so?

Then I come back to the starting point: let us stand in the Union and upon the Constitution; and if anybody is to leave this Union, or violate its guarantees, it shall be those who have taken the initiative, and passed their personal liberty bills. I am in the Union, and intend to stay in it. I intend to hold on to the Union, and the guarantees under which this Union has grown; and I do not intend to be driven from it, nor out of it, by their unconstitutional enactments.

Then, Mr. President, suppose, for instance, that a fugitive is arrested in the State of Vermont tomorrow, and under the personal liberty bill of that State, or the law—I do not remember its precise title now—which prevents, or is intended to prevent, the faithful execution of that law, Vermont undertakes to rescue him, and prevent the enforcement of the law: what is it? It is nullification; it is resistance to the laws of the United States, made in conformity with the Constitution; it is rebellion; and it is the duty of the President of the United States to enforce the law, at all hazards and to the last extremity. And, to come back to the premises, if the Federal Government fails or refuses to execute the laws made in conformity with the Constitution, and those States persist in their violation and let those unconstitutional acts remain upon their statute-books and carry them into practice; if the Government, on the one hand, fails to execute those laws, and those States, by their enactments, violate them on the other, the Government is at an end, and the parties are all released from the compact.

MR. COLLAMER. Will the gentleman indulge me one moment?

MR. JOHNSON, of Tennessee. Yes, sir.

MR. COLLAMER. The gentleman has made allusion particularly to the laws of my own State.

MR. JOHNSON, of Tennessee. I will say to the Senator that his State happened to occur to my mind, and I spoke of it simply by way of illustration.

MR. COLLAMER. I claim the privilege of saying a few words about that subject, if the gentleman will indulge me.

MR. JOHNSON, of Tennessee. Certainly.

MR. COLLAMER. Mr. President, without entering into the thread of the Senator's remarks with which I generally agree, there has been a good deal said about the action of Vermont recently, in relation to refusing to repeal certain laws. Much is said about it, I see, in the papers of the South. I wish that the truth of that matter was all known together. The whole story should be told. I shall not occupy a long time. The gentleman can have a little rest; I will not occupy a great while. I wish that I could succeed in once obtaining a short attention of gentlemen on the other side, who seem to suppose that every law concerning the colored people in the free States is made against the fugitive slave law. They look at in that light; and I see that the one in Vermont which quoted is the act of 1844. I see it is quoted in the Constitution newspaper as being of the number. When Senators speak about their being in opposition to the fugitive slave law, undoubtedly gentlemen mean the fugitive slave law of 1850. Now, will gentlemen bear in mind that that very act of Vermont was made six years before that law was passed! It had nothing in the world to do with it.

It should be remembered that in 1842, in the case of *Prigg* vs. *The Commonwealth of Pennsylvania*, the Supreme Court of the United States decided that the owner of a fugitive slave had a right to go and recapture him in the same way that a man might recapture any other personal property, subject to having a suit brought about it afterwards. When a man takes a horse, a suit can be brought afterwards to try the title. The Supreme Court decided that it would be just like that, provided the man, in so taking his slave, did not violate any State law. Now, I say it is to be borne in mind that the court recognized two modes of reclaiming fugitive slaves. One of them is according to the fugitive slave laws of Congress, and the other is the one I have just spoken of. Now, the laws that are made in my State, so far as I understand them, with regard to the recapture or reclamation of slaves, have nothing whatever to do with proceedings under the fugitive slave law; they relate to this other branch; this other mode of getting back slaves. The law was passed before the present fugitive slave law was enacted. There was a fugitive slave law in 1793; but any man who will read this act of Vermont that is now quoted, and read it in the light of what I have now suggested to him, will see that it does not relate at all to any action under the law of Congress. It goes upon the basis that every State is bound to protect its own citizens; its own people that are residents of the State; those who are commorant [sic] in the State, let their color be what it may. That, I presume, no one will deny. Then, when it was said that a man had a right to go and take his slave in a free State by mere manucaption, without resorting to any legal process whatever, cannot any man have candor enough to see that it was utterly impossible to protect our colored people against those persons who are kidnappers? Hence it was that we did what in effect the Supreme Court of the United States invited should be done; that is, make such laws as would secure our people in their rights against the assertion of the rights of those who go to take upon their own strength.

MR. JOHNSON, of Tennessee. I would ask the Senator, before he concludes what he has to say, if the Legislature of his State did not pass an additional law in 1858?

MR. COLLAMER. I was about to remark that there are some other laws; but the one which is quoted, the one which is relied upon—

MR. JOHNSON, of Tennessee. Well, sir, I was alluding to their laws generally, the steps they have taken either in former times or recently, which come in conflict with the execution of that provision of the Constitution which provides for the restoration of fugitive slaves.

MR. COLLAMER. Before I get through, the gentleman will hear all that I have got to say on that. I do not want to occupy his time much; but to complete my explanation, I must say a little more. I say that if any man will read the law to which I have alluded — the one that is quoted in the papers — and read it in the light of this decision, and in view of the facts of history, as they have transpired, he will see that it was not dictated by any enmity to the fugitive slave law; because, while it imposes severe penalties upon the taking away of colored people, and subjects to punishment all who participate in such transactions, it goes on to provide, in the last section of it, that this statute shall not be construed to extend to any judge of the United States court, or to any marshal of the United States, or to any of his assistants. It has nothing to do with the United States law. I concede that there have been two or three laws passed since the compromise measures of 1850, though I have not examined them much; and they were produced, particularly the act of 1858, which is now referred to, by what our people understood the Supreme Court to say, that a colored man, a descendant of an African, is a man without any rights that any white person is bound to respect at all. I have never examined these recent statutes fully. It is very likely that there may be features in them that are exceptional. But, Mr. President, it is to be borne in mind that the people of the free States have never held the doctrine that a State can nullify a United States law. I can easily see why the people in the extreme South, who hold that a State can nullify a United States law, think that here is an attempt to nullify a law of Congress. Our people never have held such a doctrine in the world. The profession have [sic] paid very little attention to these statutes at any rate. We look upon them just in this light: that if there are any of them which are in any way inconsistent with the provisions of the United States Constitution, they are simply waste paper and void. We deny that a State, by passing an unconstitutional law, can take itself out of the Union; and we deny, too, that if one State passes such a law, it can justify another State in going out of the Union. Such laws are simply void under the Constitution. That is our view of it, and therefore they are treated before our courts, whenever they come before them, as they would be treated anywhere else—we judge of their constitutionality with perfect fidelity.

Now Mr. President, one word in relation to the recent proposition for their repeal which I have seen mentioned. A gentleman in the State Legislature presented a bill for the repeal of these personal liberty bills, so far as they were inconsistent with the United States Constitution, or something to that effect. It was referred to a committee, of which he was made the chairman—a special committee. They made a report. It lay upon the table, and was not called up. When they had had their usual session, and came to the last day but one of the sitting, having already fixed a day to adjourn, he called up his bill. What was the result? I ought to state, further, that it is the practice of the State of Vermont, about once in twenty years, to have a careful revision of her statutes. The time had come to have it; the twenty years had passed since the last revision. In the course of the session, the Legislature had raised a commission of revision, and had appointed upon it three gentlemen, as good as we can furnish, and I do not know that it would be much arrogance to say, as good as any State could furnish. Two of them were judges of the supreme court, the other a very distinguished lawyer, formerly a member of Congress—men holding no places, wanting none—men of high position and ability. These gentlemen were appointed to revise our statutes. On the last day of the session, when the bill to repeal the personal liberty laws was called up, the gentleman who had presented it made a long argument upon it, but there was no time to consider it. They wanted all their statutes revised and considered. A motion was made in the House to dismiss the bill, and it was dismissed. The Senate immediately, on the same day, took up and passed a resolution referring all of these statutes that were said to be exceptional by people abroad, to that board of revision, to report to the next session of the Legislature if any of those laws were in any way inconsistent with the United States Constitution, or the United States laws passed according to the Constitution. It was passed, all saying "we desire no unconstitutional statutes on our books; we will endure none; we shall have them examined by a competent body, and we have just raised one." The Senate passed the proposition unanimously; they sent it to the House in the shape of a joint resolution; it was passed there unanimously, and the subject was referred to the board of revision. In all candor, is not this the dealing with the subject fairly and candidly, and on our own motion? It is no foundation for ground of objection abroad that the State of Vermont is dealing unkindly or unfairly or uncandidly.

Mr. JOHNSON, of Tennessee. Mr. President, I think that I am rather unfortunate to-day. In the first instance I gave way for an hour, and in the next place a quite lengthy speech to be injected into mine. However, as the Senator has made an explanation on the subject, I wish to ask him if he believes the law passed in 1858 by the State of Vermont in reference to persons of color in that State is constitutional or unconstitutional?

Mr. COLLAMER. The gentleman puts to me a question, and he is entitled to have that sort of candid answer which I take it the putting of the question implies. I said when I was up before that I have never examined those laws much myself. I never have. I do not know precisely what their condition is, nor what their provisions may be exactly. I have this, however, to say about it: it may be, after all, that though upon its face some of its provisions may look exceptionable, they may not really be so. It comes to this: I believe that the statute declares, in effect, that all persons held to slavery who come into Vermont, voluntarily or involuntarily, who come there of their own accord, or are brought there by their masters, shall be considered and regarded as free persons. I rather think that is the amount of it, according to my recollection. Now, what is the reason for that? I have already suggested that the Supreme Court have intimated, as our people understand the Chief Justice, that colored persons have no rights that the white man is bound to respect at all.

Mr. BENJAMIN (Louisiana). Will the Senator from Vermont permit me to—

Mr. COLLAMER. I have heard the gentleman's explanation of that several times.

Mr. BENJAMIN. Will the Senator tell us that any man in New England honestly believes the Supreme Court did decide that? Does he know any man who believes it?

Mr. COLLAMER. I can say that I believe the body of them honestly say they read it so. It reads just so.

Mr. BENJAMIN. Does the Senator say that that decision reads so?

Mr. COLLAMER. The opinion. The gentleman and myself, as

lawyers, understand the difference between an opinion and a decision. The opinion of the Chief Justice, in reciting the history of the Declaration of Independence and of the Constitution, and the condition of society at the time when those instruments were formed, comes to the result that that notion was entertained at that period, stating it in about those words which I have before repeated; and he leaves it to be understood that nothing has transpired since to change that condition of things. That is the way it is in the opinion of the court; that is the way we read it; that is the way I understand it myself.

Mr. BENJAMIN. Does the Senator say that he understands the Supreme Court to say in the opinion, that now, at this day, colored men have no rights that white men are bound to respect?

Mr. COLLAMER. The gentleman gives his version to my own statement. I choose my own version for my own statement. I understand the Chief Justice to say, as I have already stated, that in the history of these transactions, speaking of the period of time and the condition of society at the period of the adoption of the Constitution, that then—

Mr. DOOLITTLE (Wisconsin). Here is the decision, which I will hand to my friend.

Mr. BENJAMIN. Read the whole paragraph.

Mr. COLLAMER. Speaking of the condition of the colored race at the period of the Declaration of Independence and of the formation of the Constitution, the Chief Justice, in his opinion, says:

> They had for more than a century before been regarded as beings of an inferior order, and altogether unfit to associate with the white race, either in social or political relations; and so far inferior, that they had no rights which the white man was bound to respect; and that the negro might justly and lawfully be reduced to slavery for his benefit.

These are the words, and this is all there is to qualify that clause. He does not say anywhere in the opinion that the *status* of the black man has been changed since. He says nothing of the kind. Now, I say that I believe the body of the people of Vermont read that, and, understanding the English language, understand it to mean just what it says. However, that diverts me from the question put by the Senator from Tennessee. I have answered the Senator from Louisiana, and I have read the paragraph.

Now, Mr. President, to go on with the question from the Senator from Tennessee, the State of Vermont, in legislating in reference to the action of her own tribunals, having nothing to do with the United States law in regard to fugitive slaves, but simply in relation to the conduct and directions to her own tribunals in regard to this business of reclaiming slaves by the act of the master himself, has said—her language to her tribunals is—you are to presume every colored man as free until the contrary appears. In the South, we understand, they presume every colored man to be a slave until the contrary is shown. Now, we say to you in our law that you shall regard every colored man free, we care not how he gets here, until the contrary is shown. I say to you, Mr. President, that I do not believe the people of the State of Vermont, or their Legislature, ever thought of infringing the United States Constitution. They did not suppose they had done it; they never tried to do it; they never intended to do it; and what precise version they would give to their words as merely a law for their own courts, I am not prepared to say; but I do say that that law, like every other law in Vermont, whenever a question arises, will receive a fair construction. When gentlemen say that our laws have aided in the escape of a fugitive slave, I deny it. I do not believe there has been a fugitive slave in Vermont for these forty years. I never heard of one. I do not believe there has been one there. I know that one fellow claimed to be a runaway slave; but he was an impostor, and was not a runaway slave, and did not even from extremists get public sympathy for that, only for a short time. Nor has our law aided in any way to affect or impair the fugitive slave law of Congress. But, Mr. President, whether it has or has not, if our law is in any way inconsistent with the provisions of the United States Constitution, or the constitutional laws of Congress, I tell you it will be set aside, whenever a question arises before a court of Vermont, as quickly as it would before a court of the United States. So, too, if there is anything in it which is at all inconsistent with the Constitution, or the constitutional laws of Congress, I tell you that our board of revision will see that it is not kept on the statute-book—no doubt of it.

Mr. JOHNSON, of Tennessee. Mr. President—

Mr. BRAGG (North Carolina). If the Senator will give way, I will move an adjournment. I think, considering the lateness of the hour and the fact that the Senator from Tennessee has been so frequently interrupted, it is but justice to him that we should now adjourn and allow him to conclude to-morrow.

Mr. WIGFALL (Texas). It is only three o'clock.

The PRESIDING OFFICER, (Mr. Polk in the chair.) It is moved that the Senate do now adjourn.

Mr. COLLAMER. If that is agreeable to the wishes of the gentleman from Tennessee, of course we shall make no objection.

Mr. JOHNSON, of Tennessee. I am willing to go on now if the Senate desires me to continue; but there have been a good many interruptions; it is late in the day; and, if such be the pleasure of the Senate, I prefer resuming my remarks in the morning.

The motion was agreed to; and the Senate adjourned.

December 19, 1860

Mr. JOHNSON, of Tennessee. Mr. President, yesterday, while I was pursuing a line of argument to prove that a State had no constitutional power to secede from the Union without the consent of the other States, I was diverted from it to some extent by making use of an illustration in reference to the law of the State of Vermont upon the subject of fugitive slaves, which led to the Senator from Vermont [Mr. COLLAMER] making an explanation in reference to that law. I did not think that his explanation was entirely satisfactory; and the answer that he made to the direct question that I propounded to him, I think is more unsatisfactory than the preceding portion of his remarks. That Senator being a gentleman of legal attainments, having presided in the courts of the country, and having been for a long time in the councils of the country, I asked him a plain question in regard to a law of his own State, about which there had been much controversy in the newspapers. I asked him whether he was of opinion that it was a constitutional law, or whether it did not come in conflict with the fugitive slave law which was passed by the Congress of the United States in strict conformity with the Constitution of the country. I do not see him in his place; but if I remember his reply, it was an evasion. He said that it might or might not be unconstitutional. I did not ask him what it might or might not be; I asked simply what was his opinion upon the subject, and there was no reply given to that explicit question.

I think it will be determined by the courts, and will be determined by the judgment of the country, that the acts passed in 1850 and 1858 by the Legislature of Vermont are a violation, a gross palpable violation of the Constitution of the United States. It is clear and conclusive to my mind, that a State passing an unconstitutional act intended to impede or to prevent the execution of a law passed by the Congress of the United States which is constitutional, is thereby placed, so far as the initiative is concerned, in a state of rebellion. It is an open act of nullification. It is true that, so far as my information goes, I am not aware that there has been any attempt in Vermont to wrest any person out of the hands of the officers of the United States, or to imprison or to fine any person under the operation of this law; but the passage of such an act is to initiate rebellion. I think it comes in conflict directly with the spirit and letter of the Constitution of the United States, and to that extent is an act of nullification, and places the State in open rebellion to the United States.

I stated yesterday that there was no power conferred upon the Congress of the United States, by the Constitution, to coerce a State in its sovereign capacity; that there was no power on the part of the Congress of the United States even to bring a State into the supreme tribunal of the country. You cannot put a State at the bar of the Supreme Court of the United States. But, in this connection, I did say that the Congress of the United States had the power to pass laws to operate upon individuals within the limits of a State, by which all the functions of this Government could be executed and carried out. Then, in this case, if Vermont, either by an act of secession, which I take to be unconstitutional, or without first having seceded from the Union of the States by open force, in conformity with the laws of the State, should resist or attempt to resist the execution of the laws of the United States, it would be a practical rebellion, an overt act; and this Government has the power and authority under the Constitution to enforce the laws of the United States, and it has the power and authority to call to its aid such means as are deemed necessary and proper for the execution of the laws, even if it was to lead to the calling out of the militia, or calling into service the Army and Navy of the United States to execute the laws. While I make this application to Vermont, I say the same principle applies to every other State placing herself in a like attitude in opposition to, and in contravention of, the execution of the laws of the United States.

I do not think it necessary, in order to preserve this Union, or to keep a State within its sphere, that the Congress of the United States should have the power to coerce a State. All that is necessary for the Government to have the power to execute and carry out all the powers conferred upon it by the Constitution, whether they apply to the State or otherwise. This, I think, the Government clearly has the power to do; and so long as the Government executes all the laws in good faith, denying the right of a State constitutionally to secede, so long the State is in the Union, and subject to all the provisions of the Constitution and the laws passed in conformity with it. For example: the power is conferred on the Federal Government to carry mails through the several States; to establish post offices and post roads; the power is conferred on the Federal Government to establish courts in the respective States; the power is conferred on the General Government to lay and collect taxes in the several States; and so on. The various powers are enumerated, and each and every one of these powers the Federal Government has the constitutional authority to execute within the limits of the States. It is not an invasion of a State for the Federal Government to execute its laws, to take care of its public property, and to enforce the collection of its revenue; but if, in the execution of the laws; if, in the enforcement of the Constitution, it meets with resistance, it is the duty of the Government, and it has the authority, to put down resistance, and effectually to execute the laws as contemplated by the Constitution of the country.

But this was a diversion from the line of my argument. I was going to show that, according to the opinions of the fathers, not only of the country but of the Constitution itself, no State, of its own volition, had the right to withdraw from the Confederacy after having entered into the compact. I referred yesterday to the last letter Mr. Madison wrote upon this subject—at least it is the last one that I have been able to find—in which he summed up this subject in a conclusive and masterly manner. In his letter to Mr. Webster of March 15, 1833, upon the receipt of Mr. Webster's speech, after the excitement had subsided to some extent and the country had taken its stand, Mr. Madison said:

> The Constitution of the United States being established by a competent authority, by that of the sovereign people of the several States who were parties to it, it remains only to inquire what the Constitution is; and here it speaks for itself. It organizes a Government into the usual legislative, executive, and judiciary departments; invests it with specified powers, leaving others to the parties to the Constitution. It makes the Government, like other Governments, to operate directly on the people; places at its command the needful physical means of executing its powers; and finally proclaims its supremacy, and that of the laws made in pursuance of it, over the constitutions and laws of the States, the powers of the Government being exercised, as in other elective and responsible Governments, under the control of its constituents, people, and the Legislatures of the States, and subject to the revolutionary rights of the people in extreme cases.
>
> Such is the Constitution of the United States *de jure* and *de facto;* and the name, whatever it be, that may be given to it, can make it nothing more or less than what it is.

This is clear and conclusive, so far as Mr. Madison goes on the subject. I showed yesterday that in 1789, in making his report upon the Virginia resolutions, he gave the true interpretation to those resolutions, and explained what was meant by the word "respective" before "States." In his letter, in 1832, to Mr. Rives, and in his letter of 1832, to Mr. Trist, (to which I referred yesterday,) having had time to reflect on the operation of the various provisions of the Constitution upon the country, in the decline of life, when he had seen the experiment fairly made, when his mind was matured upon every single point and provision in the Constitution, he, at the late period, sums up the doctrine and comes to the conclusion that I am contending for on the present occasion.

In addition to this, Mr. Jefferson, who prior to the formation of the Constitution was in Paris, writing letters on the subject of the formation of a stable Government here, saw the great defect in the Federal head under the old Articles of Confederation, and he pointed with the unerring finger of philosophy and certainty to what is now in the Constitution, as what was wanting in the old Articles of Confederation. Mr. Jefferson, in his letter to Colonel Monroe, dated Paris, August 11, 1786, speaks thus:

> There will never be money in the Treasury till the Confederacy shows its teeth. The States must see the rod; perhaps it must be felt by some one of them. I am persuaded all of them would rejoice to see every one obliged to furnish its contributions. It is not the difficulty of furnishing them which beggars the Treasury, but the fear that others will not furnish as much. Every rational citizen must wish to see an effective instrument of coercion, and should fear to see it on any other element than the water.

Here Mr. Jefferson, seeing the difficulty that, under the old Articles of Confederation, the Federal Government had not the power to execute its laws, that it could not collect revenue, points to what should be in the Constitution of the United States when formed. Mr. Jefferson, upon the same idea which was in his mind, and which was afterwards embodied in the Constitution, said, in a letter to E. Carrington, dated Paris, August 4, 1787:

> I confess I do not go as far in the reforms thought necessary, as some of my correspondents in America; but if the convention should adopt such propositions, I shall suppose them necessary. My general plan would be, to make the States one as to everything connected with foreign nations, and several as to everything purely domestic. But, with all the imperfections of our present Government, it is without comparison the best existing, or that ever did exist. Its greatest defect is the imperfect manner in which matters of commerce have been provided for. It has been so often said, as to be generally believed, that Congress have [sic] no power by the Confederation to enforce anything—for example, contributions of money. It was not necessary to give them that power expressly; they have it by the law of nature. When *two parties make a compact, there results to each a power of compelling the other to execute it.*

"When two parties make a compact, there results to each a power of compelling the other to execute it." This is Jefferson's language. If it was not even expressed in the Constitution, the power to preserve itself and maintain its authority would be possessed by the Federal Government from the very existence of the Government itself, upon the great principle that it must have the power to preserve its own existence. But we find that, in plain and express terms, this authority is delegated. The very powers that Mr. Jefferson pointed out as being wanting in the old Government, under the Articles of Confederation, are granted by the Constitution of the United States to the present Government by express delegation. Congress has the power to lay and collect taxes; Congress has the power to pass laws to restore fugitives from labor escaping from one State into another; Congress has the power to establish post offices and post roads; Congress has the power to establish courts in the different States; and having these powers, it has the authority to do everything necessary to sustaining the collection of the revenue, the enforcement of the judicial system and the carrying of the mails. Because Congress, having the power, undertakes to execute its laws, it will not do to say that the Government is placed in the position of an aggressor. Not so. It is only acting within the scope of the Constitution, and in compliance with its delegated powers. But a State that resists the exercise of those powers becomes the aggressor, and places itself in a rebellious or nullifying attitude. It is the duty of this Government to execute its laws in good faith. When the Federal Government shall fail to execute all the laws that are made in strict conformity with the Constitution, if our sister States shall pass laws violative of that Constitution, and obstructing the laws of Congress passed in conformity with it, then, and not till then, will this Government have failed to accomplish the great objects of its creation. Then it will be at an end, and all the parties to the compact will be released.

But I wish to go a little further into the authorities as to the power of a State to secede from the Union, and to quote an opinion of Judge Marshall, given at a very early day. I know it is very common to denounce him as a Federalist; but I care not where the truth comes from, or where a sound argument may be found to sustain a proposition that is right in itself, I am willing to adopt it; and I have put myself to the trouble to hunt up these unquestionable authorities on this subject, knowing that they would have more influence before the country, and before my constituents, than anything that I could say. Though I am not a lawyer, though I have not made the legal profession my study and my pursuit, I claim to have some little common sense and understanding as to the application of general principles. I find that Judge Marshall, in speaking on the question of the right of a State upon its own volition to go out of the Confederacy, in the case of *Cohens* vs. *Virginia*, said:

"It is very true, that whenever hostility to the existing system shall become universal"—

That is, the system of our Government—

"it will be also irresistible. The people made the Constitution, and the people can unmake it."

I care not whether he speaks here of the people in the aggregate or not. The application of the principle is just as clear, whether you say the people, through the States, made the Constitution, or leave out the qualifying words "through the States."

> It is the creature of their will, and lives only by their will. But this supreme and irresistible power to make and unmake resides only in the whole body of the people; not in any subdivision of them. The attempt of any of the parts to exercise it is usurpation, and ought to be repelled by those to whom the people have delegated their power of repelling it.—*Wheaton's Reports,* vol. 6, p. 389.

Now, whether you apply that, in a general sense, to the people in the aggregate, or to the States occupying the same relation to the Federal Government that the people do to the States, the principle is just the same; and when you speak of States ratifying and making the Constitution of the United States, one State, an ingredient—one of the community that made the Constitution—has no right, without the consent of the other States, to withdraw from the compact, and set the Constitution at naught. It is the principle that I seek; and the principle applies as well to a community of individuals. Admitting that this Federal Government was made by a community of States, can one of that community of States, of its own will, without the consent of the rest, where the compact is reciprocal, set aside, and withdraw itself from the operation of the Government? I have given you the opinion of Judge Marshall, one of the most distinguished jurists that ever presided in this country, though he is called by some a Federalist. His mind was clear; he lived in that day when the Constitution should be understood, and when it was understood—in the days of Madison and Jefferson; and this is his opinion upon that subject, as far back as 1821.

In this connection I would call the attention of the Senate to General Jackson's views upon this subject; and I would also call their attention to Mr. Webster's views, if it were necessary, for he is conceded, by some at least, to be one of the most able expounders of the Constitution of the United States. General Jackson, though not celebrated for his legal attainments, was celebrated for his sagacity, his strong common sense, his great intuitive power of reaching correct conclusions, and understanding correct principles. In 1833, General Jackson, in his proclamation, takes identically the same ground; and declares that, first, a State has no power of itself to nullify a law of Congress within its limits; and next, that notwithstanding a State may claim to have seceded, it has no constitutional power to withdraw itself from the Union of the States, and thereby set at naught the laws and the Constitution. He argues this question forcibly and clearly; and comes to the unerring conclusion, according to my judgment, that no State has the constitutional power to withdraw itself from this Confederacy without the consent of the other States; and it may do good to reproduce his views on the subject. He says, in his famous proclamation, speaking of the nullification ordinance of South Carolina:

> And whereas the said ordinance prescribes to the people of South Carolina a course of conduct in direct violation of their duty as citizens of the United States, contrary to the laws of their country, subversive of its Constitution, and having for its object the destruction of the Union—that Union which, coeval with our political existence, led our fathers, without any other ties to unite them than those of patriotism and a common cause, through a sanguinary struggle to a glorious independence—that sacred Union, hitherto inviolate, which, perfected by our happy Constitution, has brought us, by the favor of Heaven, to a state of prosperity at home, and high consideration abroad, rarely, if ever, equaled in the history of nations. To preserve this bond of our political existence from destruction; to maintain inviolate this state of national honor and prosperity, and to justify the confidence my fellow-citizens have reposed in me, I, ANDREW JACKSON, *President of the United States*, have thought proper to issue this my proclamation, stating my views of the Constitution and the laws applicable to the measures adopted by the convention of South Carolina, and to the reasons they have put forth to sustain them, declaring the course which my duty will require me to pursue, and, appealing to the understanding and patriotism of the people, warn them of the consequences that must inevitably result from an observance of the dictates of the convention.

He argues the question at length:

> This right to secede is deduced from the nature of the Constitution, which, they say, is a compact between sovereign States, who have preserved their whole sovereignty, and therefore are subject to no superior; that because

they made the compact they can break it when, in their opinion, it has been departed from by other States. Fallacious as this course of reasoning is, it enlists State pride, and finds advocates in the honest prejudices of those who have not studied the nature of our Government sufficiently to see the radical error on which it rests.

The people of the United States formed the Constitution, acting through State Legislatures in making the compact, to meet and discuss its provisions, and acting in separate conventions when they ratified those provisions; but the terms used in its construction show it to be a Government in which the people of all the States collectively are represented. We are ONE PEOPLE in the choice of the President and Vice President. Hence the States have no other agency than to direct the mode in which the votes shall be given. The candidates having the majority of all the votes are chosen. The electors of a majority of the States may have given their votes for one candidate, and yet another may be chosen. The people, then, and not the States, are represented in the executive branch.

The Constitution of the United States, then, forms a *Government*, not a league; and whether it be formed by compact between the States, or in any other manner, its character is the same. It is a Government in which all the people are represented; which operates directly on the people individually, not upon the States—they retained all the power they did not grant. But each State having expressly parted with so many powers as to constitute, jointly with the other States, a single nation, cannot from that period, possess any right to secede; because such secession does not break a league but destroys the unity of the nation; and any injury to that unity is not only a breach, which would result from the contravention of a compact, but it is an offense against the whole Union. To say that any State may, at pleasure, secede from the Union, is to say that the United States are not a nation; because it would be a solecism to contend that any part of a nation might dissolve its connection with the other parts, to their injury or ruin, without committing any offense. Secession, like any other revolutionary act, may be morally justified by the extremity of oppression; but to call it a constitutional right, is confounding the meaning of terms, and can only be done through gross error, or to deceive those who are willing to assert a right but would pause before they made a revolution, or incurred the penalties consequent on a failure.

Because the Union was formed by compact, it is said the parties to that compact may, when they feel themselves aggrieved, depart from it; but it is precisely because it is a compact that they cannot. A compact is an agreement or binding obligation. It may by its terms have a sanction of penalty for its breach, or it may not. If it contains no sanction, it may be broken, with no other consequence than moral guilt; if it have a sanction, then the breach insures the designated or implied penalty. A league between independent nations, generally, has no sanction other than a moral one; or if it should contain a penalty, as there is no common superior, it cannot be enforced. A Government, on the contrary, always has a sanction expressed or implied; and in our case, it is both necessarily implied and expressly given. An attempt, by force of arms, to destroy a Government, is an offense by whatever means the constitutional compact may have been formed, and such Government has the right, by the law of self-defense, to pass acts for punishing the offender, unless that right is modified, restrained, or resumed by the constitutional act. In our system, although it is modified in the case of treason, yet authority is expressly given to pass all laws necessary to carry its powers into effect, and under this grant, provision has been made for punishing acts which obstruct the due administration of the laws.

The States, severally, have not retained their entire sovereignty. It has been shown that in becoming parts of a nation, not members of a league, they surrendered many of their essential parts of sovereignty. The right to make treaties, declare war, levy taxes, exclusive judicial and legislative powers, were all of them functions of sovereign power. The States, then, for all these purposes were no longer sovereign. The allegiance of their citizens was transferred, in the first instance, to the Government of the United States: they became American citizens, and owed obedience to the Constitution of the United States and to laws made in conformity with the powers it vested in Congress. This last position has not been, and cannot be, denied. How, then, can that State be said to be sovereign and independent whose citizens owe obedience to laws not made by it, and whose magistrates are sworn to disregard those laws when they come in conflict with those passed by another? What shows conclusively that the States cannot be said to have reserved an undivided sovereignty is, they expressly ceded the right to punish treason, not treason against their separate power, but treason against the United States. Treason is an offense against *sovereignty*, and sovereignty must reside with the power to punish it. But the reserved rights of the States are no less sacred because they have, for their common interest, made the General Government the depository of those powers.

So obvious are the reasons that forbid this secession that it is necessary only to allude to them. The Union was formed for the benefit of all. It was produced by mutual sacrifices of interest and opinions. Can these sacrifices be recalled? Can the States, who magnanimously surrendered their title to the territories of the West, recall the grant? Will the inhabitants of the inland States agree to pay the duties that may be imposed without their assent by those on the Atlantic or the Gulf for their own benefit? Shall there be a free port in one State, and onerous duties in another? No man believes that any right exists in a single State to involve all the others in these and countless other evils, contrary to the engagement solemnly made. Every one must see that the other States, in self-defense, must oppose it at all hazards.

Having traveled thus far, the question arises, in what sense are we to construe the Constitution of the United States? I assume what is assumed in one of Mr. Madison's letters, that the Constitution was formed for perpetuity; that it never was intended to be broken up. It was commenced, it is true, as an experiment; but the founders of the Constitution intended that this experiment should go on and on and on; and by way of making it perpetual, they provided for its amendment. They provided that this instrument could be amended and improved, from time to time, as the changing circumstances, as the changing pursuits, as the changing notions of men might require; but they made no provision for its destruction. The old Articles of Confederation were formed for the purpose of making "a perpetual union." In 1787, when the convention concluded their deliberations and adopted the Constitution, what do they say in the very preamble of the Constitution? Having in their mind the idea that was shadowed forth in the old Articles of Confederation, that the Union was to be perpetual, they say, at the commencement, that it is to make "a more perfect union" than the union under the old Articles of Confederation, which they called "perpetual."

What furthermore do we find? The Constitution of the United States contains a provision that it is to be submitted to the States respectively for their ratification; but on nine States ratifying it, it shall be the Constitution for them. In that way the Government was created; and in that way provision was made to perfect it. What more do we find? The Constitution, as I have just remarked, provides for its own amendment, its improvement, its perpetuation, its continuance, by pointing out and prescribing the mode and manner in which improvements shall be made. That still preserves the idea that it is to be perpetual. We find, in addition, a provision that Congress shall have power to admit new States.

Hence, in traveling along through the instrument, we find how the Government is created, how it is to be perpetuated, and how it may be enlarged in reference to the number of States constituting the Confederacy; but do we find any provision for winding it up, except on that great inherent principle that it may be wound up by the States—not by a State, but by the States which spoke it into existence—and by no other means. That is a means of taking down the Government that the Constitution could not provide for. It is above the Constitution; it is beyond any provision that can be made by mortal man.

Now, to expose the absurdity of the pretension that there is a right to secede, let me press this argument a little further. The Constitution has been formed; it has been made perfect, or, in other words, means have been provided by which it can be made perfect. It was intended to be perpetual. In reference to the execution of the laws under it, what do we find? As early as 1795, Congress passed an excise law, taxing distilleries throughout the country, and, what were called the whisky boys of Pennsylvania, resisted the law. The Government wanted means. It taxed distilleries. The people of Pennsylvania resisted it. What is the difference between a portion of the people resisting a constitutional law, and all of the people of a State doing so? But because you can apply the term coercion in one case to a State, and in the other call it simply the execution of the law against individuals, you say there is a great distinction! We do not assume the power to coerce a State, but we assume that Congress has the power to lay and collect taxes, and Congress has the right to enforce that law when obstructions and impediments are opposed to its enforcement. The people of Pennsylvania did object; they did resist and oppose the legal authorities of the country. Was that law enforced? Was it called coercion at that day to enforce it? Suppose all the people of the State of Pennsylvania had resisted: would not the law have applied with just the same force, and would it not have been just as constitutional to execute it against all the people of the State, as it was to execute it upon a part of their citizens?

George Washington, in his next annual message to the Congress of the United States, referred to the subject; and if my friend from California will read two or three paragraphs for me, he will do me a favor, for I cannot see by this light. It will be seen from the reading of these paragraphs what George Washington considered to be his duty in the execution of the laws of the United States upon the citizens of the States.

Mr. LATHAM read as follows:

> Thus, the painful alternative could not be discarded. I ordered the militia to march, after once more admonishing the insurgents, in my proclamation of the 25th of September last.

> It was a task too difficult, to ascertain with precision the lowest degree of force competent to the quelling of the insurrection. From a respect, indeed, to economy, and the ease of my fellow citizens belonging to the militia, it would have gratified me to accomplish such an estimate. My very reluctance to subscribe too much importance to the opposition, had its extent been accurately seen, would have been a decided inducement to the smallest sufficient numbers. In this uncertainty, therefore, I put in motion fifteen thousand men, as being an army which, according to all human calculation, would be prompt and adequate in every view, and might, perhaps, by rendering resistance desperate, prevent the effusion of blood. Quotas had been assigned to the States of New Jersey, Pennsylvania, Maryland, and Virginia; the Governor of Pennsylvania having declared, on this occasion, an opinion which justified a requisition to the other States.

> As commander-in-chief of the militia, when called into the actual service of the United States, I have visited the places of general rendezvous, to obtain more exact information, and to direct a plan for ulterior movements. Had there been room for persuasion that the laws were secure from obstruction; that the civil magistrate was able to bring to justice such as the most culpable as have not embraced the proffered terms of amnesty, and may be deemed fit objects of example; that the friends to peace and good government were not in need of that aid and countenance which they ought always to receive, and, I trust, ever will receive, against the vicious and turbulent; I should have caught with avidity the opportunity of restoring the militia to their families and homes. But succeeding intelligence has

tended to manifest the necessity of what has been done; it being now confessed by those who were not inclined to exaggerate the ill conduct of the insurgents, that their malevolence was not pointed merely to a particular law, but that a spirit inimical to all order has actuated many of the offenders. If the state of things had afforded reason for the continuance of my presence with the Army, it would not have been withholden. But every appearance assuring such an issue as will redound to the reputation and strength of the United States, I have judged it most proper to resume my duties at the seat of Government, leaving the chief command with the Governor of Virginia.

While there is cause to lament that occurrences of this nature should have disgraced the name or interrupted the tranquillity of any part of our community, or should have diverted to a new application any portion of the public resources, there are not wanting real and substantial consolations for the misfortune. It has demonstrated that our prosperity rests on solid foundations, by furnishing an additional proof that my fellow-citizens understand true principles of Government and liberty; that they feel their *inseparable union*; that notwithstanding all the devices which have been used to sway them from their interest and duty, they are now as ready to maintain the authority of the laws against licentious invasions as they were to defend their rights against usurpation. It has been a spectacle, displaying to the highest advantage the value of republican Government, to behold the most and least wealthy of our citizens standing in the same ranks as private soldiers, preeminently distinguished by being the army of the Constitution, undeterred by a march of three hundred miles over rugged mountains, by the approach of an inclement season, or by any other discouragement. Nor ought I to omit to acknowledge the efficacious and patriotic cooperation which I have experienced from the Chief Magistrates of the States to which my requisitions have been addressed.—*American State Papers—Miscellaneous*, vol. 1., p. 85.

Mr. JOHNSON, of Tennessee. We see that in this instance President Washington thought there was power in this Government to execute its laws. We see, too, that George Washington considered the militia the army of the Constitution. We see, too, that George Washington refers to this Union as being inseparable. This is the way that the laws were executed by the Father of his Country, the man who sat as President of the Convention that made the Constitution. Here was the resistance interposed—opposition to the execution of the laws; and George Washington, then President of the United States, went in person at the head of the militia; and it showed his sagacity, his correct comprehension of men, and the effect that an immediate movement of that kind would have upon them. He ordered fifteen thousand of his countrymen to the scene of action, and went there in person, and stayed there till he was satisfied that the insubordination was quelled. That was the manner in which he executed the laws.

Here, then, we find General Washington executing the law, in 1795, against a portion of the citizens of Pennsylvania who rebelled; and, I repeat the question, where is the difference between executing the law upon a part and upon the whole? Suppose the whole of Pennsylvania had rebelled and resisted the excise law; had refused to pay taxes on distilleries: was it not as competent and as constitutional for General Washington to have executed the law against the whole as against a part? Is there any difference? Governmental affairs must be practical as well as our own domestic affairs. You may make nice metaphysical distinctions between practical operations of Government and its theory; you may refine upon what is a State, and point out a difference between a State and a portion of a State; but what is it when you reduce it to practical operation, and square it by common sense?

In 1832, resistance was interposed to laws of the United States in another State. An ordinance was passed by South Carolina, assuming to act as a sovereign State, to nullify a law of the United States. In 1833, the distinguished man who filled the executive chair, who now lies in his silent grave, loved and respected for his virtue, his honor, his integrity, his patriotism, his undoubted courage, and his devotion to his kind, with an eye single to the promotion of his country's best interest, issued the proclamation extracts from which I have already presented. He was sworn to support the Constitution, and to see that the laws were faithfully executed; and he fulfilled the obligation. He took all the steps necessary to secure the execution of the law, and he would have executed it by the power of the Government if the point of time had arrived when it was necessary to resort to power. We can see that he acted upon similar principles to those acted upon by General Washington. He took the precaution of ordering a force there sufficient for the purpose of enabling him to say effectually to the rebellious, and those who were interposing opposition to the execution of the laws: "The laws which we made according to the Constitution, the laws that provide for the collection of the revenue to sustain this Government, must be enforced, and the revenue must be collected. It is part of the compact; it is part of the engagement you have undertaken to perform, and you of your own will have no power or authority to set it aside." The duties were collected; the law was enforced; and the Government went on. In his proclamation, he made a powerful appeal. He told them what would be done; and it would have been done, as certain as God rules on high, if the time had arrived which made it necessary.

Then we see where General Washington stood, and where General Jackson stood. Now, how does the present case stand? The time has come when men should speak out. Duties are mine; consequences are God's. I intend to discharge my duty, and I intend to avow my understanding of the Constitution and the laws of the country. Have we no authority or power to execute the laws in the State of South Carolina as well as in Vermont and Pennsylvania? I think we have. As I before said, although a State may, by an ordinance, or by a resolve, or by an act of any other kind, declare that they absolve their citizens from all allegiance to this Government, it does not release them from the compact. The compact is reciprocal; and they, in coming into it, undertook to perform certain duties and abide by the laws made in conformity with the compact. Now, sir, what is the Government to do in South Carolina? If South Carolina undertake to [sic] drive the Federal courts out of that State, yet the Federal Government has the right to hold those courts there. She may attempt to exclude the mails, yet the Federal Government has the right to establish post offices and post roads and to carry the mail there. She may resist the collection of revenue at Charleston, or any other point that the Government has provided for its collection; but the Government has the right to collect it and enforce the law. She may undertake to take possession of the property belonging to the Government which was originally ceded by the State, but the Federal Government has the right to provide the means for retaining possession of that property. If she makes an advance to either dispossess the Government of that which it purchased, or to resist the execution of the revenue laws, or of our judicial system, or the carrying of the mails, or the exercise of any other power conferred on the Federal Government, she puts herself in the wrong, and it will be the duty of the Government to see that the laws are faithfully executed. By reference to the records, it will be seen that, on

> December 19, 1805, South Carolina granted all the right, title, and claim of the State to all the lands reserved for Fort Moultrie, on Sullivan's Island, not exceeding five acres, with all the forts, fortifications, &c., thereon; canal, &c.; the high lands, and part of the marsh, belonging to Fort Johnson, not exceeding twenty acres; the land on which Fort Pickney is built, and three acres around it; a portion of the sandbank on the southeasternmost point of Charleston, not exceeding two acres; not exceeding four acres for a battery, or fort, &c., on Blythe's Point, at the mouth of Sampit River; Mustard Island, in Beaufort river, opposite Parris's Island; not exceeding seven acres of land on St. Helena Island for a principal fort; the whole on condition that the United States to compensate individuals for property; the lands, &c., to be free from taxes to the State.

Here is a clear deed of cession. The Federal Government has complied with all the conditions, and has, in its own right, the land on which these forts are constructed. The conditions of the cession have been complied with; and the Government has had possession from that period to the present time. There are forts; there is its arsenal; there are its dock-yards; there is the property of the Government; and now, under the Constitution, and under the laws made in pursuance thereof, has South Carolina the authority and the right to expel the Federal Government from its own property that has been given to it by her own act, and of which it is now in possession? By resisting the execution of the laws; by attempting to dispossess the Federal Government, does she not put herself in the wrong? Does she not violate the Constitution? Does she not put herself, within the meaning and purview of the Constitution, in the attitude of levying war against the United States? The Constitution defines and declares what is treason. Let us talk about things by their right names. I know that some hotspur or madcap may declare that these are not times for a government of law; that we are in a revolution. I know that Patrick Henry once said, "if this is treason, make the most of it." If anything can be treason in the scope and purview of the Constitution, is not levying war upon the United States treason? Is not an attempt to take its property treason? Is not an attempt to expel its soldiers treason? Is not an attempt to resist the collection of revenue, or to expel your mails, or to drive your courts from her borders, treason? Are not these powers clearly conferred in the Constitution on the Federal Government to be exercised? What is it, then, I ask in the name of the Constitution, in the meaning of the term as there defined? It is treason and nothing but treason; and if one State, upon its own volition, can go out of this Confederacy without regard to the effect it is to have upon the remaining parties to the compact, what is your Government worth? what will it come to? and in what will it end? It is no Government at all upon such a construction.

But it is declared and assumed that, if a State secedes, she is no longer a member of the Union, and that, therefore, the laws and the Constitution of the United States are no longer operative within her limits, and she is not guilty if she violates them. This is a matter of opinion. I have tried to show, from the origin of the Government down to the present time, what this doctrine of secession is, and there is but one concurring and unerring conclusion reached by all the great and distinguished men of the country. Madison, who is called the Father of the Constitution, denies the doctrine. Washington, who was the Father of his country, denies the doctrine. Jefferson, Jackson, Clay, and Webster, all deny the doctrine; and yet all at once it is discovered and ascertained that a State, of its own volition, can go out of this Confederacy, without regard to consequences, without regard to the injury and woe that may be inflicted on the remaining members from the act!

Suppose this doctrine to be true, Mr. President, that a State can withdraw from this Confederacy; and suppose South Carolina has seceded, and is now out of the Confederacy: in what an attitude does she place herself? There might be circumstances under which the States ratifying the compact might tolerate the secession of a State, she taking the consequences of the act. But there might be other circumstances under which the States could not allow one to secede. Why do I say so? Some suppose—and it is a well-founded supposition—that by secession of a State all the remaining States might be involved in disastrous consequences; they might be involved in war; and by the secession of one State, the existence of the remaining States might be involved. Then, without regard to the Constitution, dare the other States permit one to secede when it endangers and involves all the remaining States? The question arises in this connection, whether the States are in a condition to tolerate the secession of South Carolina. This is a matter to be determined by the circumstances; that is a matter to be determined by the emergency; that is a matter to be determined when it comes up. It is a question which must be left open to be determined by the surrounding circumstances, when the occasion arises.

But conceding, for argument's sake, the doctrine of secession, and admitting that the State of South Carolina is now upon your coast, a foreign Power, absolved from all connection with the Federal Government, out of the Union: what then? There was a doctrine inculcated in 1823, by Mr. Monroe, that this Government, keeping in view the safety of the people and the existence of our institutions, would permit no European Power to plant anymore colonies on this continent. Now, suppose that South Carolina is outside of the Confederacy, and this Government is in possession of the fact that she is forming an alliance with a foreign Power—with France, with England, with Russia, with Austria, or with all the principal Powers of Europe; that there is to be a great naval station established there; an immense rendezvous for their army, with a view to ulterior objects, with a view to making advances upon the rest of these States: let me ask the Senate, let me ask the country, if they dare permit it? Under and in compliance with the great law of self-preservation, we dare not let her do it; and if she were a sovereign Power to-day, outside of the Confederacy, and was forming an alliance that we deemed inimical to our institutions, and the existence of our Government, we should have a right to conquer and hold her as a province—a word which is so much used with scorn.

Mr. President, I have referred to the manner in which this Government was formed. I have referred to the provision of the Constitution which provides for the admission of new States. Now, let me ask, can anyone believe that, in the creation of this Government, its founders intended that it should have the power to acquire territory and form it into States, and then permit them to go out of the Union? Let us take a case. How long has it been since your armies were in Mexico? How long has it been since your brave men were exposed to the diseases, the privations, the sufferings, which are incident to a campaign of that kind? How long has it been since they were bearing your eagles in a foreign land, many of them falling at the point of a bayonet, consigned to their long, narrow home, with no winding-sheet but their blankets saturated with their blood? How many victories did they win? how many laurels did they acquire? how many trophies did they bring back? The country is full of them. What did it cost you? One hundred and twenty million dollars. What did you pay for the country you acquired, besides? Fifteen million dollars. Peace was made; territory was acquired; and, in a few years, from that territory California erected herself into a free and independent State, and, under the provisions of the Constitution, we admitted her as a member of this Confederacy. After having expended $120,000,000 in the war; after having lost many of our bravest and most gallant men; after having paid $15,000,000 to Mexico for the territory, and admitted it into the Union as a State, now that the people of California have got into the Confederacy and can stand alone, according to this modern doctrine, your Government was just made to let them in, and then to let them step out. Is not the conclusion illogical? Is it not absurd to say that, now that California is in, she, on her own volition—without regard to the consideration paid for her; without regard to the policy which dictated her acquisition by the United States—can walk out and bid you defiance? Is it not an absurdity, if you take the reason and object of Government?

But we need not stop here; let us go to Texas. Texas was engaged in a revolution with Mexico. She succeeded in the assertion and establishment of her independence; and she became a sovereign and independent Power outside of this Union. She applied for admission, and she was admitted into this family of States. After she was in, she was oppressed by the debts of the war which resulted in her separation from Mexico; she was harassed by the Indians upon her border; and in 1850, by way of relief to Texas, what did we do? There was an extent of territory that lies north, if my memory serves me right, embracing what is now called the Territory of New Mexico. Texas had it not in her power to protect the citizens that were there. It was a dead limb, paralyzed, lifeless. The Federal Government came along as a kind of physician, saying, "We will take this dead limb from your body, and vitalize it, by giving protection to the people, and incorporating it into a territorial government: and in addition to that, we will give you $10,000,000, and you may retain your own public lands;" and the other States were taxed in common to pay the $10,000,000. Now, after all this is done, Texas, forsooth, upon her own volition, is to say, "I will walk out of this Union!" Were there no other parties to that compact? We are told the compact is reciprocal. Did we take in California, did we take in Texas, just to benefit them? No; but to add to this great family of States; and it is apparent, from the fact of their coming in, that the compact is reciprocal; and having entered into the compact, they have no right to withdraw without the consent of the remaining States.

Again: take the case of Louisiana. What did we pay for her in 1803, and for what was she wanted? Just to get Louisiana into the Confederacy? Just for the benefit of that particular locality? Was not the mighty West looked to? Was it not to secure the free navigation of the Mississippi river, the mouth of which was then in the possession France, shortly before of Spain, passing about between those two powers? Yes, the navigation of that river was wanted. Simply for Louisiana? No, but for all the States. The United States paid $15,000,000, and France passed the country to the United States. It remained in a territorial condition for a while, sustained and protected by the strong arm of the Federal Government. We acquired the territory and the navigation of the river; and the money was paid for the benefit of all the States, and not of Louisiana exclusively. And now that this great valley is filled up; now that the navigation of the Mississippi is one hundred times more important than it was then; now, after the United States have paid the money, have acquired title to Louisiana, and have incorporated her into the Confederacy, it is proposed that she shall go out of the Union! In 1815, when her shores were invaded; when her city was about to be sacked; when her booty and her beauty were about to fall prey to British aggression, the brave men of Tennessee, and of Kentucky, and of the surrounding States, rushed into her borders and upon her shores, and under the lead of their own gallant Jackson, drove the invading forces away. And now, after all this; after the money has been paid; after the free navigation of the river has been obtained—not for the benefit of Louisiana alone, but for her in common with all the States—Louisiana says to the other States, "We will go out of this Confederacy; we do not care if you did fight our battles; we do not care if you did acquire the free navigation of this river from France; we will go out if we think proper, and constitute ourselves as an independent Power, and bid defiance to the other States." It is an absurdity; it is a contradiction; it is illogical; it is not deducible from the structure of the Government itself.

Mr. SLIDELL. Will the Senator permit me to make a single remark?

Mr. JOHNSON, of Tennessee. The Senator knows how I was interrupted yesterday.

Mr. SLIDELL. I merely wish to say to the Senator that I do not know a citizen of any south-western State bordering on the Mississippi who does not acknowledge the propriety and necessity of extending to every citizen of the country whose streams flow into the Mississippi the free navigation of the river and the free interchange of all of the agricultural products of the valley of the Mississippi. Such a course is dictated not only by every consideration of justice, but by the recognized and well-understood interests of the south-western States. On this point I can speak with entire confidence of the sentiment of Louisiana.

Mr. JOHNSON, of Tennessee. That may all be very true; and I do not suppose that, at this moment, there is a citizen in the State of Louisiana who would think of obstructing the free navigation of the river; but are not nations controlled by their interests in varying circumstances? It strikes me so; and hereafter, when a conflict of interest arises; when difficulty may spring up between two separate Powers, Louisiana, having control of the mouth of the river, might feel disposed to tax our citizens going down there. It is a power that I am not willing to concede to be exercised at the discretion of any authority outside of this Government. The Senator's assurance does not amount to anything. It depends entirely on the interest and condition of the surrounding country as to what power Louisiana would want to exercise in reference to that river. So sensitive have been the people of my State upon the free navigation of that river, that as far back as 1796, now sixty-four years ago, in their bill of rights, before they passed under the jurisdiction of the United States, they declared:

> That an equal participation of the free navigation of the Mississippi is one of the inherent rights of the citizens of this State; it cannot, therefore, be connected to any prince, potentate, Power, person, or persons whatever.

This shows the estimate that the people fixed on this stream sixty-four years ago; and now we are told, if Louisiana does go out, it is not her intention at this time to tax the people above. Who can tell what may be the intention of Louisiana hereafter? Are we willing to place the rights of our citizens, are we willing to place the travel and commerce of our citizens, at the discretion of any Power outside of this Government? I will not; I do not care whether the other Powers be in Louisiana or the moon.

But, then, as we go on, let us follow the circle, and see where this doctrine will carry us. How long has it been since Florida lay out on our coast an annoyance to us? And now she has got entirely feverish about being an independent and separate Government, while she has not as many qualified voters as there are in one congressional district. What condition did Florida occupy in 1811? She stood in the possession of Spain. What did the United States think about having adjacent territory outside of their jurisdiction? Let us turn to the authorities, and see what proposition they were willing to act upon. I find, in the statutes of the United States, this joint resolution:

> Taking into view the peculiar situation of Spain, and of her American provinces, and considering the influence which the destiny of the territory adjoining the southern border of the United States may have upon their security, tranquillity, and commerce: Therefore,
>
> *Resolved by the Senate and House of Representatives of the United States of America in Congress assembled,* That the United States, under the peculiar circumstances of the existing crisis, cannot, without serious inquietude, see any part of the said territory pass into the hands of any foreign Power; and that a due regard to their own safety compels them to provide, under certain contingencies, for the temporary occupation of the said territory. They, at the same time, declare that the same territory shall, in their hands, remain subject to future negotiation.

What principle is set forth there? Florida was in the possession of Spain. English spies were harbored in her territory. Spain was inimical to the United States; and in view of the great principle of self-preservation, the Congress of the United States passed a resolution declaring that if Spain attempted to transfer Florida into the hands of any other Power, the United States would take possession of it. Yet Congress were [sic] gracious and condescending enough to say that it should remain open to future negotiation. That is to say, "Hereafter, if we can make a negotiation that will suit us, we will make it; if we do not, we will keep the territory;" that is all. There was the territory lying upon our border, outside of the jurisdiction of the United States; and we declared, by an act of Congress, that no foreign Power should possess it.

We went still further and appropriated $100,000, and authorized the

President to enter and take possession of it with the means placed in his hands. Afterwards, we did negotiate with Spain, and gave $6,000,000 for the Territory; and we established a territorial government for it. What next? We undertook to drive out the Seminole Indians, and we had a war in which this Government lost more than it lost in all the other wars it was engaged in; and we paid the sum of $25,000,000 to get the Seminoles out of the swamps, so that the Territory could be inhabited by white men. We paid for it, we took possession of it; and I remember, when I was in the other House, and Florida was knocking at the door for admission, how extremely anxious her then able Delegate was to be admitted. He now sits before me, [Mr. YULEE.] I remember how important he thought it was then to come under the protecting wing of the United States as one of the stars of our Confederacy. But now the Territory is paid for, England is driven out, $25,000,000 have been expended; and they want no longer the protection of this Government, but will go out without consulting the other States, without reference to the effect upon the remaining parties to the compact. Where will she go? Will she attach herself to Spain again? Will she pass back under the jurisdiction of the Seminoles? After having been nurtured and protected and fostered by all these States, now, without regard to them, is she to be allowed, at her own volition, to withdraw from the Union? I say she has no constitutional right to do it; and when she does it, it is an act of aggression. If she succeeds, it will only be a successful revolution. If she does not succeed, she must take the penalties and terrors of the law.

But, sir, there is another question that suggests itself in this connection. Kansas, during the last Congress, applied for admission into this Union. She assumed to be a State, and the difficulty in the way was a provision in her constitution, and the manner of its adoption. We did not let Kansas in. We did not question her being a State; but on account of the manner of forming her constitution and its provisions, we kept Kansas out. What is Kansas now? Is she a State, or is she a Territory? Does she revert back to her territorial condition of pupilage? Or, having been a State, and having applied for admission and been refused, is she standing out a State? You hold her as a territory; you hold her as a province. You prescribe the mode of electing the members of her Legislature, and pay them out of your own Treasury. Yes, she is a province controlled by Federal authority, and her laws are made in conformity with the acts of Congress. Is she not a Territory? I think she is.

Suppose the State of California withdraws from the Union. We admitted her. She was a territory acquired by the United States, by our blood and our treasure. Now, suppose she withdraws from the Confederacy; does she pass back into a territorial condition, remain a dependency upon the Federal Government, or does she stand out as a separate government? Let me take Louisiana, for which we paid $15,000,000. That was a Territory for a number of years—yes, a province. It is only another name for a province. It is a possession held under the jurisdiction of the United States. We admitted Louisiana into the Union as a State. Suppose we had refused to admit her: would she still not have remained a Territory? Would she not have remained under the protection of the United States? But now, if she has the power to withdraw from the Union, does she not pass back into the condition in which she was before we admitted her into the Union? In what condition does she place herself? When those States which were at first Territories cease their connection with this Government, do they pass back into the territorial condition? When Florida is going out, when Louisiana is going out, and these other States that were originally Territories go out of the Union, in what condition do they place themselves? Are they Territories or States? Are they merely on probation to become members of this Confederacy, or are they States outside of the Confederacy?

Mr. YULEE. Will the Senator allow me to ask a single question in this connection?

Mr. JOHNSON, of Tennessee. I hope the Senator will not interrupt me. I do not refuse out of any discourtesy.

Mr. WIGFALL. Let him alone.

Mr. JOHNSON, of Tennessee. Remarks of that kind never affect me in the slightest degree; I never hear them. But, Mr. President, I have referred to the acts of Congress for acquiring Florida as setting forth a principle. Let me read another of those acts:

An act to enable the President of the United States, under certain emergencies, to take possession of the country lying east of the river Perdido, and south of the State of Georgia and the Mississippi Territory, and for other purposes.

Be it enacted by the Senate and House of Representatives of the United States of America in Congress assembled, That the President of the United States be, and is hereby, authorized to take possession and occupy all or any part of the territory lying east of the river Perdido, and south of the State of Georgia and the Mississippi Territory, in case an arrangement has been or shall be made with the local authorities of the said territory for the delivering up the possession of the same or any part thereof to the United States, or in the event of an attempt to occupy the said territory or any part thereof by any foreign Government; and he may, for the purpose of taking possession and occupying the territory aforesaid, in order to maintain therein

the authority of the United States, employ any part of the Army and Navy
of the United States which he may deem necessary.

What is the principle avowed here? That from the geographical
relations of this territory to the United States, from its importance to
the safety and security of the institutions of the United States, we
authorize the President to expend $100,000 to get a foothold there,
and especially take possession of it if it were likely to pass to any
foreign Power. We see the doctrine and principle there established
and acted upon by our Government. This principle was again avowed
by distinguished men at Ostend. A paper was drawn up there by Mr.
Buchanan, Mr. Soulé of Louisiana, and Mr. Mason of Virginia, our
ministers to the three principal courts in Europe. They met at Ostend
and drew up a paper in which they laid down certain doctrines in
strict conformity with the act of Congress that I have just read. They
say in that paper, signed by James Buchanan, J. Y. Mason, Pierre
Soulé:

Then, 1. It must be clear to every reflecting mind, that, from the peculiarity
of its geographical position, and the considerations attendant on it, Cuba is
as necessary to the North American Republic as any of its present members,
and that it belongs, naturally, to that great family of States of which the
Union is the providential nursery.

From its locality it commands the mouth of the Mississippi, and the immense
and annually increasing trade which must seek this avenue to the ocean.

On the numerous navigable streams, measuring an aggregate course of
some thirty thousand miles, which disembogue themselves through this
magnificent river into the Gulf of Mexico, the increase of the population
within the last ten years amounts to more than that of the entire Union at
the time Louisiana was annexed to it.

The natural and main outlet to the products of this entire population, the
highway of their direct intercourse with the Atlantic and Pacific States, can
never be secure, but must ever be endangered while Cuba is a dependency
of a distant Power in whose possession it has proved to be a source of
constant annoyance and embarrassment to their interests.

The system of immigration and labor lately organized within its limits, and
the tyranny and oppression which characterize its immediate rulers, threaten
an insurrection at any moment which may result in direct consequences to
the American people.

Cuba has thus become to us an unceasing danger, and a permanent cause
of anxiety and alarm.

Self-preservation is the first law of nature, with States as well as with individuals. All nations have, at different periods, acted upon this maxim. Although it has been made the pretext for committing flagrant injustice, as in the partition of Poland, and other similar cases which history records, yet the principle itself, though often abused, has always been recognized." * * * * "Our past history forbids that we should acquire the Island of Cuba without the consent of Spain, unless justified by the great law of self-preservation. We must, in any event, preserve our own conscious rectitude, and our own self-respect.

Mark you, we are never to acquire Cuba unless it is necessary to our self-preservation:

While pursuing this course we can afford to disregard the censures of the world, to which we have been so often and so unjustly exposed.

After we shall have offered Spain a price for Cuba far beyond its present value, and this shall have been refused, it will then be time to consider the question does Cuba, in possession of Spain, seriously endanger our internal peace and the existence of our cherished Union?

Should this question be answered in the affirmative, then, by every law, human and divine, we shall be justified in wresting it from Spain if we possess the power; and this upon the very same principle that would justify an individual in tearing down the burning house of his neighbor, if there were no other means of preventing the flames from destroying his own home.

Now, this is all pretty sound doctrine. I am for all of it.

Under such circumstances we ought neither to count the cost nor regard the odds which Spain might enlist against us. We forbear to enter into the question, whether the present condition of the island would justify such a measure? We should, however, be recreant to our duty, be unworthy of our gallant forefathers, and commit base treason against our posterity, should we permit Cuba to be Africanized and become a second St. Domingo, with all its attendant horrors to the white race, and suffer the flames to extend to our own neighboring shore, seriously to endanger or actually to consume the fair fabric of our Union.

We find in this document, signed by our three ministers, and approved by the American people, the doctrine laid down clearly that if the United States believed that Cuba was to be transferred by Spain to England or to France, or to some other Power inimical to the United States, the safety of the American people, the safety of our institutions, the existence of the Government, being imperiled, we should have a right, without regard to money or blood, to acquire it.

Where does this carry us? We find that this doctrine was not only laid down, but practiced, in the case of Florida. Suppose Louisiana was now out of the Confederacy, holding the key to the Gulf, the outlet to the commerce of the great West: under the doctrine laid down by these ministers, and practiced by the Congress of the United States, would not this Government have the right, in obedience to the great principle of self-preservation, and for the safety of our institutions, to seize it and to pass it under the jurisdiction of the United States, and hold it as a province subject to the laws of the United States? I say it would. The same principle applied to Florida. The same principle would apply to South Carolina. I regret that she occupies the position that she has assumed, but I am arguing a principle, and do not refer to her out of any disrespect. If South Carolina were outside of the Confederacy, an independent Power, having no connection with the United States, and our institutions were likely to be endangered, and the existence of the Government imperiled by her remaining a separate and independent Power, or by her forming associations and alliances with some foreign Power that would injure our free institutions, I say we should have a right, on the principle laid down by Mr. Mason, Mr. Buchanan, and Mr. Soulé, and by the principle practiced by the Congress of the United States in the case of Florida, to seize her, pass her under the jurisdiction of the United States, and hold her as a province.

Mr. President, I have spoken of the possibility of a State standing in the position of South Carolina making alliances with a foreign Power. What do we see now? Ex-Governor Manning, of that State, in a speech made not long since at Columbia, made these declarations:

> Cotton is king, and would enable us in peace to rule the nations of the world, or successfully to encounter them in war. The millions in France and England engaged in its manufacture, are an effectual guarantee of the friendship of those nations. If necessary, their armies would stand to guard its uninterrupted and peaceful cultivation, and their men-of-war would line our coasts to guard it in its transit from our ports.

Ah! are we prepared in the face of doctrines like these, to permit a State that has been a member of our Confederacy to go out, and erect herself into an independent Power, when she points to the time when she will become a dependent of Great Britain, or when she will want the protection of France? What is the doctrine laid down by Mr. Buchanan and Mr. Mason and Mr. Soulé? If Cuba is to pass into the hands of an unfriendly Power, or any Power inimical to the United States, we have a right to seize and to hold her. Where is the difference between the two cases?

If South Carolina is outside of the Confederacy as an independent Power, disconnected from this Government, and we find her forming alliances to protect her, I ask what becomes of that great principle, the law of self-preservation? Does it not apply with equal force? We are told, upon pretty high authority, that Great Britain is operating in the United States; that she is exerting a powerful influence. I find that, in a paper issued from the executive office, Little Rock, Arkansas, and addressed to the militia of the State of Arkansas, the following language is used:

> It is my opinion, that the settled and secret policy of the British Government is to disturb the domestic tranquillity of the United States; that its object is to break up and destroy our Government, get rid of a powerful rival, extend the area of the British dominions on this Continent, and become the chief and controlling Power in America.

I will not read it all. He gives us many reasons why it is so. He says:

> I believe that such a conspiracy exists against our Federal Government, and that, if all the secret facts and transactions connected with it, and the names of the secret agents and emissaries of the British Government, distributed throughout the United States, could be ascertained, well authenticated, and made public, the patriotic people of the United States would be filled with astonishment; and having discovered the *real author and instigator* of the mischief, all discord between the free States and the slave States would at once be allayed, if not entirely cease, and that then they would become fraternally and more firmly united; and that the united indignation of the patriotic citizens of the whole Union against the British Government and its agents and emissaries would be so great that war would be declared against the British Government in less than twelve months.

The Governor of the State of Arkansas says, that if all the secret workings of Great Britain in this country could be ascertained, war would be declared in less than twelve months against the Government of Great Britain. What further does he say:

> Entertaining these opinions, I deem it my duty to the people of the State of Arkansas, to warn them to go to work *in earnest* and make *permanent and thorough preparations*, so that they may at all times be ready to protect themselves and our State against evils which I believe the British Government intends shall not be temporary and trifling, but continuous and aggravated, "irrepressible" and terrible.

This is signed by "Elias N. Conway, Governor of the State of Arkansas, and commander-in-chief of the army of the said State, and of the militia thereof." But ex-Governor Manning, of South Carolina, declares that cotton is king, and that the armies of Great Britain, and the fleets of France, and their men of war, would protect them; the one in the peaceful production of cotton, and the other in its exportation to the ports of the world. What sort of times are we falling on? Where are we going? Are these the threats that we are to be met with?

Is the United States to be told by one of the States attempting to absolve itself from its allegiance, without authority, and in fact in violation of the Constitution of the United States, that being disconnected with the Confederacy, it will place itself upon our coast to form an alliance with France and with England, which will protect her more securely than the protection which she now receives from the United States? The question recurs, have we not an existence, have we not institutions, to preserve; and in compliance with the great law of self-preservation, can we permit one of these States to take the protection of a foreign Power that is inimical and dangerous to the peaceful relations of this Government? Can we do it? I do not believe that we can. I repeat, for fear it may be misunderstood, that there are certain circumstances and conditions under which the remaining States, parties to the compact, might tolerate the secession of one State; and there are other circumstances and other conditions under which they dare not do it, in view of the great principle of self-preservation of which I have been speaking. When any State takes such an attitude what will be our course of policy? The case must be determined by the existing circumstance at the time.

But it is said by some that South Carolina, in making this movement, intends to carry the other States along with her; that they will be drawn into it. Now, Mr. President, is that the way for one sister, for one rebellious State, to talk to others! Is that the language in which they should be addressed? I ask my friend from California to read an extract from the message of Governor Gist, of South Carolina. He will do me a favor by so doing; and then we shall see the basis upon which we stand, and the attitude in which we are to be placed. Not only is South Carolina to go out of the Union in violation of the Constitution, impeding and resisting the execution of the laws, but the other States are to be dragged along with her, and we are all to be involved in one common ruin.

Mr. LATHAM read the following extract from the message of Governor Gist to the Legislature of South Carolina:

> The introduction of slaves from other States which may not become members of the southern confederacy, and particularly the border States, should be prohibited by legislative enactment; and by this means they will be brought to see that their safety depends upon a withdrawal from their

enemies, and an union with their friends and natural allies. If they should continue their union with the non-slaveholding States, let them keep their slave property in their own borders, and the only alternative left them will be emancipation by their own act, or by the action of their own confederates. We cannot consent to relieve them from their embarrassing situation by permitting them to realize the money value for their slaves by selling them to us, and thus prepare them, without any loss of property, to accommodate themselves to the northern free-soil idea. But should they unite their destiny with us, and become stars in the southern galaxy—members of a great southern confederation—we will receive them with open arms and an enthusiastic greeting.

All hope, therefore, of concerted action by a southern convention being lost, there is but one course left for South Carolina to pursue consistent with her honor, interest, and safety, and that is, to look neither to the right or [sic] the left, but go straight forward to the consummation of her purpose. It is too late now to receive propositions for a conference; and the State would be wanting in self-respect, after having deliberately decided on her own course, to entertain any proposition looking to a continuance of the present Union. We can get no better or safer guarantee than the present Constitution; and that has proved impotent to protect us against the fanaticism of the North. The institution of slavery must be under the exclusive control of those directly interested in its preservation, and not left to the mercy of those that believe it to be their duty to destroy it.

Mr. JOHNSON, of Tennessee. If my friend will read an extract from the speech of Mr. KEITT, of South Carolina, it will show the determination and policy to be pursued. It is done with all respect to him; for he is a man upon whom I look as a perfect and entire gentleman, from all my acquaintance with him; but I merely want to quote from his speech to get at the policy they wish to pursue.

Mr. LATHAM read, as follows:

Hon. L. M. Keitt was serenaded at Columbia on Monday evening; and in response to the compliment he spoke at considerable length in favor of separate State action. He said that South Carolina could not take one step backward now without receiving the curses of posterity. South Carolina, single and alone, was bound to go out of this accursed Union: he would take her out if but three men went with him, and if slaves took her back it would be to her graveyard. Mr. Buchanan was pledged to secession, and he meant to hold him to it. The policy of the State should be prudent and bold. His advice was, move on, side by side. He requested union and harmony among those embarked in the same great cause; but yield not a day too long, and when the time comes let it come speedily. Take your destinies in your own hands, and shatter this accursed Union. South Carolina could do it alone. But if she could not, she could at least throw her arms around the pillars of the Constitution, and involve all the States in a common ruin. Mr. Keitt was greatly applauded throughout his address.

Mr. JOHNSON, of Tennessee. Mr. President, I have referred to these extracts to show the policy intended to be pursued by our seceding sister. What is the first threat thrown out? It is an intimidation to the border States, alluding especially, I suppose, to Virginia, Maryland, Kentucky, and Missouri. They constitute the first tier of the border slave States. The next tier would be North Carolina and Tennessee and Arkansas. We in the South have complained of and condemned the position assumed by the Abolitionists. We have complained that their intention was to hem slavery in, so that, like the scorpion when surrounded by fire, if it did not die from the intense heat of the scorching flames, it would perish in its own poisonous skin. Now, our sister, without consulting her sisters, without caring for their interest or their consent, says that she will move forward; that she will destroy the Government under which we have lived, and that hereafter, when she forms a Government or a Constitution, unless the border States come in, she will pass laws prohibiting the importation of slaves into her State from those States, and thereby obstruct the slave trade among the States, and throw the institution back upon the border States, so that they will be compelled to emancipate their slaves upon the principle laid down by the Abolition Party. That is the rod held over us!

I tell our sisters in the South that so far as Tennessee is concerned, she will not be dragged into a southern or any other confederacy until she has had time to consider; and then she will go when she believes it to be her interest, and not before. I tell our northern friends who are resisting the execution of the laws made in conformity with the Constitution, that we will not be driven on the other hand into their confederacy, and we will not go into it unless it suits us, and they give us such guarantees as we deem right and proper. We say to you of the South, we are not to be frightened or coerced. Oh, when one talks about coercing a State, how maddening and insulting to the State; but when you want to bring the other States to terms, how easy to point out a means by which to coerce them! But, sir, we do not intend to be coerced.

We are told that certain States will go out and tear this accursed Constitution into fragments, and drag he pillars of this mighty edifice down upon us, and involve us all in one common ruin. Will the border States submit to such a threat? No. If they do not come into the movement, the pillars of this stupendous fabric of human freedom and greatness and goodness are to be pulled down, and all will be involved in one common ruin. Such is the threatening language used. "You shall come into our confederacy, or we will coerce you to the emancipation of your slaves." That is the language which is held toward us.

There are many ideas afloat about this threatened dissolution, and it is time to speak out. The question arises in reference to the protection and preservation of the institution of slavery, whether dissolution is a remedy or will give to it protection. I avow here, to-day, that if I were an Abolitionist, and wanted to accomplish the overthrow of the institution of slavery in the southern States, the first step that I would take would be to break the bonds of this Union, and dissolve this Government. I believe the continuance of slavery depends upon the preservation of this Union, and a compliance with all the guarantees of the Constitution. I believe an interference with it will break up the Union; and I believe a dissolution of the Union will, in the end, though it may be some time to come, overthrow the institution of slavery. Hence we find so many in the North who desire the dissolution of these States as the most certain and direct and effectual means of overthrowing the institution of slavery.

What protection would it be to us to dissolve this Union? What protection would it be to us to convert this nation into two hostile Powers, the one warring with the other? Whose property is at stake? Whose interest is endangered? Is it not the property of the border States? Suppose Canada were moved down upon our border, and the two separated sections, then different nations, were hostile: what would the institution of slavery be worth on the border? Every man who has common sense will see that the institution would take up its march and retreat, as certainly and as unerringly as general laws can operate. Yes; it would commence to retreat the very moment this Government was converted into hostile Powers, and you made the line between the slaveholding and non-slaveholding States the line of division.

Then, what remedy do we get for the institution of slavery? Must we keep a standing army? Must we keep up forts bristling with arms along the whole border? This is a question to be considered, one that involves the future; and no step should be taken without mature reflection. Before this Union is dissolved and broken up, we in Tennessee, as one of the slave States, want to be consulted; we want to know what protection we are to have; whether we are simply to be made outposts and guards to protect the property of others, at the same time that we sacrifice and lose our own. We want to understand this question.

Again: if there is one division of the States, will there not be more than one? I heard a Senator say the other day that he would rather see this Government separated into thirty-three fractional parts than to see it consolidated; but when you once begin to divide, when the first division is made, who can tell when the next one will be made? When these States are turned loose, and a different condition of things is presented, with complex and abstruse interests to be considered and weighed and understood, what combinations may take place no one can tell. I am opposed to the consolidation of Government, and I am as much for the reserved rights of States as any one; but rather than see this Union divided into thirty-three petty Governments, with a little prince in one, a potentate in another, a little aristocracy in a third, a little democracy in a fourth, and a republic somewhere else; a citizen not being able to pass from one State to another without a passport or a commission from his Government; with quarreling and warring amongst the little petty Powers, which would result in anarchy; I would rather see this Government to-day—I proclaim it here in my place—converted into a consolidated Government. It would be better for the American people; it would be better for our kind; it would be better for humanity; better for Christianity; better for all that tends to elevate and ennoble man, than breaking up this splendid, this magnificent, this stupendous fabric of human government, the most perfect that the world ever saw, and which has succeeded thus far without a parallel in the history of the world.

When you come to break up and turn loose the different elements, there is no telling what combinations may take place in the future. It may occur, for instance, to the middle States that they will not get so good a Government by going a little further South as by remaining where we are. It may occur to North Carolina, to Tennessee, to Kentucky, to Virginia, to Maryland, to Missouri—and perhaps Illinois might fall in, too—that, by erecting themselves into a central, independent republic, disconnected either with the North or the South, they could stand as a peace-maker—could stand as a great breakwater, resisting the heated and surging waves of the South, and the fanatical abolitionism of the North. They might think that they could stand there and lift themselves up above the two extremes, with the sincere hope that the time would arrive when the extremes would come together, and reunite once more, and we could reconstruct this greatest and best Government the world has ever seen. Or it might so turn out, our institution of slavery being exposed upon the northern line, that by looking to Pennsylvania, to New York, and to some of the other States, instead of having them as hostile Powers upon our frontiers, they might come to this central republic, and give us such constitutional guarantees, and such assurances that they would be executed, that it might be to our interests to form an alliance with them, and have a protection on our frontier.

I throw these out as considerations. There will be various projects and various combinations made. Memphis is now connected with Norfolk, in the Old Dominion; Memphis is connected with Baltimore within two days. Here is a coast that lets us out to the commerce of the world. When we look around in the four States of Tennessee, Kentucky, Virginia, and Maryland, there are things about which our memories, our attachments, and our associations linger with pride and with pleasure. Go down into the Old Dominion; there is the place where, in 1781, Cornwallis surrendered his sword to the immortal Washington. In the bosom of her soil are deposited her greatest and best sons. Move along in that trail, and there we find Jefferson and Madison and Monroe, and a long list of worthies.

We come next to old North Carolina, my native State, God bless her! She is my mother. Though she was not my cherishing mother, to use the language of the classics, she is the mother whom I love, and I cling to her with undying affection, as a son should cling to an affectionate mother. We find Mecklen, who was associated with our early history, deposited in her soil. Go to King's Mountain, on her borders, and you there find the place on which the battle was fought that turned the tide of the Revolution. Yes, within her borders the signal battle was fought that turned the tide which resulted in the surrender of Cornwallis at Yorktown, in the Old Dominion.

Travel on a little further, and we get back to Tennessee. I shall be as modest as I can in reference to her, but she has some associations that make her dear to the people of the United States. In Tennessee we have our own illustrious Jackson. There he sleeps—that Jackson who issued his proclamation in 1833, and saved this Government. We have our Polk and our Grundy, and a long list of others who are worthy of remembrance.

And who lie in Kentucky? Your Hardings, your Boons, your Roanes, your Clays, are among the dead; your Crittenden among the living. All are identified and associated with the history of the country.

Maryland has her Carroll of Carrollton, and a long list of worthies, who are embalmed in the hearts of the American people. And you are talking about breaking up this Republic, with this cluster of associations, these ties of affection, around you. May we not expect that some means may be devised by which they can be preserved together?

Here, too, in the center of the Republic, is the seat of Government, which was founded by Washington, and bears his immortal name. Who dare appropriate it exclusively? It is within the borders of the States I have enumerated, in whose limits are found the graves of Washington, of Jackson, of Polk, of Clay. From them is it supposed that we will be torn away? No, sir; we will cherish these endearing associations with the hope, if this Republic shall be broken, that we may speak words of peace and reconciliation to a distracted, a divided, I may add, a maddened people. Angry waves may be lashed into fury on the one hand; on the other blustering winds may rage; but we stand immovable upon our basis, as on our own native mountains—presenting their craggy brows, their unexplored caverns, their summits "rocked-ribbed and as ancient as the sun"—we stand speaking peace, association, and concert, to a distracted Republic.

But, Mr. President, will it not be well before we break up this great Government, to inquire what kind of a government this new government in the South is to be, with which we are threatened unless we involve our destinies with this rash and precipitate movement. What intimation is there in reference to its character? Before my State and those States of which I have been speaking, go into a southern or northern confederacy, ought they not to have some idea of the kind of government that is to be formed? What are the intimations in the South, in reference to the formation of a new government? The language of some speakers is that they want a southern government obliterating all State lines—a government of consolidation. It is alarming and distressing to entertain the proposition here. What ruin and disaster would follow, if we are to have a consolidated government here! But the idea is afloat and current in the South that a southern government is to be established, in the language of some of the speakers in the State of Georgia, "obliterating all State lines;" and is that the kind of entertainment to which the people are to be invited? Is that the kind of government under which we are to pass; and are we to be forced to emancipate our slaves unless we go into it? Another suggestion in reference to a southern government is, that we shall have a southern confederacy of great strength and power, with a constitutional provision preventing any State from changing its domestic institutions without the consent of three fourths, or some great number to be fixed upon. Is that the kind of government under which we want to pass? I avow here, that so far as I am concerned, I will never enter, with my consent, any government, North or South, less republican, less democratic, than the one under which we now live.

Where are we drifting? What kind of breakers are ahead? Have we a glimpse through the fog that develops the rock on which the vessel of State is drifting? Should we not consider maturely, in giving up this old Government, what kind of government is to succeed it? Ought we not to have time to think? Are we not entitled to respect and consideration? In one of the Georgia papers we find some queer suggestions; and, as miners would say, these may be considered as mere surface indications, that develop what is below. We ought to know the kind of government that is to be established. When we read the allusions made in various papers, and by various speakers, we find that there is one party who [sic] are willing to give up this form of government; to change its character; and, in fact, to pass under a monarchical form of government. I hope that my friend will read the extracts which I will hand him.

Mr. LATHAM read the following extracts:

If the Federal system is a failure, the question may well be asked, *is not the whole republican system a failure?* Very many wise, thinking men, say so. We formed the Federal Government because the separate States, it was thought, were not strong enough to stand alone, and because they were likely to prove disadvantageous, if not dangerous, each to the other, in their distinct organization, and with their varying interests. When we break up, will the disadvantages and dangers of separate States be such as to require the formation of a new confederacy of those which are, at present, supposed to be homogeneous? If we do form a new confederacy, when the old is gone, *it would seem to be neither wise, prudent, nor statesmanlike to frame it after the pattern of the old.* New safeguards and guarantees must necessarily be required, and none but a heedless maniac would seek to avoid looking this matter squarely in the face.

It is true that we might make a constitution for the fifteen southern States, which would secure the rights of all, *at present*, from harm, or, at least, which would require a *clear violation of its letter*, so plainly that the world could discern it, when unconstitutional action was consummated. But then, in the course of years, as men changed, times changed, interests changed, business changed, productions changed, a violation of the *spirit might* occur, which would not be clearly a violation of the letter. It may be said that the constitution might provide for its own change as times changed. Well, that was the design when our present Constitution was formed, and, still, we say, it was a failure. How more carefully could a new one be arranged? Men will say that we of the South *are one*, and that we shall get along well enough. But they who say it know neither history nor human nature. When the Union was formed, twelve of the thirteen States were slaveholding; and if the cotton gin had not been invented there would not probably to-day have been an African slave in North America.

But how about the State organizations? This is an important consideration, for whether we consult with the other southern States or not, it is certain that each State must act for itself, in the first instance. When any State goes out of the present Federal Union, it then becomes a *Foreign Power* as to all the other States, as well as to the world. Whether it will unite again with any of the States, or stand alone, is for it to determine. The new Confederacy must then be made by those States which desire it—and if Georgia, or any other State, does not find the proposed terms of federation agreeable, she can maintain her own separate form of government, or at least try it. Well, what form of government shall we have? This is more easily asked than answered.

Some of the wisest and best citizens propose a HEREDITARY

CONSTITUTIONAL MONARCHY; but however good that may be in itself, the most important point to discover is, whether or not the people are prepared for it. It is thought again, by others, that we shall be able to go on for a *generation or two*, in a new confederacy, with additional safeguards; such, for instance, as an *Executive for life, a vastly restricted suffrage, Senators elected for life, or for a long period, say twenty-one years,* and the most popular branch of the assembly elected for *seven years*, the judiciary absolutely independent, and for life, or good behavior. The frequency of elections, and the universality of suffrage, with the attendant arousing of the people's passions, and the necessary sequence of demagogues being elevated to high station, are thought by many to be *the great causes* of trouble among us.

We throw out these suggestions that the people may think of them, and act as their interests require. Our own opinion is that the South might be the greatest nation on earth, and might maintain, on the basis of African slavery, not only a splendid Government, but a *secure republican* Government. *But still our fears are that through anarchy we shall reach the despotism of military chieftains, and finally be raised again to a monarchy* —*Augusta (Georgia) Chronicle and Sentinel of December 8, 1860.*

[From the Columbus (Georgia) Times]

LET US REASON TOGETHER—Permit a humble individual to lay before you a few thoughts that are burnt into his heart by their very truth.

The first great thought is this: The institution known as the 'Federal Government,' established by the people of the United States *of* America, is a *failure*. This is a fact which cannot be gainsayed. It has *never* been in the power of the 'Federal Government' to enforce all its own laws within its own territory; it has, therefore, been measurably a failure from the beginning; but its first convincing evidence of weakness was in allowing one branch of its organization to pass an unconstitutional law, (the Missouri compromise.) Its next evidence of decrepitude was its inability to enforce a constitutional law, (the fugitive slave law,) the whole fabric being shaken to its foundation by the only attempt of enforcement made by its chief officer, (President Pierce.) I need not enlarge in this direction. The 'Federal Government' *is a failure*.

What then? The States, of course, revert to their original position, each sovereign within itself. There can be no other conclusion. This, then, being our position, the question for sober, thinking, earnest men is, what shall we do for the future? I take it for granted that no man in his senses would advocate the remaining in so many petty sovereignties. We should be worse than Mexicanized by that process. What, then, shall we do? In the first place, I would say, let us look around and see if there is a government of an enlightened nation that has not yet proven a failure, but which is now, and has ever been, productive of happiness to all its law-abiding people. If such a government can be found—a government whose first and only object is the *good*, the REAL GOOD (not *fancied good*, an *ignis fatuus* which I fear both our fathers and ourselves have too much run after in this country) of all its people—if such a government exists, let us examine it carefully; if it has apparent errors, (as what human institution has not?) let us avoid them. Its beneficial arrangements let us adopt. Let us not be turned aside by its name, nor be lured by its pretensions. Try it by its works, and adopt or condemn it by its fruits. *No more experiments.* 'I speak as to wise men: judge ye what I say.'

I am one of the few who have ever dared to think that republicanism was a failure from its inception, and I have never shrunk from giving my opinion when it was worthwhile. I have never wished to see this Union disrupted; but if it must be, then I raise my voice for a return to a "CONSTITUTIONAL MONARCHY."

COLUMBIA, SOUTH CAROLINA, *December* 5, 1860. Yesterday the debate in the House of Representatives was unusually warm. The parties arrayed against each other in the matter of organizing the army, and the manner of appointing the commanding officers, used scathing language, and debate ran high throughout the session. So far as I am able to judge, both the opposing parties are led by bitter prejudices. The Joint Military Committee, with two or three exceptions, have pertinaciously clung to the idea that a standing army of paid volunteers, to be raised at once, to have the power of choosing their officers, up to captain, and to require all above to be appointed by the Governor, is the organization for the times. Mr. Cunningham, of the House, who is put forward by the committee to take all the responsibility of extreme sentiments, has openly avowed his hatred of democracy in the camp. He considered the common soldier as incapable of an elective choice. He and others of his party wage [sic] a bitter war against democracy, and indicate an utter want of faith in the ability of the people to make proper choice in elections.

The party opposed to this, the predominate party, is ostensibly led in the House by Mr. McGowan, of Abbeville, and Mr. Moore, of Anderson. These gentlemen have a hard fight of it. They represent the democratic sentiments of the rural districts, and are in opposition to the Charleston clique, who are urged on by Edward Rhett, Thomas Y. Simmons, and B. H. Rhett, Jr., of the Charleston Mercury. The tendencies of these gentlemen are all towards a dictatorship, or monarchical form of government; at least it appears so to my mind, and I find myself not alone in the opinion. They fight heart and soul for an increase of gubernatorial power; and one of their number, as I have already stated, openly avows his desire to make the Governor a military chieftain, with sovereign power.—*Correspondence of the Baltimore American.*

Mr. JOHNSON, of Tennessee. Mr. President, I have merely called attention to these surface indications for the purpose of sustaining the assumption that even the people in the southern States ought to consider what kind of government they are going to pass under, before they change the present one. We are told that the present Constitution would be adopted by the new confederacy, and in a short time everything would be organized under it. We find here other indications, and we are told from another quarter that another character of government is more preferable. We know that, North and South, there is a portion of our fellow-citizens who are opposed to a government based on the intelligence and will of the people. We know that power is always stealing from the many to the few. We know that it is always vigilant and on the alert; and now that we are in a revolution, and great changes are to be made, should we not, as faithful sentinels, as men who are made the guardians of the interests of the Government, look at these indications and call the attention of the country to them? Is it not better to

"Bear those ills we have, Than to fly to others that we know not of?"

We see, by these indications, that it is contemplated to establish a monarchy. We see it announced that this Government has been a failure from the beginning. How has it been a failure? Now, in the midst of a revolution, while the people are confused, while chaos reigns, it is supposed by some that we can be induced to return to a constitutional or absolute monarchy. Who can tell that we may not have some Louis Napoleon among us, who may be ready to make a *coupe d'etat*, and enthrone himself upon the rights and upon the liberties of the people? Who can tell what kind of government may grow up? Hence the importance, in advance, of considering maturely and deliberately before we give up the old one.

I repeat again that the people of Tennessee will never pass under another government that is less republican, less democratic in all its bearings, than the one under which we now live, I care not whether it is formed in the North or the South. We will occupy an isolated, a separate and distinct position, before we will do it. We will pass into that fractional condition to which I have alluded before we will pass under an absolute or a constitutional monarchy. I do not say that this is the design North or South, or perhaps of all but a very small portion; but it shows that there are some who, if they could find a favorable opportunity, would fix the description of government I have alluded to on the great mass of the people. Sir, I will stand by the Constitution of the country as it is, and by all its guarantees. I am not for breaking up this great Confederacy. I am for holding on to it as it is, with mode and manner pointed out in the instrument for its own amendment. It was good enough for Washington, for Adams, for Jefferson, and for Jackson. It is good enough for us. I intend to stand by it, and to insist on a compliance with all its guarantees, North and South.

Notwithstanding we want to occupy the position of a breakwater between the northern and the southern extremes, and bring all together if we can, I tell our northern friends that the constitutional guarantees must be carried out; for the time may come when, after we have exhausted all honorable and fair means, if this Government still fails to execute the laws, and protect us in our rights, it will be at an end. Gentlemen of the North need not deceive themselves in that particular; but we intend to act in the Union and under the Constitution, and not out of it. We do not intend that you should drive us out of this house that was reared by the hands of our fathers. It is our house. It is the constitutional house. We have a right here; and because you come forward and violate the ordinances of this house, I do not intend to go out; and if you persist in the violation of the ordinances of the house, we intend to eject you from the building and retain the possessions ourselves. We want, if we can, to stay the heated, and I am compelled to say, according to my judgment, the rash and precipitate action of some of our southern friends, that indicates red hot madness. I want to say to those in the North, comply with the Constitution and preserve its guarantees, and in so doing save this glorious Union and all that pertains to it. I intend to stand by the Constitution as it is, insisting upon a compliance with all its guarantees. I intend to stand by it as the sheet anchor of the Government; and I trust and hope, though it seems to be now in the very vortex of ruin, though it seems to be running between Charybdis and Scylla, the rock on the one hand and the whirlpool on the other, that it will be preserved, and will remain a beacon to guide, and an example to be imitated by all the nations of the earth. Yes, I intend to hold onto to it as the chief ark of our safety, as the palladium of our civil and religious liberty. I intend to cling to it as the shipwrecked mariner clings to the last plank, when the night and the tempest close around him. It is the last hope of human freedom. Although denounced as an experiment by some who want to see a constitutional monarchy, it has been a successful experiment. I trust and hope it will be continued; that this great work may go on.

Why should we go out of the Union? Have we anything to fear? What are we alarmed about? We say that you of the North have violated the Constitution; that you have trampled under foot its guarantees; but we intend to go to you in a proper way, and ask you to redress the wrong, and comply with the Constitution. We believe the time will come when you will do it, and we do not intend to break up the Government until the fact is ascertained that you will not do it. Where is the grievance, where is the complaint that presses on our sister, South Carolina, now? Is it that she wants to carry slavery into the Territories; that she wants protection to slavery there? How long has it been since, upon this very floor, her own Senators voted that it was not necessary to make a statute now for the protection of slavery in the Territories? No longer ago than the last session. Is that a good reason? They declared, in the resolution adopted by the Senate, that when it was necessary they had the power to do it; but that it was not necessary then. Are you going out for a grievance that has not occurred, and which your own Senators then said had not occurred? Is it because you want to carry slaves into the Territories? You were told that you had all the protection needed; that the courts had decided in your behalf, under the Constitution; and that, under the decisions of the courts, the law must be executed.

Mr. DAVIS. I do not understand the Senator perhaps correctly, as asserting that any Senator from South Carolina said that.

Mr. JOHNSON, of Tennessee. I said they voted for the resolution.

Mr. DAVIS. They did not. They voted against both the resolution and the amendment, and voted for the resolution which declared the duty to protect.

Mr. JOHNSON, of Tennessee. The duty to protect now?

Mr. DAVIS. They did declare the duty to protect at all times and in every place, under all circumstances, wherever protection was needed.

Mr. JOHNSON, of Tennessee. When necessary.

Mr. DAVIS. And I suppose, if the Senator intends to make a plea on that word, that they intended to nail to the cross the miserable miscreants who would claim protection when it was not necessary, and shrink from it when it was.

Mr. JOHNSON, of Tennessee. The test was made before the Senate upon Senator Brown's proposition to give protection now.

Mr. WIGFALL. It was not. I corrected that the other day.

Mr. JOHNSON, of Tennessee. Well, you just corrected it the way it was not—that is all. [Laughter.]

Mr. WIGFALL. Mr. President—

The PRESIDING OFFICER, (Mr. Fitzpatrick in the chair.) Does the Senator from Tennessee yield the floor to the Senator from Texas?

Mr. JOHNSON, of Tennessee. No. I will continue my remarks.

Mr. WIGFALL. Well, if the Senator chooses to pervert facts, and go on and publish them in his speech, I have nothing to say.

Mr. JOHNSON, of Tennessee. I will publish them as the records show them to be. I say that on Senator Brown's proposition to carry protection into the Territories now, it received but three votes.

Mr. WIGFALL. I say that never was proposed or voted on.

Mr. JOHNSON, of Tennessee. The record will settle it.

Mr. WIGFALL. Turn to it. I will read it for you.

Mr. JOHNSON, of Tennessee. I do not want to be interrupted now.

Mr. WIGFALL. I know you do not. You do not want the facts stated.

Mr. JOHNSON, of Tennessee. I know what the facts were, and in this Senate we voted for the passage of resolutions that Congress had the power to protect slavery when necessary and wherever protection was needed. Was there not a majority on this floor for it; and if it was necessary then, could we not have passed a bill for that purpose without passing a resolution saying that it should be protected whenever necessary? I was here; I know what the substance of the proposition was, and the whole of it was simply to declare the principle that we had the power, and that it was the duty of Congress, to protect slavery when necessary, in the Territories or wherever else protection was needed. Was it necessary then? If it was, we had the power, and why did we not pass the law?

Mr. GREEN (Missouri). Will the Senator allow me to make one suggestion?

Mr. JOHNSON, of Tennessee. I hope the Senator will not interrupt me. I do not refuse out of any discourtesy. The journal of the Senate records that on the 25th of May last—

> On motion by Mr. Brown, to amend the resolution by striking out all after the word 'resolved,' and in lieu thereof inserting:
>
> That experience having already shown that the Constitution and the common law, unaided by statutory enactments, do not afford adequate and sufficient protection to slave property; some of the Territories having failed, others having refused, to pass such enactments, it has become the duty of Congress to interpose and pass such laws as will afford to slave property in the Territories that protection which is given to other kinds of property.
>
> It was determined in the negative—yeas 3, nays 42.
>
> On motion by Mr. Brown, the yeas and nays being desired by one fifth of the Senators present. Those who voted in the affirmative, are:
>
> Messrs. Brown, Johnson of Arkansas, and Mallory.
>
> Those who voted in the negative, are:
>
> Messrs. Benjamin, Bigler, Bragg, Bright, Chesnut, Clark, Clay, Clingman, Crittenden, Davis, Dixon, Doolittle, Fitzpatrick, Foot, Foster, Green, Grimes, Gwin, Hamlin, Harlan, Hemphill, Hunter, Iverson, Johnson of Tennessee, Lane, Latham, Mason, Nicholson, Pearce, Polk, Powell, Pugh, Rice, Sebastian, Slidell, Ten Eyck, Thomson, Toombs, Trumbull, Wigfall, Wilson, and Yulee.

I was going on to say that the want of protection to slavery in the Territories cannot be considered a grievance now. That is not the reason why she is going out, and going to break up the Confederacy. What is it then? Is there any issue between South Carolina and the Federal Government? Has the Federal Government failed to comply with, and to carry out, the obligations that it owes to South Carolina? In what has the Federal Government failed? In what has it neglected the interest of South Carolina? What law has it undertaken to enforce upon South Carolina that is unconstitutional and oppressive?

If there are grievances, why cannot we all go together, and write them down, and point them out to our northern friends after we have agreed on what those grievances were, and say, "here is what we demand; here our wrongs are enumerated; upon these terms we have agreed; and now, after we have given you a reasonable time to consider these additional guarantees in order to protect ourselves against these wrongs, if you refuse them, then, having made an honorable effort, having exhausted all other means, we may declare the association to broken up, and we may go into an act of revolution." We can then say to them, "You have refused to give us guarantees that we think are needed for the protection of our institutions and for the protection of our other interests." When they do this, I will go as far as he who goes the furthest.

I tell them here to-day, if they do not do it, Tennessee will be found standing as firm and unyielding in her demands for those guarantees in the way a State should stand, as any other State in this Confederacy. She is not quite so belligerent now. She is not making quite so much noise. She is not as blustering as Sempronious was in the council in Addison's play of Cato, who declared that his "voice was still for war." There was another character there, Lucius, who was called upon to know what his opinions were; and when he was called upon, he replied that he must confess his thoughts were turned on peace; but when the extremity came, Lucius, who was deliberative, who was calm, and whose thoughts were upon peace, was found true to the interests of his country. He proved himself to be a man and a soldier; while the other was a traitor and a coward. We will do our duty; we will stand upon principle, and defend it to the last extremity.

We do not think, though, that we have just cause for going out of the Union now. We have just cause of complaint; but we are for remaining in the Union, and fighting the battle like men. We do not intend to be cowardly, and turn our backs on our own camps. We intend to stay and fight the battle here upon this consecrated ground. Why should we retreat? Because Mr. Lincoln has been elected President of the United States? Is this any cause why we should retreat? Does not every man, Senator or otherwise, know that if Mr. Breckinridge had been elected, we should not be to-day for dissolving the Union? Then what is the issue? It is because we have not got our man. If we had got our man, we should not have been for breaking up the Union; but as Mr. Lincoln is elected, we are for breaking up the Union! I say no. Let us show ourselves men, and men of courage.

How has Mr. Lincoln been elected, and how have Mr. Breckinridge and Mr. Douglas been defeated? By the votes of the American people, cast according to the Constitution and the forms of law, though it has been upon a sectional issue. It is not the first time in our history that two candidates have been elected from the same section of the country. General Jackson and Mr. Calhoun were elected on the same tickets; but nobody considered that cause of dissolution. They were from the South. While I oppose the sectional spirit that has produced the election of Lincoln and Hamlin, yet it has been done according to the Constitution and according to the forms of law. I believe we have the power in our own hands, and I am not willing to shrink from the responsibility of exercising that power.

How has Lincoln been elected, and upon what basis does he stand? A minority President by nearly a million votes; but had the election taken place upon the plan proposed in my amendment of the Constitution, by districts, he would have been this day defeated. But it has been done according to the Constitution and according to law. I am for abiding by the Constitution; and in abiding by it I want to maintain and retain my place here and put down Mr. Lincoln and drive back his advances upon southern institutions, if he designs to make any. Have we not got the brakes in our hands? Have we not got the power? We have. Let South Carolina send her Senators back; let all the Senators come; and on the 4th of March next we shall have a majority of six in this body against him. This successful sectional candidate, who is in a minority of a million, or nearly so, on the popular vote, cannot make his Cabinet on the 4th of March next unless this Senate will permit him.

Am I to be so great a coward as to retreat from duty? I will stand here and meet the encroachments upon the institutions of my country at the threshold; and as a man, as one that loves my country and my constituents, I will stand here and resist all encroachments and advances. Here is the place to stand. Shall I desert the citadel, and let the enemy come in and take possession? No. Can Mr. Lincoln send a foreign minister, or even a consul, abroad, unless he receives the sanction of the Senate? Can he appoint a postmaster whose salary is over a thousand dollars a year without the consent of the Senate? Shall we desert our posts, shrink from our responsibilities, and permit Mr. Lincoln to come with his cohorts, as we consider them, from the North, to carry off everything? Are we so cowardly that now that we are defeated, not conquered, we shall do this? Yes, we are defeated according to the forms of law and the Constitution; but the real victory is ours—the moral force is with us. Are we going to desert that noble and that patriotic band who have stood by us at the North? Who have stood by us upon principle? who have stood by us upon the Constitution? They stood by us and fought the battle upon principle; and now that we have been defeated, not conquered, are we to turn our backs upon them and leave them to their fate? I, for one, will not. I intend to stand by them. How many votes did we get in the North? We got more votes in the North against Lincoln than the entire southern States cast. Are they not able and faithful allies? They are; and now, on account of this temporary defeat, are we to turn our backs upon them to their fate, as they have fallen for us in former controversies?

We find, when all the North is summed up, that Mr. Lincoln's majority there is only about two hundred thousand on the popular vote; and when that is added to the other vote cast throughout the Union, he stands to-day in a minority of nearly a million votes. What, then, is necessary to be done? To stand to our posts like men, and act upon principle; stand for the country; and in four years from this day, Lincoln and his administration will be turned out, the worst defeated and broken-down party that ever came into power. It is an inevitable result from the combination of elements that now exist. What cause, then, is there to break up the Union? What reason is there for deserting our posts and destroying the greatest and best Government that was ever spoken into existence?

I voted against him; I spoke against him; I spent my money to defeat him; but I still love my country; I love the Constitution; I intend to insist upon its guarantees. There, and there alone, I intend to plant myself, with the confident hope and belief that if the Union remains together, in less than four years the new triumphant party will be overthrown. In less time, I have the hope and belief that we shall unite and agree upon our grievances here and demand their redress, not as suppliants at the footstool of power, but as parties to a great compact; we shall say that we want additional guarantees, and that they are necessary to the preservation of this Union; and then, when they are refused deliberately and calmly, if we cannot do better, let the South go together, and let the North go together, and let us have a division of this Government without the shedding of blood, if such a thing be possible; let us have a division of the property; let us have a division of the Navy; let us have a division of the Army and of the public lands. Let it be done in peace and in a spirit that should characterize and distinguish this people. I believe that we can obtain all our guarantees. I believe that there is too much good sense, too much intelligence, too much patriotism, too much capability, too much virtue, in the great mass of the people to permit this Government to be overthrown.

I have an abiding faith, I have an unshaken confidence in man's capability to govern himself. I will not give up this Government that is now called an experiment, which some are prepared to abandon for a constitutional monarchy. No, I intend to stand by it, and I entreat every man throughout the nation who is a patriot, and who has seen, and is compelled to admit, the success of this great experiment, to come forward, not in haste, not in precipitancy, but in deliberation, in full view of all that is before us, in the spirit of brotherly love and fraternal affection, and rally around the altar of our common country, and lay the Constitution upon it as our last libation, and swear by our God and all that is sacred and holy, that the Constitution shall be saved, and the Union preserved. Yes, in the language of the departed Jackson, let us exclaim that the Union, "the Federal Union, it must be preserved."

Are we likely, when we get to ourselves, North and South, to sink into brotherly love? Are we likely to be so harmonious in that condition as some suppose? What did we find here the other day among our brother Senators, one of whom referred to a southern Governor? I allude to it only to show the feeling that exists even among ourselves. I am sometimes impressed with the force of Mr. Jefferson's remark, that we may as well keep the North to quarrel with, for if we have no North to quarrel with, we shall quarrel among ourselves. We are a sort of quarrelsome, pugnacious people; and if we cannot get a quarrel from one quarter, we shall have it from another; and I would rather quarrel a little now with the North than be quarreling with ourselves. Because the Governor of a southern State was refusing to convene the Legislature to hasten this movement that was going on throughout the South; and because he objected to that course of conduct, what did a Senator say here in the American Senate? The question was asked if there was not some Texan Brutus that would rise up and rid the country of the hoary-headed traitor! This is the language that a Senator used. This is the way we begin to speak of southern Governors. Yes; to remove an obstacle in our way, we must have a modern Brutus who will go to the capital of a State and assassinate a Governor to accelerate the movement that is going on. If we are so unscrupulous in reference to ourselves, and in reference to the means we are willing to employ to consummate this dissolution, then it does not look very much like harmony among ourselves after we get out of it.

Mr. President, I have said much more than I anticipated when I commenced; and I have said more now (though external appearances seem different) than I have the strength or health to say; but if there is any effort of mine that would preserve this Government till there is time to think, till there is time to consider, even if it cannot be preserved any longer; if that end could be secured by making a sacrifice of my existence and offering up my blood, I would be willing to consent to it. Let us pause in this mad career; let us hesitate; let us consider well what we are doing before we make a movement. I believe that, to a certain extent, dissolution is going to take place. I say to the North, you ought to come up in the spirit which should characterize and control the North on this question; and you ought to give those indications in good faith that will approach what the South demands. It will be no sacrifice on your part. It is no suppliancy on ours, but simply a demand of right. What concession is there in doing right? Then, come forward. We have it in our power—yes, this Congress here to-day has it in its power to save this Union, even after South Carolina has gone out. Will they not do it? You can do it. Who is willing to take the dreadful alternative without making an honorable effort to save this Government? This Congress has it in its power to-day to arrest this thing, at least for a season, until there is time to consider about it, until we can act discreetly and prudently, and I believe arrest it all together.

Shall we give all this up to the Vandals and the Goths? Shall we shrink from our duty, and desert the Government as a sinking ship, or shall we stand by it? I, for one, will stand here until the high behest of my constituents demands me to desert my post; and instead of laying hold of the columns of this fabric and pulling it down, though I may not be much of a prop, I will stand with my shoulder supporting the edifice as long as human effort can do it. Then, cannot we agree? We can, if we will, and come together and save the country.

In saying what I have said on this occasion, Mr. President, I have done it in view of a duty that I felt I owed to my constituents, that I owed to my children, that I owed to myself. Without regard to consequences, I have taken the position I have; and when the tug comes, when Greek shall meet Greek, and our rights are refused after all honorable means have been exhausted, then it is that I will perish in the last breach; yes, in the language of the patriot Emmet, "I will dispute every inch of ground; I will burn every blade of grass; and the last intrenchment [sic] of freedom shall be my grave." Then, let us stand by the Constitution; and in preserving the Constitution we shall save the Union; and in saving the Union, we save this, the greatest Government on earth.

I thank the Senate for their kind attention.

5

War Will Follow

Senator George E. Pugh, Ohio
December 20, 1860

Senator Pugh (1822-1876) attended private schools and in 1840 graduated from Miami University at Oxford, Ohio. He was admitted to the bar and commenced the practice of law in 1843. He was a captain in the Mexican War. He served as a member of the Ohio house of representatives from 1848-1850, was Cincinnati city solicitor in 1850, state attorney general from 1852-1854, and was elected as a Democrat to the U.S. Senate and served from 1855-1861. From 1860 to 1864 he was unsuccessful in his reelection bid to the U.S. Senate, election as Ohio's Lieutenant Governor, and to the thirty-ninth Congress. The Senator maintained that the Republican Party intentionally provoked Southern apprehensions and exhorted the Republicans that the vast responsibility for resolving the crisis rested on their shoulders.

Mr. PUGH. James Madison, who recorded with so much fullness and accuracy the protracted debates of the convention which formed the Constitution of the United States, at the close of his labors thought it not beneath the dignity of a historian to report an anecdote, scarcely less memorable from the fact that he reported it, than from its connection with two of the most illustrious characters of the time. He tells us, that while the members of the convention were signing the Constitution, on Monday, the 17th of September, 1787, Dr. Franklin, looking towards the President's chair, at the back at which a rising sun happened to be painted, observed to a few members near him that painters had found it difficult to distinguish, in their art, a rising from a setting sun. I have, said he, often and often [sic], in the course of the session, and in the vicissitudes of my hopes and fears as to its issue, looked at that behind the President, without being able to tell whether it was rising or setting; but now, at length, I have the happiness to know that it is a rising, and not a setting, sun. (Madison Papers, vol. 3, page 1624.)

Senators, our millions of constituents, with all the nations of the civilized world as witnesses, are gazing at the lurid sky overhead, fearing, and almost expecting, that the sun which Franklin saw rising behind the chair of Washington, will be at once, and forever, extinguished in mid-heaven, instead of continuing to shine more and more brightly, if not in endless day, until we, and our children, and our children's children, have perished and been forgotten.

My colleague, [Mr. WADE] in addressing the Senate on Monday last, told us that when he left his home in Ohio, he had heard of no discontent, and apprehended no evil; that all seemed to be quiet and prosperous and cheerful. Such was not my fortune, nor was such the condition of the people with whom I reside, and whom I especially represent. On the contrary, for a month past, in the city of Cincinnati, we have listened, from day to day, while strange tempests gathered and muttered above us. It is a year of plentiful harvests, and yet all the departments of our trade and industry are obstructed, and all our energies are paralyzed. Laboring men find no employers; merchants have no customers; and property of every description is depreciated almost beyond example. The credit and the confidence of a great commercial center have sustained some shock of unwonted violence. My colleague cannot persuade me, therefore, that all is well, and that those who are alike his constituents and mine, in the southern portion of Ohio, have only to fold their arms and assure themselves that no mischief is about to happen.

As to the causes of so much calamity, if the resolution proposed by the Senator from Kentucky [Mr. POWELL] had been adopted at once, and as my distinguished friend from Illinois [Mr. DOUGLAS] pertinently suggested, in a spirit of concord, with no crimination from either side, I would not now allude to them. But my colleague does not permit me thus to remain silent. He has, himself, put the Republican party upon trial; and, without waiting for any attack, has challenged the entire Senate to say wherein the leaders of that party are at all responsible for what has occurred, or what may shortly occur; announcing, in the same breath, that he, at least, has no terms of compromise to propose or to accept.

He assumes, that, inasmuch as it never had the administration of our Federal Government, the accession of his party to power, on the 4th of March next, can afford no reasonable ground for complaint. Certainly, sir, that is no ground of complaint; but it is, and may be, ground for apprehension and alarm. The very fact that a political party has attained control of any Government, for the first time, is enough to provoke inquiry and uneasiness. That must be the case in regard to all parties; and it is especially the case, as we have been told so frequently, here and elsewhere, all past maxims of administration are to be dispensed with, and all past usages abolished.

But the real cause of apprehension, as my colleague must be aware, lies deeper than that. No complaint of injustice or unfaithfulness, heretofore, in administering the Federal Government, is made by the people of the slaveholding States; they have been satisfied with it, or, at least ninety-nine hundredths of them have been. Their apprehension is from the conduct of the Republican party in the States in which it has had absolute control, for years past, that it will so administer the Government of the United States hereafter, as to undermine their institutions, diminish their prosperity, and even destroy their tranquillity and happiness.

My colleague declares that all such apprehensions are unfounded, and that his party does not intend to impair the security or the prosperity of the slaveholding States in any manner. Well, Mr. President, I hope that is so; and in order to prove it—in order that misapprehension may be corrected—I call upon him and his fellow-partisans here in the Senate to redress those grievances which have been inflicted, as well as to remove all causes of future uneasiness. Why not express your intention by deeds, rather than by mere words? I do not ask it for their sake alone, but for your sake and mine—for the sake of our whole country, and of generations unborn. You have elected a President of the United States; and, as I dare say, expect much at his hands. I wish him to enter upon the duties of that office not merely without opposition, but with the entire confidence, the cordial good wishes, of the people, South and North, whose Chief Executive Magistrate he aspires to be.

My colleague is of opinion, however, that the invincible distrust of the southern people in him, and others like him, is due to the false accusations of certain northern men; that if they would only listen to Republican orators, or even read Republican newspapers, their minds would be altogether disabused. The Senator from New Hampshire [Mr. HALE] was greatly troubled also about these same northern men, speaking of them, if I recollect rightly, as "traitors" to their own section. Well, Mr. President, as I do not see that Senator in the Chamber, I will not say what otherwise might have been appropriate. But the fact that any northern man is a "traitor" to his own section, in the estimation of the Republican leaders, merely because he defends the rights of the southern people—as he supposes them to be—under a form of government in which the South and the North have common interests; what accusation could be made against the Republican party, in the ears of a southern audience, or any audience of fair-minded men anywhere, more condemnatory than that? And why would a citizen of Alabama credit me, for example, more than he credits my colleague? He has accused me, and those who act with me politically in the State of Ohio, as much, at least, as we have ever accused him and those who support him. What means of gaining credence have we in the South or elsewhere to which he and his followers have not equal access? He cannot be ignorant of the fact, that the opponents of the Democratic party in every southern State were his political allies when he belonged to the Whig party, and never were mine. Nor can he shut his eyes to the fact, that rather than unite with me, and with the Democratic party of Ohio, in the late presidential canvass, a large majority of Democrats in every slaveholding State, except Missouri, voted for other candidates. What absolute folly, therefore, to pretend that the South can be any more prone to believe my accusations against him, except from their intrinsic truth, than to believe his accusations against me!

Why, sir, the whole Senate listened to the speech of my colleague on Monday last. Those Senators who represent the slaveholding States, do they not hear him and his fellow-partisans day to day and from year to year? Is there no record of his votes; no report of his sayings here and elsewhere? Cannot the southern people read a Republican newspaper, if they wish, as readily as any other? Ah! sir, the South has read and heard and seen too much; it may not agree, and occasionally does not, in my opinions; but as for my colleague, having known him for the last nine years as a Senator in Congress, they regard an Administration over which he can exercise influence with absolute abhorrence.

But, gentlemen of the Republican party, what has ever been said of you by the northern Democracy that you would now deny? Give me the specification. Do you deny that you are in favor of excluding the southern people from all the Territories of the United States, except on condition of leaving their slaves at home? Do you deny that you are in favor of such exclusions, even where the inhabitants of the Territory oppose it? My colleague avowed that distinctly in his speech of Monday last. Do you deny that you are in favor of surrounding the present slaveholding States with new States and with Territories from which slavery is thus excluded? And what can be your purpose in all this, unless it be to render the institution of slavery so insecure in the States where it now exists as to compel them, by an instinct of self-preservation, to emancipate their slaves? Did not my colleague boast in his speech that when the slaveholding States had seceded—if, unfortunately, they ever should secede—from our present Union, and formed another union of their own, he and his Republican allies would conquer, or else annex, the remainder of Mexico, and thus secure a government better than we now have—a government "more magnificent, more powerful, and more just" than the world had ever seen? Whether the free-negro colonies which my colleague proposed to establish in Central America and southern Mexico were to be the subjects of or equal participants in this new government, I did not exactly understand.

Do you deny that you are unfavorable to the execution of the several acts of Congress now in force for the redelivery of fugitive slaves? What mean those various acts of legislation, in nearly all the States which you control, referring to that subject? They do not, perhaps, directly assail the right of a master to the service and labor of his slave; but their manifest design is to encompass every claimant with penalties and snares and pitfalls on every side, that he will abandon his claim under the Constitution and laws of the United States, rather than assume such risks in pursuing it.

Do you deny that, in the States which you control, you are in favor of conferring the right of suffrage, with all other political rights, upon negroes and mulattos? No such legislation prevails in any State which you do not control. I do not say that it now prevails in every State which you control, but certainly it prevails in most of them. It is a distinct feature of your partisan policy; so much so that, in the State of Ohio, despite the language of our constitution and laws, written as plainly as language could be written, your partisan court has, within the last twelve months, conferred the right of suffrage upon a sufficient number of persons tainted with African blood to control the result of our last October election.

These are the accusations I have brought against you; and I have made them—not to the people of any southern State, whom I seldom address, but to my own constituents—to the free and qualified electors of Caucasian blood in the State of my own birth and residence. I shall repeat them, knowing them to be true, year after year, as long as I live, or until you repent of such enormous and shameless transgressions.

A few words more, Mr. President, in regard to those personal liberty bills. I have characterized them sufficiently in general terms; they are of little, if any, practical effect or operation. The State of Vermont, where, according to the confession of her Senator, [Mr. COLLAMER] there has not been a fugitive slave in forty years, found it necessary (as he would persuade us) to enact a law of stringent penalties, lest, perchance, a slave might be reclaimed within her limits otherwise than as the acts of Congress prescribe. What could be the motive for such an enactment? Nothing, sir, nothing, unless it be to insult the feelings, and outrage the sentiments, of our fellow-citizens in the southern States. The Senator acknowledged that it could have no other intention; because he acknowledged, almost in terms, that no human being, white or black, would ever come within the operation of such a law. In the border States, like my own, whenever such legislation has been attempted, except in a few notorious localities, the people, of all parties, thoroughly despise such pitiful, quibbling, and tricky schemes, and therefore do not observe them. For example: in 1857, a Republican Legislature of Ohio enacted that if any person should bring a slave into the State for a single instant, even with the slave's consent, he or she would be punished with fine and imprisonment. More than a thousand persons violated that act in the city of Cincinnati within less than six months; but nothing came of it. They went from Cincinnati in every direction through the State, seeking places of sojournment for the summer. What decent man would enforce such law? Suppose that some mother, carrying her infant from the heat and peril of July or August in Louisiana, should fly to a place of refreshment in Ohio, and having no other nurse, (as, in Louisiana, they have not,) should be accompanied by some faithful slave; where is the man—for I know that my colleague would not—who would subject that mother to fine and imprisonment? Yet, sir, gentlemen like the Senator from Vermont [Mr. COLLAMER] and my colleague, who profess devotion to the Union of the States, and would not violate the courtesies of daily life, adhere to a political party which thus reduces an act of mercy to the grade of arson, rape, and robbery, and threatens outrages which by the comity, if not the law, of nations, would furnish a justifiable war.

Those bills, I repeat, have no practical operation; but they exasperate our fellow-citizens of the southern States by exposing them and their institutions to derision. I accord, therefore, and fully, with the venerable and eminent Senator from Kentucky, [Mr. CRITTENDEN,] that, first of all, as an obvious duty, not so much to the southern people, as because it concerns our own decency and honor, we, of the non-slaveholding States, should expunge from our statute-books, at once and forever, all such enactments. The Democratic party of Ohio discharged that duty, plainly, faithfully, and nobly, two years ago. What we have to fear at present is, that the Republican Legislature, about to reassemble at Columbus, on the first Monday of January, will restore what has been expunged. My colleague promised the Senator from Georgia [Mr. TOOMBS] last winter, in so many words, that those laws should be restored. I wait to learn whether his party will sustain or repudiate him.

My colleague said, also, that I had testified "magnanimously" to the fidelity of the Republican party in respect to the restoration of fugitive slaves. He does me honor over much. I intended no such testimony, and do not, if that be its price, deserve his compliment. I did reply to an extravagance of the Senator from Georgia, [Mr. IVERSON,] last week, when he declared that the fugitive slave act had not been, and could not be, executed in any non-slaveholding State, unless by force of arms; because I thought an assertion of that sort, uncontradicted, might aid in exciting the people of Georgia, at a time of already too much excitement and alarm. They might well credit, if that were allowed to pass without challenge, his assertion that the people of the northern States had lost all honesty and truthfulness. I told the Senator from Georgia, therefore, that a large majority of the people of Ohio were, this day, in favor of a strict and faithful execution of the fugitive slave law; but I did not tell him, and never imagined for one instant, that a majority of the Republican party were [sic]. No sir; a minority of the Republicans, with all the Democratic party in Ohio, and all the American or Union men, are so; and our strength is principally in the southern and central portions of the State. I erred, and, strangely enough, will convict myself in that, when I told the Senator from Georgia we never had more than one mob in Ohio resisting the execution of that law; because there was another case, at least, in which I was retained as counsel, beside the one to which I alluded. The fact escaped my recollection at the instant; but the law was, nevertheless, carried into substantial effect. The point of my allusion to the supreme court of Ohio, in what is commonly known as the Oberlin case, was not that the Republican party, but three out of five judges, in spite of their partisan affinities, obeyed the law. My colleague has not forgotten the sequel of that decision, nor how the Republican party, in State convention, with himself as presiding officer, in less than a week, dismissed the chief justice, Joseph R. Swan, from any further employment. The gentleman nominated and elected in Judge Swan's place is, I believe, in favor of executing the fugitive slave act; but no thanks to Republican leaders and managers—they did not know it at the time of his nomination. Now, sir, my colleague, having officiously called me to the stand as a witness, can make the most—he cannot deny it—of what I have testified.

With respect to fugitives from justice—of which so much has been said—I will make one observation. The behavior of Governor Dennison, in refusing to comply with the requisition of Governor Magoffin, is utterly indefensible; but the Senator from Kentucky [Mr. POWELL] attaches entirely too much importance to the case. It is not the first case of that kind, nor the second, nor the fiftieth. On the contrary, in most of the States, a miserable habit has grown upon Governors of sacrificing the plainest obligation of the Constitution of the United States, to appease some local and perhaps temporary excitement. Instead of observing, as every one of them ought to observe, that the Constitution is a treaty of universal extradition, and that each State is under the most solemn compact to assist in executing the laws of every other State, so far as fugitives are concerned; the Governors, and even the courts, of nearly all the States, seem to have arrived at the conclusion that a fugitive from justice shall not be surrendered upon constitutional demand unless the crime with which he has been charged is cognizable at common law, or is alike a crime in the State of refuge and in the State from which the party fled. It is wholly indefensible, Mr. President, in every case; and New Jersey is the only border State, so far as I now recollect, which has truly discharged her obligation in this particular. But now, if we should be able to amend the Constitution at all, I trust that my honorable friend from Kentucky, [Mr. CRITTENDEN,] under whom I have enlisted for this campaign, will propose some words of amendment so plain as to obviate all such unseemly controversies hereafter.

Thus much [sic], sir, because if I had not corrected my colleague, I should have appeared in a false position. I did not interrupt him on Monday last, because others interrupted him too much, and hardly allowed him to develop, as he might otherwise had done, the whole scope of his argument.

My colleague declared also that the Republican party had taught no new doctrine with regard to the subject of slavery in the Territories. Suppose that were all true; suppose, after ever so long an acquiescence in its policy, or ever so cordial an approval, the people of fifteen States had now ascertained, for the first time, that such a policy must be injurious to them, to their interests, to their future prosperity: what reasonable objection has my colleague to assign (or any one else) for not rendering the Union as beneficial to those States as it can possibly be rendered, without injury to others, in any respect whatsoever? But the declaration of my colleague is not true. The policy of our Confederation, from the beginning, was to allow the slaveholding as well as the non-slaveholding States an equal opportunity for colonization and development. The Senator from Massachusetts [Mr. WILSON] shakes his head. Well, sir, I understand the history of our country quite as well as he does; and I say that it was foreseen, in 1787, by the legislative action, or, at least, the legislative tendency of the several States, that the line between Delaware, Maryland, and Virginia upon one side, and Pennsylvania upon the other, would be established as a line of separation indefinitely between the slaveholding and the non-slaveholding States of the Confederacy; and that suggested the Ohio river [sic] as a fixed and natural boundary westward to what was then our westernmost line of limitation. The territory northwest of the Ohio river was devoted to colonization from the non-slaveholding States, or those about to become such; while Kentucky, then part of Virginia, but expecting soon to be a separate State, together with the territories now embraced by Tennessee, Mississippi, and Alabama, remained to slaveholding immigration and settlement. Afterwards, at the time of the Missouri compromise, in March, 1820, President Monroe yielded his doubts in regard to the constitutionality of that arrangement, because it carried into effect substantially what the original States had themselves foreordained. It was, in truth, a partition of the territory between tenants in common. And now, the Republican party, which has ever justified its own origin and existence, and more than all, its intensely sectional character, by arguments drawn from the abrogation of the Missouri compromise line, in 1854, must either accept the proposition of my distinguished and venerable friend from Kentucky, [Mr. CRITTENDEN,] or confess itself a delusion and a snare from the commencement. I accept his proposition, and in good faith shall vote for it. Yet, sir, except the Senator from Connecticut [Mr. DIXON] who addressed us so pertinently and so eloquently, and with such honor to his constituents, in the early part of last week, I have not heard one man upon the Republican side of this Chamber pronounce a syllable of approbation, or even of compromise. Senators, it is time for you to speak; and may God grant that you will speak wisely for yourselves, as well as for me!

Why cannot we of the non-slaveholding States consent, immediately and cordially, that the slaveholding States of the Union shall have as ample scope and verge, proportional to their numbers, as we have, for the development of their form of civilization. If you, Republicans, believe (as I do not) that there is any antagonism between their civilization and ours, within the same organized community, then divide the public domain, and allow them, as well as ourselves, equally and separately, to have room. Our present Territories are large enough, and most of them are uninhabited; but if you think otherwise, we can purchase or conquer more. You must either agree with me, or you must answer me distinctly this great question; is the institution of African servitude, as it now prevails in the southern States, so hateful to you, so barbarous and sinful in your estimation, that you cannot suffer it to exist, with your tolerance, anywhere? If so, how can we ever hope for peace in a Union of slaveholding and non-slaveholding States? Is it impossible that two great sections, the one fervently attached to an institution which the other so much abhors, can arrive at any terms of conciliation. You cannot adopt that alternative, therefore, without expressing yourselves disunionists in principle and disunionists at heart.

The question becomes very material also in view of another clause in the proposition which my venerable friend from Kentucky [Mr. CRITTENDEN] has submitted, namely: that Congress shall never prohibit the existence of African slavery in the forts, arsenals, and dock-yards, situated within the limits of a slaveholding State, and shall not abolish it in the District of Columbia, so long as the institution prevails in the adjacent States of Maryland and Virginia, nor even when they shall have abolished it, except with the consent of the people residing here, and upon terms of just compensation. If you can agree to that proposition—as I hope you will—you can agree, by the very same argument, to divide our common Territories between slaveholding and non-slaveholding civilization. Do not attempt to avoid me, Senators, even in the secrecy of your own hearts. What you have to decide now, and to decide for all time, is whether, in your estimation, slavery is or is not so hateful that you are under a conscientious obligation to abolish it or prevent it wherever you have the power. If yea, the Union is in fact dissolved; it never, in fact, had any but a nominal existence.

Observe, Senators, if this be your doctrine, that you are only absolved, in the light of your own consciences, from the duty of abolishing slavery in the States where it now exists, by the fact that you have no constitutional power respecting it. But is it not your duty, under such admonitions of conscience, to divide the States, New York, Pennsylvania, and Ohio, or by the admission of new States, with or without adequate population, to arm yourselves, through an amendment of the Federal Constitution, with whatever powers may be requisite?

I propound to you this alternative, as deciding the whole controversy in the simplest terms. It includes every thing [sic], and puts everything to an immediate and decisive and eventful issue.

My colleague said that the character of Mr. Lincoln, the President elect, from his youth upward, ought to afford a sufficient guarantee that he would never infringe, by his administration, the rights or the security of the people, South or North, in any particular. Well, sir, I know nothing to Mr. Lincoln's personal discredit; I hope well of him, and even desire to think well of him. But I must be permitted to say, despite all this, despite the assurance of my colleague, that singularly enough, Mr. Lincoln is the most obscure man ever elected to the Presidency of the United States. He may be an excellent man, worthy in all respects, but he has had less experience in public affairs, and is less known to the country at large, than any of his predecessors. My colleague may have learned Mr. Lincoln's character since the nomination at Chicago; but I think it safe to affirm that, of the million who voted for him in November last, ninety-nine hundredths never heard of him until his contest with my friend from Illinois, [Mr. DOUGLAS,] about two years ago.

Mr. WADE. I ask the Senator whether he had well studied Mr. Buchanan's character before he voted for him?

Mr. PUGH. Yes, sir, I had; but where is the pertinency of such a question?

Mr. WADE. I only wished to know.

Mr. PUGH. Mr. Buchanan had a record of more than twenty-five years of public service. I voted for him, therefore, without the least hesitation; but when my colleague demands that I shall accept Mr. Lincoln's character, not as an individual, but as a public man, I may well ask what he has ever done or ever said. Mr. Lincoln may be the wisest man of our age—I do not deny it, because I know nothing of him; he may be, for aught I know, an angel in disguise; but of thirty millions of people, north and south, whose Chief Magistrate he is to be, nine hundred thousand in each million never heard of him until the Senator from Illinois rendered him suddenly famous. Mr. Lincoln must approve [sic] himself in the future, consequently, and not from the past. If the convention at Chicago had nominated my colleague, for instance, or any other Senator upon that side—I do not wish to engage in your quarrels, and am only speaking in supposition—I might have known what to expect. As the matter stands at present, the character of Mr. Lincoln, whatever his character may be, affords no guarantee at all. He was the least notable of all the aspirants for the Chicago nomination; and that, I imagine, secured his ultimate success.

But, sir, except Mr. Lincoln's extraordinary luck in thus securing a presidential nomination, and afterwards (by what causes I need not specify) an election, I know nothing to his credit or discredit, as a politician, except the paragraph quoted by the Senator from Oregon [Mr. LANE] yesterday afternoon. That may be, and is, very essential in connection with what I have just now inquired. In a speech, delivered upon sufficient deliberation, at a State-convention of his party, in Springfield, Illinois, on the 17th of June, 1858, Mr. Lincoln used language which now requires, at least, some explanation. He referred to what is called, in ordinary parlance, the slavery agitation. He said:

> In my opinion, it will not cease until a crisis shall have been reached and passed. 'A house divided against itself cannot stand.' I believe this Government cannot endure, permanently, half slave and half free. I do not expect the Union to be dissolved—I do not expect the house to fall—but I do expect it will cease to be divided. I will become all one thing, or all the other. Either the opponents of slavery will arrest the future spread of it, and place it where the public mind shall rest in the belief that it is in the course of ultimate extinction; or its advocates will push it forward till it shall become alike lawful in all the States, old as well as new, North as well as South.

Mr. Lincoln spoke here indubitably and entirely of slavery in the States where it now exists. We have no question respecting the extension of slavery into Territories, inhabited or uninhabited. Mr. Lincoln compares our Federal Government to a divided house, which, in his opinion, cannot stand. Now, sir, what divides our house? Only the existence of slavery in some States and its non-existence in others. That division always existed; it existed at the first hour of the Federal Government, when merely eleven States out of thirteen had ratified our present Constitution. It will continue to exist as long as there is one State in the whole Union maintaining the institution of slavery while others do not. It is not a question, therefore, whether the institution of slavery shall or shall not be extended into Territories now free. My colleague might as well abandon such disputations. The division of which Mr. Lincoln speaks in our house always existed; and, in all human probability, if the house should stand, will continue forever. Mr. Lincoln confesses, in terms, that it is slavery which divides the house:

"I believe [he said] this Government cannot endure, *permanently*, half slave and half free."

That is a curious style of adjective, and I give him credit for its invention.

"I do not expect the Union to be dissolved, [he said;] I do not expect the house to fall."

Why not? Why should not our divided house fall in pieces? Why does not a Government which cannot endure permanently, and therefore must fall, now fall all at once? Mr. Lincoln avoids the logical conclusion of his own premises, in a simple, and, if true, a conclusive manner. That is, to extirpate slavery wherever it now exists.

"I do not expect the house to fall," [he said,] "but I do expect it will cease to be divided."

How can it cease to be divided? Only, as all must answer, by the emancipation of slaves within the States where they are now enthralled. The division cannot cease in any other way; and Mr. Lincoln, with a boldness which I admire, confesses the fact:

> It will become all one thing or all the other. Either the opponents of slavery will arrest the future spread of it, and place it where the public mind shall rest in the belief that it is in the course of *ultimate* extinction, or its advocates will push it forward till it shall become alike lawful in all the States, old as well as new, North as well as South.

Mr. Lincoln preludes all this by a sentence which I have once read, and now read again:

"In my opinion it will not cease until a crisis shall have been reached and passed."

Senators, we are in that "crisis" now; we are passing through it. The "crisis" of Mr. Lincoln has come on us, and upon the whole country, by the fact of his election. It is for him, consequently, and for his political supporters, here and elsewhere, to affirm or repudiate the doctrine which

I have elaborated. I implore you, Senators of the Republican party, for your own sakes, for the sake of your wives and children, as well as mine, for the sake of our country, North and South, to unite with the Senator from Kentucky, [Mr. CRITTENDEN,] in terms of honorable conciliation and settlement. I am no partisan; I was once; but, as you all know, my party is distracted, and I fear, hopelessly destroyed. I ask you to give the people of the slaveholding States additional guarantees—such as they ought to have, under the Constitution of the United States, and such as it is eminently proper, in the circumstances, that you should propose, or, at least, should accept.

Heretofore, under the administration of other Presidents, and of all other parties, Federal and Republican, Whig and Democratic, slavery in some of the States has never been thought so to divide our national house that it should necessarily either be abolished or extended. It has been regarded as a subject of local concernment; and so far from estimating it as a source of weakness, all parties have heretofore concurred in estimating it as an essential element of strength.

My colleague objects that the complaints of the southern people are indefinite, and their apprehensions extremely vague. Perhaps so; but the question ought to be not how an account can be settled between them and us, as between two hucksters; but whether, in a spirit of amity, of generous earnestness, aye, sir, in a spirit of wisdom, we will now redress complaints which, although indefinite, are not unfounded, and soothe apprehensions which are all the more dangerous, because they are inexpressible. I commend my colleague to these words of a man who wrote as elegantly as he thought profoundly:

> As for discontentments, they are in the politic body like to humors in the natural, which are apt to gather a preter-natural heat, and to inflame; and let no prince measure the danger of them by this, whether they be just or unjust, for that were to imagine people to be too reasonable, who do often spurn at their own good; nor yet by this, whether the griefs whereupon they rise be, in fact, great or small; for they are the most dangerous discontentments, where the fear is greater than the feeling: *Dolendi modus, timendi non item*. Besides; in great oppressions, the same things that provoke the patience do withal mate the courage: but in fears it is not so. Neither let any prince or State be secure concerning discontentments, because they have been often, or have been long, and yet no peril hath ensued; for as it is true that every vapor or fume doth not turn into a storm, so it is nevertheless true that storms, though they blow over divers times, yet may fall at last; and, as the Spanish proverb noteth well, the cord breaketh at the last by the weakest pull.—*Bacon, Essay on Seditions and Troubles*.

In this case, also, the people of the slaveholding States are under greater apprehension for the future than resentment for the past. I ask you of the Republican party, therefore, to express by some constitutional amendment, what you are now so profuse in declaring by speeches. You must do that; nothing else can be effectual or give any satisfaction. Do not flatter yourselves because there have been controversies respecting slavery in time past, and these have been safely settled. We are now at the end of such controversies, one way or another. Mr. Lincoln's election may be no substantial grievance; but remember the Spanish proverb, and beware lest that prove "the weakest pull" by which, at last, the silver cord of our Union is broken forever.

Senators, I do not wish to offend you, but I assure you that a vast responsibility is upon your shoulders, and you cannot escape it. Why should you not join the rest of us in some reasonable plan of adjustment and conciliation? You have the power this day to save or destroy the Government. You represent a victorious party, and can afford to be generous. All other political organizations have been shivered to fragments within the last twelve months; and to that, more than to any other cause, your success is due. You are about to become the Administration party, and may, if you act wisely, continue in power for a long time. But you cannot continue as you have commenced.

The subject of slavery must cease to be a subject of partisan dispute. It involves questions too dangerous to be longer agitated. If we do not settle this controversy now, and upon a fair basis, it will find a solution of its own, and at our expense.

Mr. WADE. We are to be on bail for good behavior, I suppose?

Mr. PUGH. Well, sir, what is the objection to your giving such bail? It cannot be forfeited while your good behavior continues.

Mr. WADE. Not till you break the peace.

Mr. PUGH. The peace has been broken already, and you must aid us in restoring it. If you intend to behave well for the next four years, you can have no reasonable objection to giving bail; if you do not, there is all the more necessity for it. Here is a controversy comparable to none other. If your party had no mission except to wage it for six or seven years past, your party is now dead. You have gained a victory; but by the very necessities of the case, that victory must be the last. You cannot proceed another step in that direction; whereas, by disposing of the controversy at once, and before Mr. Lincoln's term, you will have an opportunity for initiating other and more profitable issues. The advantage of a party in administration, is that it can choose the best side of every new question; the opposition must take the other side, or decline any contest. You have it in your power, Senators, thus to found a great political party; but if you adhere to the policy which my colleague announced, there will be nothing left of all your strength in two years.

Consider, also, the imminency of this crisis. The telegraph may report, in five minutes, that one State has abandoned our Confederacy; abandoned it, at all events, as far as she can. Five other States, Alabama, Florida, Georgia, Mississippi, and Louisiana, are soon to choose delegates and assemble conventions in order to follow the path by which South Carolina has gone. Arkansas and Texas, I doubt not, will join them. The Legislature of North Carolina is now in session, and has taken measures to arm and equip the militia of that State for immediate service. The Legislatures of Virginia and Tennessee have been summoned by the Governors of those States, and will be in session very soon. Is it not your duty, as men upon whom the responsibility of administration will be devolved in less than three months, to avoid now, by conciliation, what you may not be able to avoid hereafter, even by drawing the sword? It would be a crown of honor to any man, for all his lifetime, that he had relieved such earnest apprehension, and given peace to so many thousands.

My colleague declares, however, that the day of COMPROMISE is past. Then, sir, the day of Union is past; for the Union was founded upon compromise, and cannot be maintained without compromise. The most essential provisions of the Constitution are compromises; the Government itself, in all its shape and proportions, is a vast compromise. One of the noblest legacies bequeathed to us, by the Father of his country, is the letter with which he communicated the Constitution of the United States to the old Congress of the Confederation; and from that let us ascertain the principles upon which the Constitution was inaugurated:

In Convention, *September* 17, 1787.

SIR: We have now the honor to submit to the consideration of the United States in Congress assembled that Constitution which has appeared to us the most advisable.

The friends of our country have long seen and desired, that the power of making war, peace, and treaties; that of levying money and regulating commerce; and the correspondent executive and judicial authorities, should be fully and effectually vested in the General Government of the Union; but the impropriety of delegating such extensive trusts to one body of men, is evident. Hence results the necessity of a different organization.

It is obviously impracticable, in the Federal Government of these States, to secure all rights of independent sovereignty to each, and yet provide for the interests and safety of all. Individuals entering into society must give up a share of liberty to preserve the rest. The magnitude of the sacrifice must depend as well on situation and circumstances, as on the object to be obtained. It is at all times difficult to draw with precision the line between those rights which must be surrendered, and those which may be reserved; and on the present occasion this difficulty was increased by a difference among the several States as to their situation, extent, habits, and particular interests. In all our deliberations on this subject, we kept steadily in our view that which appears to be the greatest interest of every true American, the consolidation of our Union, in which is involved our prosperity, felicity, safety, perhaps our national existence. This important consideration, seriously and deeply impressed on our minds, led each State in the convention to be less rigid on points of inferior magnitude than might have been otherwise expected; and thus the Constitution which we now present, is the result of a spirit of amity and that of mutual deference and concession which the peculiarity of our political situation rendered indispensable.

That it will meet the full and entire approbation of every State, is not, perhaps, to be expected; but each will doubtless consider that, had her interest been alone consulted, the consequences might have been particularly disagreeable or injurious to others. That it is liable to as few exceptions as could reasonably have been expected, we hope and believe; that it may promote the lasting welfare of that country so dear to us all, and secure her freedom and happiness, is our most ardent wish.

With great respect, we have the honor to be, sir, your Excellency's most obedient and humble servants.

GEORGE WASHINGTON
President, (by unanimous order of the Convention.)

His Excellency, the PRESIDENT OF CONGRESS.

Those gentlemen upon both sides who declare that the day of compromise is past, avow sentiments clearly unconstitutional; for it was by means of compromise and conciliation, regard being had to all the States, and to their different habits, interests, and situation, that the Constitution was formed; and in that spirit, at all times, should the legislation of Congress proceed.

But my colleague complains of the weakness of past compromises; and the Senator from New Hampshire, taking up the piteous tale, wished to know whether, in case the proposition of my honorable friend from Kentucky should be adopted, it would be more or less sacred than the act of Congress by which the Missouri compromise line was first established. Mr. President, I will not engage in crimination on this subject; but, granting the truth of all that my colleague and the Senator from New Hampshire have said, now answer: *Let us revive the Missouri compromise in all its principle and effect; let us put it into the Constitution of the United States; and let us declare that it shall be unalterable, except by the consent of all the States.* We shall thus avoid the weakness of which my colleague complains, and restore to the Senator from New Hampshire the lost one for whom he has mourned.

But my colleague says that he will not amend the Constitution of the United States, because it is quite good enough for him. I doubt not; it is good enough for me also, or for any one else. But, sir, there is a vast difference between altering the principles of our Constitution and merely supplying such omissions as time and actual experience have disclosed. That is necessary, oftentimes, in order that the principles may be preserved, or, at least, be carried into full effect. The whole subject of territorial government is extra-constitutional. It was not foreseen, in 1787, that our domains would extend from the Atlantic to the Pacific ocean [sic]; and, therefore, no provision was made respecting the government of Territories or colonies.

In regard to the delivery of fugitive slaves, the fault is not in Congress, or anywhere in the Federal Government; it is that some of the States have aggressed upon the terms of compacts as well as upon the rights of their confederates. The Constitution lacks a power of self-vindication in that particular.

It appears to me that the proposition of my honorable friend from Kentucky ought to be accepted at once, by both sections, by all parties, and even fragments of parties. The northern States, for which the Republican party claims to speak, desire Territories suitable to free labor, and from which slavery is excluded. The proposition complies with that demand. The southern States desire colonies also, and that property in slaves shall be rendered secure while the territorial organization continues. Both demands are granted by the proposition. In addition, the two forms of colonization are so separated that there never can be any conflict between them. I hope that the Senator from Kentucky will express his proposition in such words that it will execute its own purpose, and exclude all legislation by Congress, one way or another. I never wish to hear of the subject again in these halls.

My honorable friend from Illinois [Mr. DOUGLAS] will thus obtain the principle of non-intervention by Congress with slavery in the Territories. The whole question will be taken hence; and, at last, after more than forty years of tribulation, of unseemly quarrels and wrangles, in this House and in the other, we may hope for eternal peace. I obtain "squatter sovereignty" also by the proposition; although that, I hope, will not prejudice the Senator from Texas [Mr. WIGFALL] against it. The Territorial Legislatures of Nebraska and Kansas, upon the one side, and of New Mexico, including Arizona, upon the other, have provided, by their enactments, precisely what is here declared. Thus, all ought to be satisfied, and an end of controversy made. The adjustment will not be disturbed in our time, and probably never.

My colleague thinks it would be dishonorable in Mr. Lincoln's friends to accept terms of compromise before his assumption of the presidential chair. I think not. The question is not so much whether a compromise shall be made before or after Mr. Lincoln's inauguration, as whether, at this session of Congress, in view of so much agitation and alarm throughout the country; in view of a long recess from the 4th of March until the first Monday of December next; in view of the fact, also, that this compromise, if it should be adopted here, will require ratification by the Legislatures, or by conventions of the several States, we will now commence the good work of conciliation and peace. Mr. Jefferson did not think himself dishonored because his own election, in 1800, disclosed a defect in the Constitution. On the contrary, at once, and with his approbation, measures were taken to amend it.

I shudder, Mr. President and Senators, at the evil times on which we have fallen. To-day, as I said, or, at furthest, to-morrow, the State of South Carolina will separate from our Union, so far as she has any power of separation. Five, and probably seven, other States will follow her in less than a month. Is that all? I know not. God only knows. We may acquiesce in the separation of six, eight, or twelve States; acquiesce peaceably, and make such divisions as we choose, or can make, of the property owned by all the States in common. That happens ordinarily with persons who cannot be reconciled. Or—and that is what I hope and fondly desire—we can so adjust all controversy in regard to fugitive slaves, in regard to slavery in the Territories, in regard to protection and domestic tranquillity of the slaveholding States, as to prevent further separation. We may retain all the States, except South Carolina; and in time, if not immediately, win her back. She has acted rashly, and, I might almost say, ungovernably; but she has acted in a moment of overwhelming apprehension. Or, last of all, we can wage war on South Carolina, and every other State which secedes. The Senator from Illinois [Mr. TRUMBULL] inquired, this morning, who had proposed to make war. Well, sir, war generally makes itself, and before the parties intend it. Congress may declare war; may declare that war actually exists, or shall exist; but the shedding of blood is scarcely an affair of so much calculation.

It is not of the slightest consequence, in my estimation, whether we send the Army of the United States to disperse the Legislature or the convention of South Carolina, or, as I understood my friend from

Tennessee [Mr. JOHNSON] to propose on yesterday, send it to carry the mails in that State; whether we make hostile demonstrations against the city of Charleston, or insist on levying taxes from a people who do not, and will not, obey our Government. It can make no difference. We are not children; and we ought to be men of practical sense. Why endeavor to disguise a fact with mere words? I care not whether you call it coercion, or collecting the revenue, or defending public property, or enforcing the laws: you know, and I know, that it means war; and that war will follow it. South Carolina will be supported by other States; and, in a little while, by all in which slavery exists. I call upon you, Senators, from the northern and from the southern extremes, to remember those of us whose homes and families are upon the border of the slaveholding and non-slaveholding States. Assist us in averting a calamity which must fall chiefly upon us; you may reason upon the subject; we cannot.

Mr. President, I do not engage in the discussion whether or not South Carolina, or any other State, can rightfully secede from the Confederation. I will not stretch forth my hand rashly to draw aside the vail [sic] behind which I know there stands also the ATLAS OF STATE SOVEREIGNTY, supporting upon his shoulders alone the entire firmament of our Federal system. That giant has been mute for nearly the life of a generation; but, if you will listen, he seems to move uneasily, and as if he were about to speak. I do not wish to hear his voice; it is the voice of the earthquake or the avalanche. Instead of putting aside the vail which now hides him, I content myself with reading the inscription, which should warn every man not to intrude, unnecessarily, into those sacred precincts:

"The enumeration, in the Constitution, of certain rights, shall not be construed to deny or disparage others retained by the people. The powers not delegated to the United States by the Constitution, nor prohibited by it to the States, are reserved to the States respectively, or to the people."

If my honorable friend from Tennessee [Mr. JOHNSON] ever has occasion to speak on the subject again, I advise him to look in the Constitution, not for the authority of a State to secede, but for a prohibition of it.

Let us by all means avoid the discussion of such topics; they do not belong to us. In Great Britain, questions of constitutional law are only questions of principle, because Parliament is said to be omnipotent; and a law may be unconstitutional without being void. But in our country of written constitutions and limited legislative powers, we are so much accustomed to compare text with text merely, that we argue the most solemn issues rather as lawyers than as politicians. The Senator from

Texas [Mr. WIGFALL] appealed to me, for instance, to vindicate the constitutional right of South Carolina to secede without being attacked. Well, sir, when South Carolina secedes—as I doubt not she will—what further interest has she, by the terms of her own argument, in the Constitution of the United States? And if she should thus become, as she claims, a wholly independent sovereignty, I must decide all questions of peace and war without any consideration of her welfare—because she, by her own act, excludes herself from my consideration—and solely with regard to the welfare and interests of the States which remain. It is all a political and not a legal question. No constitution ever included the means of its own destruction; and nine tenths of the human family avoid making wills or testaments, because they abhor the contemplation of death. Whether a State can or cannot secede, and what others may do toward her, or she toward them—these are questions behind the Constitution of the United States, and, if I may say without irreverence, far above it. They are questions of political science, and not of constitutional construction; questions upon which empires are often dismembered and dynasties overthrown. Our question should be one of avoiding civil war; of restoring brotherhood and peace; of rebuilding the Union upon its former foundations. Why spend our precious moments in abstract disquisition; in citing the text of constitutions and laws; in searching old musty precedents, which can have no pertinency in so fearful a crisis? I take leave to doubt, Mr. President and Senators, whether it be the part of wisdom, at any time, to decide upon controversies affecting the life of our Government, or the essential order of society, as if these were questions of customary legislation, or could ever be resolved by processes of strict and regular analysis. An eminent scholar, as well as a profound metaphysician, Sir James Mackintosh, has aptly admonished us on that subject. I commend it to those who would wisely ponder the issue of our time:

> The causes which the politician has to consider are, above all others, multiplied, mutable, minute, subtle, and, if I may so speak, evanescent; perpetually changing their form, and varying their combinations; losing their nature, while they keep their name; exhibiting the most different consequences in the endless variety of men and nations on whom they operate; in one degree of strength producing the most signal benefit, and, under a slight variation of circumstances, the most tremendous mischiefs. They admit, indeed, of being reduced to theory; but to a theory formed on the most extensive views, of the most comprehensive and flexible principles, to embrace all their varieties, and to fit all their rapid transmigrations—a theory of which the most fundamental maxim is distrust in itself, and deference for practical prudence.—*Discourse on the Law of Nature and*

Nations.

And so, sir, in what I have been accustomed to consider as one of the ablest numbers of the Federalist, written by Alexander Hamilton, I find some words more immediately applicable. In exhibiting the defects of the old Confederation, Mr. Hamilton said:

> Even in those confederacies which have been composed of members smaller than many of our counties, the principle of legislation for sovereign States, supported by military coercion, has never been found effectual. It has rarely been attempted to be employed but against the weaker members; and in most instances attempts to coerce the refractory and disobedient have been the signals of bloody wars, in which one half of the confederacy has displayed its banners against the other.

He argues thence the necessity of a new Government which can act upon individuals directly, and anticipates the objection that the Legislature of some State might interpose its authority to defeat the execution of a Federal law. There is, he wisely observed, an important difference between non-action and interposition. If the Federal Government cannot proceed without the assistance of the State Legislatures—as it could not under the Articles of Confederation—mere neglect, or inattention, or carelessness, will constantly frustrate all measures of common defense and general welfare; whereas, in regard to the interposition of any State, affirmatively, he thought the instances would be very few, and hardly capable of redress. But you shall hear his own words:

> If opposition to the national Government should arise from the disorderly conduct of refractory or seditious individuals, it could be overcome by the same means which are daily employed against the same evil under the State governments. The magistracy being equally the ministers of the law of the land, from whatever source it might emanate, would doubtless be as ready to guard the national as the local regulations from the inroads of private licentiousness. As to those partial commotions and insurrections, which sometimes disquiet society from the intrigues of an inconsiderable faction, or from sudden or occasional ill-humors that do not affect the great body of the community, the General Government could command more extensive resources for the suppression of disturbances of that kind, than would be in the power of any single member. And as to those feuds, which in certain conjunctures spread a conflagration through a whole nation, or through a very large portion of it, proceeding either from weighty causes of discontent given by the Government or from the contagion of some violent popular paroxysm, they do not fall within any ordinary rules of calculation. When they happen they commonly amount to revolutions and dismemberments of empire. No form of government can always either avoid or control them. It is in vain to hope to guard against events too mighty for human foresight or precaution; and it would be idle to object to a

Government because it could not perform impossibilities.

I will also refer to the authority of John Quincy Adams. In his fourth annual message, on 2d of December, 1828, alluding to the controversy between the United States and the State of Georgia respecting the Cherokee lands, Mr. Adams said:

> The United States of America, and the people of every State of which they are composed, are each of them sovereign Powers. The legislative authority of the whole is exercised by Congress under authority granted them in the common Constitution. The legislative power of each State is exercised by Assemblies deriving their authority from the constitution of the State. Each is sovereign within its own province. The distribution of power between them presupposes that these authorities will move in harmony with each other. The members of the State and General Government are all under oath to support both, and allegiance is due to the one and to the other. The case of a conflict between these two Powers has not been supposed; nor has any provision been made for it in our institutions, as a virtuous nation of ancient times existed more than five centuries without a law for the punishment of parricide.
>
> More than once, however, in the progress of our history, have the people and Legislatures of one or more States, in moments of excitement, been instigated to this conflict; and the means of effecting this impulse have been allegations that acts of Congress to be resisted were unconstitutional. The people of no one State have ever delegated to their Legislature the power of pronouncing an act of Congress unconstitutional; but they have delegated to them powers by the exercise of which the execution of the laws of Congress within the State may be resisted. If we suppose the case of such conflicting legislation sustained by the corresponding executive and judicial authorities, patriotism and philanthropy turn their eyes from the condition in which the parties would be placed, and from that of the people of both, which must be its victims.

My friend from Tennessee laid great stress upon the authority of Jackson. In the farewell address of that eminent chieftain, March 3, 1837, I find a paragraph worthy to be forever remembered:

> But the Constitution cannot be maintained, nor the Union preserved in opposition to public feeling, by the mere exertion of the coercive powers confided to the General Government. The foundations must be laid in the affections of the people; in the security it gives to life, liberty, character, and property, in every quarter of the country; and in the fraternal attachments which the citizens of the several States bear, one to another, as members of one political family, mutually contributing to promote the happiness of each other. Hence, the citizens of every State should studiously avoid everything calculated to wound the sensibility or offend the just pride of the people of other States; and they should frown upon any proceedings within their own borders likely to disturb the tranquillity of their political brethren in other

portions of the Union. In a country so extensive as the United States, and with the pursuits so varied, the internal regulations of the several States must frequently differ from one another in important particulars; and this difference is unavoidably increased by the varying principles upon which the American colonies were originally planted; principles which had taken deep root in their social relations before the Revolution, and therefore, of necessity, influencing their policy since they became free and independent States. But each State has the unquestionable right to regulate its own internal concerns according to its own pleasure; and while it does not interfere with the rights of the people of other States, or the rights of the Union, every State must be the sole judge of the measures proper to secure the safety of its citizens and promote their happiness; and all efforts on the part of the people of other States to cast odium upon their institutions, and all measures calculated to disturb their rights of property, or to put in jeopardy their peace and internal tranquillity, are in direct opposition of the spirit in which the Union was formed, and must endanger its safety. Motives of philanthropy may be assigned for this unwarrantable interference; and weak men may persuade themselves, for a moment, that they are laboring in the cause of humanity, and asserting the rights of the human race; but every one, upon sober reflection, will see that nothing but mischief can come from these improper assaults upon the feelings and rights of others. Rest assured, that the men found busy in this work of discord are not worthy of your confidence, and deserve your strongest reprobation.

One more authority, Mr. President, and for my colleague's benefit. Others may object to it, but he cannot. On the 11th of June, 1858, the Senator from Georgia [Mr. TOOMBS] engaged in some discussion with my colleague respecting the reserved rights of the States. The Senator from Georgia said:

When this Government was formed there was great difficulty, in the convention that framed the Constitution, about what should be the relations of the States to the General Government. They were entirely equal under the Confederation. Many of the lesser States struggled to retain their equality, but finally they yielded it in one branch of the National Legislature, and maintained it in the other. That was the result of the struggle. They agreed that numbers, that population throughout the United States, should govern in one branch of Congress, but that the other branch should represent the sovereignty of the States. I am quite sure my friend from Ohio, [Mr. WADE,] who has very fairly argued this question on his side, cannot place a higher estimate—it is impossible for any man to place a higher estimate— on the importance of the absolute sovereignty of the States in this Union than I do. I have maintained it throughout my political life, in good fortune and in evil fortune, that they were sovereign; that they were judges of the infraction of the compact, and of the mode and measure of redress; and I take it that he would be too afraid of the term 'nullifier,' to extend his devotion to the sovereignty of the States as far as I claim that my own goes.

Mr. WADE. I am as good a nullifier as you are.

Mr. TOOMBS. I am glad to hear it. It is good doctrine. I think it is a good sign to hear the Senator make that declaration, especially after our troubles for the last eight or ten years. I have seen the time when I could not find a man in either branch of Congress to adopt that he was one.

Mr. WADE. I was not here then.—*Congressional Globe, first session Thirty-Fifth Congress*, part three, page 2943.

Mr. President, my colleague employed the phrase "make war," in speaking of a controversy which might arise between the State of South Carolina and the Federal Government. If it be a cause of war, as my colleague supposed, why not war according to the usage of civilized nations? They do not, as my colleague proposed, hang the prisoners. The Senator from Illinois [Mr. TRUMBULL] inquired this morning for a definition of rebellion. Was not George Washington a rebel? And yet, sir, when the British commander threatened to treat American prisoners, taken in battle, as my colleague threatens to treat our Carolina prisoners, if we should have any, General Washington gave notice of retaliation at once. That ended the affair on both sides.

It is of no real importance, I repeat, whether we commence, or South Carolina commences. It will be a case of actual war in either event. The questions we have to decide, consequently, are those which I propounded: shall we acquiesce in the peaceful separation of six States from the rest, or shall we engage in a war in which we cannot see the end; or shall we now address ourselves to the noble and higher duty of attempting measures of conciliation, reconstructing and laying more deeply, more firmly than ever, the foundations of the Union as at present constituted, redressing all complaints, silencing every discontent, and doing this, not as partisans, but (if there be no better motive) by an instinct of self-preservation, and an earnest desire to perpetuate the Government which has been so valuable to us, the best Government which the heart of man could crave? It is no time, sir, in the very crisis of our national existence, to stand upon the question, who should propose, or who should accept terms of conciliation.

My colleague seems to imagine it the duty of the President , under his oath of office, to precipitate our whole country into civil war. He said that the President had sworn not to know that any State had seceded, or attempted to secede. Well, sir, I should like to be informed whereabouts an affidavit of such ignorance has been recorded. I am not advised of anything like it. The President is under obligation, assuredly, to execute the laws of the land; but can we not suspend the execution of any law upon the statute-book? Can we not suspend it for a week, or a month, or six months, or six years, if the attempt to execute it, by force of arms, will provoke interminable war? In this regard, also, I commend the counsels of John Quincy Adams. He did not imagine, while he occupied the presidential chair, that he was under any obligation to provoke or accept, such dire extremity. He did not believe that the Constitution of the United States bound him, inevitably, to precipitate the country into civil war. On the contrary, in his special message of February 5, 1827, Mr. Adams said:

> In abstaining, at this stage of the proceedings, from the application of any military force, I have been governed by considerations which will, I trust, meet the concurrence of the Legislature. Among them, one of paramount importance has been that these surveys have been attempted and partly effected under color of legal authority from the State of Georgia; that the surveyors are, therefore, not to be viewed in the light of individual and solitary transgressors, but as the agents of a sovereign State, acting in obedience to authority which they believed to be binding upon them. Intimations had been given that, should they meet with interruption, they would, at all hazards, be sustained by the military force of the State; in which event, if the military force of the Union should have been employed to enforce its violated law, a conflict must have ensued, which would, in itself, have inflicted a wound upon the Union, and have presented the aspect of one of these confederated States at war with the rest. Anxious, above all, to avert this state of things, yet at the same time impressed with the deepest conviction of my own duty to take care that the laws shall be executed, and the faith of the nation preserved, I have used the means intrusted [sic] to the Executive for that purpose only those which, without resorting to military force, may vindicate the sanctity of the law by the ordinary agency of the judicial tribunals.

And yet, sir, that was a case in which the Government was striving to maintain the plighted faith of a treaty, as against infraction by one of the States. When my colleague, or the Senator from Tennessee, assumes, therefore, to treat the act of persons bearing the commission of South Carolina as if it were only the act of individuals, I entreat them to consider the pertinent suggestions of Mr. Adams in a similar case. Such acts cannot be viewed as the acts of individual and solitary transgressions, but as the acts of persons obeying the mandates of a sovereignty, and to an extent (which they believe, at least) it is binding upon them.

It will end in war; begin as it may, it will end in war. This idea of my colleague, that the Constitution of the United States, *ex proprio vigore*, compels the Executive, and even compels Congress, to engage in hostilities with a part of our own people; it is amazing to me, and utterly revolting. Why, sir, we have absolute discretion whether to declare war or to maintain peace in regard to foreign nations. If our citizens are abused, if our territory is invaded, or even possessed, by hostile array, we, the

Congress of the United States, consisting of a Senate and a House of Representatives, may, if we deem it essential, to our own interests, decline to authorize hostilities. Does anyone deny that? Why, then, are we told that we have not as much liberty in deciding questions of war and peace with our fellow citizens in South Carolina, as in deciding such questions with foreign nations—a war, too, in which, if my colleague be right, the unfortunate captives are not to be treated as we treat prisoners of another nation, but are to be executed in the most ignominious manner? Mr. President, I have not the words to express my abhorrence of such a conclusion.

It is the lesson of history, that whenever a man would commit some atrocity without being responsible to his own conscience, he styles it doing God's service. Persecutors, in all time, have burned or slain the body of their victim in order, as they alleged, to save his soul. What no Senator would do, upon his own responsibility, or from his own inclination—draw the sword upon a whole community of our people, scatter desolation and carnage throughout a State which, be her conduct ever so unjustifiable, has, at least, some cause of complaint—must it occur as if by the inexorable laws of fate? Where, in our senatorial oath, can such an obligation be distinguished? No, sir; we cannot avoid the responsibility of such calamities, if they should occur, by charging it upon the Constitution of the United States, or upon our oath of office. We will be responsible for bloodshed, for civil war, for anarchy, if we do not avoid them. We can avoid them; but our responsibility we cannot avoid—responsibility to God and our country, and to all the civilized world.

My colleague thinks it is of no consequence whether the mails be or be not carried in South Carolina; the people need not have them, he says, if they do not wish them. Nor does he consider it of any consequence whether the district or circuit courts of the United States are open or closed in that State from this time forth. But, sir, the people of all the States are interested in the carriage of mails through South Carolina, and the receipt and delivery of letters within it. And so in regard to the administration of justice. It is of more importance to the citizens of other States than to the citizens of South Carolina that the courts of the Federal Government should be kept open; because a citizen of South Carolina cannot be plaintiff in those courts except in a few cases.

We must decide the whole proposition one way or another. Shall we employ soldiers to carry the mail and deliver letters within the limits of South Carolina? Shall we appoint as judges the citizens of another State;

and shall we surround them, while sitting upon the bench, with Federal bayonets? This will cost money, at least, and a great deal of it. We must burden and tax our own constituents, therefore, to meet an expenditure so enormous. Why should we impoverish ourselves in order to enforce our laws against an unwilling people; and that, too, when we might win them back with no loss of money, and only an expenditure of kindness?

My colleague's idea seems to be that, because an act of Congress for collecting duties at Charleston may not be executed for two or three months, or even for a longer time, it behooves us to employ arms, and engage in war. Granted that South Carolina will violate the Constitution of the United States: must we, for that reason, and without any regard to consequences, draw the sword? The Senator from New Hampshire [Mr. CLARK] seems afraid that the "public property" in Fort Moultrie and Fort Sumter is not safe, and wishes the President to inform us immediately how many soldiers are in garrison at each; whether they are able to defend themselves against an attack; what arms and ammunition they have; and above all, what orders, secret or otherwise, have been transmitted to them. He could not even see the force of what was so well suggested by the Senator from Mississippi [Mr. DAVIS] in response, namely: that if any attack be apprehended, the worst thing we could do, possibly, would be to inform the assailants, through the newspapers, the number of each garrison; the commands under which it must act; what is the armament of the fortresses, or their capacity to be defended. I apprehend no attack at present, unless additional troops be ordered thither; and, rather than do that, as an act of mercy to the officers and soldiers now stationed at Charleston, I would have them withdrawn. God forbid that the glories of Fort Moultrie, won from the British fleet and army in 1776, should ever be washed away in the blood of our own soldiers and citizens! We are magnanimous enough, I hope, if we must have war with South Carolina, not to point the guns of any fortress erected for the defense of Charleston harbor against foreign enemies, into the streets of the city before which they stand.

As to this idea that we must vindicate the Constitution of the United States by force of arms, upon all occasions and without alternative, when we know that civil war will inevitably ensue, I deny it. Why, sir, let us examine the Constitution by the rule. Here, for example, is the tenth section of the first article: *"No State shall enter into any treaty, alliance, or confederation."* Suppose a state should do so: it would be a palpable breach of duty on her part; but would any Congress of the United States declare war against her? *"Or grant letters of marque; coin money."* That is a vital power; it is delegated to Congress in terms by another clause, and here, as we observe, it is expressly forbidden to the States. I believe that some States have coined money nevertheless, and one of them may attempt it, for aught we can do, to-morrow. You would not attack any State government: so my colleague said. What then? Will you send our Army to tear down the mint; and, in case an officer of the State resists, will you prosecute him for treason? *"Emit bills of credit."* Several States have emitted them; but no punishment was ever proposed. *"Make anything but gold and silver coin a tender in payment of debts; pass any bill of attainder, ex post facto law, or law impairing the obligation of contracts; or grant any title of nobility."* Suppose that South Carolina should grant a title of nobility to some man—I understood the Senator from Tennessee to be apprehensive yesterday on that point: will you disperse the Legislature by force of arms, or only enact a law requiring the man to renounce his title, or suffer the penalty of treason? You would not, I fancy, do any of these things. Subsequently, in the same section, I read:

> No State shall, without the consent of Congress, lay any duty of tonnage; keep troops or ships of war in time of peace; enter into any agreement or compact with another State or with a foreign Power; or engage in war, unless actually invaded, or in such imminent danger as will not admit of delay.

I presume there is no doubt that South Carolina now has troops, and, perhaps, ships of war. I observe, by the newspapers, also that the Legislature of North Carolina has appropriated money for arming and equipping certain military companies. Does any one propose to treat the officers and privates of such companies as guilty of treason, or to disperse the companies wherever assembled by armed force? Obviously, then, Senators, it cannot be that a mere violation of the Federal Constitution, and far less of Federal laws, would leave to Congress no discretion whether actual war should or should not be levied.

This having been shown, as I conceive, why should we not avoid war, if possible, with the authorities and people of South Carolina? "Oh!" some objector will say, "we must collect the revenue." Yes, sir, men who care nothing whether the mails are or are not carried; whether justice be administered in the Federal courts or not; whether the people of South Carolina have any representation in Congress or any other advantage from the Government, insist, vigorously, and at all events, (most sacred constitutional vindication,) that we shall make as much money from those people, levy as much tribute on them, all of them; disperse the convention and the Legislature by arms; execute as traitors all officers of the State: is *that* maintaining the Union? The Senator from Tennessee appeared to think so yesterday, if I rightly heard his speech. I think not. I think the Union would at once and necessarily be destroyed. We should have so much territory from the Atlantic ocean to the Savannah river as our conquered province; we should have so many prisoners, and, if we spare their lives, so many helpless subjects; but we should certainly have overthrown THE GOVERNMENT of the State, and South Carolina would be no more. We might erect some false image, instead of the State so demolished; our true confederate—our sister—is dead.

> "Labitur exsanguis, labuntuy frigida leto
> Lumina, purpureus quondam color ora reliquit."

Mr. President, I am for peace, and not for war; least of all, for a war so unnatural as this would be. I am for conciliation; and therefore, in good faith, will stand at the side of my honorable friend from Kentucky, [Mr. CRITTENDEN,] and earnestly endeavor to keep the door of compromise open as long as possible. Others may debate the abstract right, as they call it, of a State to secede; but my voice shall not engage in a clamor so dreadful. I esteem the path I have chosen to be the path of safety for all the States, and therefore the path of wisdom; not, indeed, the wisdom by which the people are sometimes betrayed, under specious phrases and soft pretexts, to their own ruin, kindling their hearts with hatred, and staining their hands with blood; but that wisdom founded upon humane thoughts, by which nations continue to flourish and long maintain their liberties. I am opposed to the scheme, under what name soever disguised, of plunging our country into the abyss of violence, anarchy, and fatal dismemberment.

If the Prince of Wales, when lately admiring the magnificence of our domain, our luxurious cities, our noble rivers and lakes, our vast prairies, our somber mountains, our smiling fields and plains, our stupendous works of public improvement, remembered—as, being doubtless familiar with all the glories of English literature, he may have remembered—the speech delivered by Edmund Burke, in the House of Commons, on the 22d of March, 1775, in favor of conciliation with the American colonies, he probably said to himself, or possibly to others: "Alas! alas! had my great-grandfather, George III, listened to such counsels in time, and followed them, instead of attempting to collect the revenue and enforce the laws by mere violence, while a complaining people stood before him with angry countenances and hearts almost turned to despair, this matchless jewel might have glittered this day as the proudest in my mother's diadem."

Mr. President, from that very speech allow me to give you the substance of the objections which I have urged at length:

> First, sir, permit me to observe that the use of force alone is but temporary. It may subdue for a moment, but it does not remove the necessity of subduing again; and a nation is not governed, which is perpetually to be conquered.

> My next objection is uncertainty. Terror is not always the effect of force, and an armament is not victory. If you do not succeed, you are without resource; for, conciliation failing, force remains; but, force failing, no further hope of reconciliation is left. Power and authority are sometimes bought by kindness; but they can never be begged, as alms, by an impoverished and defeated violence.

> A further objection to force is, that you impair the object by your very endeavor to preserve it. The thing you fought for is not the thing which you recover; but depreciated, sunk, wasted, and consumed, in the contest. Nothing less will content me than *whole* America. I do not choose to consume its strength along with our own; because, in all parts, it is the British strength that I consume. I do not choose to be caught, by a foreign enemy, at the end of this exhausting conflict; and, still less, in the midst of it. I may escape; but I can make no insurance against such an event.

Senators, I did hope, fondly hope, that instead of refusing to accept terms of conciliation and honorable compromise; instead of madly provoking whole States and millions of people to what some of you call treason and rebellion; instead of giving them and ourselves to destruction upon the fatal conceit that our oaths to support the Constitution of the United States do not even allow us to pause in the presence of an unexampled crisis, we should have all agreed, ere this, in the adoption of measures calculated to stay the alarm which now pervades the country, and threatens our Union with perpetual overthrow. There is yet time; but time is very precious. Let us determine, first of all, that we will have no war, no bloodshed, if we are able in any manner to avoid it. War is no remedy in such a case; it is always a horrible visitation—horrible when waged for the best and holiest cause; but horrible indeed, and inexpressibly wicked, when waged without any cause, and by one portion of our people against another. Let us not hesitate to suspend the execution of whatever laws cannot be executed, at present, without violence; submit, if necessary, to a diminution of revenue; and thus, or further, if necessary, through acts of generous confidence, avoid all dangers of collision between Federal and State authorities, soothe apprehension everywhere, and be enabled calmly to proceed, by constitutional amendment, to the duty of securing forever the Union we shall have rescued, and ultimately restored, if not absolutely preserved.

Whether I have or have not spoken wisely, for my own sake, as an individual, I have now discharged my duty, as I understand it, toward God and my country; beyond that, in all sincerity, I have not inquired. I believe that the policy which my colleague announced—of entertaining no terms of conciliation and compromise, and, at the same time, endeavoring to avoid the responsibility of civil war by charging it upon the Constitution and the oath we have taken—will drive us all, North as well as South, into an abyss where reunion is impossible, where peace never can be restored, where the liberties of all the states will be utterly and hopelessly ingulfed [sic]. If my colleague has truly expressed the determination of his and my constituents, I shall esteem it no loss, but an eminent and glorious distinction, to retire from public service while the flag of the Union yet floats above this Capitol, and calls together, in annual session, the embassadors [sic] and representatives of thirty-three independent, free, and equal sovereignties. I have once declared to you, Senators, and now repeat, that your separate confederacies, northern or southern, have no charms for me; their promises of liberty, security, and endurance, kindle not my imagination, nor satisfy the desire of my heart. Let me, at least, no more frequent this palace after its proud GENIUS shall have departed; lest where now, in niche and upon column, or station, or pediment, I behold the sculptured effigies of past glory, there blaze forth, as by some horrible enchantment, from stony eyes and distorted features, the demon of discord and fraternal strife; while, instead of gorgeous inscriptions to THE UNION displayed on every side—above, beneath, and around—I see only the fingers of a man's hand writing over against the candlestick, upon the plaster of the wall, such dreadful words as pronounced the doom of Babylon:

GOD HATH NUMBERED THY KINGDOM, AND FINISHED IT; THOU ART WEIGHED IN THE BALANCES, AND ART FOUND WANTING; THY KINGDOM IS DIVIDED, AND GIVEN TO THE MEDES AND PERSIANS.

It may be, for a while, that genial suns and refreshing showers and the providence of times and seasons will continue to repay the husbandman for his toil; that art and science and the comforts of civilization will bless our people as now; but over all the destroying angel, which has turned so many realms to deserts, will slowly, silently, inevitably, extend his pinions, until the fair places of this continent become like the faded seats of once imperial Republics in the Old World.

6

The Reign of Sectionalism

Senator Alfred P. Nicholson, Tennessee
December 24, 1860

Senator Nicholson (1808-1876) graduated from the University of North Carolina in 1827 and was admitted to the bar in 1831. He began his law practice in Columbia, Tennessee; edited the Western Mercury *from 1832-1835 and served in the Tennessee state legislature until his appointment as a Democrat to the U.S. Senate in 1840 to fill the vacancy resulting from the death of the incumbent. In 1842 his term expired. From 1842 to 1859, he served as editor of several newspapers, bank president, and state legislator. In 1859 he was elected to the U.S. Senate and served until his March 3, 1861, retirement, and was formally expelled on July 11, 1861. From 1870-1876 he served as Chief Justice of the Tennessee Supreme Court. In this speech the Senator forewarned the Republicans that if they refuse to address in good faith the legitimate concerns of the South, "all is lost; civil war is inevitable; and that physical force must settle the conflict."*

Mr. NICHOLSON. Mr. President, I took the floor the other day with no expectation that the bill for the admission of Kansas would be the question for consideration by the Senate. Another question, however, somewhat germane to it in the views which I shall present, was expected to be before the Senate. The remarks which I shall make, though they will not be directed particularly to the propriety or impropriety of the admission of Kansas, will have a bearing upon one of the consequences of that admission—the increase in the number of free States. I shall therefore proceed to pursue the line of argument in reference to the present crisis in our country, which I had designed pursuing before this change in the order of business.

In the course of the speech delivered by the Senator from Ohio, [Mr. WADE,] the other day, he made the following remarks:

> I have listened to the complaints on the other side patiently, and with an ardent desire to ascertain what was the particular difficulty under which they were laboring. Many of those who had supposed themselves aggrieved have spoken; but I confess that I am now totally unable to understand precisely what it is of which they complain.

And further on, the same Senator said:

> But what has caused this great excitement? Sir, I will tell you what I suppose it is. I do not (and I say it frankly) so much blame the people of the South; because they believe, and they are led to believe by all the information that ever comes before them, that we, the dominant party to-day, who have just seized upon the reins of this Government, are their mortal enemies, and stand ready to trample their institutions underfoot. They have been told so by our enemies at the North. Their misfortune, or their fault, is that they have lent a too easy ear to the insinuations of those who are our mortal enemies, while they would not hear us.

And again, in the same speech, the Senator said:

> Now, what do you complain of? You are going to break up this Government; you are going to involve us in war and blood, from a mere suspicion that we shall justify that which we stand everywhere pledged not to do. Would you be justified in the eyes of the civilized world in taking so monstrous a position, and predicating it on a bare, groundless suspicion?

It seems, then, Mr. President, that this gloom which hangs over the country, and which is seen and felt by us all, and freely admitted by the Senator himself, has no better a foundation, in his estimation, than the groundless suspicion that the party soon to take possession of the Government intends to do something wrong. Is it possible that this feeling which pervades the whole country; which manifest itself in all our intercourse; which is seen in the countenances of all men; and which indicates the fearful looking for of some sad calamity that is about to befall the country, is only the result of an idle delusion? Is it possible that this wide-spread, disastrous, pecuniary and commercial revulsion that has taken place; this destruction of private and public credit which within the last sixty days has actually diminished the actual value of the estates of men in this country from twenty five to fifty per cent., is it possible, I say, that all these consequences, these apprehension, these dangers, are the fruits of an idle, baseless, groundless suspicion on the part of southern men? If it be so, then it becomes us all with promptness and fairness and candor, at once to relieve the country from so strange and so ruinous a delusion.

But, while the Senator can find no better ground for this wide-spread feeling of alarm and danger, he concedes that southern men are not so much to blame. He concedes that we *believe* that the Republican party are [sic] our mortal enemies, and, believing that, he does not think we are so much to blame; but in the next breath he says we believe this upon unfounded information; that we listen to none but the mortal enemies of the Republican party at the North, and that we will not hear the party itself. I suppose the Senator alludes to those in the North as mortal enemies who stand opposed to the Republican party. As a matter of course, he embraces within this designation the Democratic party of the North. While I freely concede that he is right in saying that we of the South believe his party our are mortal enemies, I deny that that conviction is made on our minds from information, either true or false, derived exclusively or mainly even, from our friends of the North.

We have for them the highest appreciation. In regard to them it is my pleasure to say, that in the South we have for years confided in them as faithful friends and true patriots. We have regarded them as standing as a barrier between our rights and the interests and the aggressions of our enemies; and but for their faithful and efficient exertions and devotion to the constitutional rights of all sections, this crisis which is now upon us would have come years ago. It would at least have come in 1856. My only regret is that they have not been able still to stem the current of sectionalism and fanaticism that has overwhelmed them and brought full to our view the terrors of a dissolving Union. Whatever may come in the future—though this Union may be dissolved; though we may separate into two confederacies—there is one thing that will always be remembered by southern men; and that is the fidelity and bravery and disinterestedness with which northern men have stood by and sustained and defended our rights, until the power of sectionalism has at last crushed them down.

But, Mr. President, it is true, as assumed by the Senator from Ohio, that there does exist in the South a deep and wide-spread conviction that the Republican party is the mortal enemy of the institutions and rights of the South. That conviction, as I have said, does not arise from the misrepresentations, as some have said, of northern national men, of whatever party, but it has been produced by stubborn facts, and by information derived from the most authentic and reliable sources. It comes from the leading men of the Republican party; from their speeches made here and elsewhere; from the acts of their Legislatures; from all the sources, authentic and reliable, from which the truth as to public sentiment is to be ascertained. Among those from whom, and by whom, this conviction has been produced on the southern mind, there are few, if any, who have contributed more than the Senator from Ohio himself. His own speeches here and elsewhere have made the impression at the South that, so far as his opinions are concerned, (and we regard him as a representative man,) that portion of the northern people represented in sentiment by him, are our mortal enemies. The people of the South know the characters of the leading men of the North of all parties. I tell the distinguished Senator from Ohio that in the South we regard him not only as a representative man, as a strong-minded man, but as a bold, blunt, brave man; a man of candor; and when he speaks, when he tells the country that there is now *"really no union* between the North and the South;" that there is a *"bitter rancor"* of feeling existing between the two sections that does not characterize the feeling existing between any other two foreign Governments; when he says that "the only salvation of this Union is to be found in divesting it entirely from all taint of slavery, what are we to infer but that he and those whose opinions he represents are the mortal enemies of interests and rights with which our lives and our happiness and our all are identified?

I have alluded, Mr. President, to the evidence of a hostile feeling in the North against the South furnished by the Senator from Ohio, because he has assumed that the only evidence on which the southern mind relies for its convictions on this subject is derived from the enemies of Republicanism in the North. I could pile up the proof, in refutation of his remark, by referring to the declarations of other representatives and leading men of the Republican party, in this body and in the other House, and out of them; by referring to the facilities well known to be constantly furnished to the free States for the escape of fugitive slaves; by referring to the difficulty and danger of executing the fugitive slave law; by referring to the statutes passed by many of the free State Legislatures for the acknowledged purpose of obstructing the successful execution of a plain obligation imposed by the Constitution; by referring to the well-known fact that anti-slavery societies are tolerated in the free States, while the avowed purposes of their association are to scatter incendiary publications through the South, tending directly to the production of discontent, rebellion, and insurrection among the slaves; but I forbear. It is only necessary to allude to the facts to repel the allegation of the Senator from Ohio, that our convictions as to the hostility of his party are unfounded, and based only on the information derived from the enemies of his party in the North.

But, Mr. President, without going outside of the most authentic sources of information, relying upon no facts stated by the friends of the South at the North; but upon the acknowledged evidences furnished by the Republican party itself, I shall proceed to state, as briefly as possible, what I understand to be the complaints of the South.

Mr. President, in regard to the sentiments of a majority of the northern people upon the subject of slavery as an abstract proposition, either morally or politically, I presume there can be no diversity of opinion. Looking to all the sources of propositions to present fairly the sentiment of the northern mind—I mean the prevailing sentiment—in reference to the subject of slavery:

1. That slavery, as it exists in the southern States, is a moral as well as social and political evil.

2. That the owners and their slaves are created equal; that they are endowed alike with the inalienable rights of life, liberty, and the pursuit of happiness; and that to secure these rights equally to both governments are instituted, deriving their just power from the consent of the governed.

3. That as the owners and their slaves are created equal, the former cannot rightfully acquire or hold dominion over, or property in, the latter without his consent.

Now, Mr. President, these I understand to be the prevalent sentiments of the northern mind in reference to the question of slavery, viewed either socially, morally, or politically. These sentiments have prevailed from the beginning of the Government. They have characterized no particular sect or party prior to the year 1856. I make no complaint against the entertaining by northern men of these opinions. Under the freedom of speech and the freedom of conscience, they have a full and perfect right to entertain these opinions. It is no cause of quarrel between us and them. On the other hand, we of the South entertain directly antagonistic opinions as matters of conscience and as matter of political opinions, on each one of these propositions. We claim the right under the same high sanction to entertain these opinions, and we say that it is no cause of quarrel, and should be none.

These opinions, Mr. President, prevailed, as we all know, in the convention that framed our Government. There was precisely the same antagonism then and there that exists to-day between the North and South on these questions; yet it was no cause of disruption; it was no cause of quarrel; it was no insuperable obstacle to the formation of this Government. Men who believed, as does the Senator from Ohio, that slavery is a moral, social, and political evil, in that convention, sanctioned the Constitution, and labored for its adoption and ratification; yet in that Constitution we all know the legality and the rightfulness of property in slaves are conceded in more than one clause; that it even goes the length of conceding the right to increase the number of slaves by importations for twenty years. How can it be, then, that we who stand now in the same position, cannot settle these conflicting opinions upon the same principle that they did? That principle was to leave every man to the enjoyment of his own conscientious opinion, and to require every man to agree that the Constitution of the country is the supreme law of the land, and in the discharge of his obligations as a citizen, to yield to this supremacy of the Constitution.

What we now complain of is, that in the year 1856 these questions, known to be questions of antagonism, morally and socially, if not politically, incapable of reconciliation between the North and South, were seized upon by political leaders at the North and incorporated as the basis, as the "central idea," of a political association which, rising upon the strength of this prevailing sentiment at the North, has finally taken possession of the Government of the country. Mr. President, the first fatal stab to this Union was made at the Philadelphia convention, in 1856, when these propositions were incorporated as a part of Republicanism, and there was the birth of organized sectionalism; its legitimate fruits are agitation, dissension, alienation, and, finally, disunion, in some form or other. In my honest conviction, there is to be found the true origin of disunionism, and there the real responsibility for that catastrophe.

Mr. President I desire now to turn the attention of the Senate to the Republican platform, for the purpose of showing that the surprise which is expressed here at the prevalence of the feeling of resistance in the South ought to have no existence. The resolution in that platform to which I particularly refer is this:

> *Resolved*, That, with our republican fathers, we hold it to be self-evident that all men are endowed with the inalienable rights to life, liberty, and the

pursuit of happiness; and that the primary object and ulterior designs of our Federal Government were to secure these rights to all persons within its exclusive jurisdiction; that as our republican fathers, when they had abolished slavery in all our national territory, ordained that no person should be deprived of life, liberty, or property, without due process of law, it becomes our duty to maintain this provision of the Constitution against all attempts to violate it for the purpose of establishing slavery in any Territory of the United States, by positive legislation, prohibiting its existence or extension therein. That we deny the authority of Congress, of a Territorial Legislature, of any individual or association of individuals to give legal existence to slavery in any Territory of the United States while the present Constitution shall be maintained.

There, Mr. President, in my estimation, is the incorporation into a political platform of principles which make up an issue between the North and the South which I fear is wholly irreconcilable. There is sectionalism in its length and breadth; and I regret to add, sectionalism largely impregnated with fanaticism. Who was the author of that platform? I think I have seen it stated recently that a distinguished gentleman, late a member of Congress from Ohio, Mr. Giddings, claims the honor of having inserted this plank in the Republican platform. It is a plank in that platform worthy of that prominent man's known hostility to southern institutions. He has succeeded in incorporating a principle which, sooner or later, must result in the destruction of our Federal system of government, unless we can return, in truth and in honesty, to the real sentiments and patriotism of our fathers who framed it.

Mr. President, when the principle was incorporated into the Republican platform, there was a distinguished citizen of the State of New York, then, or soon after, a candidate for the Presidency, who spoke words of warning on this subject which it will now be of use to recur to for more purposes than one—I allude to Mr. Fillmore. In his criticisms upon this party and its organization, he stated in plain, simple, and few words, the truth, the whole truth, and the end of this sectional organization. Listen to him:

But we now see a party organized in the North for the first time selecting candidates for the President and Vice President exclusively from the northern States, with the avowed intention of electing them to govern the South as well as the North.

And again:

The North is, beyond all question, the most populous, the most wealthy, and has the most voters; and therefore has the power to inflict this injustice upon the South. But we can best judge of its consequences by reversing the case. Suppose the South was the most populous, the most wealthy, and possessed the greatest number of electoral votes; and that it should declare that, for some fancied or real injustice done at the North, it would elect none but a President and Vice President of slaveholders from the South to rule over the North: do you think, fellow-citizens, you would submit to this injustice? ["No!" "No!"] No, truly you would not; but one universal ery [sic] cry of "no!" would rend the skies! And can you suppose your southern brethren less sensitive than yourselves, or less jealous of their rights? If you do, let me tell you that you are mistaken; and you must therefore perceive that the success of such a party, with such an object, must be—

What?

"a dissolution of the Union."

There, Mr. President, is the truth spoken in plain, unmistakable words. What is the complaint? It is that the majority of the people of one section of the Union, having the numerical power to obtain possession of the Government, form themselves into a political organization upon principles that exclude the minority section from cooperation, for the purpose of governing that minority section. That is a species of dominion in this case connected with the aggravating circumstances attending sectionalism, combined with fanaticism, that no brave and high-minded people would long endure. Hence, Mr. Fillmore said truly, when this party was organized, and organized upon this purely sectional principle, that the necessary result of its triumph would be a dissolution of the Union. His words would have been verified in 1856, but for the brave and successful exertions of those very northern men whom the Senator from Ohio regards as his mortal enemies. It was the men of Pennsylvania and of New Jersey and of Indiana and of Illinois who then averted the catastrophe which hung over the country. Mr. Fillmore's sentiment was responded to throughout the whole South, and receive as a declaration of patriotism that placed him high in the estimation of southern men. It was responded to everywhere as a sentiment worthy of a patriot. Why? That he was a dissolutionist, a disunionist? No; but that he saw that it was an act of despotism on the part of the majority to adopt a principle or principles which necessarily made their organization sectional, necessarily excluded the minority from any actual participation in the Government, and held them, therefore, as mere subjects, in the event of the permanent triumph of that organization.

Why can gentlemen express surprise at the state of things now existing, when we all know that precisely the same state of things would have occurred if the Republican party had been successful in 1856? The same ground which existed then exists now in a more aggravated form; for, in addition to the same platform substantially, the candidate placed upon it, in my estimation, makes the triumph even more offensive than it would have been in 1856.

Now, Mr. President, let us see what it is in this platform that is so offensive to the South; for the real foundation of our complaint is to be found here. Gentlemen of the North seem not to comprehend this. They even take up the idea that it is a mere suspicion that some wrong may be done; some, that it is merely because we were defeated in the election; because we have lost our candidates; because we have failed in holding the Government which we have held so long, that we manifest such deep concern. I tell them, in all candor, that they are mistaken in this. If Mr. Lincoln had entertained opinions and stood upon a platform that did not, in our estimation, involve our final destruction—I mean the destruction of our southern interests and institutions—we should have acquiesced in his election as cheerfully as in that of any other man. What, then, is it in this platform to which we take exception? The first thing is, that it recognizes the general principle that ALL men are created equal; and, in recognizing this, asserts, as a fact, that Governments are made for the purpose of securing alike the rights of life and liberty and the pursuit of happiness to the slave and to his owner. That general principle, if applied in the States, would liberate four million slaves. This is a necessary deduction from the assertion of the principle of the equality of the two races. But the Republican party, I must do them the justice to say, do not in their platform make the application of this general principle to the States. They confine it to those places within which Congress has, according to the platform of 1856, "exclusive jurisdiction." Then, the position is this: you concede that in the States we have a right to enjoy this property, and you profess to be willing that this constitutional guarantee shall be maintained; yet, in doing so, you avow a principle to be applied to all other places within which Congress has jurisdiction, which principle places a stigma on every southern man who is the owner of a slave; which principle would, if applied, (and which, you had the power, it is fair to infer, you would apply,) would set free every slave of the South. Without undertaking to say that this would be done without regard to other consequences than the loss of property, yet to a southern mind these other consequences are so frightful, that when a party plants itself on a principle so alarming and so destructive, if carried out to all its legitimate results, we can but feel that our security is small when all we have to repose upon is the professions of that party that it will regard our rights within the States, when the same party tells us that rights which we regard the same outside of the States, it intends to disregard. This party promises us, as the inducement to our repose, that our rights of property in slaves shall not be interfered with in the States, *because* the Constitution recognizes those rights. But they refuse to extend that promise to our rights of property in slaves outside of the States, although, upon the authority of the high judicial tribunal of the country for deciding constitutional questions, we have exactly the same rights outside of the States, within the jurisdiction of the Federal Government, as the owners of any other species of property have. They concede our rights in the one case, because they are expressly recognized by the Constitution; they deny them in the other, and in so doing, repudiate the authoritative adjudication of the Supreme Court.

But, suppose this general principle be carried out within those places where Congress has jurisdiction: then it would be carried out in this District, for here Congress has jurisdiction; it will be carried out in the forts and arsenals, for Congress there has jurisdiction; it will be carried in the Territories, for Congress there has jurisdiction. Suppose a State makes application for admission into the Union with the recognition of slavery in its constitution: is not that another case within your jurisdiction? And do you not stand, at least by implication from the principle you assert, pledged to reject the admission of such a State?

These are vital points with southern men. Suppose your party gets possession of both branches of Congress: then, under this platform, and under your pledge to carry out this general principle of yours, what guarantee have we, what hope have we, that this district will not at once be visited with your power? And so of the forts and arsenals within the slave States. We know that in the Territories you would at once erect an impassable barrier. We believe that you would exclude every other slave State from the Union. Will any fair-minded man deny that these measures, in their practical consequences, work not only to the prevention of the spread of slavery, but to its final extinguishment in the States where it now exists? Will any candid man deny that these principles and measures are expected and intended by the Republican party to result in the universal emancipation of the slaves?

But, Mr. President, while these measures, if carried out into practice under the feeling that you manifest, look, as we honestly believe, to a period when they will result naturally, legitimately, and necessarily, without any violence upon the Constitution, according to your mode of construing it, in the final extinction of slavery,—a more fearful aspect of the case is presented when it is remembered that, without any violation of the Constitution, the operation of these measures is to swell the already formidable disparity between the two sections, by increasing the number of free States. The same power that will enable you to carry out these measures will enable you to hasten the introduction of free States to the number that will enable you to adopt such amendments to the Constitution as your party may desire. Is it strange to you that southern men, looking to the final catastrophe which they believe is the ultimate end of your organization, shall look to the period when you obtain the power to make these amendments as the end of the institution of slavery?

Mr. President, these, in my estimation, are the grounds on which the southern mind is now resting, and upon which the southern people have come to the settled conviction that the election of Mr. Lincoln to the Presidency, on the principles laid down in the Republican platform, is tantamount to a declaration of war against an institution which, in the South, is identified with all our interests, will all our happiness, with all our prosperity, socially, politically, and materially. This is our conviction, and this conviction is strengthened when we turn to the antecedents, politically, of the candidate whom you have succeeded in electing. Against him personally, I have not a word to say. He may be all that his friends represent him, and I shall not controvert it; but the point is, is he a fair representative in his antecedents of these principles and these measures which we look upon as threatening our institutions. When I turn to his record, I find a most remarkable coincidence in all respects between his position, as deliberately and frequently repeated by him, and the principle to which I have referred as constituting the "central idea" of the platform of the Republican party. Upon a careful examination of Mr. Lincoln's sentiments, as declared again and again in his celebrated controversy, in 1858, with Judge DOUGLAS, and other speeches of his published and relied upon by his friends in the late contest, in the volume which is before me, I come to the conclusion that he entertains these opinions: He hates slavery as much as an Abolitionist hates it; he says so in many words. He believes that the slave has the same right to be protected in his life, LIBERTY, and *pursuit of happiness*, as his owner. He believes that man cannot have property in man without his consent; that is Mr. Lincoln's "central idea," his "sheet-anchor" of Republicanism. He believes that slavery is a social, moral, and political evil. He desires its ultimate extinction. He looks to the Republican party to adopt and carry out such a policy, not inconsistent with the Constitution as he construes it, as will induce the public mind to repose on the conviction that slavery will be finally extinguished. He believes that such a policy is compatible with the continued existence of the Federal Union. He believes the Constitution can be so construed, administered, and executed, that it will be, if not the instrument, at least no obstruction to the final extinction of slavery.

Now, Mr. President, in the triumph of the Republican party they have placed in the presidential chair a President who entertains these views, in strict accordance, I agree, with the principles and sentiments which characterize his party. In all seriousness and earnestness, I ask gentlemen on the other side if it is surprising that the southern mind is moved, is disturbed, is alarmed at the triumph of a party entertaining these opinions and at the election of a candidate avowing these sentiments?

The whole import and purport, therefore, of your triumph is plainly this: that you have formed and intend to perpetuate a political organization which must, from its principles, be confined to one section, and that the stronger section, with the avowed purpose of so construing and administering the Constitution as finally to extinguish the institution of slavery. You have the voting power to carry out your principles; I mean you have the voting power *in the North*, and you have succeeded in combining that power into a political organization, and you have taken the first great steps towards the ultimate accomplishment of your purpose. You have secured the executive department of Government; you have the whole power and patronage of that Department, with its millions upon millions of dollars, for the next four years. Is it, then surprising, I again ask, with all these facts, that the southern mind is disturbed; that question of disunion is agitated; that the question of secession is the great absorbing question of the day?

Mr. President, what Mr. Fillmore referred to as the great point of danger of this organization, we have now to look full in the face. The reign of sectionalism now begins. Under the permanent dominion of the Republican party, what is the condition of the South? Suppose she continues to send her representatives here: what is her condition? She is nominally represented; actually, she is without representation. She has no voice in electing the Executive—none that is counted; none that is potent. She has no voice in making the law; for if this sectional majority chooses to combine in the enactment of laws as it does in the election of a President, though every southern State is here represented and casts its vote, that vote does not weigh a feather in the enactment of any law, or in the prevention of its enactment. In view of consequences like these, and the commencement of a reign of political sectionalism, rendered doubly terrible from its connection with religious fanaticism, I am amazed that the gentlemen on the other side, with cool indifference, express their inability to understand why southern men manifest so much uneasiness and so much concern, and meet us with no disposition to aid in promoting any measure for averting the calamities that threaten our country.

We are asked to repose quietly, because the President elect is said to be a conservative man. I do not believe he intends to violate the Constitution, as he construes it; but where is the necessity of his violating it? The measures that he proposes to carry out, and that party stand [sic] pledged to carry out, require no violation of the Constitution, as they construe that instrument, for their ultimate success. It is only a matter of time. The end may be hastened under the administration of a fanatical President and Congress; but the result is fixed; it is inevitable. Mr. Lincoln desires to place this Government in a condition in which the public mind will repose upon the conviction that the institution of slavery is finally to be extinguished. What sort of appeal is that to southern men, whose interests and happiness are identified with this institution? What sort of appeal is it to those men in the extreme South, where not only all they have is identified with this institution and is involved in it, but where the lives of themselves and their families are constantly liable to be destroyed and sacrificed by some misguided fanatic or monomaniac, who, feeling restive and unwilling to await the slow process of the Republican mode of liberating slaves, chooses to resort to the torch and to insurrection? Is it not a most astonishing appeal to make to them, to say to them, "We expect you to repose quietly upon the conviction that in five years, ten years, twenty years, or thirty years, all that you have is to be swept away?"

Repose is the great object desired by the South. It is essential to the peace, happiness, and prosperity of her people. To them the constant agitation of the slavery question is full of danger. It was to secure repose that the South sought for years, and with earnestness, to secure the recognition of congressional non-intervention as the established policy of the country. Although this principle has been declared by the Supreme Court to be the true intent and meaning of the Constitution, we have failed to secure repose, because the Republican party repudiated that solemn adjudication, and resolved to continue the agitation of the question until its reversal could be secured. We can never have repose until the right to hold slaves as other property is placed beyond discussion and agitation. This can only be accomplished by an express constitutional recognition of that right. It is for that reason that the South now demands this express recognition as a necessary condition to a final and satisfactory settlement of the issue between the North and the South, and to the preservation and perpetuation of the Federal Union.

Without going outside of your platform and the declarations of your President elect, we find ample justification for the feeling now pervading the southern States. Under as solemn conviction that the permanent ascendancy of a purely sectional organization, looking necessarily, by its principles, though carried out without violation of the letter of the Constitution, to the overthrow of our domestic institutions and the revolutionizing of all our social relations, the sentiment is largely, overwhelmingly predominant in the southern States that nothing short of full and explicit and unalterable constitutional guarantees can avert a disruption of the Confederacy. I admit that there are some who, while they deprecate the result of an election as a fearful calamity, yet, from their ardent devotion to the Union and their dread of the sad consequences of its dissolution, are willing to acquiesce so far as to wait for some open act of aggression on the part of the new Administration. I confess that I do not look for danger so much in open aggressions as the insidious and covert attacks upon our rights. According to my information and observation, this portion of the southern people constitutes a meager minority. No State in the Confederacy has been more conservative in its sentiments or more earnestly attached to the Federal Union than that which I represent in part. To a just, constitutional Union that attachment is as ardent and as earnest to-day as it ever was. But the late election has been followed by the wide-spread conviction that the principles on which the Republican party triumphed are incompatible with the continued existence of a just, constitutional Union; and hence, in my judgment, the sentiment that is predominant in that State is, that new guarantees for the future, to be ingrafted on the Constitution, and to be unalterable, explicitly recognizing, among others, the principles as to the rights of property in slaves announced by the Supreme Court, in the late Dred Scott case, as the supreme law of the land, must be obtained, or that a sacred regard for the constitutional rights of her people will impel a majority of them to demand a severance of her connection with a Union which will then have ceased to be entitled to their allegiance. Acting upon this conviction as to the predominant sentiment of my State, agreeing fully as it does with my own, I shall earnestly sustain every effort made here to secure such guarantees; and, failing in that, I will zealously cooperate in other measures that may be resorted to in the southern States for accomplishing the same end. Without indulging in profuse professions of devotion to the Union, it is enough for me to say that I shall exhaust all reasonable efforts for its preservation upon terms that will give assurance that it will hereafter secure to all sections and every State and every citizen the enjoyment of all their just rights; and when these have failed, I shall have no hesitancy in choosing secession or revolution, rather than acquiesce in or submission to the domination of sectionalism.

Now, Mr. President, while I speak thus of the position of my own State, and my concurrence in it, as I understand that position to be, I repeat, I regard the overwhelming sentiment of the South to be that of demanding guarantees that shall be unalterable—that shall recognize distinctly and fully the right of the southern man to his slave as property—and others of much importance connected with the fugitive slave law. I believe the overwhelming sentiment of the South demands this, or it demands secession and revolution. That is my honest conviction of the prevailing sentiment of the South.

Mr. President, there is one thing connected with these movements at the South that I most deeply regret. I regret that the whole southern mind had not been consulted deliberately and solemnly as to the best means of obtaining the redress or the security which we demand. There is an identity of sentiment in the South, there is an identity of conviction there, which, in my judgment, ought to have been consulted and ascertained. If there had been a southern consultation, representing fairly and honestly the sentiments of each State, in the most solemn manner known to the expression of the sovereign will, and if such a consultation had prepared, as I think they ought, declarations on which they should ask the action of their northern confederates in this Government, I have hoped—I have believed even—that such an appeal, with all this moral force connected with it as the sentiment of the whole South, could not have been resisted by our northern brethren. That is my view of the true mode of obtaining the relief or the guarantees which we demand, and which ought to have been adopted.

That mode, however, was not satisfactory to some of the extreme southern States. They have less immediate interest in this question, so far as the escape and the loss by the escape of fugitives is concerned, than we of the middle and border States have. For this reason, I think there should have been concert between all the southern States. I admit, however, that in the ultimate question of the final extinction of slavery, their interest is immensely greater than ours. I can see, in this fact, why it is they have been more sensitive and less willing to wait the more tardy, but, as I think it would have been, the more certain and peaceful process of an entire consultation with the southern States. They have adopted their own course; and now, in my judgment, the remaining border and middle States ought to concert measures for making their united appeal to the people of the northern States. I think there is too much involved in this question of dissolution to justify any man in failing to do all that within the bounds of reason can be done to avert so fearful a calamity as that of a dissolution of our Government. I think this appeal should also be made with earnestness and promptness to the people of the southern States, with a view of urging upon them to delay the final consummation of their secession movements until our appeal to the northern people can have a response.

Our extreme southern brethren disagree with us as to the best mode of meeting the crisis. I am willing to believe that all of us are aiming at the same end. I am not willing yet to believe that the policy adopted by them has been resorted to from a feeling of disunion *per se*; but I regard them as viewing separate secession as the best means of awaking the sentiment of the whole North, and of the whole country, to the real danger, and the importance of a satisfactory adjustment. While I differ with them in that policy, I am not prepared to pronounce judgment of censure and condemnation upon them. They are sovereign and independent States. It is their right to do on this subject as their judgments dictate. But having taken their course, the duty devolves upon us who live in the middle and border States to take our course.

Our people are not prepared—at least I can speak for my own State—until every reasonable effort is exhausted, to resort to the last remedy. What, then, shall we do? In my judgment, the middle and border States have a plain duty to meet together in consultation, in the most solemn manner that such consultation can be gotten up, and to present to the North their demand for guarantees on these questions. Will the North not grant them? Judging from what I see here; judging from the efforts now being made by leading organs of the Republican party to prevent even the inauguration of propositions to be submitted to the States on this question, I confess that I scarcely see a ray of hope of anything being accomplished; but if there is any hope, it is in an appeal to the people themselves. I think the middle and border States ought to make that appeal. What will that demand be? Mr. President, I am bound as a man of candor, to say that one essential feature in that guarantee must be the constitutional recognition of our right to property in slaves in the Territories; and that this right of property shall never be disturbed by any future amendment of the Constitution.

Now, I know that presents the great point of difference between us. It was the great point of difference when our Government was formed. Our fathers had patriotism enough to settle it. We have lived happily, and prosperously, and grown great under that settlement for over sixty years. Why can we not settle the same question again? Why will the northern mind refuse to do it? Is it a matter of conscience that we ask them to surrender? Was it not a matter of conscience with our fathers that slavery was a social and moral evil? And yet they could settle it. They could concede the right of property in slaves, without doing violence to their consciences. They could authorize the increase of the number of slaves by new immigrations for twenty years. They could provide for the existence of this right of property, even outside of the slave States, when the slaves escape into a free State. Will anyone presume to say that our fathers were less conscientious than we are? Yet I am told that if the recognition of our right of property in slaves be the *sine qua non* of our demand, then all is hopeless. I think that may be the sentiment of gentlemen who have ridden upon the current of sectionalism into power, and now occupy official places; but I prefer, at least, before I give up all hope, to see whether or not, on an appeal to the popular sovereignty of the North, there is not patriotism enough there again to make this concession as our fathers did, and to close up and settle forever this question of agitation between the two sections.

These, Mr. President, are my views as to our duty in the present crisis, entertained from a deep sense of their correctness, as well as from an ardent attachment to this Government, and a most determined opposition to seeing it destroyed until every reasonable effort to maintain it upon principles of justice and equality shall be exhausted.

But, Mr. President, whatever may be the results in future growing out of the efforts here or elsewhere to obtain satisfactory guarantees in the way of amendments to the Constitution, we are called upon for present action as to an event which, though looked for, has produced a profound sensation throughout the Confederacy. I refer, of course, to the ordinance unanimously adopted by the people of South Carolina, in convention assembled at Charleston, on the 20th instant, by which that State has repealed all ordinances and acts ratifying the Constitution of the United States and the amendments thereto, and declared that the Union now subsisting between South Carolina and the other States of America is thereby dissolved. This is the act of one of the sovereign States of the Confederacy—of one of the original members of that Confederacy. It is an act consummated in the most solemn and imposing form in which the voice and the will of a sovereign people can be pronounced.

The occasion calls for no discussion as to the character of the right which the people of South Carolina have exercised in thus deliberately resuming those attributes of their sovereignty which in 1788 they, in the same solemn and deliberate form, delegated to the Federal Government. I shall enter into no such discussion. I allude to it only as a great accomplished fact which must soon present practical questions of the most momentous character. I shall content myself now with briefly stating, without argument, the course which, in my judgment, ought to be taken on that phase of these questions which may look to a resort to force.

This question must arise either in a proposition to resort to force for the purpose of executing the laws of the United States within the territorial limits of South Carolina, or for the subduing the people of that State and coercing them back to their allegiance to the United States. Whatever technical distinction there may be in the two propositions, I regard them practically as amounting to the same thing—as resort to force for either purpose amounts, in my estimation, to war upon the State of South Carolina.

I discard any distinction on this subject, because the effect of the ordinance adopted by their convention is to constitute for the people of South Carolina a separate and independent government—not, in my estimation, a separate and independent government *de jure*, but *de facto*. This government has absolved its people, as far as it can be done, from all allegiance to the Government of the United States, and has thereby interposed between each one of its citizens and Government of the United States on any question of allegiance that may hereafter arise between them. As the Constitution of the United States recognizes the existence of the States as States in all the departments of the Government— legislative, judicial, and executive—as the Constitution was ratified by the States as States, and as the State of Carolina [sic], meaning thereby the people of South Carolina in their sovereign capacity, has demanded of every citizen thereof an undivided allegiance, when the Federal Government resorts to force against one of those citizens who resists on the ground that he is obeying the command of South Carolina, the Federal Government cannot decline to treat the resistance as the act of South Carolina in her character as a government. If hostility ensue, therefore, it becomes war. Hence, practically, I regard the resort to force either for the purpose of executing the laws in South Carolina or for the purpose of reducing her people to their allegiance to the United States, as resulting in war.

The question then arises whether, in the attitude in which South Carolina now stands, war ought to be made against her people? With a full appreciation of the importance of executing the laws when obstructed or resisted, I am constrained to the conclusion that, even if the power to resort to force were subject to no controversy, the reasons and considerations against such a resort are so weighty and controlling as to induce me unhesitatingly to declare against it; and, in so declaring, I am thoroughly satisfied that I have the concurrence of the people of my State. Against one of the sovereign States whose people, in the most solemn and deliberate manner known to the exercise of sovereignty, decide and declare that their grievances and oppressions are intolerable, or that they have good reasons to believe that the necessary results of the policy of a sectional organization about to take the reigns of the Federal Government, with every prospect of holding these reins perpetually, must be ruinous to her interests and destructive of the objects for which the Government was formed, and who, for reasons like these, claim the right to resume her delegated sovereignty, or to seek for redress or self-preservation in revolution, I cannot consent to make war, unless the subjection of such State is imperatively demanded for the general welfare and safety of the other members of the Federal Government. In every such case, the interests of the States remaining in the Union, as well as those of the State proposing to withdraw, must be involved. Both parties to the case have rights to look to, and obligations to discharge; all the surrounding circumstances must be examined with an eye to all the consequences. It would require a strong case to induce me to incur all the horrors of a civil war, either to execute the laws against the people of a sovereign State, or to conquer such people to their former allegiance. I cannot forget that the Union was not formed by force, and I know it can never be maintained and perpetuated by force. Resting on fraternal feelings among its members it was created. If it is to be preserved, it must be done by the persuasive but efficient instrumentalities of kindness, forbearance, patience, and fraternity. If South Carolina stood alone in this crisis, I would see no blood spilled to coerce her; but knowing, as we all do, that in the grievances on which she is taking so responsible a step, fourteen of the other members of the Confederacy are strongly sympathizing with her, and are earnestly considering what measures for redress and safety they will adopt, it cannot be doubted for a moment that war upon South Carolina would involve the entire Confederacy in the conflict, and destroy forever all hope of either preserving or reconstructing the Federal Union. In this connection, I do not pause to contemplate the horrors of the civil war that will follow an attempt to coerce South Carolina. If nothing else can be saved; if the Union must perish; if the members of the Confederacy must be severed, let us, at least, save the blood of our countrymen.

Instead of considering the question of war upon one of our sister States, it rather becomes us, the representatives of the other sisters of the Confederacy, to elevate our thoughts, our feelings, our hearts, into the atmosphere of a pure and unadulterated patriotism, and from that elevation look down with calmness, with kindness, with unprejudiced minds, upon the causes which have impelled South Carolina to this fearful experiment, and which are impelling fourteen other sovereign States to seek remedies for great evils with which they feel they are threatened; and upon this view to see whether it is not possible for us to find a peaceful and effectual solution of the frightful catastrophe of civil war and destruction of our Government which is impending over us. It surely cannot be that the people of fifteen States are so deeply moved and so painfully intent upon having additional securities for their rights in the Union without some just and substantial cause for their grievances and their demands. If the people of the other States can see no ground for this alarming state of things, or if, seeing it, they are resolved finally and unalterably that they cannot accede to the demands for guarantees, then it will become us to look the consequence full in the face; that consequence is, that there is an antagonism of interest, or of sentiment, between the dominant party in the North and the people of the South, which is wholly and entirely irreconcilable, and which must end in separation, either violently or peacefully. I am not willing yet, as discouraging as are all the present signs, to admit the existence of such a irreconcilable antagonism. I do fear that, so far as the decision of the question depends upon us here, now, there is scarcely a ray of hope for a favorable solution. What then? Shall we make up our minds that all is lost; that civil war is inevitable; that physical force must settle the conflict, and that the work of blood shall commence in South Carolina? I trust in God that if we cannot agree upon a remedy for the evils that already overwhelm us, we can at least agree to such measures of forbearance and conciliation as will allow an appeal to the people of the North before we superadd to them the horrors of a civil war. If we must see the Union perish, let us at least resolve that we will bury it in peace and with bloodless hands. If we cannot agree to live together in harmony as brothers of one Confederacy, let us separate in peace, showing, by our justice to each other in the act of separation, that we are determined so to live as neighbors that a hope of a future reconstruction of our Confederacy, and of the resurrection at no distant day of our Federal Union to an immortality of grandeur and prosperity, may not be forever destroyed.

7

Slavery Agitation As Partisan Warfare

Senator Stephen A. Douglas, Illinois
January 3, 1861

Stephen A. Douglas (1813-1861) was born in Vermont, began the study of law in 1832 in New York, and then moved to Winchester, Illinois, where he taught school and continued to study law. He was admitted to the bar in 1834 and commenced practice in Jacksonville, Illinois. He served as state attorney (1835), state legislator (1836-1837), secretary of state (1840), and state supreme court judge (1841); he served in the U.S. House of Representatives from 1843-1847; he was elected to the U.S. Senate in 1847 as a Democrat and reelected in 1853 as a Popular Sovereignty Democrat, and again in 1857 defeating Abraham Lincoln. In 1852 and 1856 he was an unsuccessful candidate for the Democratic presidential nomination; he was nominated for President by the Democratic National Convention at Baltimore in 1860 and received twelve electoral college votes in the general election.

The occasion of this January 3, 1861, speech was the inability of the Select Committee of Thirteen to agree upon a plan to remedy the escalating crisis. In this speech Senator Douglas delineates his understanding of the nature of the crisis and why the Senate has thus far been unsuccessful in its attempts to place the Union back on terra firma.

Douglas traces the development of sectional strife through the Congressional compromises of 1820, 1850, 1854, and the election of 1860. He proposed several constitutional amendments, claiming that if ratified they would peacefully reestablish the Union on the basis of sectional integrity and national commercial prosperity. Emphasizing the unconstitutionality of southern secession, Douglas maintained that once a State has seceded the United States must deal with it according to the laws of nations. He articulated a realpolitik of coercion, premised upon the midwestern States' interests in unimpeded access to the Mississippi River and the Gulf of Mexico.

Mr. DOUGLAS. Mr. President: No act of my public life has ever caused me so much regret as the necessity of voting in the special committee of thirteen for the resolution reporting to the Senate our inability to agree upon any general plan of adjustment, which would restore peace to the country and insure the integrity of the Union. If we wish to understand the real causes which have produced such wide-spread and deep-seated discontent in the slaveholding States, we must go back beyond the recent presidential election, and trace the origin and history of the slavery agitation from the period when it first became an active element in Federal politics. Without fatiguing the Senate with tedious details, I may be permitted to assume, without the fear of successful contradiction, that whenever the Federal Government has attempted to decide and control the slavery question in the newly acquired Territories, regardless of the wishes of the inhabitants, alienation of feeling, sectional strife, and discord have ensued; and whenever Congress has refrained from such interference, harmony and fraternal feeling have been restored. The whole volume of our nation's history may be confidently appealed to in support of this proposition. The most memorable instances are the fearful sectional controversies which brought the Union to the verge of disruption in 1820, and again in 1850. It was the territorial question in each case which presented the chief points of difficulty, because it involved the irritating question of the relative political power of the two sections. All the other questions, which entered into and served to increase the slavery agitation, were deemed of secondary importance, and dwindled into insignificance so soon as the territorial question was definitely settled.

From the period of the organization of the Federal Government, under the Constitution, in 1789, down to 1820, all the territorial governments had been organized upon the basis of non-interference by Congress with the domestic institutions of the people. During that period several new

Territories were organized, including Tennessee, Louisiana, Missouri, Mississippi, and Alabama. In no [sic] one of these Territories did Congress attempt to interfere with the question of slavery, either to introduce or exclude, protect or prohibit it. During the whole of this period there was peace and good-will between the people of all parts of the Union so far as the question of slavery was concerned.

But the first time Congress ever attempted to interfere with and control that question, regardless of the wishes of the people interested in it, the Union was put in jeopardy, and was only saved from dissolution by the adoption of the compromise of 1820. In the famous Missouri controversy, the majority of the North demanded that Congress should prohibit slavery forever in all the territory acquired from France, extending from the State of Louisiana to the British possessions on the north, and from the Mississippi to the Rocky Mountains. The South and the conservative minority of the North, on the contrary, stood firmly upon the ground of non-intervention, denying the right of Congress to touch the subject. They did not ask Congress to interfere for protection nor for any purpose; while they opposed the right and justice of exclusion. Thus, each party, with their respective positions distinctly defined—the one for and the other against congressional intervention—maintained its position with desperate persistency until disunion seemed inevitable, when a compromise was effected by an equitable partition of the territory between the two sections on the line of 36° 30′, prohibiting slavery on the one side and permitting it on the other.

In the adoption of this compromise, each party yielded one half of its claim for the sake of the Union. It was designed to form the basis of perpetual peace on the slavery question by establishing a rule in accordance with which all future controversy would be avoided. The line of partition was distinctly marked so far as our territory might extend; and, by irresistible inference, the spirit of the compromise required the extension of the line on the same parallel whenever we should extend our territorial limits. The North and the South—although each was dissatisfied with the terms of the settlement, each having surrendered one half of its claim—by common consent agreed to acquiesce in it, and abide by it as a permanent basis of peace upon the slavery question. It is true, that there were a few discontented spirits in both sections who attempted to renew the controversy from time to time; but the deep Union feeling prevailed, and the masses of the people were disposed to stand by the settlements as the surest means of averting future difficulties.

Peace was restored, fraternal feeling returned, and we were a happy and united people so long as we adhered to, and carried out in good faith, the Missouri compromise [sic], according to its spirit as well as its letter. In 1845, when Texas was annexed to the Union, the policy of an equitable partition on the line of 36° 30′ was adhered to, and carried no effect by the extension of the line as far westward as the new acquisition might reach. It is true, there was much diversity of opinion as to the propriety and wisdom of annexing Texas. In the North the measure was opposed by large numbers upon the distinct ground that it was enlarging the area of slave territory within the Union; and in the South it probably received much additional support for the same reason; but, while it may have been opposed and supported, in some degree, north and south, from these considerations, no considerable number in either section objected to it upon the ground that it extended and carried out the policy of the Missouri compromise. The objection was solely to the acquisition of the country, and not to the application of the Missouri compromise to it, if acquired. No fair-minded man could deny that every reason which induced the adoption of the line in 1820 demanded its extension through Texas, and every new acquisition, whenever we enlarged our territorial possessions in that direction. No man would have been deemed faithful to the obligations of the Missouri compromise at that day, who was opposed to its application to future acquisitions.

The record shows that Texas was annexed to the Union upon the express condition that the Missouri compromise should be extended and made applicable to the country, so far as our new boundaries might reach. The history of that acquisition will show that I not only supported the annexation of Texas, but that I urged the necessity of applying the Missouri compromise to it, for the purpose of extending it through New Mexico and California to the Pacific ocean [sic], whenever we should acquire those Territories, as a means of putting an end to the slavery agitation forever.

The annexation of Texas drew after it the war with Mexico, and the treaty of peace left us in possession of California and New Mexico. This large acquisition of new territory was made the occasion for renewing the Missouri controversy. The agitation of 1849-50 was a second edition of that of 1819-20. It was stimulated by the same motives, aiming at the same ends, and enforced by the same arguments. The northern majority invoked the intervention of Congress to prohibit slavery everywhere in the Territories of the United States—both sides of the Missouri line—south as well as north of 36° 30′. The South, together with a conservative minority in the North, stood firmly upon the ground of non-intervention, denying the right of Congress to interfere with the subject, but avowing a willingness, in the spirit of concession for the sake of peace and the Union, to adhere to and carry out the policy of an equitable partition on the line of 36° 30′ to the Pacific ocean, in the same sense in which it was adopted in 1820, and according to the understanding when Texas was annexed in 1845. Every argument and reason, every consideration of patriotism and duty, which induced the adoption of the policy in 1820, and its application to Texas in 1845, demanded its application to California and New Mexico in 1848. The peace of the country, the fraternal feelings of all its parts, the safety of the Union, all were involved.

Under these circumstances, as chairman of the Committee on Territories, I introduced into the Senate the following proposition, which was adopted by a vote of 33 to 21 in the Senate, but rejected in the House of Representatives. I read from the Journal, August 10, 1848, page 563:

> On a motion by Mr. DOUGLAS to amend the bill, section four, line one, by inserting after the word 'enacted:'

> That the line of 36° 30′ of north latitude, known as the Missouri compromise line, as defined by the eighth section of an act entitled 'An act to authorize the people of the Missouri Territory to form a constitution and State government, and for the admission of such State into the Union on an equal footing with the original States, and to prohibit slavery in certain Territories, approved March 6, 1820,' be, and the same is hereby, declared to extend to the Pacific ocean; and the said eighth section, together with the compromise therein effected, is hereby revived, and declared to be in full force and binding, for the future organization of the Territories of the United States, in the same sense, and with the same understanding, with which it was originally adopted;

> It was determined in the affirmative—yeas 33, nays 21.

> On the motion by Mr. Baldwin, the yeas and nays being desired by one fifth of the Senators present, those who voted in the affirmative are:

> Messrs.. Atchison, Badger, Bell, Benton, Berrien, Borland, Bright, Calhoun, Cameron, Davis of Mississippi, Dickinson, Douglas, Downs, Fitzgerald, Foote, Hannegan, Houston, Hunter, Johnson of Maryland, Johnson of Louisiana, Johnson of Georgia, King, Lewis, Mangum, Mason, Metcalfe, Pearce, Sebastian, Spruance, Sturgeon, Turney, Underwood.

> Those voted in the negative are:

> Messrs. Allen, Atherton, Baldwin, Bradbury, Breese, Clark, Corwin, Davis of Massachusetts, Dayton, Dix, Dodge, Felch, Green, Hale, Hamlin, Miller, Niles, Phelps, Upham, Walker, Webster.

So the proposed amendment was agreed to.

The bill, as amended, was then ordered to be engrossed for a third reading, by a vote of 33 to 22, and was read a third time, and was passed on the same day. By the classification of the votes for my proposition to carry out the Missouri compromise, it will be seen that all the southern Senators, twenty-six in number, including Mr. Calhoun, voted in the affirmative, and of the northern Senators, seven voted in the affirmative and twenty-one in the negative. The proposition was rejected in the House of Representatives by almost a sectional vote, the whole South voting for it, and a large majority of the North against it.

It was the rejection of that proposition—the repudiation of the policy of an equitable partition of the territory between the two sections, on the line of 36° 30′—which reopened the floodgate of slavery agitation and deluged the whole country with sectional strife and bitterness, until the Union was again brought to the verge of disruption, before the swelling tide of bitter waters could be turned back, and passion and prejudice could be made to give place to reason and patriotism.

Had the Senate's proposition been concurred in by the House of Representatives; had the policy of an equitable partition been adhered to; had the Missouri compromise been carried out in good faith, through our newly acquired territory, to the Pacific ocean, there would have been an end to the slavery agitation forever. For, the line of partition between free and slave territory being once firmly established and distinctly defined from the Atlantic to the Pacific, all new acquisitions, whether on the North or the South, would have conformed to that adjustment, without exciting the passions, or wounding the sensibilities, or disturbing the harmony of our people. I do not think it would have made any material difference in respect to the condition of the new States to be formed out of such territory, for I have always believed, and often said, that the existence or non-existence of African slavery depends more upon the necessities of climate, health, and productions, than upon congressional and territorial enactments. It was in reference to this great truth that Mr. Webster said that the condition of all the territory acquired from Mexico, so far as the question of slavery was concerned, was irrevocably fixed and settled by an irrepealable law—the law of climate, and of physical geography, and the formation of the earth. You might as well by act of Congress to compel cotton to grow upon the tops of the Rocky Mountains and rice upon the summits of the Sierra Nevada, as to compel slavery to exist, by congressional enactment, where neither climate, nor health, nor productions, will render it necessary and self-sustaining. Yet the desire, on the one hand, for the extension of slavery into regions where it is physically impossible to sustain it, and, on the other hand, to abolish and exclude it from those countries where the white man cannot endure the climate and cultivate the soil, threatens to keep the agitation of this question perpetually in Congress, until the passions of the people shall become so inflamed that civil war and disunion shall become inevitable. It is the territorial question—whether slavery shall exist in those vast regions, in utter disregard of the wishes and necessities of the people inhabiting them—that is convulsing and dissolving the Republic; a question in which we have no direct interest, about which we have very little knowledge, and which the people of those Territories must and will eventually decide for themselves and to suit themselves, no matter what Congress may do. But for this territorial question there would be very little difficulty in settling the other matters in controversy. The Abolitionists could never endanger the peace of the country or the existence of the Union by the agitation of the slavery question in the District of Columbia by itself, or in the dock-yards, forts, and arsenals in the slaveholding States, or upon the fugitive slave law, or upon any minor issue, or upon them all together, if the territorial question could be finally and irrevocably settled.

I repeat, it was the repudiation of the policy of the Missouri compromise, the refusal to apply it to the territory acquired from Mexico, when offered by me, and supported by the whole South, in August, 1848, which reopened and revived the Missouri controversy. The compromise of 1820 once repudiated, the policy of an equitable partition of the territory abandoned, the proposition to extend it to the Pacific being rejected, and the original controversy reopened with increased bitterness, each party threw itself back on its original extreme position—the one demanding its exclusion everywhere, and the other insisting upon its right to go everywhere in the Territories, regardless of the wishes of the people inhabiting them. All the arguments, *pro* and *con.*, [sic] used in 1819-20 were repeated in 1849-50. The question was the same, and the relative position of the two sections the same.

Such was the condition of things at the opening of the session of 1849-50, when Mr. Clay resumed his seat in this body.

The purest patriots in the land had become alarmed for the fate of the Republic. The immortal Clay, whose life had been devoted to the rights, interests, and glory of his country, had retired to the shades of Ashland to prepare for another and a better world. When, in his retirement, hearing the harsh and discordant notes of sectional strife and disunion, he consented, at the earnest solicitation of his countrymen, to resume his seat in the Senate, the theater of his great deeds, to see if, by his experience, his wisdom, the renown of his great name, and his strong hold upon the confidence and affections of the American people, he could not do something to restore peace to a distracted country. From the moment of his arrival among us he became, by common consent, and as a matter of course, the leader of the Union men. His first idea was to revive and extend to the Pacific ocean the Missouri compromise line, with the same understanding and legal effect in which it had been adopted in 1820, and continued through Texas in 1845. I was one of his humble followers and trusted friends in endeavoring to carry out that policy, and in connection with others, at his special request, carefully canvassed both Houses of Congress to ascertain whether it was possible to obtain a majority vote in each House for the measure. We found no difficulty with the southern Senators and Representatives, and could secure the cooperation of a minority from the North; but not enough to give us a majority in both Houses. Hence the Missouri compromise was abandoned by its friends, NOT *from choice*, but from INABILITY *to carry it into effect in good faith*. It was with extreme reluctance that Mr. Clay, and those of us who acted with him and shared his confidence, were brought to the conclusion that we must abandon, from inability to carry out, the line of policy which had saved the Union in 1820, and given peace to the country for many happy years.

Finding ourselves unable to maintain that policy, we yielded to a stern necessity, and turned our attention to the discovery of some other plan by which the existing difficulties could be settled, and future troubles avoided. I need not detail the circumstances under which Mr. Clay brought forward his plan of adjustment, which received the sanction of the two Houses of Congress and the approbation of the American people, and is familiarly known as the compromise measures of 1850. These measures were designed to accomplish the same results as the act of 1820, but in a different mode. The leading feature and chief merit of each was to banish the slavery agitation from the Halls of Congress and the arena of Federal politics. The act of 1820 was intended to attain this end by an equitable partition of the Territories between the contending sections. The acts of 1850 were designed to attain the same end by remitting the whole question of slavery to the decision of the people of the Territories, subject to the limitations of the Constitution, and let the Federal courts determine the validity and constitutionality of the territorial enactments from time to time, as cases should arise and appeals be taken to the Supreme Court of the United States. The one, proposed to settle the question by a geographical line and an equitable partition; the other by the principles of popular sovereignty in accordance with the Constitution. The object of both being the same, I supported each in turn as a means of attaining a desirable end.

After the compromise measure of 1850 had become the law of the land, those who opposed their enactment appealed to their constituents to sustain them in their opposition, and implored them not to acquiesce in the principles upon which they were founded, and never to cease war upon them until they should be annulled and effaced from the statute-book. The contest before the people was fierce and bitter, accompanied sometimes with acts of violence and intimidation; but fortunately, Mr. Clay lived long enough to feel and know that his last great efforts for the peace of the country and the perpetuity of the Union—the crowning acts of a brilliant and glorious career in the public service—had met the approval and received the almost unanimous indorsement [sic] of his grateful countrymen. The response which the country was permitted to enjoy for a brief period proved to be a temporary truce in the sectional conflict, and not a permanent peace upon the slavery question. The purpose of reopening the agitation for a congressional prohibition of slavery in all the Territories whenever an opportunity or excuse could be had, seems never to have been abandoned by those who originated the scheme for partisan purposes, in 1819, and were baffled in their designs by the adoption of the Missouri compromise in 1820; and who renewed the attempt in 1848, but were again doomed to suffer a mortifying defeat in the adoption of the compromise measures of 1850. The opportunity and pretext for renewing the agitation was discovered by those who had never abandoned the design, when it became necessary, in 1854, to pass the necessary laws for the organization of the Territories of Kansas and Nebraska. The necessity for the organization of these Territories, in order to open and protect the routes of emigration and travel to California and Oregon could not be denied. The measure could not be postponed longer without endangering the peace of the frontier settlements, and incurring the hazards of an Indian war, growing out of the constant collisions between the emigrants and the Indian tribes through whose country they were compelled to pass.

Early in December, 1853, Senator Dodge, of Iowa, introduced a bill for the organization of the Territory of Nebraska, which was referred to the Committee on Territories, of which I was chairman. The committee did not volunteer their services on the occasion. The bill was referred to us by a vote of the Senate, and our action was in discharge of a plain duty imposed upon us by an express command of the body.

The first question which addressed itself to the calm and deliberate consideration of the committee was: upon what basis shall the organization of the territory be formed? Whether upon a theory of a geographical line and an equitable partition of the territory in accordance with the compromise of 1820, which had been abandoned by its supporters not from choice, but from our inability to carry it out; or upon the principle of non-intervention and popular sovereignty, according to the compromise measures of 1850, which had taken the place of the Missouri compromise?

The committee, upon mature deliberation, and with great unanimity, decided that all future territorial organizations should be formed upon the principles and model of the compromise measures of 1850, inasmuch as the recent presidential election (1852) both of the great political parties of the country, (Whig and Democratic,) of which the Senate was composed, stood pledged to those measures as a substitute for the act of 1820; and the committee instructed me, as their organ, to prepare a report and draft a substitute for Mr. Dodge's bill in accordance with these views. I will now read from the record, at the hazard of being somewhat tedious, in order that the Senate and the country may judge with what fidelity I performed this duty:

> January 4th, 1854, Mr. DOUGLAS made the following report: The Committee on Territories, to which was referred a bill for an act to establish the Territory of Nebraska, have given the same that serious and deliberate consideration which its great importance demands, and beg leave to report it back to the Senate, with various amendments, in the form of a substitute bill.

> The principal amendments which your committee deem it their duty to commend to the favorable action of the Senate, in a special report, are those in which the principles established by the compromise measures of 1850, so far as they are applicable to territorial organizations, are proposed to be affirmed and carried into practical operation within the limits of the new Territory.

> The wisdom of those measures is attested, not less by their salutary and beneficial effects in allaying sectional agitation and restoring peace and harmony to an irritated and distracted people, than by the cordial and almost universal approbation with which they have been received and sanctioned by the whole country. In the judgment of your committee, *those measures were intended to have a far more comprehensive and enduring effect than the mere adjustment of the difficulties arising out of the recent acquisition of Mexican territory.* THEY WERE DESIGNED TO ESTABLISH CERTAIN GREAT PRINCIPLES, WHICH WOULD NOT ONLY

FURNISH ADEQUATE REMEDIES FOR EXISTING EVILS, BUT IN
ALL TIME TO COME TO AVOID THE PERILS OF A SIMILAR
AGITATION, BY WITHDRAWING THE QUESTION OF SLAVERY
FROM THE HALLS OF CONGRESS AND THE POLITICAL ARENA,
AND COMMITTING IT TO THE ARBITRAMENT OF THOSE WHO
WERE IMMEDIATELY INTERESTED IN, AND ALONE
RESPONSIBLE FOR, ITS CONSEQUENCES. With the view of
conforming their action to what they regard the settled policy of the
Government, sanctioned by the approving voice of the American people,
your committee have deemed it their duty to incorporate and perpetuate in
their territorial bills the principles and spirit of those measures.

After reviewing the provisions of the legislation of 1850, the
committee conclude [sic] as follows:

From these provisions it is apparent that the compromise measures of
1850 affirm and rest upon the following propositions:

First, That all questions pertaining to slavery in the Territories, and in the
new States to be formed therefrom, are to be left to the decision of the
people residing therein, by their appropriate representatives, to be chosen
by them for that purpose.

Second, That 'all cases involving title to slaves,' and 'questions of personal
freedom,' are referred to the adjudication of the local tribunals, with the
right of appeal to the Supreme Court of the United States.

Third, That the provision of the Constitution of the United States, in respect
to fugitives from service, is to be carried into faithful execution in all 'the
organized Territories,' the same as in the States.

The substitute for the bill which your committee have prepared, and which
is commended to the favorable action of the Senate, *proposes to carry
those propositions and principles into practical operation*, IN THE
PRECISE LANGUAGE OF THE COMPROMISE MEASURES OF 1850.

No sooner was this report and bill printed and laid upon the tables of
Senators, than an address was prepared and issued over the signatures of
those party leaders who had always denounced "the Missouri compromise
as a crime against freedom, and a compact with infamy," in which the
bill was "arraigned as a gross violation of a sacred pledge;" "as a criminal
betrayal of precious rights;" and the report denounced as "a mere
invention, designed to cover up from public reprehension mediated bad
faith."

The Missouri compromise was "infamous," in their estimation, so
long as it remained upon the statute-book and was carried out in good
faith, as a means of preserving the peace of the country and preventing
slavery agitation in Congress. But it suddenly became "a sacred pledge,"

a "solemn compact for the preservation of precious rights," the moment they had succeeded in preventing its faithful execution and in causing it to be abandoned when it ceased to be an impregnable barrier against slavery agitation and sectional strife. The bill against which the hue and cry was raised, and the crusade preached, did not contain a word about the Missouri compromise, nor in any manner refer to it. It simply allowed the people of the Territory to legislate for themselves on all rightful subjects of legislation, and left them free to form and regulate their domestic institutions in their own way, subject only to the Constitution. So far as the Missouri act, or any other statute might be supposed to conflict with this right of self-government in the Territories, it was, by inference, rendered null and void to that extent, and for no other purpose. Several weeks afterwards, when a doubt was suggested whether, under the bill as it stood, the people of the Territory would be authorized to exercise this right of self-government upon the slavery question, *during the existence of the territorial government*, an amendment was adopted, on my motion, for the sole and avowed purpose of removing that doubt and securing that right, in accordance with the compromise measures of 1850, as stated by me and reported in the debates at the time. The amendment will be found in the fourteenth section of the act, and is as follows:

> That the Constitution and all laws of the United States which are not locally inapplicable, shall have the same force and effect within the said Territory of Nebraska as elsewhere within the United States, except the eighth section the act preparatory to the admission of Missouri into the Union, approved March 6, 1820, *which, being inconsistent with the principle of nonintervention by Congress with slavery in the States and Territories,* AS RECOGNIZED BY THE LEGISLATION OF 1850, commonly called the compromise measures, is hereby declared inoperative and void; it being the true intent and meaning of this act not to legislate slavery into any Territory or State, nor to exclude it therefrom, *but to leave the people thereof perfectly free to form and regulate their domestic institutions in their own way,* subject only to the Constitution of the United States.

In my opinion this amendment did not change the legal effect of the bill as reported by the committee. Its object was to render its meaning certain, by removing all doubts in regard to the right of the people to exercise the privileges of self-government on the slavery question, as well as all others consistent with the Constitution, during their territorial condition, as well as when they should become a State. From that day to this, there has been a fierce and desperate struggle between the supporters and opponents of the territorial policy inaugurated under the auspices of

Mr. Clay, in 1850, and affirmed in the Kansas-Nebraska act in 1854—the one to maintain and the other to overthrow the principle of non-intervention and popular sovereignty, as the settled policy of the government in reference to the organization of Territories, and the admission of new States. This sketch of the origin and progress of the slavery agitation as an element of political power and partisan warfare, covers the entire period from the organization of the Federal Government under the Constitution, in 1789, to the present, and is naturally divided into three parts:

First. From 1789, when the Constitution went into operation, to 1819-20, when the Missouri controversy arose, the Territories were all organized upon the basis of non-intervention by the Congress with the domestic affairs of the people, and especially upon the question of African slavery. During the whole of this period, domestic tranquillity and fraternal feeling prevailed.

Second. From 1820, when the Missouri compromise was adopted, to 1848 and 1850, when it was repudiated and finally abandoned, all the Territories were organized with reference to the policy of an equitable partition between the two sections upon the line of 36° 30′. During this period there was no serious difficulty upon the territorial question, so long as the Missouri compromise was adhered to, and carried out in good faith.

Third. From 1850, when the original doctrine of non-intervention, as it prevailed during the first thirty years, was reestablished as the policy of the Government in the organization of Territories, and the admission of new States, to the present time, there has been a constant struggle, except for a short interval, to overthrow and repudiate the policy and principles of the compromise measures of 1850, for the purpose of returning to the old doctrine of congressional intervention for the prohibition of slavery in all the Territories, south as well as north of the Missouri line, regardless of the wishes and condition of the people inhabiting the country.

In view of these facts, I feel authorized to reaffirm the proposition with which I commenced my remarks, that whenever the Federal Government has attempted to control the slavery question in our newly acquired Territories, alienation of feeling, discord, and sectional strife, have ensued; and whenever Congress has refrained from such interference, peace, harmony, and good will, have returned. The conclusion I draw from these premises is, that the slavery question should be banished forever from the Halls of Congress and the arena of Federal politics by an irrepealable constitutional provision. I have deemed this exposition of the origin and progress of the slavery agitation essential to a full comprehension of the difficulties with which we are surrounded, and the remedies for the evils which threaten the disruption of the Republic. The immediate causes which have precipitated the southern country into revolution, although inseparably connected with, and flowing from, the slavery agitation, whose history I portrayed, are to be found in the result of the recent presidential election. I hold that the election of any man, no matter who, by the American people, according to the Constitution, furnishes no cause, no justification, for the dissolution of the Union. But we cannot close our eyes to the fact that the southern people have received the result of that election as furnishing conclusive evidence that the dominant party of the North, which is soon to take possession of the Federal Government under that election, are determined to invade and destroy their constitutional rights. Believing that their domestic institutions, their hearthstones, and their family alters, are to be assailed, at least by indirect means, and that the Federal Government is to be used for the inauguration of a line of policy which shall have for its object the ultimate extinction of slavery in all the States, old as well as new, south as well as north, the southern people are prepared to rush wildly, madly, as I think, into revolution, disunion, war, and defy the consequences, whatever they may be, rather than to wait for the development of events, or submit tamely to what they think is a fatal blow impending over them and all they hold dear on earth. It matters not, so far as we and the peace of the country and the fate of the Union are concerned, whether these apprehensions are real or imaginary, whether they are well founded or wholly without foundation, so long as they believe them and are determined to act upon them. The Senator from Ohio, [Mr. WADE,] whose speech was received with so much favor by his friends the other day, referred to these serious apprehensions, and acknowledged his belief that the southern people were laboring under the conviction that they were well founded. He was kind enough to add that he did not blame the southern people much for what they were doing under this fatal misapprehension; but cast the whole blame upon the northern Democracy; and referred especially to his colleague and myself, for having misrepresented and falsified the purposes and policy of the Republican party, and for having made the southern people believe our misrepresentations! He does not blame the southern people for acting on their honest convictions in resorting to revolution to avert an impending but imaginary calamity. No; he does not blame them, because they believe in the existence of the danger; yet he will do no act to undeceive them; will take no step to relieve their painful apprehensions; and will furnish no guarantees, no security against the dangers which they believe to exist, and the existence of which he denies; but, on the contrary, he demands unconditional submission, threatens war, and talks about armies, navies, and military force, for the purpose of preserving the Union and enforcing the laws! I submit whether this mode of treating the question is not calculated to confirm the worst apprehensions of the southern people, and force them into the most extreme measures of resistance!

I regret that the Senator from Ohio, or any other Senator, should have deemed it consistent with his duty, under present circumstances, to introduce partisan politics, and attempt to manufacture partisan capital out of a question involving the peace and safety of the country. I regret what I have said on another occasion, that, if I know myself, my action will be influenced by no partisan considerations, until we shall have rescued the country from the perils which environ it. But since the Senator has attempted to throw the whole responsibility of the present difficulty upon the northern Democracy, and has charged us with misrepresenting and falsifying the purposes and policy of the Republican party, and thereby deceiving the southern people, I feel called upon to repel the charge, and show that it is without a shadow of foundation. No man living would rejoice more than myself in the conviction, if I could only be convinced of the fact, that I have misunderstood, and consequently misrepresented, the policy and designs of the Republican party. Produce the evidence and convince me of my error, and I will take more pleasure in making the correction and repairing the injustice, than I ever have taken in denouncing what I believed to be an unjust and ruinous policy.

With the view of ascertaining whether I have misapprehended or misrepresented the policy and purposes of the Republican party, I will now inquire of the Senator, and yield the floor for an answer: whether it is not the policy of his party to confine slavery within its present limits by the action of the Federal Government? Whether they do not intend to abolish and prohibit slavery by act of Congress, notwithstanding the decision of the Supreme Court to the contrary, in all the Territories we now possess, or may hereafter acquire? Whether he and his party are in favor of returning to their master the fugitive slaves that may escape? In short, I will give the Senator an opportunity now to say—

Mr. WADE. Mr. President—

Mr. DOUGLAS. One other question, and I will give way.

Mr. WADE. Very well.

Mr. DOUGLAS. I will give the Senator an opportunity of saying now whether it is not the policy of his party to exert all the powers of the Federal Government under the Constitution, according to their interpretation of the instrument, to restrain and cripple the institution of slavery, with a view to its ultimate extinction in all the States, old as well as new, south as well as north.

Are not these the views and purposes of the party, as proclaimed by their leaders, and understood by the people, in speeches, addresses, sermons, newspapers, and public meetings? Now, I will hear his answer.

Mr. WADE. Mr. President, all these questions are most pertinently answered in the speech the Senator is professing to answer. I have nothing to add to it. If he will read my speech, he will find my sentiments upon all these questions.

Mr. DOUGLAS. Mr. President, I did not expect an unequivocal answer. I know too well that the Senator will not deny that each of these interrogatories do express his individual policy and the policy of the Republican party as he understands it. I should not have propounded the interrogatories to him if he had not accused me and the northern Democracy of having misrepresented the policy of the Republican party, and with having deceived the southern people by such misrepresentations. The most obnoxious sentiments I ever attributed to the Republican party, and that not in the South, but in northern Illinois and in the strongholds of Abolitionism, was that they intended to exercise the powers of the Federal Government with a view to the ultimate extinction of slavery in the southern States. I have expressed my belief, and would be glad to be corrected if I am in error, that it is the policy of that party to exclude slavery from all the Territories we now possess or may acquire, with a view of surrounding the slave States with a cordon of abolition States, and thus confine the institution within such narrow limits that, when the number increases beyond the capacity of the soil to raise food for their subsistence, the institution must end in starvation, colonization, or servile insurrection. I have often exposed the enormities of this policy, and appealed to the people of Illinois to know whether this mode of getting rid of the evils of slavery could be justified in the name of civilization, humanity, and Christianity? I have often used these arguments in the strongest abolition portions of the North; but never in the South. The truth is, I have always been very mild and gentle upon the Republicans when addressing a southern audience; for it seemed ungenerous to say behind their backs, and where they dare not go to reply to me, those things which I was in the habit of saying to their faces, and in the presence of their leaders, where they were in the majority.

But inasmuch as I do not get a direct answer from the Senator who makes this charge against the northern Democracy, as to the purposes of that party to use the power of the Federal Government under their construction of the Constitution, with a view to the ultimate extinction of slavery in the States, I will turn to the record of their President elect, and see what he says on that subject. The Republicans have gone to the trouble to collect and publish in pamphlet form, under the sanction of Mr. Lincoln, the debates which took place between him and myself in the senatorial canvass of 1858. It may not be improper here to remark that this publication is unfair towards me, for reasons that Mr. Lincoln personally revised and corrected his own speeches, without giving me an opportunity to correct the numerous errors in mine. Inasmuch as the publication is made under the sanction of Mr. Lincoln himself, accompanied by a letter from him that he has revised the speeches by verbal corrections, and thereby approved them, it becomes important to show what his views are, since he is in the daily habit of referring to those speeches for his present opinions.

Mr. Lincoln was nominated for United States Senator by a Republican State convention at Springfield in June, 1858. Anticipating the nomination, he had carefully prepared a written speech, which he delivered on the occasion, and which, by order of the convention, was published among the proceedings as containing the platform of principles upon which the canvass was to be conducted. More importance is due to this speech than to those delivered under the excitement of debate in joint discussions by the exigencies of the contest. The first few paragraphs which I will now read, may be taken as a fair statement of his opinion and feelings upon the slavery question. Mr. Lincoln said:

> Mr. President and Gentlemen of the convention, if we could first know where we are and whither we are tending, we could better judge what to do and how to do it. We are now far into the fifth year since a policy was initiated with the avowed object and confident promise of putting an end to slavery agitation. Under the operation of that policy, that agitation has not only not ceased, but has constantly augmented. In my opinion, it will not cease until a crisis shall have been reached and passed. A house divided against itself cannot stand! I believe this Government cannot endure permanently half slave and half free. I do not expect the Union to be dissolved—but I do expect it will cease to be divided. It will become all one thing or all the other. Either the opponents of slavery will arrest the further spread of it, and place it where the public mind shall rest in the belief that it is in the course of ultimate extinction, or its advocates will push it forward, till it shall alike become lawful in all the States, old as well as new, North as well as South.

There you are told by the President elect that this Union cannot permanently endure divided into free and slave States; that these States must all become free or all slave, all become one thing or all become the other; that this agitation will never cease until the opponents of slavery have restrained its expansion, and have placed it where the public mind will be satisfied that it will be in the course of ultimate extinction. Mark the language:

"Either the opponents of slavery will arrest the further spread of it?"

We are now told that the object of the Republican party is to prevent the extension of slavery. What did Mr. Lincoln say? That the opponents of slavery must first prevent the further spread of it. But that is not all. What else must they do?

"And place it where the public mind can rest in the belief that it is in the course of ultimate extinction."

The ultimate extinction of slavery, of which Mr. Lincoln was then speaking, related to the States of this Union. He had reference to the southern States of this Confederacy; for, in the next sentence, he says that the States must all become one thing or the other—"old as well as new, north as well as south"—showing that he meant that the policy of the Republican party was to keep up this agitation in the Federal Government until slavery in the States was placed in the process of ultimate extinction. Now, sir, when the Republican committee have [sic] published an edition of Mr. Lincoln's speeches containing sentiments like these, and circulated it as a campaign document, is it surprising that the people of the South should suppose that he was in earnest, and intended to carry out the policy which he had announced?

I regret the necessity which has made it my duty to reproduce these dangerous and revolutionary opinions of the President elect. No consideration could have induced me to have done so but the attempt of his friends to denounce the policy which Mr. Lincoln has boldly advocated, as gross calumnies upon the Republican party, and as base inventions by the northern Democracy to excite rebellion in the southern country. I should like to find one Senator on that side of the Chamber, in the confidence of the President elect, who will have the hardihood to deny that Mr. Lincoln stands by his public speeches, to which he now refers constantly as containing his present opinions, to carry out the policy indicated in the speech from which I have read. I take great pleasure in saying, however, that I do not believe the rights of the South will materially suffer under the administration of Mr. Lincoln. I repeat what I have said on another occasion, that neither he nor his party will have the power to do any act prejudicial to southern rights and interests, if the Union shall be preserved, and the southern States shall retain a full delegation in both Houses of Congress. With a majority against them in this body and in the House of Representatives, they can do no act, except to enforce the laws, without the consent of those to whom the South has confided her interests, and even his appointments for that purpose are subject to our advice and confirmation. Besides, I still indulge the hope that when Mr. Lincoln shall assume the high responsibilities which will soon devolve upon him, he will be fully impressed with the necessity of sinking the politician in the statesman, the partisan in the patriot, and regard the obligations which he owes to his country as paramount to those of his party. In view of these considerations, I had indulged the fond hope that the people of the southern States would have been content to remain in the Union and defend their rights under the Constitution, instead of rushing madly into revolution and disunion, as a refuge from apprehended dangers which may not exist.

But this apprehension has become wide-spread and deep-seated in the southern people. It has taken possession of the southern mind, sunk deep in the southern heart, and filled them with the conviction that their firesides, their family altars, and their domestic institutions, are to be ruthlessly assailed through the machinery of the Federal Government. The Senator from Ohio says he does not blame you, southern Senators, nor the southern people, for believing those things; and yet, instead of doing those acts which will relieve your apprehensions, and render it impossible that your rights should be invaded by Federal power under any Administration, he threatens you with war, armies, military force, under the pretext of enforcing the laws and preserving the Union. We are told that the authority of the Government must be vindicated; that the Union must be preserved; that rebellion must be put down; the insurrection must be suppressed, and the laws must be enforced. I agree to all this. I am in favor of doing these things according to the Constitution and laws. No man will go further than I to maintain the just authority of the Government, to preserve the Union, to put down rebellion, to suppress insurrection, and to enforce the laws. I would use all the powers conferred by the Constitution for this purpose. But, in the performance of these important and delicate duties, it must be borne in mind that those powers only must be used, and such measures employed, as are authorized by the Constitution and laws. Things should be called by right names; and facts, whose existence can no longer be denied, should be acknowledged.

Insurrections and rebellions, although unlawful and criminal, frequently become successful revolutions. The strongest Governments and proudest monarchs on earth have often been reduced to the humiliating necessity of recognizing the existence of Governments *de facto*, although not *de jure*, in their revolted States and provinces, when rebellion has ripened into successful revolution, and the national authorities have been expelled from their limits. In such cases the right to regain possession and exact obedience to the laws remains; but the exercise of that right is war, and must be governed by the laws of war. Such was the relative condition of Great Britain and the American colonies for seven years after the Declaration of Independence. The rebellion had progressed and matured into revolution, with a Government *de facto*, and an army and navy to defend it. Great Britain, regarding the complaints of the colonies unfounded, refused to yield to their demands, and proceeded to reduce them to obedience; not by the enforcement of the laws, but by military force, armies and navies, according to the rules of war. Captives taken in battle with arms in their hands, fighting against Great Britain, were not executed as traitors, but held as prisoners of war, and exchanged according to the usages of civilized nations. The laws of nations, the principles of humanity, of civilization, and Christianity, demanded that the Government *de facto* should be acknowledged and treated as such. While the right to prosecute the war for the purpose of reducing the revolted provinces to obedience still remained, yet it was a military remedy, and could only be exercised according to the established principles of war.

It is said that after one of the earliest engagements, the British general threatened to execute as traitors all the prisoners he had taken in battle; and that General Washington replied that he, too, had taken some prisoners, and would shoot two for one until the British general should respect the laws of war, and treat his prisoners accordingly. May Divine Providence, in His infinite wisdom and mercy, save our country from the humiliation and calamities which now seem almost inevitable! South Carolina has already declared her independence of the United States; has expelled the Federal authorities from her limits, and established a Government *de facto*, with a military force to sustain it. The revolution is complete, there being no man within her limits who denies the authority of her government or acknowledges allegiance to that of the United States. There is every reason to believe that seven other States will soon follow her example; and much ground to apprehend that the other slaveholding States will follow them.

How are we going to prevent an alliance between these seceding States by which they may establish a Federal government, at least *de facto*, for themselves? If they shall do so, and expel the authorities of the United States from their limits, as South Carolina has done, and others are about to do, so that there shall be no human being within their boundaries who acknowledges allegiance to the United States, how are we going to enforce the laws? Armies and navies can make war, but cannot enforce laws in this country. The laws can be enforced only by the civil authorities, assisted by the military as a *posse comitatus*, when resisted when executing judicial process. Who is to issue the judicial process in a State where there is no judge, no court, no judicial functionary? Who is to perform the duties of marshal in executing the process where no man will or dare accept office? Who is to serve on juries while every citizen is *particeps criminis* with the accused? How are you going to comply with the Constitution in respect to a jury trial, where there are no men qualified to serve on the jury? I agree that the laws should be enforced. I hold that our Government is clothed with the power and duty of using all the means necessary to the enforcement of the laws, *according to the Constitution and laws*. The President is sworn to the faithful performance of this duty. I do not propose to inquire, at this time, how far, and with what fidelity, the President has performed that duty. His conduct and duty in this regard, including acts of commission and omission, while the rebellion was in its incipient stages, and when confined to a few individuals, present a very different question from that which we are now discussing—after the revolution has become complete, and the Federal authorities have been expelled, and the Governments *de facto* put into practical operation, and in the unrestrained and unresisted exercise of all the powers and functions of Government, local and national.

But we are told that secession is wrong, and that South Carolina had no right to secede. I agree that it is wrong, unlawful, unconstitutional, criminal. In my opinion South Carolina had no right to secede; *but she has done it.* She has declared her independence of us, effaced the last vestige of our civil authority, established a foreign Government, and is now engaged in the preliminary steps to open diplomatic intercourse with the great powers of the world. What next? If her act was illegal, unconstitutional, and wrong, have we no remedy? Unquestionably we have the right to use all the power and force necessary to regain possession of that portion of the United States, in order that we may again enforce our Constitution and laws upon the inhabitants. We can enforce our laws in those States, Territories, and places only which are within our possession. It often happens that the territorial rights of a country extend beyond the limits of their actual possessions. That is our case at present in respect to South Carolina. Our right of jurisdiction over that State for Federal purposes, according to the Constitution, has not been destroyed or impaired by the ordinance of secession, or any act of the convention, or of the *de facto* government. The right remains; but the possession is lost, for the time being. "How shall we regain the possession?" is the pertinent inquiry. It may be done by arms, or by a peaceable adjustment of the matters in controversy.

Are we prepared for war? I do not mean that kind of preparation which consists of armies and navies, and supplies, and munitions of war; but are we prepared IN OUR HEARTS for war with our own brethren and kindred? I confess I am not. While I affirm that the Constitution is, and was intended to be, a bond of perpetual Union; while I can do no act and utter no word that will acknowledge or countenance the right of secession; while I affirm the right and duty of the Federal Government to use all legitimate means to enforce the laws, put down rebellion, and suppress insurrection, I will not mediate war, nor tolerate the idea, until every effort at peaceful adjustment shall have been exhausted, and the last ray of hope shall have deserted the patriot's heart. Then, and not till then, will I consider and determine what course my duty to my country may require me to pursue in such an emergency. In my opinion, war is disunion, certain, inevitable, irrevocable. I am for peace to save the Union.

I have said that I cannot recognize nor countenance the right of secession. Illinois, situated in the interior of the continent, can never acknowledge the right of the States bordering on the seas to withdraw from the Union at pleasure, and form alliances among themselves and with other countries, by which we shall be excluded from all access to the ocean, from all intercourse and commerce with foreign nations. We can never consent to be shut up within the circle of a Chinese wall, erected and controlled by others without our permission; or to any other system of isolation by which we shall be deprived of any communication with the rest of the civilized world. Those States which are situated in the interior of the continent can never consent to any such doctrine. Our rights, our interests, our safety, our existence as a free people, forbid it! The northwestern States were ceded to the United States before the

Constitution was made, on condition of perpetual union with the other States. The Territories were organized, settlers invited, lands purchased, and homes made, on the pledge of your plighted faith of perpetual union.

When there were but two hundred thousand inhabitants scattered over that vast region, the navigation of the Mississippi was deemed by Mr. Jefferson so important and essential to their interests and prosperity, that he did not hesitate to declare that if Spain or France insisted upon retaining possession of the mouth of that river, it would become the duty of the United States to take it by arms, if they failed to acquire it by treaty. If the possession of that river, with jurisdiction over its mouth and channel, was indispensable to the people of the Northwest when we had two hundred thousand inhabitants, is it reasonable to suppose that we will voluntarily surrender it now when we have ten million people? Louisiana was not purchased for the exclusive benefit of the few Spanish and French residents in the territory, nor for those who might become residents. These considerations did not enter into the negotiations and formed no inducement to the acquisition. Louisiana was purchased with the national treasure, for the common benefit of the whole Union in general, and for the safety, convenience, and prosperity of the Northwest in particular. We paid $15,000,000 for the territory. We have expended much more than that sum in the extinguishment of Indian titles, the removal of Indians, the survey of lands, the erection of custom-houses, light-houses, forts, and arsenals. We admitted the inhabitants into the Union on an equal footing with ourselves. Now we are called upon to acknowledge the moral and constitutional right of those people to dissolve the Union without the consent of the other States; to seize forts, arsenals, and other public property, and appropriate them to their own use; to take possession of the Mississippi river, and exercise jurisdiction over the same, and to reannex herself to France, or remain an independent nation, or to form alliances with such other foreign Powers as she, in the plenitude of her sovereign will and pleasure, may see fit. If this thing is to be done— peaceably if you can; and forcibly, if you must—all I propose to say at this time is, that you cannot expect us of the Northwest to yield our assent to it, nor to acknowledge your right to do it, or the propriety and justice of the act.

The respectful attention with which my friend from Florida [Mr. YULEE] is listening to me, reminds me that his State furnishes an apt illustration of this modern doctrine of secession. We paid five million for the Territory. We expended marvelous sums in subduing the Indians, extinguishing Indian titles, removal of Indians beyond her borders, surveying the lands, building light-houses, navy-yards, forts, and arsenals, with untold millions for the never-ending Florida claims. I assure my friend that I do not refer to these things in an offensive sense, for he knows how much respect I have for him, and has not forgotten my efforts in the House many years ago, to secure the admission of his State into the Union, in order that he might represent her, as he has since done with so much ability and fidelity, in this body. But I will say that it never occurred to me at that time that the State whose admission into the Union I was advocating would be one of the first to join in a scheme to break up the Union. I submit to him whether it is not an extraordinary spectacle to see that State, which has cost us so much blood and treasure, turn her back on the Union which has fostered and protected her when she was too feeble to protect herself, and seize the light-houses, navy-yards, forts, and arsenals, which, although within her boundaries, were erected with national funds, for the benefit and defense of the whole Union.

I do not know if I can find a more striking illustration of this doctrine of secession than was suggested to my mind when reading the President's last inaugural message. My attention was first arrested by the remarkable passage, that the Federal Government had no power to *coerce* a State back into the Union if she did secede; and my admiration was unbounded when I found, a few lines afterwards, a recommendation to appropriate money to purchase the island of Cuba. It occurred to me instantly, what a brilliant achievement it would be to pay Spain $300,000,000 for Cuba, and immediately admit the island into the Union as a State, and let her secede and reannex herself to Spain the next day, when the Spanish Queen would be ready to sell the island again for half price, or double price, according to the gullibility of the purchaser! [Laughter.]

During my service in Congress it was one of my pleasant duties to take an active part in the annexation of Texas; and at a subsequent session to write and introduce the bill which made Texas one of the States of the Union. Out of that annexation grew the war with Mexico, in which we expended $100,000,000; and were left to mourn the loss of about ten thousand as gallant men as ever died upon a battle-field for the honor and glory of their country! We have since spent millions of money to protect Texas against her own Indians, to establish forts and fortifications to protect her frontier settlements, and to defend her against the assaults of all enemies until she became strong enough to protect herself. We are now called upon to acknowledge that Texas has a moral, just and constitutional right to rescind the act of admission into the Union; repudiate her ratification of the resolutions of annexation; seize the forts and public buildings which were constructed with our money; appropriate the same to her own use, and leave us to pay $100,000,000 and mourn the death of the brave men who sacrificed their lives in defending the integrity of her soil. In the name of Hardin, and Bissell, and Harris, and of the seven thousand gallant spirits from Illinois, who fought bravely upon every battle-field of Mexico, I protest against the right of Texas to separate herself from the Union without our consent.

Mr. HEMPHILL. Mr. President, if the Senator from Illinois will allow me, I will inquire whether there were no other causes assigned by the United States for the war with Mexico than simply the defense of Texas?

Mr. DOUGLAS. I will answer the question. We undoubtedly did assign other acts as being causes for war, which had existed for years, if we had chosen to treat them so; but we did not go to war for any other cause than the annexation of Texas, as is shown in the act of Congress recognizing the existence of war with Mexico, in which it is declared that "war exists by the act of the Republic of Mexico." The sole cause of grievance which Mexico had against us, and for which she commenced the war, was our annexation of Texas. Hence, none can deny that the Mexican war was solely and exclusively the result of the annexation of Texas.

Mr. HEMPHILL. I will inquire further, whether the United States paid anything to Texas for the annexation of her three hundred and seventy thousand square miles of territory, and whether the United States has not got $500,000,000 by the acquisition of California through that war with Mexico.

Mr. DOUGLAS. Sir, we did not pay anything for bringing Texas into the Union; for we did not get any of her lands, except that we purchased from her some poor lands afterwards, which she did not own, and paid her $10,000,000 for them. [Laughter.] But we did spend blood and treasure in the acquisition and subsequent defense of Texas.

Now, sir, I will answer his question in respect to California. The treaty of peace brought California and New Mexico into the Union. Our people moved there, took possession of the lands, settled up the country, and erected a State of which the United States have a right to be proud. We have expended millions upon millions for fortification in California, and for navy-yards, and mints, and public buildings, and land surveys, and feeding the Indians, and protecting her people. I believe the public land sales do not amount to more than one tenth of the cost of the surveys, according to the returns that have been made. It is true that the people of California have dug a large amount of gold (principally out of the lands belonging to the United States) and sold it to us; but I am not aware that we are under any more obligations to them for selling it to us, than they are to us for buying it of them. The people of Texas, during the same time, have probably made cotton and agricultural productions to a much larger value, and sold some of it to New England, and some to Old England. I suppose the benefits of the bargain were reciprocal, and the one was under just as much obligation as the other for the mutual benefits of the sale and purchase.

The question remains, whether, after paying $15,000,000 for California—as the Senator from Texas has called my attention to that State—and perhaps as much more in protecting and defending her, she has any moral, constitutional right to annul the compact between her and the Union, and form alliances with foreign Powers, and leave us to pay the cost and expenses? I cannot recognize any such doctrine. In my opinion, the Constitution was intended to be a bond of perpetual Union. It begins with the declaration in the preamble, that it is made in order "to form a more perfect Union," and every section and paragraph in the instrument implies perpetuity. It was intended to last for ever [sic], and was so understood when ratified by the people of the several States. New York and Virginia have been referred to as having ratified with the reserved right to withdraw or secede at pleasure. This was a mistake. The correspondence between Mr. Hamilton and Mr. Madison, at the time, is conclusive on this point. After Virginia had ratified the Constitution, General Hamilton, who was a member of the New York convention, wrote to Mr. Madison that New York would probably ratify the Constitution for a term of years, and reserve the right to withdraw after that time, if certain amendments were not sooner adopted; to which Mr. Madison replied that such ratification would not make New York a member of the Union; that the ratification must be unconditional,*in toto* and *forever*, or not at all; that the same question was considered at Richmond, and abandoned when Virginia ratified the Constitution. Hence the declaration of Virginia and New York, that they had not surrendered the right to resume the delegated powers, must be understood as referring to the right of revolution, which nobody acknowledges more freely than I do, and not the right of secession.

The Constitution being made as a bond of perpetual Union; its framers proceeded to provide against the necessities of revolution, by prescribing the mode in which it might be amended; so that if, in the course of time, the condition of the country should so change as to require a different fundamental law, amendments might be made peaceably, in the manner prescribed in the instrument; and thus avoid the necessity of ever resorting to revolution. Having provided for a perpetual Union, and for amendments to the Constitution, they next inserted a clause for admitting new States, *but no provision for the withdrawal of any of the other States*. I will not argue the question of the right of secession any further than to enter my protest against the whole doctrine. I deny that there is any foundation for it in the Constitution, in the nature of the compact, in the principles of the Government, or in justice, or in good faith.

Nor do I sympathize at all in all the apprehensions and misgivings I hear expressed about *coercion*. We are told that inasmuch as our Government is founded upon the will of the people, or the consent of the governed, therefore coercion is incompatible with republicanism. Sir, the word government means coercion. There can be no Government without coercion. Coercion is the vital principle upon which all Governments rest. Withdraw the right of coercion, and you dissolve your Government. If every man would perform his duty and respect the rights of his neighbors voluntarily, there would be no necessity for any Government on earth. The necessity of government is found to consist in the fact that some men will not do right unless coerced to do so. The object of all government is to coerce and compel every man to do his duty, who would otherwise not perform it. Hence I do not subscribe at all to this doctrine that coercion is not to be used in a free Government. It must be used in all Governments, no matter what their form or what their principles.

But coercion must always be used in the mode prescribed in the Constitution and laws. I hold that the Federal Government is, and ought to be, clothed with the power and duty to use all the means necessary to coerce obedience to all laws made in pursuance of the Constitution. But the proposition to subvert the *de facto* government of South Carolina, and reduce the people of that State into subjection to our Federal authority, no longer involves the question of enforcing the laws in a country within our possession; but it does involve the question whether we will make war on a State which has withdrawn her allegiance and expelled our authorities, with a view of subjecting her to our possession for the purpose of enforcing our laws within her limits.

We are bound, by the usages of nations, by the laws of civilization, by the uniform practice of our own Government, to acknowledge the existence of a Government *de facto*, so long as it maintains its undivided authority. When Louis Philippe fled from the throne of France, and Lamartine suddenly one morning found himself the head of a provisional

Government, I believe it was but three days until the American minister recognized the Government *de facto*. Texas was a Government *de facto*, not recognized by Mexico, when we annexed her; and Mexico was a Government *de facto*, not recognized by Spain, when Texas revolted. The laws of nations recognize Governments *de facto* where they exercise and maintain undivided sway, leaving the question of their authority *de jure* to be determined by the people interested in the Government. Now, as a man who loves the Union, and desires to see it maintained forever, and to see the laws enforced, and rebellion put down, and insurrection suppressed, and order maintained, I desire to know of my Union-loving friends on the other side of the Chamber how they intend to enforce the laws in the seceding States, except by making war, conquering them first, and administering the laws in them afterwards.

In my opinion, we have reached a point where disunion is inevitable, unless some compromise, founded upon mutual concession, can be made. I prefer compromise to war. I prefer concession to dissolution of the Union. When I avow myself in favor of compromise, I do not mean that one side should give up all that it has claimed, nor that the other side should give up everything for which it has contended. Nor do I ask any man to come to my standard; but I simply say that I will meet every one half way who is willing to preserve the peace of the country, and save the Union from disruption upon principles of compromise and concession.

In my judgment, no system of compromise can be effectual and permanent which does not banish the slavery question from the Halls of Congress and the arena of Federal politics, by irrepealable constitutional provision. We have tried compromises by law, compromises by act of Congress; and now we are engaged in the small business of crimination and recrimination, as to who is responsible for not having lived up to them in good faith, and for having broken faith. I want whatever compromise is agreed to, placed beyond the reach of party politics and partisan policy, by being made irrevocable in the Constitution itself, so that every man who holds office will be bound by his oath to support it.

There are several modes in which this irritating question may be withdrawn from Congress, peace restored, the rights of the States maintained, and the Union rendered secure. One of them—one to which I can cordially assent—has been presented by the venerable Senator from Kentucky, [Mr. CRITTENDEN.] The journal of the committee of thirteen shows that I voted for it in committee. I am prepared to vote for it again. I shall not occupy my time now in discussing the question whether my vote to make a partition between the two sections, instead of referring the question to the people, will be consistent with my previous record or not. The country has no very great interest in my consistency. The preservation of this Union, the integrity of this Republic, is of more importance than party platforms or individual records. Hence I have no hesitation in saying to Senators on all sides of this Chamber, that I am prepared to act on this question with reference to the present exigencies of the case, as if I had never given a vote, or uttered a word, or had an opinion upon the subject.

Why cannot you Republicans accede to the re-establishment and extension of the Missouri compromise line? You have sung peans enough in its praise, and uttered imprecations and curses enough on my head for its repeal, one would think, to justify you now in claiming a triumph by its reestablishment. If you are willing to give up your party feelings—to sink the partisan in the patriot—and help me to reestablish and extend that line, as a perpetual bond of peace between the North and the South, I will promise you never to remind you in the future of your denunciations of the Missouri compromise so long as I was supporting it, and of your praises of the same measure when we removed it from the statute-book, after you have caused it to be abandoned, by rendering it impossible for us to carry it out. I seek no partisan advantage; I desire no personal triumph. I am willing to let by-gones be by-gones with every man who, in this exigency, will show by his vote that he loves his country more than his party.

I presented to the committee of thirteen, and also introduced into the Senate, another plan by which the slavery question may be taken out of Congress and the peace of the country maintained. It is, that Congress shall make no law on the subject of slavery in the Territories, and that the existing *status* of each Territory on that subject, as it now stands by law, shall remain unchanged until it has fifty thousand inhabitants, when it shall have the right of self-government as to its domestic policy; but with only a Delegate in each House of Congress until it has the population required by the Federal ratio for a Representative in Congress, when it shall be admitted into the Union on an equal footing with the original States. I put the number of inhabitants at fifty thousand before the people of the Territory shall change the *status* in respect to slavery as a fair compromise between the conflicting opinions upon this subject. The two extremes, North and South, unite in condemning the doctrine of popular sovereignty in the Territories upon the ground that the first few settlers ought not to be permitted to decide so important a question for those who are to come after them. I have never considered that objection well taken, for the reason that no Territory should be organized with the right to elect a Legislature and make its own laws upon rightful subjects of legislation, until it contained a sufficient population to constitute a political community; and whenever Congress should decide that there was a sufficient population, capable of self-government, by organizing the Territory, to govern themselves upon all other subjects, I could never perceive any good reason why the same political community should not be permitted to decide the slavery question for themselves.

But since we are now trying to compromise our difficulties upon the basis of mutual concessions, I propose to meet both extremes halfway, by fixing the number at fifty thousand. This number, certainly, ought to be satisfactory to those States which have been admitted into the Union with less than fifty thousand inhabitants. Oregon, Florida, Arkansas, Mississippi, Alabama, Ohio, Indiana, and Illinois, were each admitted into the Union, I believe, with less than that number of inhabitants. Surely the Senators and Representatives from those States do not doubt that fifty thousand people were enough to constitute a political community capable of deciding the slavery question for themselves. I now invite attention to the next proposition.

In order to allay all apprehension, North or South, that territory would be acquired in the future for sectional or partisan purposes, by adding a large number of free States on the North, or slave States on the South, with the view of giving the one section or the other a dangerous political ascendancy, I have inserted the provision that "No more territory shall be acquired by the United States, except by treaty or the concurrent vote of two thirds in each House of Congress." If this provision should be incorporated into the Constitution, it would be impossible for either section to annex any territory without the concurrence of a large portion of the other section; and hence there need be no apprehension that any territory would hereafter be acquired for any other than such national considerations as would commend the subject to the approbation of both sections.

I have also inserted a provision confining the right of suffrage and holding office to white men, excluding the African race. I have also inserted a provision for the colonization of free negroes from such Sates as may desire to have them removed, to districts of country to be acquired in Africa and South America. In addition to these, I have adopted the various provisions contained in the propositions of the Senator from Kentucky, in reference to fugitive slaves, the abolition of slavery in the forts, arsenals, and dock-yards in the slave States and in the District of Columbia, and the other provisions for the safety of the South. I believe this to be a fair basis of amicable adjustment. If you of the Republican side are not willing to accept this, nor the proposition of the Senator from Kentucky, [Mr. CRITTENDEN,] pray tell us what you are willing to do? I address the inquiry to the Republicans alone, for the reason that in the committee of thirteen, a few days ago, every member from the South, including those from the cotton States, [Messrs. TOOMBS and DAVIS,] expressed their readiness to accept the proposition of my venerable friend from Kentucky [Mr. CRITTENDEN] as a final settlement of the controversy, if tendered and sustained by the Republican members. Hence, the sole responsibility of our disagreement, and the only difficulty in the way of an amicable adjustment, is with the Republican party.

At first, I thought your reason for declining to adjust this question amicably, was that the Constitution, as it stands, was good enough, and that you would make no amendment to it. That position has already been waived. The great leader of the Republican party, [Mr. SEWARD,] by the unanimous concurrence of his friends, brought into the committee of thirteen a proposition to amend the Constitution. Inasmuch, therefore, as you are willing to amend the instrument, and to entertain propositions of adjustment, why not go further, and relieve the apprehensions of the southern people on all points where you do not intend to operate aggressively? You offer to amend the Constitution, by declaring that no further amendments shall be made which shall empower Congress to interfere with slavery in the States?

Now, if you do not intend to do any other act prejudicial to their constitutional rights and safety, why not relieve their apprehensions by inserting, in your own proposed amendment to the Constitution, such further provisions as will, in like manner, render it impossible for you to do that which you have no purpose of doing, if it be true that you have no such purpose? For the purpose of removing the apprehensions of the southern people, and for no other purpose, you propose to amend the Constitution, so as to render it impossible, in all future time, for Congress to interfere with slavery in the States where it may exist under the laws thereof. Why not insert a similar amendment in respect to slavery in the District of Columbia, and in the navy-yards, forts, arsenals, and other places within the limits of the slaveholding States, over which Congress has exclusive jurisdiction? Why not insert a similar provision in respect to the slave trade between the slaveholding States? The southern people have more serious apprehensions on these points than they have of your direct interference with slavery in the States.

If their apprehensions on these several points are groundless, is it not a duty you owe to God and your country to relieve their anxiety and remove all causes of discontent? Is there not quite as much reason for relieving their apprehensions upon these points, in regard to which they are much more sensitive, as in respect to your direct interference in the States, where they know and you acknowledge that you have no power to interfere as the Constitution now stands? The fact that you propose to give the assurance on the one point and peremptorily refuse to give it on the others, seems to authorize the presumption that you do intend to use the powers of the Federal Government for the purpose of direct interference with slavery and the slave trade everywhere else, with the view to its indirect effects upon slavery in the States; or, in the language of Mr. Lincoln, with the view of its "ultimate extinction in all the States, old as well as new, north as well as south."

If you had exhausted your ingenuity in devising a plan for the express purpose of increasing the apprehensions and inflaming the passions of the southern people, with the view of driving them into revolution and disunion, none could have been contrived better calculated than to accomplish the object than the offering of that one amendment to the Constitution, and rejecting all others which are infinitely more important to the safety and domestic tranquillity of the slaveholding States.

In my opinion, we have now reached a point where this agitation must close, and all the matters in controversy be finally determined by constitutional amendments, or civil war and the disruption of the Union are inevitable. My friend from Oregon, [Mr. BAKER,] who has addressed the Senate for the last two days, will fail in his avowed purpose to "evade" the question. He claims to be liberal and conservative; and I must confess he seems the most liberal of any gentleman on that side of the Chamber, always excepting the noble and patriotic speech of the Senator from Connecticut, [Mr. DIXON;] and the utmost extent to which the Senator from Oregon would consent to go, was to devise a scheme by which the real question at issue could be evaded.

I regret the determination, to which I apprehend the Republican Senators have come, to make no adjustment, entertain no proposition, and listen to no compromise of the matters in controversy.

I fear, from all the indications, that they are disposed to treat the matter as a party question, to be determined in caucus with reference to its effects upon the prospects of their party, rather than upon the peace of the country and the safety of the Union. I invoke their deliberate judgment whether it is not a dangerous experiment for any political party to demonstrate to the American people that the unity of their party is dearer to them than the Union of these States. The argument is, that the Chicago platform having been ratified by the people in a majority of the States must be maintained at all hazards, no matter what the consequences to the country. I insist that they are mistaken in the fact when they assert that this question was decided by the American people in the late election. The American people have not decided that they preferred the disruption of this Government, and civil war with all its horrors and miseries, to surrendering one iota of the Chicago platform. If you believe that the people are with you on this issue, let the question be submitted to the people on the proposition offered by the Senator from Kentucky, or mine, or any other fair compromise, and I will venture the prediction that your own people will ratify the proposed amendments to the Constitution, in order to take this slavery agitation out of Congress, and restore peace to the country, and insure the perpetuity of the Union.

Why not give the people a chance? It is an important crisis. There is now a different issue presented from that in the presidential election. I have no doubt that the people of Massachusetts, by an overwhelming majority, are in favor of a prohibition of slavery in the Territories by an act of Congress. An overwhelming majority of the same people were in favor of the instant prohibition of the African slave trade, on moral and religious grounds, when the Constitution was made. When they found that the Constitution could not be adopted and the Union preserved, without surrendering their objections on the slavery question, they, in the spirit of patriotism and of Christian feeling, preferred the lesser evil to the greater, and ratified the Constitution without their favorite provision in regard to slavery. Give them a chance to decide now between the ratification of these proposed amendments to the Constitution and the consequences which your policies will inevitably produce.

Why not allow the people to pass on these questions? All we have to do is to submit them to the States. If the people reject them, theirs will be the responsibility, and no harm will have been done by the reference. If they accept them, the country will be safe, and at peace. The political party which shall refuse to allow to the people to determine for themselves at the ballot-box the issue between revolution and war on the one side, and obstinate adherence to a party platform on the other, will assume a fearful responsibility. A war upon a political issue, waged by the people of eighteen States against the people and domestic institutions of fifteen sister States, is a fearful and revolting thought. The South will be a unit, and desperate, under the belief that your object in waging war is their destruction, and not the preservation of the Union; that you mediate servile insurrection, and the abolition of slavery in the southern States, by fire and sword, in the name and under the pretext of enforcing the laws and vindicating the authority of the Government. You know that such is the prevailing, and, I may say, unanimous opinion at the South; and that ten million people are preparing for the terrible conflict under that conviction.

When there is such an irrepressible discontent pervading ten million people, penetrating the bosom of every man, woman, and child, and, in their estimation, involving everything that is valuable and dear on earth, is it not time to pause and reflect whether there is not some cause, real or imaginary, for apprehension? If there be a just cause for it, in God's name, in the name of humanity and civilization, let it be removed. Will we not be guilty, in the sight of Heaven and posterity, if we do not remove all just cause before proceeding to extremities? If, on the contrary, there be no real foundation for these apprehensions; if it all be a mistake, and yet they, believing it to be a solemn reality, are determined to act on that belief, is it not equally our duty to remove the misapprehension? Hence the obligation to remove the causes of discontent, whether real or imaginary, is alike imperative upon us, if we wish to preserve the peace of the country and the Union of the States.

It matters not, so far as the peace of the country and the preservation of the Union are concerned, whether the apprehensions of the southern people are well founded or not, so long as they believe them, and are determined to act upon that belief. If war comes, it must have an end at some time; and that termination, I apprehend, will be a final separation. Whether the war last one year, seven years, or thirty years, the result must be the same—a cessation of hostilities when the parties become exhausted, and a treaty of peace recognizing the separate independence of each section. The history of the world does not furnish an instance, where war has raged for a series of years between two classes of States, divided by a geographical line under the same national Government, which has ended in reconciliation and reunion. Extermination, subjugation, or separation, one of these three must be the result of the war between the northern and southern States. Surely, you do not expect to exterminate or subjugate ten million people, the entire population of one section, as a means of preserving amicable relations between the two sections!

I repeat, then, my solemn conviction, that war means disunion— final, irrevocable, eternal separation. I see no alternative, therefore, but a fair compromise, founded on the basis of mutual concessions, alike honorable, just, and beneficial to all parties, or civil war and disunion. Is there anything humiliating in a fair compromise of conflicting interests, opinions, and theories, for the sake of peace, union, and safety? Read the debates of the Federal convention, which formed our glorious Constitution, and you will find noble examples, worthy of imitation; instances where sages and patriots were willing to surrender cherished theories and principles of government, believed to be essential to the best form of society, for the sake of peace and unity.

I never understood that wise and good men ever regarded mutual concessions by such men as Washington, Madison, Franklin, and Hamilton, as evidences of weakness, cowardice, or want of patriotism. On the contrary, this spirit of conciliation and compromise has ever been considered, and will in all time be regarded as the highest evidence which their great deeds and immortal services ever furnished of their patriotism, wisdom, foresight, and devotion to their country and their race. Can we not afford to imitate their example in this momentous crisis? Are we to be told that we must not do our duty to our country lest we injure the party; that no compromise can be effected without violating the party platform upon which we were elected? Better that all party platforms be scattered to the winds; better that all political organizations be broken up; better that every public man and politician in America be consigned to political martyrdom, than that the Union be destroyed and the country plunged into civil war.

It seems that party platforms, pride of opinion, personal consistency, fear of political martyrdom, are the only obstacles to a satisfactory adjustment. Have we nothing else to live for but political position? Have we no other inducement, no other incentive to our efforts, our toils, and our sacrifices? Most of us have children, the objects of our tenderest affections and deepest solicitude, whom we hope to leave behind us to enjoy the rewards of our labors in a happy, prosperous, and united country, under the best Government the wisdom of man ever devised or the sun of heaven ever shone upon. Can we make no concessions, no sacrifices, for the sake of our children, that they may have a country to live in, and a Government to protect them, when party platforms and political honors shall avail us nothing in the day of final reckoning?

In conclusion, I have only to renew the assurance that I am prepared to cooperate cordially with the friends of a fair, just, and honorable compromise, in securing such amendments to the Constitution as will expel the slavery agitation from Congress and the arena of Federal politics forever, and restore peace to the country, and preserve our liberties and Union as the most precious legacy we can transmit to our posterity.

8

Pulling Down the Political Temple

Senator Jefferson Davis, Mississippi
January 10, 1861

Jefferson Davis (1808-1889) was born in Kentucky and moved to Mississippi the same year. He attended schools in Kentucky and Mississippi, including Transylvania University in Lexington. He graduated from West Point in 1828, served in the Black Hawk War from 1830-1831, resigned from the military in 1835, and moved to his plantation in Warren County, Mississippi. He was elected to the U.S. House of Representatives in 1845 and resigned in 1846 to command the First Regiment of Mississippi Riflemen during the Mexican War. In 1847 he was appointed to the U.S. Senate and resigned in 1851 to conduct his unsuccessful campaign for governor of Mississippi. He was appointed Secretary of War by President Pierce and served from 1853-1857. In 1857 he was again elected to the Senate and resigned on January 21, 1861. He was chosen by the C.S.A. Provisional Congress to be President of the C.S.A. and was inaugurated on February 18, 1861; later that year he was elected President of the C.S.A. for a six year term and inaugurated on February 22, 1862. On May 10, 1865, he was captured by Union troops, imprisoned, and indicted for treason on May 8, 1866. He was paroled to the custody of the court on May 13, 1867, and a nolle prosequi *was ordered by the U.S. Government in December 1868. In this speech Davis criticized the Senate for discussing abstract questions and reading "patch-work from the opinions of men now mingled with the dust" rather than "manfully" and "patriotically" struggling with the difficulties oppressing the country.*

Mr. DAVIS. Mr. President, when I took the floor yesterday, I intended to engage somewhat in the argument which has heretofore prevailed in the Senate upon the great questions of constitutional right, which have divided the country from the beginning of the Government. I intended to adduce some evidences, which I thought were conclusive, in favor of the opinions which I entertain; but events, with a current hurrying on as it progresses, have borne me past the point where it would be useful for me to argue, by the citing of authorities, the question of rights. Today, therefore, it is my purpose to deal with events. Abstract argument has become among the things that are past. We have to deal now with facts; and in order that we may meet those facts and apply them to our present condition, it is well to inquire what is the state of the country. The Constitution provides that the President shall, from time to time, communicate information of the state of the Union. The message which is now under consideration gives us very little, indeed, beyond that which the world, less, indeed, than reading men generally, knew before it was communicated.

What, Senators, to-day is the condition of the country? From every quarter of it comes the wailing cry of patriotism pleading for the preservation of the great inheritance we derived from our fathers. Is there a Senator who does not daily receive letters appealing to him to use even the small power which one man here possesses to save the rich inheritance our fathers gave us? Tears now trickling down the stern face of man; and those who have bled for the flag of their country, and are willing now to die for it, stand powerless before the plea that the party about to come into power laid down a platform, and that comes what will, though ruin stare us in the face, consistency must be adhered to, even though the Government be lost.

In this state of the case, then, we turn and ask, what is the character of the Administration? What is the executive department doing? What assurance have we there for the safety of the country? But we come back from that inquiry with a mournful conviction that feeble hands now hold the reins of State; that drivelers are taken in as counselors not provided by the Constitution; that vacillation is the law; and the policy of this great Government is changed with every changing rumor of the day; nay more, it is changing with every new phase of causeless fear. In this state of the case, after complications have been introduced into the question, after we were brought to the verge of war, after we were hourly expecting by telegraph to learn that the conflict had commenced, after nothing had been done to insure the peace of the land, we are told in this last hour that the question is thrown at the door of Congress, and here rests the responsibility.

Had the garrison at Charleston, representing the claim of the Government to hold the property in a fort there, been called away thirty days, nay, ten days ago, peace would have spread its pinions over this land, and calm negotiation would have been the order of the day. Why was it not recalled? No reason yet has been offered, save that the Government is bound to preserve its property; and yet look from North to South, from East to West, wherever we have constructed forts to defend States against a foreign foe, and everywhere you find them without a garrison, except at a few points where troops are left for special purposes; not to coerce or threaten a State, but stationed in sea-coast fortifications there merely for the purposes of discipline and instruction as artillerists. You find all the other forts in the hands of fort keepers and ordnance sergeants, and before a moral and patriotic people, standing safely there as the property of the country.

I asked in this Senate weeks ago "what causes the peril that is now imminent at Fort Moultrie; is it the weakness of the garrison?" and then I answered, "no, it is its presence, not its weakness." Had an ordnance sergeant there represented the Federal Government; had there been no troops, no physical power to protect it, I would have pledged my life upon the issue that no question ever would have been made as to its seizure. Now, not only there, but elsewhere, we find movements of troops further to complicate this question, and probably to precipitate us upon the issue of civil war; and worse than all, this Government, reposing on the consent of the governed; this Government, strong in the affections of the people; this Government (I describe it as our fathers made it) is now furtively sending troops to occupy positions lest "the mob" should seize them. When before in the history of our land was it that a mob could resist the sound public opinion of the country? When before was it that an unarmed magistrate had not the power, by crying, "I command the peace," to quell a mob in any portion of the land? Yet now we find, under cover of night, troops detached from one position to occupy another. Fort Washington, standing in its lonely grandeur, and overlooking the home of the Father of his Country, near the place where the ashes of Washington repose, built there to prevent a foreign foe from coming up the Potomac with armed ships to take the capital—Fort Washington is garrisoned by marines sent secretly away from the navy-yard at Washington. And Fort McHenry, memorable in our history as the place where, under bombardment, the star-spangled banner floated through the darkness of night, the point which was consecrated by our national song—Fort McHenry, too, has been garrisoned by a detachment of marines, sent from this place in an extra train, and sent under cover of the night, so that even the mob should not know it.

Senators, the responsibility is thrown at the door of Congress. Let us take it. It is our duty in this last hour to seize the pillars of our Government and uphold them, though we be crushed in the fall. Then what is our policy? Are we to drift into war? Allow an unconfirmed head of a Department to make war? Allow a general of the Army to make war. Allow a President to make war? No, sir. Our fathers gave to Congress the power to make war, and even to Congress they gave no power to make war upon a State of the Union. It could not have been given, except as a power to dissolve the Union. When, then, we see, as is evident to the whole country, that we are drifting into a war between the United States and an individual State, does it become the Senate to sit listlessly by and discuss abstract questions, and read patch-work from the opinions of men now mingled with dust? Are we not bound to meet events as they come before us, manfully and patriotically to struggle with the difficulties which now oppress the country?

In the message yesterday we were even told that the District of Columbia was in danger. In danger of what? From whom comes the danger? Is there a man here who dreads that the deliberations of this body are to be interrupted by an armed force? Is there one who would not prefer to fall with dignity at his station, the representative of a great and peaceful Government, rather than to be protected by armed bands? And yet the rumor is—and rumors seem now to be so authentic that we credit them rather than other means of information—that companies of artillery are to be quartered in this city to preserve peace where the laws have heretofore been supreme, and that this District is to become a camp, by calling out every able-bodied man within its limits to bear arms under militia law. Are we invaded? Is there an insurrection? Are there two Senators here who would not be willing to go forth as a file, and put down any resistance which showed itself in this District against the Government of the United States? Is the reproach meant against these, my friends from the South, who advocate southern rights and State rights? If so, it is a base slander. We claim our rights under the Constitution; we claim our rights reserved to the States; and we seek by no brute force to gain any advantage which the law and the Constitution do not give us. We have never appealed to mobs. We have never asked for the Army and the Navy to protect us. On the soil of Mississippi, not the foot of a Federal soldier has been impressed since 1819, when, flying from the yellow fever, they sought refuge within the limits of our State; and on the soil of Mississippi there breathes not a man who asks for any other protection than that which our Constitution gives us, that which our strong arms afford, and the brave hearts of our people will insure in every contingency.

Senators, we are rapidly drifting into a position in which this is to become a Government of the Army and Navy; in which the authority of the United States is to be maintained, not by law, not by constitutional agreement between the States, but by physical force; and will you stand still and see this policy consummated? Will you fold your arms, the degenerate descendants of those men who proclaimed the eternal principle that government rests on the consent of the governed; and that every people have a right to change, modify, or abolish a Government when it ceases to answer the ends for which it was established, and permit this Government imperceptibly to slide from the moorings where it was originally anchored, and become a military despotism? It was well said by the Senator from New York, whom I do not now see in his seat, [Mr. SEWARD,] well said in a speech, wherein I found but little to commend, that this Union could not be maintained by force, and that a Union of force was a despotism. It was a great truth, come from what quarter it may. That was not the Government instituted by our fathers; and against it, so long as I live, with heart and hand, I will rebel.

This brings me to a great passage in the message, which says:

"I certainly had no right to make aggressive war upon any State; and I am perfectly satisfied that the Constitution has wisely withheld that power from Congress;"—

Very good.

"but the right and the duty to use military force defensively against those who resist the Federal officers in the execution of their legal functions, and against those who assail the power of the Federal

Government, is clear and undeniable."

Is it so? Where does he get it? Our fathers were so jealous of a standing army, that they scarcely would permit the organization and maintenance of any army? Where does he get the "clear and undeniable" power to use the force of the United States in the manner he there proposes? To execute a process, troops may be summoned as a *posse comitatus*; and here, in the history of our Government, it is not to be forgotten that in the earlier, and, as it is frequently said, the better days of the Republic—and painfully we feel that they were better indeed—a President of the United States did not recur to the Army; he went to the people of the United States. Vaguely and confusedly, indeed, did the Senator from Tennessee [Mr. JOHNSON] bring forward the case of the great man, Washington, as one in which he had used a power which, he argued, was equivalent to the coercion of a State; for he said that Washington used the military power against a portion of the people of a State; and why might he not as well as used it against the whole State? Let me tell that Senator that the case of General Washington has no application, as he supposes. It was a case of insurrection within the State of Pennsylvania; and the very message from which he read communicated the fact that Governor Mifflin thought it necessary to call the militia of adjoining States to aid him. President Washington cooperated with Governor Mifflin; he called the militia of adjoining States to cooperate with those of Pennsylvania. He used the militia, not as a standing army. It was by the consent of the Governor; it was by his advice. It was not the invasion of the State; it was not the coercion of the State; but it was aiding the State to put down insurrection, and in the very manner provided for in the Constitution itself.

But, I ask again, what power has the President to use the Army and the Navy except to execute process? Are we to have drum-head courts substituted for those which the Constitution and laws provide? Are we to have sergeants sent over the land instead of civil magistrates? Not so thought the elder Adams; and here, in passing, I will pay him a tribute he deserves, as the one to whom, more than any other man among the early founders of this Government, credit is due for the military principles which prevail in its organization. Associated with Mr. Jefferson originally, in preparing the rules and articles of war, Mr. Adams reverted through the long pages of history back to the empire of Rome, and drew from that foundation the very rules and articles of war which govern in our country to-day, and drew them thence because he said they had brought two nations to the pinnacle of glory—referring to the Romans and the

Britons, whose military law was borrowed from them. Mr. Adams, however, when an insurrection occurred in the same State of Pennsylvania, not only relied upon the militia, but his orders, through Secretary McHenry, required that the militia of the vicinage should be employed; and, though he did order mounted troops from Philadelphia, he required the militia of the northern counties to be employed as long as they were able to execute the laws; and the orders given to Colonel McPherson, then in New Jersey, were, that Federal troops should not go across the Jersey line except in the last resort. I say, then, when we trace our history to its early foundation, under the first two Presidents of the United States, we find that this idea of using the Army and Navy to execute the laws at the discretion of the President, was one not even entertained, still less acted upon, in any case.

Then, Senators, we are brought to consider passing events. A little garrison in the harbor of Charleston now occupies a post which, I am sorry to say, it gained by the perfidious breach of an understanding between the parties concerned; and here, that I may do justice to one who had not the power on this floor, at least, to right himself—who has no friend here to represent him—let me say that remark does not apply to Major Anderson; for I hold that, though his orders were not so designed, as I am assured, they did empower him to go from one post to another, and to take his choice of the posts in the harbor of Charleston; but, in so doing, he committed an act of hostility. When he dismantled Fort Moultrie, when he burned the carriages and spiked the guns bearing upon Fort Sumter, he put Carolina in the attitude of an enemy of the United States; and yet has not shown any just cause for apprehension. Vague rumors had reached him—and causeless fear seems now to be the impelling motive of every public act—vague rumors of an intention to take Fort Moultrie. But, sir, a soldier should be confronted by an overpowering force before he spikes his guns and burns his carriages. A soldier should be confronted by a public enemy before he destroys the property of the United States lest it should fall into the hands of such an enemy. Was that fort built to make war upon Carolina? Was an armament put into it for such a purpose? Or was it built for the protection of Charleston harbor; and was it armed to make that protection complete? If so, what right had any soldier to destroy that armament lest it should fall into the hands of Carolina?

Some time since I presented the Senate resolutions which embodied my views upon this subject, drawing from the Constitution itself the data upon which I based those resolutions. I then invoked the attention of the Senate in that form to the question as to whether garrisons should be kept within a State against the consent of that State. Clear was I then, as I am now, in my conclusion. No garrison should be kept within a State during a time of peace, if the State believes the presence of that garrison to be either offensive or dangerous. Our Army is maintained for common defense; our forts are built out of the common Treasury, to which every State contributes; and they are perverted from the purpose for which they were erected whenever they are garrisoned with a view to threaten, to intimidate, or to control a State in any respect.

Yet we are told this is no purpose to coerce a State; we are told the power does not exist to coerce a State; but the Senator from Tennessee [Mr. JOHNSON] says it is only a power to coerce individuals; and the Senator from Ohio [Mr. WADE] seems to look upon this latter power as a very harmless power in the hands of the President, though such coercion would be to destroy the State. What is a State? Is it land and houses? Is it taxable property? Is it the organization of local government? Or is it all these combined, with the people who possess them? Destroy the people, and yet not make war upon a State! To state the proposition is to answer it, by reason of its very absurdity. It is like making desolation and calling it peace.

There being, as it is admitted on every hand, no power to coerce a State, I ask what is the use of a garrison within a State where it needs no defense? The answer from every candid mind must be, there is none. The answer from every patriotic breast must be, peace requires, under all such circumstances, that the garrison should be withdrawn. Let the Senate to-day, as the responsibility is thrown at our door, pass those resolutions, or others which better express the idea contained in them, and you have taken one long step towards peace, one long stride towards the preservation of the Government of our fathers.

The President's message of December, however, had all the characteristics of a diplomatic paper, for diplomacy is said to abhor certainty, as nature abhors a vacuum; and it was not within the power of man to reach any fixed conclusion from that message. When the country was agitated, when opinions were being formed, when we are drifting beyond the power ever to return, this was not what we had a right to expect from the Chief Magistrate. One policy or the other he ought to have taken. If a federalist [sic], if believing this to be a Government of force, if believing it to be a consolidated mass and not a confederation of States, he should have said: no State has a right to secede; every State is subordinate to the Federal Government, and the Federal Government must empower me with physical means to reduce to subjugation the State asserting such a right. If not, if a State-rights man and a Democrat—as for many years it has been my pride to acknowledge our venerable Chief Magistrate to be—then another line of policy should have been taken. The Constitution gave no power to the Federal Government to coerce a State; the Constitution gave an army for the purposes of common defense, and to preserve domestic tranquillity; but the Constitution never contemplated using that army against a State. A State exercising the sovereign function of secession is beyond the reach of the Federal Government, unless we woo her with the voice of fraternity, and bring her back to the enticements of affection. One policy or the other should have been taken; and it is not for me to say which, though my opinion is well known; but one policy or the other should have been pursued. He should have brought his opinion to one conclusion or another, and to-day our country would have been safer than it is.

What is the message before us? Does it benefit the case? is there a solution offered here? We are informed in it of propositions made by commissioners from South Carolina. We are not informed even as to how they terminated. No countervailing proposition is presented; no suggestion is made. We are left drifting loosely, without chart or compass.

There is in our recent history, however, an event which might have suggested a policy to be pursued. When foreigners, having no citizenship within the United States, declared war against it, and made war upon it; when the inhabitants of a Territory disgraced by institutions offensive to the law of every State of the Union held this attitude of rebellion; when the Executive there had power to use troops, he first sent commissioners of peace to win them back to their duty. When South Carolina, a sovereign State, resumes the grants she had delegated; when South Carolina stands in an attitude which threatens within a short period to involve the country in a civil war, unless the policy of the Government be changed—no suggestion is made to us that this Government might send commissioners to her; no suggestion is made to us that better information should be sought; there is no policy of peace, but we are told the Army and the Navy are in the hands of the President of the United States, to be used against those who assail the power of the Federal Government.

Then, my friends, are we to allow events to drift onward to this fatal consummation? Are we to do nothing to restore peace? Shall we not, in addition to the proposition I have already made, to withdraw the force which complicates the question, send commissioners there in order that we may learn what this community may desire, what this community will do, and put the two Governments upon friendly relations?

I will not weary the Senate by going over the argument of coercion. My friend from Ohio, [Mr. PUGH,] I may say, has exhausted the subject. I thank him, because it came appropriately from one not identified by his position with South Carolina. It came more effectively from him than it would have done from me, had I (as I have not) a power to present it as forcibly as he has done. Sirs, let me say, among the painful reflections which have crowded me by day and by night, none weighed more heavily upon my heart than the reflection that our separation severs the ties which have so long bound us to our northern friends, of whom we are glad to recognize the Senator as a type.

Now let us return a moment to consider what would have been the state of the case if the garrison at Charleston had been withdrawn. The fort would have stood there—not dismantled, but unoccupied. It would have stood there in the hands of an ordnance sergeant. Commissioners would have come to treat of all questions with the Federal Government, of these forts as well as others. They would have remained there to answer the ends for which they were constructed—the ends of defense. If South Carolina was an independent State, then she might hold to us such a relation as Rhode Island held the dissolution of the Confederation and before the formation of the Union, when Rhode Island appealed to the sympathies existing between the States connected in the struggle of the Revolution, and asked that a commercial war should not be waged upon her. These forts would have stood there then to cover the harbor of a friendly State; and if the feeling which once existed among the people of the States had subsisted still, and that fort had been attacked, brave men from every section would have rushed to the rescue, and there imperiled their lives in the defense of a State identified with their early history, and still associated in their breasts with affection; and the first act of this time would have been one appealing to every generous motive of those people again to reconsider the question of how we could live together, and through that bloody ordeal to have brought us into the position in which our fathers left us. There could have been no collision; there could have been no question of property which that State was not ready to meet. If it was a question of dollars and cents, they came here to adjust it. If it was a question of covering an interior State, their interests were identical. In whatever way the question could have been presented, the consequences would have been to relieve the Government of the charge of maintaining the fort, and to throw it upon the State which had resolved to be independent.

Thus we see that no evil could have resulted. We have yet to learn what evil the opposite policy may bring. Telegraphic intelligence, by the man who occupied the seat on the right of me in the old Chamber, was never relied on. He was the wisest man I ever knew—a man whose prophetic vision foretold all the trials through which we are now passing; whose clear intellect elaborating everything, borrowing nothing from anybody, seemed to dive into the future, and to unveil those things which are hidden to other eyes. Need I say I mean Calhoun? No other man than he would have answered this description. I say, then, not relying upon telegraphic dispatches, we still have information enough to notify us that we are on the verge of civil war; that civil war is in the hands of men irresponsible, as it seems to us; their acts unknown to us; their discretion not covered by any existing law or usage; and we now have the responsibility thrown upon us, which justifies us in demanding information to meet an emergency in which the country is involved.

Is there any point of pride which prevents us from withdrawing that garrison? I have heard it said by a gallant gentleman, to whom I make no special reference, that the great objection was an unwillingness to lower the flag. To lower the flag! Under what circumstances? Does any man's courage impel him to stand boldly forth to take the life of his brethren? Does any man insist upon going upon the open field with deadly weapons to fight his brother on a question of courage? There is no point of pride. These are your brethren; and they have shed as much glory upon that flag as any equal number of men in the Union. They are the men, and that is the locality, where the first Union flag was unfurled, and where was fought a gallant battle before our independence was declared—not the flag with thirteen stripes and thirty-three stars, but a flag with a cross of St. George, and the long stripes running through it. When the gallant Moultrie took the British Fort Johnson, and carried it, for the first time, I believe, did the Union flag fly in the air; and that was in October, 1775. When he took the position and threw up a temporary battery with palmetto logs and sand, upon the sight called Fort Moultrie, that fort was assailed by the British fleet, and bombarded until the old logs, clinging with stern tenacity to the enemy that assailed them, were filled with balls, the flag still floated there, and though many bled, the garrison conquered. Those old logs are gone; the eroding current is even taking away the site where Fort Moultrie stood; the gallant men who held it, now mingle with the earth; but their memories live in the hearts of a gallant people, and their sons yet live, and they, like their fathers, are ready to bleed and to die for the cause in which their fathers triumphed. Glorious are the memories clinging around that old fort which now, for the first time, has been abandoned—abandoned not even at the presence of a foe, but under the imaginings that a foe might come; and guns spiked and carriages burned where the band of Moultrie bled, and, with an insufficient armament, repelled the common foe of all the colonies. Her ancient history compares proudly with the present.

Can there, then, be a point of pride upon so sacred a soil as this, where the blood of the fathers cries to Heaven against civil war? Can there be a point of pride against laying upon that sacred soil to-day the flag for which our fathers died? My pride, Senators, is different. My pride is that that flag shall not be set between contending brothers; and that, when it shall no longer be the common flag of the country, it shall be folded up and laid away like a vesture no longer used; that it shall be kept as a sacred momento of the past, to which each of us can make a pilgrimage, and remember the glorious days in which we were born.

In the answer of the commissioners, which I caused to be read yesterday, I observed that they referred to Fort Sumter as remaining a momento of Carolina faith. It is an instance of the accuracy of the opinion which I have expressed. It stood without a garrison. It commanded the harbor, and the fort was known to have the armament in it capable of defense. Did the Carolinian attack it? Did they propose to seize it? It stood there safe as public property; and there it might have stood to the end of negotiations without a question, if a garrison had not been sent into it. It was the faith on which they relied, that the Federal Government would take no position of hostility to them, that constituted its safety, and by which they lost the advantage they would have had in seizing it when unoccupied. I think that something is due to faith as well as fraternity; and I think that one of the increasing and accumulative obligations upon us to withdraw the garrison from that fort is from the manner in which it was taken—taken, as we heard by reading the paper yesterday, while Carolina remained under the assurance that the *status* would not be violated; while I was under the assurance, and half a dozen other Senators now within the sound of my voice felt secure under the same pledge, that nothing would be done until negotiations had terminated, unless it was to withdraw the garrison. Then we, the Federal Government, broke the faith; we committed the first act of hostility; and from this first act of hostility arose all those acts to which reference is made in the message as unprovoked aggression—the seizing of forts elsewhere. Why were they seized? Self-preservation is the first law of nature; and when they no longer had confidence that this Federal

Government would not seize the forts constructed for their defense, and use them for their destruction, they only obeyed the dictates of self-preservation when they seized the forts to prevent the enemy from taking possession of them as a means of coercion, for they then were compelled to believe this Federal Government had become an enemy.

Now, what is the remedy? To assure them that you do not intend to use physical force against them is your first remedy; to assure them that you intend to consider calmly all the propositions which they make, and to recognize the rights which the Union was established to secure; that you intend to settle with them upon a basis in accordance with the Declaration of Independence and the Constitution of the United States. When you do that, peace will prevail over the land, and force become a thing that no man will consider necessary.

I am here confronted with a question which I will not argue. The position which I have taken necessarily brings me to its consideration. Without arguing it, I will merely state it. It is a right of a State to withdraw from the Union. The President says it is not a constitutional right. The Senator from Ohio, [Mr. WADE,] and his ally, the Senator from Tennessee, argued it as no right at all. Well, let us see. What is meant by a constitutional right? Is it meant to be a right derived from the Constitution—a grant made in the Constitution? If that is what is meant, of course we all see at once we do not derive it in that way. Is it intended that it is not a constitutional right, because it is not granted in the Constitution? That shows, indeed, but a poor appreciation of the nature of our Government. All that is not granted in the Constitution belongs to the States; and nothing but what is granted in the Constitution belongs to the Federal Government; and keeping this distinction in view, it requires but little argument to see the conclusion at which we necessarily arrive. Did the States surrender their sovereignty to the Federal Government? Did the States agree that they never could withdraw from the Federal Union?

I know it has been argued here, that the Confederation said the Articles of Confederation were to be a perpetual bond of Union, and that the Constitution was made to form a more perfect Union; that is to say, a Government beyond perpetuity; or one day, or two or three days after doomsday. But that has no foundation in the Constitution itself; it has no basis in the nature of our Government. The Constitution was a compact between independent States; it was not a national Government; and hence Mr. Madison answered with such effectiveness to Patrick Henry, in the convention of Virginia, which ratified the Constitution, denying his proposition that it was to form a nation, and stating to him the conclusive fact, that "we sit here as a convention of the States to ratify or reject that Constitution; and how then can you say that it forms a nation, and is adopted by the mass of the people?" It was not adopted by the mass of the people, as we all know, historically; it was adopted by each State; each State voluntarily ratifying it, entered the Union; and that Union was formed whenever nine States should enter it; and in abundance of caution, it was stated in the resolutions of ratification of three of the States, that they still possessed the power to withdraw the grants which they had delegated, whenever they should be used to their injury or oppression. I know it is said that this meant the people of all of the States; but that is such an absurdity that I suppose it hardly necessary to answer it; or to speak of an elective government rendering itself injurious and oppressive to the whole body of the people by whom it is elected is such an absurdity, that no man can believe it; and to suppose that a State convention, speaking for a State, having no authority to speak for anybody else, to say that it was declaring what the people of the other States would do, would be an assumption altogether derogatory to the sound sense and well-known sentiments of the men who formed the Constitution and ratified it.

But in abundance of caution not only was this done, but the tenth amendment [sic] of the Constitution declared that all which had not been delegated was reserved to the States or to the people. Now, I ask where among the delegated grants to the Federal Government do you find any power to coerce a State; where among the provisions of the Constitution do you find any prohibition on the part of a State to withdraw; and if you find neither one nor the other, must not this power be in the great depository, the reserved rights of the States? How was it ever taken out of that source of all power to the Federal Government? It was not delegated to the Federal Government; it was not prohibited to the States; it necessarily remains, then, among the reserved powers of the States.

This question has been so forcibly argued by the Senator from Louisiana, [Mr. BENJAMIN,] that I think it unnecessary to pursue it. Three times the proposition was made to give power to coerce a State, in the convention, and as often refused; opposed as a proposition to make war on a State, and refused on the ground that the Federal Government could not make war upon a State. The Constitution was to form a Government for such States as should unite; it had no application beyond those who should voluntarily adopt it. Among the delegated powers there is none which interferes with the exercise of the right of secession by a

State. As a right of sovereignty it remained to the States under the Confederation; and if it did not, you arraign the faith of the men who framed the Constitution to which you appeal, for they provided that nine States could secede from thirteen. Eleven did secede from the thirteen, and put themselves in the very position which, by a great abuse of language, is to-day called treason, against the two States of North Carolina and Rhode Island, they still claiming to adhere to the perpetual Articles of Confederation, these eleven States absolving themselves from the obligations which arose under them.

The Senator from Tennessee, to whom I must refer again—and I do so because he is a southern Senator—taking the most hostile ground against us, refers to the State of Tennessee, and points to the time when that State may do those things which he has declared it an absurdity for any State to perform. I will read a single paragraph from his speech, showing what his language is, in order that I may not, by any possibility, produce an impression upon others which his language does not justify. Here are the expressions to which I refer. I call the Senator's attention to them:

> If there are grievances, why cannot we all go together, and write them down, and point them out to our northern friends after we have agreed on what those grievances were, and say, 'here is what we demand; here our wrongs are enumerated; upon these terms we have agreed; and now, after we have given you a reasonable time to consider these additional guarantees in order to protect ourselves against these wrongs, if you refuse them, then, having made an honorable effort—having exhausted all other means—we may declare the association to be broken up, and we may go into an act of revolution?' We can then say to them, 'you have refused to give us guarantees that we think are needed for the protection of our institutions and for the protection of our other interests.' When they do this, I will go as far as he who goes the furthest.

Now, it does appear that he will go that far; and he goes a little further than anybody, I believe, who has spoken in vindication of the right, for he says:

> We do not intend that you shall drive us out of this house that was reared by the hands of our fathers. It is our house. It is the constitutional house. We have a right here, and because you come forward and violate the ordinances of this house, I do not intend to go out; and if you persist in the violation of the ordinances of the house, we intend to eject you from the building and retain the possession ourselves.

I wonder if this is what caused the artillery companies to be ordered here, and the militia of this city to be organized. I think it was a mere figure of speech. I do not believe the Senator from Tennessee intended to kick you out of the house; and if he did, let me say to you, in all sincerity, we who claim the constitutional right of a State to withdraw from the union, do not intend to help him. He says, however, and this softens it a little:

> We do not think, though, that we have a just cause for going out of the Union now. We have just cause of complaint; but we are for remaining in the Union, and fighting the battle like men.

What does that mean? In the name of common sense, I ask how are we to fight in the Union? We take an oath of office to maintain the Constitution of the United States. The Constitution of the United States was formed for domestic tranquillity; and how, then, are we to fight in the Union? I have heard the proposition from others; but I have not understood it. I understand how men fight when they assume attitudes of hostility; but I do not understand how men remaining connected together in a bond as brethren, sworn to mutual aid and protection, still propose to fight each other. I do not understand what the Senator means. If he chooses to answer my question, I am willing to hear him, for I do not understand how we are to fight in the Union.

Mr. JOHNSON, of Tennessee. When my speech is taken altogether, I think my meaning can be very easily understood. What I mean by fighting the battle in the Union, is, I think, very distinctly and clearly set forth in my speech; and if the Senator will take it from beginning to end, I apprehend that he will have no difficulty in ascertaining what I meant. But, for his gratification upon this particular point, I will repeat, in substance, what I then said as to fighting the battle in the Union. I meant that we should remain here under the Constitution of the United States, and contend for all its guarantees; and by preserving the Constitution and all its guarantees we would preserve the Union. Our true place to maintain these guarantees, and to preserve the Constitution, is in the Union, there to fight our battle. How? By argument; by appeals to the patriotism, to the good sense, and to the judgment of the whole country; by showing the people that the Constitution has been violated; that all its guarantees were not complied with; and I have entertained the hope that when they were possessed of the fact, there would be found patriotism and honesty enough in the great mass of the people, north and south, to come forward and do what was just and right between the contending sections of the country. I meant that the true way to fight the battle was for us to remain here and occupy the places assigned to us by the Constitution of the country. Why did I make that statement? It was because, on the 4th day of March next, we shall have six majority in this body; and if, as some apprehended, the incoming Administration shall show any disposition to make encroachments upon the institution of slavery, encroachments upon the rights of the States, or any other violation of the Constitution, we, by remaining in the Union, and standing at our places, will have the power to resist all these encroachments. How? We have the power even to reject the appointment of the Cabinet officers of the incoming President. Then, should we not be fighting the battle in the Union, by resisting even the organization of the Administration in a constitutional mode; and thus, at the very start, disable an Administration which was likely to encroach on our rights and to violate the Constitution of the country? So far as appointing even a minister abroad is concerned, the incoming Administration will have no power without our consent, if we remain here. It comes into office handcuffed, powerless to do harm. We, standing here, hold the balance of power in our hands; we can resist it at the very threshold effectually; and do it inside of the Union, and in our house. The incoming Administration has not even the power to appoint a postmaster whose salary exceeds $1,000 a year, without consultation with, and the acquiescence of, the Senate of the United States. The President has not even the power to draw his salary—his $25,000 per annum—unless we appropriate it. I contend, then, that the true place to fight the battle is in the Union, and within the provisions of the Constitution. The Army and Navy cannot be sustained without appropriations by Congress; and if we were apprehensive that encroachments would be made on the southern States and on their institutions, in violation of the Constitution, we could prevent him from having a dollar even to feed his Army or his Navy.

Mr. DAVIS. I receive the answer from the Senator, and I think I comprehend now that he is not going to use any force, but it is a sort of fighting that is to be done by votes and words; and I think, therefore, the President need not bring artillery and order out the militia to suppress them. I think, altogether, we are not in danger of much bloodshed in the mode proposed by the Senator from Tennessee.

Mr. JOHNSON, of Tennessee. I had not quite done; but if the Senator is satisfied—

Mr. DAVIS. Quite satisfied. I am entirely satisfied that the answer of the Senator shows me he did not intend to fight at all; that it was a mere figure of speech, and does not justify converting the Federal capital into a military camp. But it is a sort of revolution which he proposes; it is a revolution under the forms of the Government. Now, I have to say, once for all, that, as long as I am a Senator here, I will not use the powers I possess to destroy the very Government to which I am accredited. I will not attempt, in the language of the Senator, to handcuff the President. I will not attempt to destroy the Administration by refusing any officers to administer its functions. I should vote, as I have done to Administrations to which I stood in nearest relation, against a bad nomination; but I never would agree, under the forms of the Constitution, and with the powers I bear as a Senator of the United States, to turn those powers to the destruction of the Government I was sworn to support. I leave that to gentlemen who take the oath with a mental reservation. It is not my policy. If I must have revolution, I say let it be a revolution such as our fathers made when they were denied their natural rights.

So much for that. It has quieted apprehension; and I hope the artillery will not be brought here; that the militia will not be called out; and that female schools will continue their sessions as heretofore. [Laughter.] The authority of Mr. Madison, however, was relied on by the Senator from Tennessee; and he read fairly an extract from Mr. Madison's letter to Mr. Webster, and I give him credit for reading what it seems to me destroys his whole argument. It is this clause:

> The powers of the Government being exercised, as in other elective and responsible Governments, under the control of its constituents, the people, and the Legislatures of the States, and subject to the revolutionary rights of the people in extreme cases.

Now, sir, we are confusing language very much. Men speak of revolution; and when they say revolution, they mean blood. Our fathers meant nothing of the sort. When they spoke of revolution, they spoke of an inalienable right. When they declared as an inalienable right the power of the people to abrogate and modify their form of Government whenever it did not answer the ends for which it was established, they did not mean that they were to sustain that by brute force. They meant that it was a right; and force could only be invoked when that right was wrongfully denied. Great Britain denied the right in the case of the colonies; and therefore our revolution for independence was bloody. If Great Britain had admitted the great American doctrine, there would have been no blood shed; and does it become the descendants of those who proclaimed this as the great principle on which they took their place among the nations of the earth, now to proclaim, if that is a right, it is one you can only get as the subjects of the Emperor of Austria may get their rights, by force overcoming force? Are we, in this age of civilization and political progress, when political philosophy had advanced to the point which seemed to render it possible that the millennium should now be seen by prophetic eyes; are we now to roll back the whole current of human thought, and again to return to the mere brute force which prevails between beasts of prey, as the only method of settling questions between men?

If the Declaration of Independence be true, (and who here gainsays it?) every community may dissolve its connection with any other community previously made, and have no other obligation than that which results from the breach of any alliance between States. Is it to be supposed; could any man reasoning *a priori* come to the conclusion that men who fought the battles of the Revolution for community independence—that the men who struggled against the then greatest military Power on the face of the globe in order that they might possess those inalienable rights which they had declared—terminated their great efforts by transmitting posterity to a condition in which they could only gain those rights by force? If so, the blood of the Revolution was shed in vain; no great principles were established; for force was the law of nature before the battles of the Revolution were fought.

I see, then—if gentlemen insist on using the word "revolution" in the sense of a resort to force—a very great difference between their opinion and that of Mr. Madison. Mr. Madison put the rights of the people over and above everything else; and he said this was the Government *de jure* and *de facto*. Call it what name you will, he understood ours to be a Government of the people. The people never have separated themselves from those rights which our fathers had declared to be inalienable. They did not delegate to the Federal Government the powers which the British Crown exercised over the colonies; they did not achieve their independence for any purpose so low as that. They left us to the inheritance of freemen, living in independent communities, the States united for the purposes which they thought would bless posterity. It is in the exercise of this reserved right as defined by Mr. Madison, as one to which all the powers of Government are subject; that the people of a State in convention have claimed to resume the functions which in like manner they had made to the Federal Government.

I pass from the argument of this question, which I have previously said I did not intend to enter into at large, to ask, why is the right denied? It is part of the history of our times, it is part of the condition of the country, that the right is denied, because this conflict between the sections, in which one was struggling for domination, the other for existence, has been brought to the point where the dominant section insists that it will hold the other for its purposes; where it claims that we shall not go in peace, nor remain with our rights; and if the attempt be made to hold that position by force, we accept the wager of battle.

Mississippi, in her brief history, claims to have shown at Pensacola and New Orleans something of the spirit of the freemen who achieved our independence. I was reared in a county where, when the soil of a neighboring State was invaded by a powerful foe, the draft was who should stay at home, not who should go. I also have the satisfaction to know that the present generation have not derogated from the history of those who went before it. From many a bloody field, both in foreign and Indian war, has ascended the proud spirit of a Mississippian enshrined in glory, whence they look down upon us to vindicate the honorable fame of our State; and every heart beats true to the impulse of pride and the dictate of duty. If this right were admitted, we should have less cause to exercise it than we have. If admitted, there would be less danger from a dominant section than there is; there would be less tendency to use power, when it was acquired, to the injury of others. The denial of the right is a grievance inflicted on all who fear that power will be used for aggression. The concession of the right might delay its exercise; and at the same time would restrain the dominant section from abusing its power so as to drive others to resort to it. Why is the right denied? It is an impractical question at best. If you take us out of the history of our country, throw us into a broad discussion of the natural rights of man, we may answer by the facts which are being enacted. States have gone out; and what is the use of arguing their right? The only questions which remain are for yourselves: first, have you the right to coerce them back? and secondly, have you the power?

My friend from Louisiana, in closing his remarks, referred to the disastrous scenes which might be occasioned by the invasion of the South. He did not offer the other side of the picture; and yet I have seen that, in northern papers, he has been criticized for saying even what he did. There is, however, another side to the picture. An army with banners would do but little harm in marching through a country of plantations. They would have but little power to bring away prisoners and fugitives. How stands it on the other side? In a country of populous cities, of manufacturing towns, where population is gathered from the country to the towns and villages, the torch and the sword can do their work with dreadful havoc, and starving millions would weep at the stupidity of those who had precipitated them into so sad a policy.

We do not desire these things. We seek not the injury of any one. We seek not to disturb your prosperity. We, at least to a great extent, have from time to time looked to our agricultural labor as to that to which we prefer to adhere. We have seen, in the diversity of the occupation of the States, the bond of Union. We have rejoiced in your prosperity. We have sent you our staples, and purchased your manufactured articles. We have used your ships for the purpose of transport and navigation. We have gloried in the extension of American commerce everywhere; have felt proud as yourselves in every achievement you made in art; on every sea that you carried your flag in regions to which it had hitherto not been borne; and, if we must leave you, we can leave you still with the good-will which would prefer that your prosperity should continue. If we must part, I say we can put our relations upon that basis which will give you the advantage of a favored trade with us, and still make the intercourse mutually beneficial to each other. If you will not, then it is an issue from which we will not shrink; for, between oppression and freedom, between the maintenance of right and submission to power, we will invoke the God of battles, and meet our fate, whatever it may be.

I was reading, a short time ago, an extract from the speech of the Senator from Tennessee which referred to the time when "we"—I suppose it means Tennessee—would take the position which was said to be an absurdity for South Carolina to hold. How can the change of names thus affect the question; and who is to judge in the case? Tennessee still was put, in the same speech, in the attitude of a great objector against the exercise and right of secession. Is there anything in her history which thus places her? Tennessee, born of secession, rocked in the cradle of revolution, taking her position before she was matured, and claiming to be a State because she had violently severed her connection with North Carolina, and through an act of secession and revolution to have become a State. I honor her for it. I honor the gallant old Sevier for maintaining the rights of which North Carolina attempted to deprive him, and I admire the talent which made recruits from every army which was sent to subdue him. Washington and Jackson, too, are often presented as authority against it—Washington, who led the army of the Revolution; Washington, whose reputation rests upon the fact that with the sword he cut the cord which bound the colonies to Great Britain; they not having the justification of the sovereign attributes belonging to States; Washington, who presided when the States seceded from the Confederation, and formed the Union, in disregard of the claims of the States not agreeing to it; and Jackson, glorious old soldier, who, in his minority, upon the sacred sod of South Carolina, bled for the cause of revolution and the overthrow of a Government which he believed to be oppressive; who, through his whole life, indicated the same cast of character, standing in an attitude which to-day would be called rebellion and treason, when he opposed the Federal Government, denied their power, condemned their orders to disband his troops, threatened to put any officer in irons who came into his camp to recruit, and marched his force, the Tennessee militia, back from Washington in Mississippi, to the place whence they had started. Bad authorities are these for our opponents; yet they are the names under the shadow of which we can safely repose!

If we were reduced to arguing the question on the ground of expediency; if we had to convince the dominant section that it was good for them that their best customers should leave them; if we had to convince them that they should not any longer have the power to tax us, that they should not collect the revenue which fills the Treasury and builds up their vast public works, I fear we should not succeed; but if they are sincere in believing that we are of no advantage to them; if they look upon the southern States as a burden; if they think we require their protection, then we are ready to relieve them.

The question which now presents itself to the country is, what shall we do with events as they stand? Shall we allow this separation to be total? Shall we render it peaceful, with a view to the chance that when hunger shall brighten the intellects of men, and the teaching of hard experience shall have tamed them, they may come back, in the spirit of our fathers, to the task of reconstruction? Or will they have that separation partial; will they give to each State all its military power; will they give to each State its revenue power; will they still preserve the common agent; and will they thus carry on a Government different from that which now exists, yet not separating the States so entirely as to make the work of reconstruction equal to a new creation; not separating them so as to render it utterly impossible to administer any functions of the Government in security and peace?

I waive the question of duality, considering that a dual Executive would be the institution of a king-lord. I consider a dual legislative department would be to bring into antagonism the representatives of two different countries, and thus to continue not a union, but the irrepressible conflict. There is no duality possible (unless there be two Confederacies) which seems to me consistent with the interests of either or both. It might be that two Confederacies could be so organized as to answer jointly many of the ends of our present Union; it might be that States, agreeing with each other in their internal polity—having a similarity of interests and an identity of purpose—might associate together; and that these two Confederacies might have relations to each other so close as to give them a united power in time of war against any foreign nation. These things are possibilities; these things it becomes us to contemplate; these things it devolves on the majority section to consider now; for with every motion of that clock is passing away your opportunity. It was greater when we met on the first Monday in December than it is now; it is greater now than it will be on the first day of next week. We have waited long; we have come to the conclusion that you mean to do nothing. In the committee of thirteen, where the resolutions of the Senator from Kentucky [Mr. CRITTENDEN] were considered, various attempts were made, but no prospect of any agreement on which it was possible for us to stand, in security for the future, could be matured. I offered a proposition, which was but the declaration of that which the Constitution announces; but that which the Supreme Court had, from time to time, and from an early period, asserted; but that which was necessary for equality in the Union. Not one single vote of the Republican portion of that committee was given for the proposition.

Looking then upon separation as inevitable, not knowing how that separation is to occur, or at least what States it is to embrace, there remains to us, I believe, as the consideration which is most useful, the inquiry, how can this separation be effected so as to leave to us the power, whenever we shall have the will, to reconstruct? It can only be done by adopting a policy of peace. It can only be done by denying to the Federal Government all power to coerce. It can only be done by returning to the point from which we started, and saying, "This is a Government of fraternity, a Government of consent; and it shall not be administered in a departure from those principles."

I do not regard the failure of our constitutional Union, as very many do, to be the failure of self-government; to be conclusive in all future time of the unfitness of man to govern himself. Our State governments have charge of nearly all the relations of personal property. This Federal Government was instituted mainly as a common agent for foreign purposes, for free trade among the States, and for common defense. Representative liberty will remain in the States after they are separated. Liberty was not crushed by the separation of the colonies from the mother country, then the most constitutional monarchy and the freest Government known. Still less will liberty be destroyed by the separation of these States to prevent the destruction of the spirit of the Constitution by the maladministration of it. There will be injury—injury to all; differing in degree, differing in manner. The injury to the manufacturing and navigating States will be to their internal prosperity. The injury to the southern States will be mainly to their foreign commerce. All will feel the deprivation of that high pride and power which belong to the flag now representing the greatest Government, upon the face of the globe. I would that it still remained to consider what we might calmly have considered on the first Monday in December—how this could be avoided; but events have rolled past that point. You would not make propositions when they would have been effective. I presume you will not make them now; and I know not what effect they would have if you did. Your propositions would have been most welcome if they had been made before any question of coercion, and before any vain boasting of power; for pride and passion do not often take counsel of pecuniary interest, at least among those whom I represent. But you have chosen to take the policy of clinging to words, in disregard of events, and have hastened them onwards. It is true, as shown by the history of all revolutions, that they are most precipitated and intensified by obstinacy and vacillation. The want of a policy, the obstinate adherence to unimportant things, have brought us to a condition where I close my eyes, because I cannot see anything that encourages me to hope.

In the long period which elapsed after the downfall of the great Republics of the East, when despotism seemed to brood over the civilized world, and only here and there constitutional monarchy even was able to rear its head; when all the great principles of republican and representative government had sunk deep, fathomless, into the sea of human events; it was then that the storm of our Revolution moved the waters. The earth, the air, and the sea, became brilliant; and from the foam of the ages rose the constellation which was set in the political firmament as a sign of unity and confederation and community independence, coexistent with confederate strength. That constellation has served to bless our people. Nay, more; its light had been thrown on foreign lands, and its regenerative power will outlive, perhaps, the Government as a sign for which it was set. It may be pardoned to me, sir, who, in my boyhood, was given to the military service, and who have followed under the tropical suns, and over northern snows, the flag of the Union, suffering from it as it does not become me to speak it, if I here express the deep sorrow which always overwhelms me when I think of taking a last leave of that object of early affection and proud association, feeling that henceforth it is not to be the banner which, by day and night, I am ready to follow, to hail with the rising and bless with the setting sun. But God, who knows the hearts of men, will judge between you and us, at whose door lies the responsibility of this. Men will see the efforts I have made, here and elsewhere; that I have been silent when words would not avail, and have curbed an impatient temper, and hoped that conciliatory counsels might do that which I knew could not be effected by harsh means. And yet the only response which has come from the other side has been a stolid indifference, as though it mattered not, "let the temple fall, we do not care." Sirs, remember that such conduct is offensive, and that men may become indifferent even to the objects of their early attachments.

If our Government should fail, it will not be the defect of the system, though its mechanism was wonderful, surpassing that which the solar system furnishes for our contemplation; for it had no center of gravitation; each planet was set to revolve in an orbit of its own, each moving by its own impulse, and all attracted by the affections which countervailed each other. It has been the perversion of the Constitution; it has been the substitution of theories of morals for principles of government; it has been forcing crude opinions about things not understood upon the domestic institutions of other men, which has disturbed these planets in their orbit; it is this which threatens to destroy the constellation which, in its power and its glory, has been gathering one after another, until, from thirteen, it had risen to thirty-three stars.

If we accept the argument of to-day in favor of coercion as the theory of our Government, its only effect will be to precipitate men who have pride and self-reliance into the assertion of the freedom and independence to which they were born. Our fathers would never have entered into a confederate Government which had within itself the power of coercion. I would not agree to remain one day in such a Government after I had the power to get out of it. To argue that a man who follows the mandate of his State, resuming her sovereign jurisdiction and power, is disloyal to his allegiance to the United States, which allegiance he only owed through his State, is such a confusion of ideas as does not belongs to an ordinary comprehension of our Government. It is treason to the principle of community independence. It is to recur to that doctrine of passive obedience which, in England, cost one monarch his head, and drove another into exile; a doctrine which, since the revolution of 1688, has obtained nowhere where men speak the English tongue; and yet all this it is needful to admit before we accept this doctrine of coercion, which is to send an Army and a Navy to do that which there are no courts to perform; to execute the law without a judicial decision, and without an officer to serve process. This, I say, would degrade us to the basest despotism under which man could live; the despotism of a many-headed monster, without the sensibility or regardful consideration which might belong to a hereditary king.

But the Senator found somewhere, I believe in Georgia, a newspaper article which suggested the advantages of a constitutional monarchy. Does the Senator believe there is any considerable number of people in any of the States who favor the establishment of a constitutional monarchy? If so, let me at once, speaking with that assurance which is given to me by those knowing more of that people than myself, say that the apprehension is vain. I am sure that the same feeling prevails in that State as my own; the same which exists in his State of Tennessee; and in each of them there are many like the Lucius Junius—

—"that would have brooked
The eternal Devil to keep his state in Rome,
As easily as a King"

Mr. IVERSON. As illusion has been made by the Senator from Mississippi to an article which appeared in a paper in my own town, and about which a good deal of noise has been made, and which was referred to by the Senator from Tennessee, in his celebrated speech, the other day, as evidence that there was a party in the South in favor of a constitutional monarchy, I take the liberty to say that that was a communication merely to the paper, and that it slipped in without the knowledge and consent of the proprietors of the paper; and in the very next paper the editors disclaimed and denounced it. I will take the opportunity to say, in conjunction with what the Senator from Mississippi has said, that there is not one man in a million, as far as I know and believe, in the State of Georgia, or elsewhere in the South, who would be in favor of any such principle.

Mr. DAVIS. If, Mr. President, a paper containing such a doctrine could subsist upon subscription anywhere in the United States, I should esteem it nearly as bad an indication as the adoption of the doctrine of slavish submission; and either the one or the other I should consider a far worse sign of man's incapacity to govern himself than any which is presented by the resumption of the grants that a State has made. I have no idea that there is any such feeling within the limits of the southern

States.

There are two modes, however, of dissolving the Union. One alone has been contemplated. It was that which proceeded from the States separating themselves from those to whom they are united. There is another. It is by destroying the Constitution; by pulling down the political temple; by forming a consolidated Government. Union, in the very meaning of the word, implies the junction of separate States. Consolidation would be the destruction of the Union, and far more fatal to popular liberty than the separation of the States. But, if fanaticism and sectionalism, like the blind giant of old, shall seize the pillars of the temple to tear them down, in order that they may destroy its inmates, it but remains for us to withdraw, and it will be our purpose to commence the erection of another on the same plan on which our father built this. We share no such common ruin as falls upon a people by consolidation and destruction of the principles of liberty contained in the Constitution, by interference with community and social rights; and we go out of such a Government whenever it takes that form, in accordance with the Constitution, and in defense of the principles on which the Constitution rests. We have warned you for many years that you would drive us to this alternative, and you would not heed. I believe that you still look upon it as a mere passing political move, as a device for some party end, knowing little of the deep struggle with which we have contemplated this as a necessity, not as a choice, when we have been brought to stand before the alternative—the destruction of our community independence, or the destruction of that Union which our fathers made. You would not heed us. You deemed our warning to be merely to the end of electing a candidate for the miserable spoils of office, of which I am glad to say I represent a people who have had so little indeed that they have never acquired an appetite for them. Yet you have believed—not looking to the great end to which our eyes were directed—that it was a mere political resort, by which we would intimidate some of your own voters. You have turned upon those true friends of ours at the North who have vindicated the Constitution, and pointed out to you the danger of your course, and held them responsible for the censure you received, as though you had not, in fact, aggressed. Even at this session, after forty years of debate, you have asked us what was the matter.

Your platform on which you elected your candidate denies us equality. Your votes refuse to recognize our domestic institutions which preexisted the formation of the Union, our property which was guarded by the Constitution. You refuse us that equality without which we should be degraded if we remain in the Union. You elect a candidate upon the basis of sectional hostility; one who, in his speeches, now thrown broadcast over the country, made a distinct declaration of war upon our institutions. We care not whether that war be made by armies marching for invasion, or whether it be by proclamation, or whether it be by indirect and covert process. In both modes, however, you have declared your hostility. The leading members of that party, some of them now before me, making speeches in various portions of the country during the last summer, even after the election was over, when no purpose of the canvass remained still to excite them, announcing the triumph which had been achieved, as the downfall of our domestic institutions; and still you ask us to make specifications, to file an indictment as though we intended to arraign you before a magistrate's court. Our fathers united with yours on the basis of equality, and they were prompted to form a union by the fraternity which existed between them. Do you admit that equality? Do you feel that fraternity? Do your actions show it? They united for the purpose not only of domestic tranquillity, but for common defense; and the debates in the convention which formed the Constitution set forth that the navigating and manufacturing interests of one section, and the better defense in the other, were the two great objects which drew them together. Are you willing now to fulfill the conditions on which our fathers agreed to unite?

When you use figurative language, its harshness indicates the severity of your temper and the bitterness of your hate. When you talk about having your heel on the slave power and grinding it into the dust; when you talk about the final triumph; when you talk about the extinction of slavery, an institution with which you have nothing to do and of which you know nothing, is this the fraternity, is this the Union, to which we were invited? Is that an administration of the Government under which we can live in safety? Is this a condition of things to which men, through whose veins flows the blood of the Revolution, can stoop without acknowledging that they had sunk from their birthright of freedom to become slaves?

I care not to read from your platform; I care not to read from the speeches of your President elect. You know them as I do; and the man who is regarded over this country as the directing intellect of the party to which he belongs, the Senator from New York, [Mr. SEWARD,] has, with less harshness of expression than others, but with more method, indicated this same purpose of deadly hostility in every form in which it could be portrayed. Did we unite with you in order that the powers of the

General Government should be used for destroying our domestic institutions? Do you believe that now, in our increased and increasing commercial as well as physical power, we will consent to remain united to a Government exercised for such a purpose as this?

What boots it to tell me that no direct act of aggression will be made? I prefer direct to indirect hostile measures which will produce the same result. I prefer it, as I prefer an open to a secret foe. Is there a Senator upon the other side who to-day will agree that we shall have equal enjoyment of the Territories of the United States? Is there one who will deny that we have equally paid in their purchases, and equally bled in their acquisition in war? Then, is this the observance of your compact? Whose is the fault if the Union be dissolved? Do you say that there is one of you who controverts either of these positions? Then I ask you, do you give us justice; do we enjoy equality? If we are not equals, this is not the Union to which we were pledged; this is not the Constitution you have sworn to maintain, nor this the Government we are bound to support.

There is much, too, which is exceedingly offensive in the speculations you make upon our servants when you talk about negro insurrection. Governments have tampered with slaves; bad men have gone among the ignorant and credulous people, and incited them to murder and arson; but of themselves—moving by themselves—I say history does not chronicle a case of negro insurrection. San Domingo, so often referred to, and so little understood, is not a case where black heroes rose and acquired a Government. It was a case in which the French Government, trampling upon the rights and safety of a distant and feeble colony by sending troops among them, brought on a revolution, first of the mulattoes [sic], and afterwards of the blacks. Their first army was not even able to effect this. It required a second army, and that army to be quartered on the plantations; nay, after all, it required that the master should be arrested on the charge of treason and taken to France, before the negroes could be aroused to insurrection.

Do you wonder, then, that we pause when we see this studied tendency to convert the Government into a military despotism? Do you wonder that we question the right of the President to send troops to execute the laws wherever he pleases, when we remember the conduct of France, and that those troops were sent with like avowal; and quartered on plantations, and planters arrested for treason—just such charges as are made to-day against southern men—and brought away that insurrection might be instigated among their slaves?

I seek not to exasperate or intensify the causes of difficulty. It is needful that we should understand each other. I thought we had done so before, and was surprised to hear the questioned asked, "What is the matter?" The last canvass, I thought, had expressed the feelings and the opinions of the southern States. The State of Mississippi gave warning in solemn resolutions passed by her Legislature. Those resolutions were printed elsewhere, and were generally known. She declared her purpose to take counsel with her southern sister States whenever a President should be elected on the basis of sectional hostility to them. With all this warning, you paused not. The quarrel was not of our making. Our hands are stainless; you aggressed upon our rights and our homes, and, under the will of God, we will defend them.

There is a strange similarity in the position of affairs at the present day to that which the colonies occupied. Lord North asserted the right to collect the revenue, and insisted on collecting it by force. He sent troops to Boston harbor, and to Charleston, and he quartered troops in those towns. The result was collision, and out of that collision came the separation of the colonies from the mother country. The same thing is being attempted to-day. Not the law, not the civil magistrate, but troops, are relied upon now to execute the laws. To gather taxes in the southern ports, the Army and Navy must be sent to perform the functions of magistrates. It is the old case over again. Senators of the North, you are reenacting the blunders which statesmen in Great Britain committed; but among you, there are some who, like Chatham and Burke, though not of our section, yet are vindicating our rights.

I have heard, with some surprise, for it seemed to me idle, the repetition of the assertion heretofore made that the cause of the separation was the election of Mr. Lincoln. It may be a source of gratification to some gentlemen that their friend is elected; but no individual had the power to produce the existing state of things. It was the purpose, the end; it was the declaration by himself and his friends, which constitute the necessity of providing new safeguards for ourselves. The man was nothing, save as he the was representative of opinions, of a policy, of purposes, of power, to inflict upon us those wrongs to which freemen never tamely submit.

Senators, I have spoken longer than I desired. I had supposed it was possible, avoiding argument and not citing authority, to have made to you a brief address. It was thought useless to argue a question which now belongs to the past. The time is near at hand when the places which have known us as colleagues laboring together, can know us in that relation no more forever. I have striven to avert the catastrophe which now impends over the country, unsuccessfully; and I regret it. For the few days which I may remain, I am willing to labor in order that the catastrophe shall be as little as possible destructive to public peace and prosperity. If you desire at this last moment to avert civil war, so be it; it is better so. If you will allow us to but separate from you peaceably, since we cannot live peaceably together, to leave with the rights we had before we were united, since we cannot enjoy them in the Union, then there are as many relations which may still subsist between us, drawn from the associations of our struggles from the revolutionary era to the present day, which may be beneficial to you as well as to us.

If you will not have it thus; if in the pride of power, if in contempt of reason and reliance upon force, you say we shall not go, but shall remain as subjects to you, then, gentlemen of the North, a war is to be inaugurated the like of which men have not seen. Sufficiently numerous on both sides, in close contact with only imaginary lines of division, and with many means of approach, each sustained by productive sections, the people of which will give freely both of money and of store, the conflicts must be multiplied indefinitely; and masses of men, sacrifices to the demon of civil war, will furnish hecatombs, such as the recent campaign in Italy did not offer. At the end of all this, what will you have effected? Destruction upon both sides; subjugation upon neither; a treaty of peace leaving both torn and bleeding; the wail of the widow and the cry of the orphan substituted for those peaceful notes of domestic happiness that now prevail throughout the land; and then you will agree that each is to pursue his separate course as best he may. This is to be the end of war. Through a long series of years you may waste your strength, distress your people, and get at last to the position which you might have had at first, had justice and reason, instead of selfishness and passion, folly and crime, dictated your course.

Is there wisdom, is there patriotism in the land? If so, easy must be the solution of this question. If not, then Mississippi's gallant sons will stand like a wall of fire around their State; and I go hence, not in hostility to you, but in love and allegiance to her, to take my place among her sons, be it for good or for evil.

I shall probably never again attempt to utter here the language either of warning or of argument. I leave the case in your hands. If you solve it not before I go, you will have still to decide it. Towards you individually, as well as to those whom you represent, I would that I had the power now to say there shall be peace between us forever. I would that I had the power now to say the intercourse and the commerce between the States, if they cannot live in one Union, shall still be uninterrupted; that all the social relations shall remain undisturbed; that the son in Mississippi shall visit freely his father in Maine, and the reverse; and that each shall be welcomed when he goes to the other, not by himself alone, but also by his neighbors; and that all kindly intercourse which has subsisted between the different sections of the Union shall continue to exist. It is not only for the interests of all, but it is my profoundest wish, my sincerest desire, that such remnant of that which is passing away may grace the memory of a glorious, though too brief, existence.

Day by day you have become more and more exasperated. False reports have led you to suppose there was in our section hostility to you with manifestations which did not exist. In one case, I well remember when the Senator from Vermont [Mr. COLLAMER] was serving with me on a special committee, it was reported that a gentleman who had gone from a commercial house in New York had been inhumanely treated at Vicksburg, and this embarrassed a question which we then had pending. I wrote to Vicksburg for information, and my friends could not learn that such a man had ever been there; but if he had been there, no violence had certainly been offered to him. Falsehood and suspicion have thus led you on step by step in the career of crimination, and perhaps has induced to some part of your aggression. Such evil effects we have heretofore suffered, and the consequences now have their fatal culmination. On the verge of war, distrust and passion increase the danger. To-day it is in the power of two bad men, at the opposite ends of the telegraphic line between Washington and Charleston, to precipitate the State of South Carolina and the United States into a conflict of arms without other cause to have produced it.

And still will you hesitate; still will you do nothing? Will you sit with sublime indifference and allow events to shape themselves? No longer can you say the responsibility is upon the Executive. He has thrown it upon you. He has notified you that he can do nothing; and you therefore know he will do nothing. He has told you the responsibility now rests with Congress; and I close as I began, by invoking you to meet that responsibility, bravely to act the patriot's part. If you will, the angel of peace may spread her wings, though it be over divided States; and the sons of the sires of the Revolution may still go on in friendly intercourse with each other, ever renewing the memories of a common origin, the sections, by the diversity of their products and habits, acting and reacting beneficially, the commerce of each may swell the prosperity of both, and the happiness of all be still interwoven together. Thus may it be; and thus it is in your power to make it. [Applause in the galleries.]

The PRESIDING OFFICER. (Mr. Foster in the chair.) The Sergeant-at-Arms will take care to remove disorderly persons in the gallery. Order must be preserved.

9

The Instincts of Empire

Senator Robert M. T. Hunter, Virginia
January 11, 1861

Robert M. T. Hunter (1809-1887) was born in Virginia, tutored at home, and graduated from the University of Virginia. He studied law, was admitted to the bar and commenced practice in 1830. From 1833-1837 he served in the Virginia legislature. From 1837-1847 he served in the U.S. House of Representatives, excepting 1843-1845 when his bid for reelection failed. He served in the U.S. Senate from 1847 until his withdrawal in 1861. He served as C.S.A. Secretary of State from July 1861 to February 1862 and in the C.S.A. Senate from 1862-1865. He was one of the peace commissioners who met with President Lincoln at the Hampton Roads conference in February 1865. In this speech Senator Hunter proposed a reconstruction of the Union with "a more permanent bond of alliance and fraternity than the one which is passing away" and thereby averting a civil war which would "float the land in blood.".

Mr. HUNTER. Mr. President, I have not sought to speak hitherto on the momentous question of the day, because I did not believe that any good would be accomplished by speaking. The disease seemed to me to be so deeply seated that none but the most radical remedies would suffice;

and I had no hope that the public mind of the North was in a condition to receive any such proposition. I do not know that it is even now prepared to weigh carefully such a suggestion; but surely none can no longer doubt the imminence or the extremity of the danger. All must see that the bonds which have hitherto bound together the members of this Confederacy are parting like flax before the fire of popular passion. Our political fabric is reeling and tottering in the storm; so that, if it were not based on the solid foundations of State organization, there would be every reason to expect its entire destruction. Before the end of this month, it is almost certain that six or seven of the States will have seceded from this Union. It is therefore now no more a question of saving or preserving the old Union. We cannot recall the past; we cannot restore the dead; but the hope and the trust of those who desire a Union, are that we may be able to reconstruct a new Government and a new Union, which perhaps may be more permanent and efficient than the old. I know, sir, that there are difficulties in the way; but I put my trust in the good sense and in the instincts of empire, which have heretofore characterized the American people, to accomplish that great work. If we would do it, we must not sit idly, bewailing the condition of public affairs; but in the heroic spirit of the mariner who is cast away on a distant shore, see, if we cannot find materials to build another ship, in which we may once more take the sea, and rejoin our kindred and friends. But, Mr. President, to do this, we must face and acknowledge the true evil of the day. To-day we must deal wisely with the mighty present, that we may be ready for perhaps the still more eventful future which will be on us tomorrow. New ideas, like new forces, have entered into our system; they are demanding the legitimate expression of their power, or they threaten to rend and destroy it in their wild and irregular play. There are now portions of this Union in which population already begins to press on the means of subsistence. In all of the States there is a desire—in some of them a necessity—for further expansion. It is that which has led to the warfare between the two social systems which have been brought together in our Constitution; a war raged with a bitterness and asperity that has reduced us to the sad pass in which we now find ourselves.

This Constitution was designed to unite two social systems, upon terms of equality and fairness, different in their character, but not necessarily hostile. Indeed, the very differences in these systems, it would seem, ought to have formed causes of union and mutual attraction, instead of giving rise to the "irrepressible conflict" which it is said, some law of nature has declared between them. What the one wanted, the other could supply. If the carrying States did not make their provisions, the provision-growing, on the other hand, had not the ships in which to transport their surplus productions. If the manufacturing States did not raise the raw material, the planting States, on the other hand, did not have the manufactories to convert that material into useful and necessary fabrics. Thus, what one wanted, the other could supply. The only difference of products would seem to have afforded the means for forming a perfect system of industry, which should have been stronger by the mutual dependence and support of the parts. Unfortunately, however, as those who represented the non-slaveholding system of society grew into power, they commenced a warfare upon the other system which was associated with it under the Constitution. It was commenced in 1820, when it was declared that the social system of the South was founded upon sin, was anti-republican in its character, and deserved to be repressed and suppressed by the General Government wherever it had exclusive jurisdiction. The claim was made, that so far as the Territories of the United States were concerned, they were to be given up to the exclusive expansion of one of these systems at the expense of the other. Unhappily, in that first contest, the weaker system went by the board; a law was passed which did put it under the ban of the Empire; which did exclude the South from a larger portion of the domain of the United States.

After that sprang up a party, at first not so large as it is now, which commenced a regular warfare upon the system of slavery in the South; upon the social system of the States which tolerated the institution of slavery. They commenced, a system of agitation through the press, the pulpit, and the common halls of legislation, whose object it was to wound the self-respect of the slaveholder, and to make him odious in the eyes of the rest of the world. They denied that there could be any property in slaves—the very foundation of the social system of the South—and, as a consequence, they maintained that this Government was bound to prevent its extension, and to abolish and suppress it wherever it had exclusive jurisdiction. They sought, by petition, to put an end to the slave trade between the States, that the institution might be pent up, and made dangerous and unprofitable.

In the process of time, they either evaded or they denied the constitutional obligation to return fugitive slaves; and at last it was proclaimed here in these Halls that there was a law higher than the Constitution, which nullified its obligations and its provisions. Practicing upon this preaching, the majority of the non-slaveholding States, as was shown by my friend from Georgia [Mr. TOOMBS] in his able argument on the subject, passed personal liberty bills, the practical effect of which was to nullify the fugitive slave law, which was passed in pursuance of the Constitution of the United States.

It is but a year since there was an armed invasion of my State for the purpose of creating servile insurrection; and yet not a State—and it is with the States alone that effectual remedies can be applied—has interfered, to make any such combination penal in time to come. We have heard it pronounced, sir, by a distinguished leader of that party, that there was to be an "irrepressible conflict" between the two social systems, until one or the other was destroyed. A President has been nominated and elected by a sectional majority, who was known to have avowed and to entertain such opinions; and a party has come into power, with full possession of this Government, which has elected a President and a standard-bearer who has made such declarations in regard to the rights of the South.

Is it surprising, then, that the southern States should say: "It is not safe for us to remain longer in a Government which may be directed as an instrument of hostility against us; it is not safe for us to remain longer under the rule of a Government whose President may misuse his patronage for the very purpose of stirring up civil strife among us, and also for the purpose of creating civil war in our midst?" For it is known that a large portion—and that was but a year ago—of the Republican leaders and members in the House of Representatives endorsed and recommended a book which proposed the extinction of slavery by such means. Under such circumstances, I ask, is it surprising that the southern States should say: "It is unsafe for us to remain under a Government which, instead of protecting us, may be directed against us, as an instrument of attack, unless we can be protected by some new constitutional guarantees, which will save our social system from such warfare as this?"

Mr. President, the southern people number now some thirteen million, and cover between eight hundred and nine hundred thousand square miles of territory. They have within themselves all the capacities of empire. Is it to be supposed that when they are threatened in the common Government with an attack upon their social system, upon which their very being depends, they will not withdraw from that Government— unless they can be secured within the Union—for the purpose of establishing another, which they know will and can protect them? Why, sir, what people is it that can stand a constant warfare upon their social system, waged for the purpose of dwarfing and suppressing and destroying it? The social system of a people is its moral being; and the Government which would dwarf or suppress it is like the parent who would consign his child to vice and ignorance. I know of instances in which nations have thriven [sic] under bad laws; I know of instances in which nations have thriven when their allegiance was transferred by force from one country to another; I know of none which survived the sudden and total prostration of its social system. To reduce them to that is to reduce them to anarchy, which is the death of a nation or a people.

I say, therefore, sir, that the South is bound to take this course unless it can get some guarantees which will protect it in the Union, some constitutional guarantees which will serve that end; and, I now ask, what should be the nature of the guarantees that would effectually prevent the social system from such assaults as these? I say, they must be guarantees of a kind that will stop up all the avenues through which they have threatened to assail the social system of the South. There must be constitutional amendments which shall provide: first, that Congress shall have no power to abolish slavery in the States, in the District of Columbia, in the dock-yards, forts and arsenals of the United States; second, that it shall not abolish, tax, or obstruct the slave trade between the States; third, that it shall be the duty of each of the States to suppress combinations within their jurisdiction for armed invasions of another; fourth, that States shall be admitted with or without slavery, according to the election of the people; fifth, that it shall be the duty of the States to restore fugitive slaves when within their borders, or to pay the value of the same; sixth, that fugitives from justice shall be deemed all those who have offended against the laws of a State within its jurisdiction, and who have escaped therefrom; seventh, that Congress shall recognize and protect as property whatever is held to be such by the laws or prescriptions of any State within the Territories, dock-yards, forts, and arsenals of the United States, and wherever the United States has exclusive jurisdiction; with the following exceptions: First, it may leave the subject of slavery or involuntary servitude to the people of the Territories when a law shall be passed to that effect with the usual sanction, and also with the assent of a majority of the Senators from the slaveholding States, and a majority of the Senators from the non-slaveholding States. That exception is designed to provide for the case where we might annex a Territory almost fully peopled, and whose people ought to have the right of self-government, and yet might not be ready to be admitted into the Union.

The next exception is, that "Congress may divide the Territories, to the effect that slavery or involuntary servitude shall be prohibited in one portion of the territory, and recognized and protected in another; provided the law has the sanction of a majority from each of the sections as aforesaid," and that exception is designed to provide for the case where an unpeopled Territory is annexed and it is a fair subject of division between the two sections.

Such, Mr. President, are the guarantees of principle, which, it seems to me, ought to be established by amendments to the Constitution; but I do not believe that these guarantees alone would protect the social system of the South against attack, and perhaps overthrow, from the superior North. I believe that, in addition to these guarantees of principle, there ought to be guarantees of power; because, if you do not adopt these, the South would still be subjected to the danger of an improper use of the patronage of the Executive, who might apply it for the purpose of stirring up civil strife and dissension among them. The southern States might, too, notwithstanding these provisions, find themselves in a position in which the stronger party had construed them away, and asserted, perhaps, that there was some higher law, which nullified and destroyed them. To make the South secure, then, some power ought to be given it to protect its rights in the Union—some veto power in the system, which would enable it to prevent it from ever being perverted to its attack and destruction.

And here, Mr. President, if the Senate will bear with me, I will proceed to suggest such remedies in this regard as I think ought to be applied, premising that I do not mean, by any means, to say that I suppose I am suggesting the only means on which a settlement may be made. I know there are others—others on which I would agree—but I am suggesting the means on which I think the best and most permanent settlement can be made; and I do not think that any permanent peace can be secured, unless we provide some guarantees of power, as well as of principle.

In regard to this guarantee of power, in the first place, I would resort to the dual executive, as proposed by Mr. Calhoun, not in the shape in which he recommended it, but in another form, which, I think, is not obnoxious to the objection that may be fairly taken against his plan. I would provide that each section should elect a President, to be called the first and second President; the first to serve for four years as President, the next to succeed him at the end of four years, and to govern for four other years, and afterwards to be reeligible. I would provide that, during the term of service of the first President, the second should be President of the Senate, with a casting vote in the case of a tie; and no treaty should be valid which did not have the signature of both Presidents, and the assent of two thirds of the Senate; that no law should be valid which did not have the assent of both Presidents, or in the event of a veto by one of them, the assent of a majority of the Senators of the section from which he came; that no person should be appointed to a local office in the section from which the second President was elected, unless the appointment had the assent of that President, or in the event of his veto, the assent of a majority of the Senators from the section from which he came.

And, sir, if I had the power, I would change the mode of electing these Presidents. I would provide that each State should be divided into presidential electoral districts; that each district should elect one man, and that these representatives from the whole United States should meet in one chamber, and that the two men who, after a certain number of ballots, received the highest number of votes should be submitted as the candidates to the people, and he should be declared as President who received a majority of the districts—the districts each voting singly. I would do this to destroy the opportunities which are given under our present system of nomination to the formation of corrupt combinations for purposes of plunder and patronage. I would substitutes this, instead of national conventions, which have already done so much harm in our system.

I would also diminish the temptation to such corrupt combinations for spoils and patronage, by the fact that the President, after the first election, would be elected for four years before he commenced his service as President, and in the mean time [sic] he would be training as a second President at the head of the Senate, and exercising the veto power. The fact that he was elected four years beforehand would do much to prevent such combinations; but, further than this, the effect of such a division of the Executive power would be to destroy, to a great extent, the miserable system of rotation in office, which exists at present, and to make merit the test of the fitness for office and a guarantee for his permanence in place; for, as the second President would probably keep those in office during his term of President whom he had protected by his veto power before, if they were worthy of the place, the effect would be, at least if this system were introduced, that the rotation principle would be applied, if at all, not once in four years, but once in eight years.

But this plan would have another good effect. It would save us from most of those agitations attending a presidential election which now disturb the country, which unsettle public affairs, and which are doing so much to demoralize and corrupt the people. The election would take place in one section at a time; it would take place in each section but once in eight years; and in this way we should escape those disturbances which are now dividing and destroying us.

Mr. President, I do not believe that under this system the objection would apply which has been urged against the common dual executive. I have no idea that it would get up two parties, each concentrated around the different Presidents; because the second President would exercise his veto power only for the protection of his section, and would not wish to offend the other section, whose good will would be valuable to him hereafter; nor would he wish to impair and injure the influence of the office to which he was to succeed after his predecessor had passed through his term of service. The rule between them would be the rule of justice; and the probability is, that whenever there was a dispute, it would be apt to end in adopting that course which was either just, or which seemed to be just, to both sections.

Neither, sir, would it operate to retard or delay the operation of the Government to too great an extent. In time of war, the operation would be quick enough. In time of peace, the delay would only occur where there was a dispute between the sections; and there the movements of Government ought to be slow until some means are found for conciliating and adjusting the difficulty.

But, Mr. President, I will go further. I believe, putting out of consideration these sectional questions, that the working of the present executive system of our Government will destroy it in the end, and lead either to disunion or despotism, if some amendment be not made. I believe it will do so because the working of our executive system is now such as to beget and bring up a party whose existence and foundation depend upon spoils and plunder. I have often heard Mr. Calhoun say that most of the conflicts in every Government would be found at last to result in the contests between two parties, which he denominated the tax-consuming and the tax-paying parties. The tax-consuming party, he said, was that which fed upon the revenues of the Government, the spoils of office, the benefits of unequal and class legislation; the tax-paying party was that which made the contributions to the Government by which it was supported, and expected nothing in return but the general benefits of its protection and legislation; and, he said, and said wisely, in my opinion, that whenever this tax-consuming party, as he called it, got possession of the Government, the people must decay, and the Government must either go to pieces or assume another and different form.

Now, sir, I say that the working of our present executive system is such as to produce a party of that description in the country, and give it the power of ruling its affairs. Place the predominant power in this

Government in such hands, and I say one of two things must certainly happen: the Union will go to pieces in the collision which such a state of things would occasion, or else the Government would eventuate in a despotism.

The check which I propose would not only remedy this evil, by giving a sectional check where a sectional check is necessary, but it would do more; it would do much to purify the general legislation of the country, and do much to elevate the tone of public morals and manners throughout the land. I believe that this single change would do more to give us a permanent Union, a just and efficient Government, than any other that could be made.

But, Mr. President, that is not the only check which, in a reconstruction of this Government and Union, ought, in my opinion, to be introduced. It is well known that some of the most important objects of this Constitution and Union are left simply to the discretion of the States; that there is a large class of rights, and important rights, for which there are no remedies, or next to no remedies. Those provisions which are designed to secure free trade and free intercourse between the citizens of the States can all of them be nullified or set aside by State legislation. The States can pass laws so to obstruct this free intercourse that the constitutional privilege may amount to nothing; and if this Union had endured, and these contests had continued, we should have seen laws passed in a spirit of retaliation by the States which would have broken up free trade between them. They could have taxed the commodities of the obnoxious States after the package was broken, under the decision of the Supreme Court itself. They could make it penal in their citizens to use the ships of another State, if it was obnoxious to them; and in many other ways, they could, by their legislation, destroy some of the most important objects of the Constitution.

I believe, myself, that it was intended, by the framers of that instrument, that the States should have been mainly instrumental in restoring fugitives from labor, or, to speak more plainly, fugitive slaves. We know that it is in their power, not only to refrain from discharging this duty, but actually to obstruct and impede the Government of the United States in its effort to execute the law. There are certain rights for which there are no remedies. It is provided, for instance, that no State shall maintain an army; and yet, if it does so, there is no remedy to prevent it.

Now, sir, I propose, in order to secure the proper enforcement of these rights for which, as I say, there are no adequate remedies, that the

Supreme Court should also be adjusted. It should consist of ten judges—five from each section—the Chief Justice to be one of the five. I would allow any State to cite another State before this tribunal to charge it with having failed to perform its constitutional obligations; and if the court decided a State thus cited to be in default, then I would provide, if it did not repair the wrong it had done, that any State might deny to its citizens within its jurisdiction the privileges of citizens in all the States; that it might tax its commerce and the property of its people until it ceased to be in default. Thus, I would provide a remedy without bringing the General Government into collision with the States; and without bringing the Supreme Court into collision with them. Whenever international stipulations in regard to the duties imposed on the States, as laid down in the Constitution, are violated, I would remedy the wrong by international remedies. I would give a State the right, in such cases, after the adjudication of the court, to deny to the offending State the performances of the mutual obligations which had been created for its benefit. In this way I believe that these wrongs might be remedied without producing collision in the system. A self-executing process would thus provide a remedy for the wrong, without a jar to the machinery of Government.

I have presented this scheme, Mr. President, as one which, in my opinion, would adjust the differences between the two social systems, and which would protect each from the assault of the other. If this were done, so that we were made mutually safe, I, for one, would be willing to regulate the right of secession, which I hold to be a right not given in the Constitution, but resulting from the nature of the compact. I would provide, that before a State seceded it should summon a convention of the States in the section to which it belonged, and to submit to them a statement of its grievances and wrongs. Should a majority of the States in such a convention decide the complaint to be well founded, then the State ought to be permitted to secede in peace. For, whenever a majority of the States in an entire section shall declare that good cause for secession exists, then who can dispute that it ought to take place? Should they say, however, that no good cause existed, then the moral force for such a decision, on the part of the confederates of those who are bound to the complaining State by identical and homogeneous interests, would prevent it from prosecuting the claim any further. I believe that the system thus adjusted would give us a permanent Union, and efficient, a useful, and a just Government. I think our Government would then rank among the most permanent of human institutions. It is my honest opinion that, with a Government thus balanced, and with such capacities for empire as our people possess, we should build up a political system whose power and stability and beneficial influences would be unparalleled in all the history of the past.

I know, Mr. President, it may be said that such a distribution of power does not accord with the principle of distributing power according to numbers; but I say if that be the true principle at all, it applies only to States which have a single government; it does not apply to confederacies; and if it were left to me to amend this Constitution, I would stamp upon this Government a character still more distinctly federative than that which it now bears. I say, then, that the distribution of power which I would propose would be entirely just upon the federative principle. Nor would my proposition be at all more inconsistent with the principle of distributing power according to numbers than the arrangements of the present Federal Constitution. Nothing in my scheme is more unequal than the provision which gives the six New England States twelve Senators while New York has only two, although the population of that State is as great, and I believe greater, than that of all the New England States together. There is nothing in the scheme now proposed, inconsistent with the federative principle; and if the slaveholding and non-slaveholding States had been standing apart for a dozen years in different confederacies, and there was a proposition to unite those confederacies in one, no man would think it extreme, or be surprised if each of the confederacies insisted upon such powers and such guarantees as would enable it to defend its own social system and to secure equality, together with the opportunity for expansion according to the peculiar law of its development.

But, Mr. President, as I said before, I do not mean to declare that this is the only scheme upon which I will settle. I say I believe it to afford the best basis of settlement which has yet been devised. There are other schemes upon which I would settle. I would settle upon something which would give only a truce, provided it promised to be a long truce, and then trust to public opinion and the progress of the truth to remedy future evils when they might arise. But I would prefer, when we do settle, after all this turmoil and confusion, that we should do so upon some principle which promises us a permanent adjustment, a constant and continuing peace, a safe, an efficient, and a stable Government.

Mr. President, I have founded my suggestions upon the fact, which I take to be an accomplished fact, that some of the States of this Union have already withdrawn, and that the old Union has been dissolved, and has gone. I believe there is no way of obtaining a Union except through a reconstruction, because I utterly repudiate and deny that it can be done through the system of coercion, which some have proposed. Sir, I say, if you were to attempt coercion, and by conquest to restore the Union, it would not be the Union of our fathers; but a very different one. I say it would be a Union constructed in entire opposition to the true American spirit and American principles; a Union of a number of subjugated provinces with others who governed them and wielded the whole power of the Confederacy.

But, sir, I maintain that coercion, if it were possible, is not right; and that if it were right, it is not possible. I think it can be shown that it is neither right nor possible. I believe it can be proved that the only effect of an attempt at coercion would be to destroy the chances of a reconstruction of the Union, or, in other words, to defeat all the hopes that are left to the friends of a Union in the country. I say that if it were possible, it is not right. I believe it is not right, because I believe in the right of secession in the States. It is not my purpose to repeat the argument which has been so much better made by my friend, the distinguished Senator from Louisiana, [Mr. BENJAMIN]. I do not mean to argue that question; I merely say that, to my mind, it lies in a nutshell. If it be true that our Constitution is a compact, as history demonstrates, between the States as parties; and if it be true, as Mr. Madison has demonstrated, that there is no common arbiter in disputes between these parties; and if it be true, as Mr. Webster has said, that a bargain broken on one side is broken on all sides, then it results inevitably that it is for the State to say whether the bargain has been broken, and to act accordingly. I do not say that this right of secession is laid down in the Constitution. It results from the nature of the compact. When two nations enter into a treaty of mutual obligations, and one fails to fulfill its part, the other may cancel it; not from any stipulation in the treaty, but from the nature of the compact. It is the very remedy for the very wrong; and, indeed, it is the only remedy for the wrong.

But, sir, I care not what you call it; call it revolution, if you choose; let this be the name that you give it; I still say I think I can show you from the Constitution that you have no right to interfere with it. If it be revolution, it is organized revolution; it is a revolution conducted by an organized body, and so acknowledged to be in the Constitution itself. If it be revolution, it is a revolution managed by the government which the Constitution acknowledges to be a legal government—I mean the government of the State. How, then, could this Government pretend to treat as a rebel him who obeys a government that it acknowledges to be legitimate? Especially, how can it interfere to treat him as such when he has acted under a warrant from the very power from which this Government derives its authority? How does this Government derive its authority to administer its functions within the State of Virginia? It derives it from the assent of the people of the State of Virginia, given in the convention which represented them in their sovereign capacity. How does the State government derive its authority? From the very same source; and in any dispute between the two, as to authority, it is for the source of authority to both to say whom the citizen shall obey. This Government rests and has its being in the assent of the people of the different States; and without it the Constitution has clearly created a Government which cannot exist or be administered within a State. Then, if it be true that this Constitution created a Federal Government which cannot be administered within its limits without the assent of the people of the State, it would follow that the Constitution has declared, by implication, that the only authority of that Government rests upon the assent of the people of the State; and that when this is withdrawn, it has no longer any rightful jurisdiction within it. Is it, then, true that this Government is so constructed by the Constitution that it cannot execute its functions within the State without the assent of the State, or against its authority? If so, then the Constitution clearly implies that the authority of the General Government is gone within the limits of a State when the people of that State have withdrawn their assent to its jurisdiction—a conclusion which is in entire accordance with the principles of free government as laid down by the fathers of the Constitution.

I proceed then, Mr. President, to make my proposition, that this Federal Government cannot be carried on within the limits and jurisdiction of a State, without the assent, the aid, and the sympathy of its people. In the first place, it depends on the Legislatures of the different States to elect members of this body. If a majority of the States, although they might represent a small minority of the people, were to refuse to send Senators here, your Government is gone; you have lost one of the most important arms of the system; you have no longer a Senate.

But, sir, in order to carry out the functions of this Government you must administer its judicial powers. Can you administer the judicial powers of this Government within a State if that State withdraws its assent and is determined to resist that administration? Can you do it by any means given under the Constitution? Suppose a State repeals the penalties for murder as against the officers of the General Government; suppose it repeals the penalties for false imprisonment as against those officers; suppose it should say it had reason to fear that the officers of the General

Government would be appointed under influences which would be utterly destructive to its domestic peace and social system, and that they must give bonds for good behavior, with sureties to be found in the State itself: if a State were to undertake to obstruct the course of Federal justice in that way, where would the remedy be found within the constitutional power of this Government? Would it undertake to pass a code of municipal legislation in order to protect the persons, and property, and effects of its officers? Could it say that its officers should not be answerable to the jurisdiction of the State for offenses against the laws of the State when they were within its jurisdiction? Certainly they could not do that, consistently with the Constitution. When it came to such a pass as that, they would have the same right to enact and execute a municipal code for all the people of all the States, that they would have to make one for that portion of the people who constituted the mass of the Federal officers.

But, sir, that is not all. To obtain the right of exclusive legislation within dock-yards, forts, arsenals, and other needful buildings, Congress must have, first, the consent of the States. That must be given under the Constitution. Suppose a State refuses its consent. Where would be your court-houses, your forts, your custom-houses? Where would you have the *locus in quo*, from which to administer the functions and the power of this General Government? Everywhere, if they were to refuse to give you this assent, you would be under State jurisdiction; and thus it would be in the power of the State constantly to thwart, obstruct, and prevent the administration of Federal power, within her limits and jurisdictions.

So, too, it is in the power of the States, if they choose, if they undertake to withdraw their assent from this Constitution, to defeat these great ends of the Union, which I have before described as designed to insure free intercourse and free trade between the citizens of the several States. Thus it will be found, when you come to examine the matter, that this Federal Government cannot exercise its most important and its essential functions within the limits of a State if the people of that State refuse to assent to its power, and choose to obstruct it by means which they have under the Constitution of the United States. If this be so, what is the result to be derived from that fact? The result is, that the framers of the Constitution supposed that this Federal Government would only be an authorized Government within a State so long as it had the assent of the people of that State; and that when the people of that State withdrew their assent, it was not the authorized Government; and therefore they provided no means for enforcing its powers and for exercising its jurisdiction. Is not that the inevitable conclusion, from the facts which I have just allured? Sir, the only mode in which you could protect the administration of the Federal affairs and the Federal jurisdiction within the State, would be to set aside the State government by force, and to reduce it to a territorial condition; and then what would be the result? You first coerce a State because it secedes from thirty-two other members of this Confederacy; and you turn around and secede yourselves from it by reducing it from a condition of a State to the position of a Territory!

But, Mr. President, I say that if coercion were right, it is impossible. I say that no man can doubt that if it be attempted against one of the seceding States, all the slaveholding States will rally to the aid of their sister; and the idea that you can coerce eight, or ten, or fourteen, or fifteen of the States in this Confederacy when standing in a solid body, is preposterous. I acknowledge that you may make a civil war which will produce immense disasters in both sections of the country; I acknowledge that you can inflict immeasurable evils and great calamities upon both the contending sections; but as to supposing that either one could subdue the other so as to place it under its yoke, and impose its laws upon it, I do not entertain the idea for an instant.

Why, sir, how would this war of coercion be waged? It would take $100,000,000 yearly, for you cannot wage it with less than a hundred thousand men; and where would you get this sum? Not from imports; for what would the imports for the northern portion of the Confederacy be when you took from them all that comes in return for the exports of the South? You would have to sustain the war by loans and direct taxation; and is it to be supposed that the people would bear such burdens in such a cause as that? I believe they might submit to any just and necessary taxation in the defense of their own legal and necessary rights; but would they submit to such a scheme of taxation for the purpose of enforcing their yoke upon other people—for the purpose of depriving those other people of the right of self-government? Whose would be the commerce that would be preyed upon? Not the southern commerce. That would go in foreign bottoms. The commerce to be preyed upon by privateers would be the commerce of the other section of the Confederacy. If it came to a question of plunder, which of the sections would afford the greatest temptation to plunder? Where are the cities, villages, the concentrated wealth of a community to be found in the greatest number and quantity? Those are the objects which tempt the cupidity of a soldiery. You could not steal our negroes. Your own people would not allow you to take them and set them free among them, to enter into competition with them for labor and for wages. How would you carry on such a war, sir? Where would you find the means? You would not continue the attempt for more than six months before you would find it impossible, and you would abandon it.

I say, therefore, that it is not possible, by any such means, to coerce the southern people into submission. I know there is a talk of attaining all the valuable purposes of a Union, by a simple blockade of the coast; that is, by a blockade which should collect the customs and do nothing more. Where would the ships come from to blockade the whole southern coast? And how could they effect their purposes under this Constitution, unless, indeed, they intend to violate it? Where would be their judges, their inspectors, their appraisers, their collectors? Where would they exercise their functions? On shipboard? That would be impossible. Would you transfer the cargo of the ship to another port of a collection district in another State, which had not seceded? Why, sir, the cargo would not be wanted there. How in regard to the commerce of the South during that period? You can lay no duty upon exports. They would forbid their people, under penalties, to send their commodities by any but foreign bottoms; they might forbid the people, by penalties, from consuming any goods which they did not manufacture themselves, or import from abroad; and thus you would lose your most valuable customers in the carrying of trade, and the most profitable consumers of your manufactures.

And what would you get in return? Would the customs that you thus collected pay the expenses of the blockade? Would they pay half the expenses of the blockade? It is manifest they would not. The blockade, to be effectual, would have to be a blockade of war, in which you prevented vessels from going either out or in; and is it to be supposed that foreign nations would allow this? Is it to be presumed that Great Britain, which has millions of human beings whose very existence depends upon cotton, that the great interests of civilization, would allow this grand material of human industry to be thus shut up and denied to them? Why, sir, it is not to be supposed for a moment. There are other Powers which would prevent such a blockade, in addition to the resistance which might be expected from the section that it was attempted thus to coerce.

I say, then, Mr. President, that it is idle to think of coercion. You may, if you choose, if such be your feeling, inflict evils by waging civil war; but will you inflict more on others than you receive in return? I think not. But suppose you could succeed—I put the question to you now—suppose you had succeeded according to your utmost wishes; suppose you had conquered the South; that you had subjugated the entire section; that you had reduced those States to the condition of dependent provinces: how would you exercise your power? Would you apply your doctrine, that there can be no property in slaves? In that community of eight or nine million white men and four million slaves, would you turn them loose together, and set the slaves free? Would you repeat the experiment of the British West Indies—of the Island of Jamaica? Would your people stand by and see the cultivated fields return to the bush, the white man being gradually reduced to the level of the negro, and the negro remitted and restored to his primitive condition of barbarism? Would the great interests of civilization and humanity permit such a result? Would your own interests, your manufacturers, your ship owners, agree to it? Sir, it is not to be supposed that such a thing would be permitted; and what then would be the result? You would have to maintain the social system; you would have to recognize property in slaves; and what would follow from that? If you recognize property in slaves, you must cause fugitive slaves to be restored. If you recognize a property that is under the jurisdiction of your Government, you must protect it; and if you do protect it, you must punish persons who attempt to make raids upon it, and to incite servile insurrections. And, sirs, if you once commit yourselves to the duty of protecting it throughout all of these conquered States, you would find that it followed, as a necessary consequence, that you must protect it wherever you had the exclusive jurisdiction. What, then, would become of your dogma of excluding the Territories? What would be the effect of such an experiment? You pen them up until there comes to be a surplus population in the old States; you pen up the negroes, and say the negro shall not move, but the white man may. What is the effect of that? The white man does move when the wages of labor are low; the negro remains and gains the preponderance in population until you give him the best part of the continent, and remove the white man to the worst. Could such an absurdity as this be tolerated, Mr. President? No, sir; not for a moment.

Then, if you would be forced to accede to all these things, if you succeeded according to your wishes, and conquered and subdued us, after a bloody and harassing civil war, why not do it beforehand, when it would save the Union? Why not do it now, when it would avert all these calamities? Why not avail yourself of the present opportunity, when you may do so without the dreadful inconsistency which will be charged upon you, when you may be forced to do these very things after you have carried on this cruel and harassing and distressing system of civil war?

I say, then, Mr. President, that it is impossible to coerce the southern States, if you were to attempt to do so. If you had the constitutional right to do so, it would be impossible. Why create a civil war wantonly, without purpose, without use of benefit to any one? If this be so, why not adopt the proposition in my resolution—why not cede back the forts to those States that claim to have seceded, and to have withdrawn from this Confederacy? What do you want with them? What do you want with the forts in the harbor of Charleston? If you do not mean to coerce South Carolina, they are of no use to you; if you do mean to coerce her, you ought not to have them. The whole thing lies in a nutshell; because, if you do mean to use them for the purpose of coercion, you light up the flames of civil war, and there is no telling when those flames will be extinguished; if you do attempt to use them for the purpose of coercion, you destroy the chances of the construction of another Union, which I still hope and trust may take place, and which may prove to us a more permanent bond of alliance and fraternity than the one which is passing away from us.

I say, too, sir, that you have no right, when you come to weigh the question of right, to hold on to these forts. You could not have obtained them without the consent of the Legislature of the State; that is the provision of the Constitution. Upon what consideration was that consent given? Not for pecuniary considerations. It was given upon the consideration that they were to be used for the defense of the State. Now, sir, you keep them when they can no longer be used for the defense of the State, but are proposed to be used against her. The consideration, therefore, in my opinion, has failed; and in justice and equity, you ought to restore them.

But, Mr. President, if there were no moral obligation upon you to do so, I maintain that considerations of policy ought to prompt you to do it. In no other way can you prevent the commencement of civil war. They say they have seceded; they say they are out of this Union: I believe myself that they are. You maintain a different opinion; but certain it is, that while you might give them up without inconsistency, so far as your opinions are concerned, they could not yield them without absolute inconsistency, so far as their pretensions are to be considered. If they are an independent people, they have a right to these forts. If they are an independent people, they are bound to take them, if they have the power to do so, when they believe they are in the possession of a foreign Power. But how is it with you? What inconsistency do you manifest, provided it be policy to do so, when you withdraw from them? You do not admit the doctrine of secession. In the form in which the resolution is proposed, you are not called upon to admit it. You may support the resolution upon the ground of policy; for, under the resolution, a State which did not intend to secede might apply for a retrocession of the forts, and the retrocession might be given in some cases from motives of policy, and without the least violation of the Constitution. Suppose the city of New York had said to us, at a time when the public defenses were going up at a rate which did not satisfy her, because they were too slow, "retrocede to us the jurisdiction; it is essential to us to have the forts; we will construct them rapidly; pass a law allowing us to maintain troops, and we will man them and keep them." It is obvious that there might be circumstances under which it would be polite for New York to make such a demand, and there might be circumstances under which it would be just and proper to grant it. I say, therefore, you do nothing inconsistent with your opinions against secession, when you agree to return these forts; and there is nothing impolitic in such a concession, unless you desire to use them for purposes of coercion.

Mr. President, I maintain that every consideration of policy should induce us to remove that bone of contention, that cause of strife between us; and I am especially anxious for it, because I believe that if we have civil war, we loose all hopes of reconstructing this Union. I desire myself to see it reconstructed on principles of fairness, equality, and justice, between the sections. I believe that if a drop of blood is once shed, if you do not destroy the chances of it, you postpone it to a very distant day; and for one, I do not desire to see this. I presume that we shall soon see nearly all the southern States out of the Union. I think it probable that they will unite first and form a union for the South for the sake of the South; and having done so, I hope and trust and believe that they will call a southern convention for the purpose of proposing a reaccommodation and readjustment on proper terms; and if the non-slaveholding States at the same time shall assemble in convention and exchange propositions, I hope and trust that some settlement may be had, some reconstruction to make this Union more permanent and this Government more valuable than ever it has been to us in the past. Secession does not necessarily destroy the Union, or rather the hopes of reunion; it may turn out to be the necessary path to reconstruction. The secession of the Roman people to the Sacred Mount did not destroy Rome. On the contrary, it led to a reconstruction of the constitution, to the tribunitian veto, to new securities for the equality and liberty of the people. The Roman Government became more permanent and powerful than before, and the Roman people benefited by the change. But if it should turn out that in this exchange of propositions it was impossible to accommodate the difference, still it might result in the establishment of some league, not merely commercial, but political, holding us together by a looser bond than any which has bound us heretofore, and we might thus still secure many of the benefits of this Government and this Union, while we left each section free to follow the law of its own genius, and to develop itself according to the promptings of its own nature.

I say, therefore, that, so far as I can weigh the question, it is no more a question of Union, but one of reunion. To produce reunion, it is essential that the southern States should be allowed to take that position which it is obvious they are going to take, in peace. You must give, too, all the time you can, and offer all the opportunities you may, to those who desire to make an effort for the reconstruction of this Confederacy. Sir, I say I am one of those; for while I believe that the South owes to itself first to secure its own position, to provide for its own protection, to unite in such strength as will enable it to defend itself against all goers and comers, I also believe that the interests of mankind, our own interests, and the interests of our confederacies, would then require that we should reconstruct the old Union if we can, or rather construct a new Union on terms of equality and of justice.

But, Mr. President, will this be possible if we enter into a course of civil war? If brother begins to shed the blood of brother, and people become irritated and excited at the sight of blood, will it be possible to reunite us again? And, sir, I ask if the Republicans are willing, if they mean to insist, to add civil war to the long catalogue of enormities for which they are to be held responsible hereafter? Is it not enough that they have marched into power over the ruins of the Constitution, and that they have seized this Government at the expense of the Union? Will they be contented with nothing less now than civil war, and such a strife, according to their own account of it, as is unparalleled in the history of modern and civilized warfare? It is said that this fratricidal contest is to be attended with horrors and atrocities at which even the men of Wallenstein, her "whiskered pandours and fierce hussars," would stand aghast and pale.

I would ask if they are, indeed, willing to let loose the dogs of war, hot from hell, to raven through this land; if they desire that "one spirit of the first born Cain" shall reign in every American bosom, to prepare the hearts and minds of men for blood, and to stir up fratricidal strife throughout this once happy country? What excuse, when they have returned from such a war of devastation and ruin, will they be able to give to their own consciences? How will they account with humanity for its best hopes, which they have destroyed; for having crushed out and extinguished the highest capacities for usefulness, progress, and development, which were ever bestowed on man? Sir, what judgment will posterity pronounce upon them when it comes to sit in judgment on the deeds occasioned by such unhallowed ambition? Will it not say, "You found peace, and you established war; you found an empire of the United states, and you have rent and scattered it into separate and hostile fragments."

And, more awful still, what account will they render at the bar of Heaven, when, from many a burning homestead and many a bloody battlefield, spectral hosts shall appear to accuse them there; when the last wail of suffering childhood shall rise from the very depths of the grave to make its feeble plaint against them, and tears of woman, helpless woman, shall plead against them for her wounded honor in the voiceless woe of her ineffable despair? How will they account for it before man and God, before earth and Heaven, if they close with blood this great American experiment which was inaugurated by Providence in the wilderness to insure peace on earth and good will to man; an experiment which was maintained and conducted by our fathers, not only by their blood, but with their most pious care? How will they hide themselves from the accusation, when one universal voice of misery and despair shall be heard throughout the land?

I say to them, sir, that it will be no compensation or excuse for such sins that they have succeeded in enabling themselves to wave a barren scepter over a mutilated empire, an exhausted and suffering land! Why is it that these threats are made? Is it done for the purpose of preventing the southern States from seceding? Never have been taken more ill-judged steps to secure an end. They but precipitate and hasten what they wish to prevent. Such threats of coercion as these only serve to make the southern States precipitate themselves into the arms of each other, that they may stand together in a common cause, and unite their strength to make a common defense. I say, for my own State, that she has not yet commissioned me to speak; she is taking counsel at home as to her future action; but this I do feel authorized to declare; she loves peace, and she desires to avoid war; but she will not be deterred from asserting her rights by threats of coercion or from any fear of consequences. Sir, once before in her past history, in the sacred name of honor, liberty, and equality, she staked her destiny on the war of the Revolution, when "the cause of Boston was the cause of all;" and for the same high considerations, I know that she will imperil all again, if she believes it to be her duty to do so. And if the day shall ever come when she can neither defend her honor nor assert her rights because the hand of power wields its bloody sword before her, she would feel that it would be better for her name and fame to perish with them.

Republican Senators, why are these threats of coercion sent to southern States, who are seeking to do no evil to others, but merely to protect and defend themselves? Do they go out with any purpose of attacking your rights? Do they secede with the wish to injure or disturb you in any manner? Are they not going out simply for the purpose of exercising that first law of nature and of nations, the right of self-government, because they believe they are not safe under your rule? Are they not willing to meet all the responsibilities which they have incurred while they were carrying on a joint government with you? Why, then, sirs, do you claim to pursue them with fire and sword; and why do you deny to them that right which belongs to every organized people? When we were asserting that right against the Government of Great Britain, we claimed, and we received, the sympathies of the whole civilized world. When the Spanish provinces rebelled against the mother country, we were quick to express our sympathy and regard for their cause. When Greece, distant Greece, asserted her independence, we were among the first to express our sympathy for her. Now, sir, the right which we are free to offer, and sympathy which we gladly extend, to foreigners and aliens, are refused to our own brethren; and you say that, if they attempt to exercise them, you will pursue them to the death.

Mr. President, is it to be supposed that any Anglo-Saxon people, people of our own blood and race, would submit to such demands? Is there any free people who are worthy of liberty, who would not say that sooner than yield to such demands as these we bid you to wrap in flames our dwellings, and float our land in blood? I believe if they attempt to coerce the southern people in this regard, they will meet not only with the general detestation of mankind, but with such resistance as has never been shown before in the world, except, perhaps, in the history of Holland, whose people fought behind the dykes and flooded their land with the waves of the sea, preferring death in any and every form rather than submission to such oppression and tyranny.

But, Mr. President, I do not wish to pursue this line of argument. I do not desire to engage in any discussion which so much stirs the blood as the supposition that such rights as these are to be denied to any portion of my countrymen. I choose rather to stand in the character in which I appear this day. I stand here to plead for peace; not that my State, in my opinion, has any reason to fear war more that [sic] another, but because it is in the interest of all to preserve peace. In the sacred names of humanity and of Christian civilization; in the names of thirty million human souls, men, women, and children, whose lives, whose honor, and whose happiness, depend upon the events of such a civil war as that with which we are threatened; in the name of the great American experiment, which, as I said before, was founded by Providence in the wilderness, and which, I insist, has not yet failed; I appeal to the American people to prevent the effusion of blood. It is said that the very scent of blood stirs up the animal passions of man. Give us time for the play of reason. Let us see, after the southern States have secured themselves by some united action, if we cannot bring together once more our scattered divisions; if we cannot close up our broken ranks; if we cannot find some place of conciliation, some common ground upon which we all may rally once more; and when the columns come mustering in from the distant North and the furthest South, and from the rising and from the setting sun, to take their part in that grand review, the shout of their war-cry shall shake the air until it brings down the very birds in their flight as it ascends to the heavens to proclaim to the world that we are united once more, brothers in war, and brothers in peace, ready to take our wonted place in the front line of the mighty march of human progress, and able and willing to play for the mastery in that game of nations where the prizes are power and empire, and where victory may crown our name with eternal fame and deathless renown.

10

The Enlargement of Empire

Senator William H. Seward, New York
January 12, 1861

William H. Seward (1801-1872) was born in New York, attended Farmers' Hall Academy, and graduated from Union College in 1820. He studied law and was admitted to the bar and commenced the practice of law in 1823. He served in the New York senate from 1830-1834, was an unsuccessful Whig candidate for governor in 1834, and was elected governor of New York and served from 1838-1842. He was elected to the U.S. Senate as a Whig in 1849 and reelected as a Republican in 1855. He served as U.S. Secretary of State from 1861-1869. In this speech Seward insisted that the national government had the imperative duty and ability to preserve the Union, and that "the Union cannot be saved by some insincere and cunning compact of pacification. The continuance of the Union comprehends nothing less than the fate of an empire."

Mr. SEWARD. Mr. President, Congress adjourned last summer amid auspices of national abundance, contentment, tranquillity, and happiness. It was reassembled this winter in the presence of derangement of business and disturbance of public as well as private credit, and in the face of seditious combinations to overthrow the Union. The alarm is appalling; for Union is not more the body than liberty is the soul of the nation. The American citizen has been accustomed to believe the Republic immortal. He shrinks from the sight of convulsions indicative of its sudden death. The report of our condition has gone over the seas; and we who have so long and with much complacency studied the endless agitations of society in the Old World, believing ourselves exempt from such disturbances, now, in our turn, seem to be falling into a momentous and disastrous revolution.

I know how difficult it is to decide, amid so many and so various counsels, what ought to be and even what can be done. Certainly, however, it is time for every Senator to declare himself. I, therefore, following the example of the noble Senator from Tennessee, [Mr. JOHNSON,] avow my adherence to the Union in its integrity and with all its parts, with my friends, my party, with my State, with my country, or without either, as they may determine, in every event, whether of peace or of war, with every consequence of honor or dishonor, of life or death. Although I lament the occasion, I hail with cheerfulness the duty of lifting up my voice among distracted debates, for my whole country and its inestimable Union.

Hitherto the exhibitions of spirit and resolution here, as elsewhere, have been chiefly made on the side of disunion. I do not regret this. Disunion is so unexpected and unnatural that it must plainly reveal itself before its presence can be realized. I like best, also, the courage that rises slowly under the pressure of severe provocation. If it be a Christian duty to forgive to the stranger even seventy times seven offenses, it is the highest patriotism to endure without complaint the passionate waywardness of political brethren so long as there is hope that they may come to a better mind.

I think it is easy to pronounce what measures or conduct will not save the Union. I agree with the honorable Senator from North Carolina [Mr. CLINGMAN] that mere eulogiums will not save it. Yet I think that as prayer brings us closer to God, though it cannot move him toward us, so there is healing and saving virtue in every word of devotion to the Union that is spoken, and in every sigh that its danger draws forth. I know, at least, that, like virtue, it derives its strength from every irreverent act that is committed and every blasphemous phrase that is uttered against it.

The Union cannot be saved by mutual criminations concerning our respective share of responsibility for the present evils. He whose conscience acquits him will naturally be slow to accuse others whose cooperation he needs. History only can adjust the great account.

A continuance of the debate on the constitutional power of Congress over the subject of slavery in the Territories will not save the Union. The opinions of parties and sections on that question have become dogmatical, and it is this circumstance that has produced the existing alienation. A truce, at least during the debate on the Union, is essential to reconciliation.

The Union cannot be saved by proving that secession is illegal or unconstitutional. Persons bent on that fearful step will not stand long enough on forms of law to be dislodged; and loyal men do not need such narrow ground to stand upon.

I fear that little more will be gained from discussing the right of the Federal Government to coerce seceding States into obedience. If disunion is to go on, this question will give place to the more practical one, whether many seceding States have a right to coerce the remaining members to acquiesce in a dissolution.

I dread, as in my innermost soul I abhor, civil war. I do not know what the Union would be worth if saved by the use of the sword. Yet, for all this, I do not agree with those who, with a desire to avert this great calamity, advise a conventional or unopposed separation, with a view to what they call a reconstruction. It is enough for me, first, that in this plan, destruction goes before reconstruction; and secondly, that the strength of the vase in which the hopes of the nation are held consists chiefly in its remaining unbroken.

Congressional compromises are not likely to save the Union. I know, indeed, that tradition favors this form of remedy. But it is essential to its success, in any case, that there be found a preponderating mass of citizens, so far neutral on the issue which separates parties, that they can intervene, strike down clashing weapons, and compel an accommodation. Moderate concessions are not customarily asked by a force with its guns in battery; nor are liberal concessions apt to be given by an opposing force not less confident of its own right and its own strength. I think, also, that there is a prevailing conviction that legislative compromises which sacrifice honestly cherished principles, while they anticipate future exigencies, even if they do not assume extra-constitutional powers, are less sure to avert imminent evils than they are certain to produce ultimately even greater dangers.

Indeed, Mr. President, I think it will be wise to discard two prevalent ideas or prejudices, namely: first, that the Union is to be saved by somebody in particular; and secondly, that it is to be saved by some cunning and insincere compact of pacification. If I remember rightly, I said something like this here so long ago as 1850, and afterwards in 1854.

The present danger discloses itself in this form. Discontented citizens have obtained political power in certain States, and they are using this authority to overthrow the Federal Government. They delude themselves with a belief that the State power they have acquired enables them to discharge themselves of allegiance to the whole Republic. The honorable Senator from Illinois [Mr. DOUGLAS] says we have a right to coerce a State, but we cannot. The President says that no State has a right to secede, but we have no constitutional power to make war against a State. The dilemma results from an assumption that those who, in such a case, act against the Federal Government, act lawfully as a State; although manifestly they have perverted the power of the State to an unconstitutional purpose. A class of politicians in New England set up this theory and attempted to practice upon it in our war with Great Britain. Mr. Jefferson did not hesitate to say that the States must be kept within their constitutional sphere by impulsion, if they could not be held there by attraction. Secession was then held to be inadmissible in the face of a public enemy. But if it is untenable in one case, it is necessarily so in all others. I fully admit the originality, the sovereignty, and the independence of the several States within their sphere. But I hold the Federal Government to be equally original, sovereign, and independent within its sphere. And the government of the State can no more absolve the people residing within its limits from allegiance to the Union, than the Government of the Union can absolve them from allegiance to the State. The Constitution of the United States, and the laws made in pursuance thereof, are the supreme law of the land, paramount to all legislation of the States, whether made under the Constitution, or even by their organic conventions. The Union can be dissolved, not by secession, with or without armed force, but only by the voluntary consent of the people of the United States, collected in the manner prescribed by the Constitution of the United States.

Congress, in the present case, ought not to be impassive. It ought, if it can, to redress any real grievances of the offended States, and then it ought to supply the President with all the means necessary to maintain the Union in the full exhibition and discreet exercise of its authority. Beyond this, with the proper activity on the part of the Executive, the responsibility of saving the Union belongs to the people, and they are abundantly competent to discharge it.

I propose, therefore, with great deference, to address myself to the country upon the momentous subject, asking a hearing, not less from the people within what are called the seceding, than from those who reside within the adhering States.

Union is an old, fixed, settled habit of the American people, resulting from convictions of its necessity, and therefore not likely to be hastily discarded. The early States, while existing as colonies, were combined, though imperfectly, through a common allegiance to the British Crown. When that allegiance ceased, no one was so presumptuous as to suppose political existence compatible with disunion; and, therefore, on the same day that they declared themselves independent, they proclaimed themselves also confederated States. Experience in war and in peace, from 1776 until 1787, only convinced them of the necessity of converting that loose Confederacy into a more perfect and perpetual Union. They acted with a coolness very different from the intemperate conduct of those who now on one side threaten, and those who on the other side rashly defy disunion. They considered the continuance of the Union as a subject comprehending nothing less than the safety and welfare of all the parts of which the country was composed, and the fate of an empire in many respects the most interesting in the world. I enter upon the subject of continuing the Union now, deeply impressed with the same generous and loyal conviction. How could it be otherwise, when, instead of only thirteen, the country is now composed of thirty-three parts; and the empire embraces, instead of only four million, no less than thirty million inhabitants.

The founders of the Constitution moreover regarded the Union as no mere national or American interest. On the contrary, they confessed with deep sensibility that it seemed to them to have been reserved for the people of this country to decide whether societies of men are really capable of establishing good government upon reflection and choice, or whether they are forever destined to depend for their political constitutions on accident and force. They feared, therefore, that their failure to continue and perfect the Union would be a misfortune to the nations. How much more, sir, would its overthrow now be a calamity to mankind!

Some form of government is indispensable here as elsewhere. Whatever form we have, every individual and every State must cede to it some natural rights, to invest the Government with requisite power. The simple question, therefore, for us now to decide, while laying aside all pique, passion, and prejudice, is: whether it conduces more to the interests of the people of this country to remain, for the general purposes of peace and war, commerce inland and foreign, postal communication at home and abroad, the care and disposition of the public domain, colonization, the organization and admission of new States, and generally, the enlargement of empire, one nation under our present Constitution, than it would do to divide themselves into separate Confederacies or States.

Our country remains now as it was in 1787—composed not of detached and distant Territories, but of one whole well-connected and fertile region lying within the temperate zone, with climates and soils hardly more various than those of France or of Italy. This slight diversity quickens and amplifies manufacture and commerce. Our rivers and valleys, as improved by art, furnish us a system of highways unequaled in the world. The different forms of labor, if slavery were not perverted to purposes of political ambition, need not constitute an element of strife in the Confederacy.

Notwithstanding recent vehement expressions and manifestations of intolerance in some quarters, produced by intense partisan excitement, we are, in fact, a homogeneous people, chiefly of one stock, with accessions well assimilated. We have, practically, only one language, one religion, one system of Government, and manners and customs common to all. Why, then, shall we not remain henceforth, as hitherto, one people?

The first object of every human society is safety or security, for which, if need be, they will, and they must, sacrifice every other. This security is of two kinds: one, exemption from foreign aggression and influence; the other, exemption from domestic tyranny and sedition.

Foreign wars come from either violations of treaties or domestic violence. The Union has, thus far, proved itself an almost perfect shield against such wars. The United States, continually enlarging their diplomatic acquaintance, have now treaties with France, the Netherlands, Great Britain, Sweden, Prussia, Spain, Russia, Denmark, Mexico, Brazil, Austria, Turkey, Chili, Siam, Muscat, Venezuela, Peru, Greece, Sardinia, Ecuador, Hanover, Portugal, New Granada, Hesse Cassel, Wurtemburg, China, Bavaria, Saxony, Nassau, Switzerland, Mecklenburg-Schwerin, Guatemala, the Hawaiian Islands, San Salvador, Borneo, Costa Rica, Peru, Bremen, the Argentine Confederation, Loo Choo, Japan, Brunswick, Persia, Baden, Belgium, and Paraguay. Nevertheless, the United States, within their entire existence under the Federal Constitution, have had flagrant wars with only four States, two of which were insignificant Powers, on the coast of Barbary, and have had direct hostilities, amounting to reprisals, against only two or three more; and they are now at peace with the whole world. If the Union should be divided into only two Confederacies, each of them would need to make as many treaties as we have now; and, of course, would be liable to give as many causes of war as we now do. But we know, from the sad experiences of other nations, that disintegration, once begun, inevitably continues until even the greatest empire crumbles into many parts. Each Confederation that shall ultimately arise out of the ruin of the Union will have necessity for as many treaties as we have now, and will incur liabilities for war as often as we now do, by breaking them. It is the multiplication of treaties, and the want of confederation, that makes a war the normal condition of society in Western Europe and in Spanish America. It is union that, notwithstanding our world-wide intercourse, makes peace the habit of the American people.

I will not descend so low as to ask whether new confederacies would be able or willing to bear the grievous expense of maintaining the diplomatic relations which cannot be dispensed with except by withdrawing from foreign commerce.

Our Federal Government is better able to avoid giving just causes of war than several confederacies, because it can conform the action of all the States to compacts. It can have only one construction, of every treaty. Local and temporary interests and passions, or personal cupidity and ambition, can drive small confederacies or States more easily than a Great Republic into indiscreet violations of treaties.

The United States being a great and formidable Power, can always secure favorable and satisfactory treaties. Indeed, every treaty we have was voluntarily made. Small confederacies or States must take such treaties as they can get, and give whatever treaties are exacted. A humiliating, or even an unsatisfactory treaty, is a chronic cause of foreign war.

The chapter of wars resulting from unjustifiable causes would, in case of division, amplify itself in proportion to the number of new confederacies and their irritability. Our disputes with Great Britain about Oregon, the boundary of Maine, the patriot insurrection in Canada, and the Island of San Juan; the border strifes between Texas and Mexico, the incursions of the late William Walker into Mexico and Central America; all these were cases in which war was prevented only by the imperturbability of the Federal Government.

This Government not only gives fewer causes of war, whether just or unjust, than smaller confederacies would; but it always has a greater ability to accommodate them by the exercise of more coolness and courage, the use of more various and more liberal means, and the display, if need be, of greater force. Every one knows how placable we ourselves are in controversies with Great Britain, France, and Spain; and yet how exacting we have been in our intercourse with New Granada, Paraguay, and San Juan de Nicaragua.

Mr. President, no one will dispute our forefathers' maxim, that the common safety of all is the safety of each of the States. While they remain united, the Federal Government combines all the materials and all the forces of the several States; organizes their defenses on one general principle; harmonizes and assimilates them with one system; watches for them with a single eye, which it turns in all directions, and moves all agents under the control of one executive head. A nation so constituted is safe against assault or even insult.

War produces always [sic] a speedy exhaustion of money and a severe strain upon credit. The treasuries and credits of small confederacies would often prove inadequate. Those of the Union are always ample.

I have thus far kept out of view the relations which must arise between the confederacies themselves. They would be small and inconsiderable nations bordering on each other, and therefore, according to all political philosophy, natural enemies. In addition to the many treaties which each must make with foreign Powers, and the causes of war which they would give by violating them, each of the confederacies must also maintain treaties with all the others, and so be liable to give them frequent offense. They would necessarily have different interests resulting from their establishment of different policies of revenue, of mining, manufactures, and navigation, of immigration, and perhaps the slave trade. Each would stipulate with foreign nations for advantages peculiar to itself and injurious to its rivals.

If, indeed, it were necessary that the Union should be broken up, it would be in the last degree important that the new confederacies to be formed should be as nearly as possible equal in strength and power, that mutual fear and mutual respect might inspire them with caution against mutual offense. But such equality could not long be maintained; one confederacy would rise in the scale of political importance, and the others would view it thenceforward with envy and apprehension. Jealousies would bring on frequent and retaliatory wars, and all these wars, from the peculiar circumstances of the confederacies, would have the character and nature of civil war. Dissolution, therefore, is, for the people of this country, perpetual civil war. To mitigate it, and obtain occasional rest, what else could they accept but the system of adjusting the balance of power which has obtained in Europe, in which the few strong nations dictate the very terms on which all the others shall be content to live. When this hateful system should fail at last, foreign nations would intervene, now in favor of one and then in aid of another; and thus our country having expelled all European Powers from the continent, would relapse into an aggregated form of its colonial experience, and, like Italy, Turkey, India, and China, become the theater of transatlantic intervention and rapacity.

If, however, we grant to the new confederacies an exemption from complications among each other and with foreign States, still there is too much reason to believe that not one of them could long maintain a republican form of government. Universal suffrage and the absence of a standing army are essential to the republican system. The world has yet to see a single self-sustaining State of that kind, or even any confederation of such States, except our own. Canada leans on Great Britain not unwillingly, and Switzerland is guarantied [sic] by interested monarchical States. Our own experiment has thus far been successful; because, by the continual addition of new States, the influence of each of the members of the Union is constantly restrained and reduced. No one, of course, can foretell the way and manner of travel; but history indicates with unerring certainty the end which the several confederacies would reach. Licentiousness would render life intolerable; and they would sooner or later purchase tranquillity and domestic safety by the surrender of liberty, and yield themselves up to the protection of military despotism

Indulge me, sir, in one or two details under this head. First, it is only sixty days since this disunion movement began; already those who are engaged in it have canvassed with portentous freedom the possible recombinations of the States when dissevered, and the feasible alliances of those recombinations with European nations; alliances as unnatural, and which would prove ultimately as pestilential to society here as that of the Tlascalaus with the Spaniard, who promised them revenge upon their ancient enemies, the Aztecs.

Secondly. The disunion movement arises partly out of a dispute over the common domain of the United States. Hitherto the Union has confined this controversy within the bounds of political debate by referring it, with all other national ones, to the arbitrament of the ballot-box. Does any one suppose that disunion would transfer the whole domain to either party, or that any other umpire than war would, after dissolution, be invoked?

Thirdly. This movement arises, in another view, out of the relation of African slaves to the domestic population of the country. Freedom is to them, as to all mankind, the chief object of desire. Hitherto, under the operation of the Union, they have practically remained ignorant of the controversy, especially of its being on themselves. Can we hope that flagrant civil war shall rage among ourselves in their very presence, and yet they will remain stupid and idle speculators? Does history furnish us any satisfactory instruction upon the horrors of civil war among a people so brave, so skilled in arms, so earnest in conviction, and so intent in purpose, as we are? Is it a mere chimera which suggests an aggravation of those horrors beyond endurance when, on either side, there shall occur the intervention of an uprising ferocious African slave population of four, or six, perhaps twenty million?

The opinions of mankind change, and with them policies of nations. One hundred years ago all the commercial European States were engaged in transferring negro slaves from Africa to this hemisphere. To-day all those States are firmly set in hostility to the extension and even to the practice of slavery. Opposition to it takes two forms: one European, which is simple, direct abolition, effected, if need be, by compulsion; the other American, which seeks to arrest the African slave trade, and resist the entrance of domestic slavery into the Territories where it is yet unknown, while it leaves the disposition of existing slavery to the considerate action of the States by which it is retained. It is the Union that restricts the opposition to slavery in this country within these limits. If dissolution prevail, what guarantee shall there be against the full development here of the fearful and uncompromising hostility to slavery which elsewhere pervades the world, and of which the recent invasion of Virginia was an illustration?

Mr. President, I have designedly dwelt so long on the probable effects of disunion upon the safety of the American people as to leave me little time to consider the other evils which must follow in its train. But practically, the loss of safety involves every other form of public calamity. When once the guardian angel has taken flight, everything is lost.

Dissolution would not only arrest, but extinguish the greatness of our country. Even if separate confederacies could exist and endure, they could severally preserve no share of the common *prestige* of the Union. If the constellation is to be broken up, the stars, whether scattered widely apart or grouped in smaller clusters, will thenceforth shed forth feeble, glimmering, and lurid lights. Nor will great achievements be possible for the new confederacies. Dissolution would signalize its triumph by acts of wantonness which would shock and astound the world. It would provincialize Mount Vernon and give this Capitol over to desolation at the very moment when the dome is rising over our heads that was to be crowned with the statue of Liberty. After this there would remain for disunion no act of stupendous infamy to be committed. No petty confederacy that shall follow the United States can prolong, or even renew, the majestic drama of national progress. Perhaps it is to be arrested because its sublimity is incapable of continuance. Let it be so, if we have indeed become degenerate. After Washington, and the inflexible Adams, Henry, and the peerless Hamilton, Jefferson, and the majestic Clay, Webster, and the acute Calhoun, Jackson, the modest Taylor, and Scott, who rises in greatness under the burden of years, and Franklin, and Fulton, and Whitney, and Morse, have all performed their parts, let the curtain fall!

While listening to these debates, I have sometimes forgotten myself in marking their contrasted effects upon the page who customarily stands on the dais before me, and the venerable Secretary who sits behind me. The youth exhibits intense but pleased emotion in the excitement, while at every irreverent word that is uttered against the Union the eyes of the aged man suffused with tears. Let him weep no more. Rather rejoice, for yours has been a lot of rare felicity. You have seen and been a part of all the greatness of your country, the towering national greatness of all the world. Weep only you, and weep with all the bitterness of anguish, who are just stepping on the threshold of life; for that greatness perishes prematurely and exists not for you, nor for me, nor for any that shall come after us.

The public prosperity! how [sic] could it survive the storm? Its elements are industry in the culture of every fruit; mining of all the metals; commerce at home and on every sea; material improvement that knows no obstacle and has no end; invention that ranges throughout the domain of nature; increase of knowledge as broad as the human mind can explore; perfection of art as high as human genius can reach; and social refinement working for the renovation of the world. How could our successors prosecute these noble objects in the midst of brutalizing civil conduct? What guarantees will capital invested for such purposes have, that will outweigh the premium offered by political and military ambition? What leisure will the citizen find for study, or invention, or art, under the reign of conscription; nay, what interest in them will society feel when fear and hate shall have taken possession of the national mind? Let the miner in California take heed; for its golden wealth will become the prize of the nation that can command the most iron. Let the borderer take care; for the Indian will again lurk around his dwelling. Let the pioneer come back into our denser settlements; for the railroad, the post road, and the telegraph, advance not one furlong further into the wilderness. With standing armies consuming the substance of our people on the land, and our Navy and our postal steamers withdrawn from the ocean, who will protect or respect, or who will even know by name our petty confederacies? The American man-of-war is a noble spectacle. I have seen it enter an ancient port in the Mediterranean. All the world wondered at it, and talked of it. Salvos of artillery, from forts and shipping in the harbor, saluted its flag. Princes and princesses and merchants paid it homage, and all the people blessed it as a harbinger of hope for their own ultimate freedom. I imagine now the same noble vessel again entering the same haven. The flag of thirty-three stars and thirteen stripes has been hauled down, and in its place a signal is run up, which flaunts the device of a lone star or a palmetto tree. Men ask, "Who is the stranger that thus steals into our waters?" The answer contemptuously given is, "She comes from one of the obscure republics of North America. Let her pass on."

Lastly, public liberty, our own peculiar liberty, must languish for a time, and then cease to live. And such a liberty! free [sic] movement everywhere through our own land and throughout the world; free speech, free press, free suffrage; the freedom of every subject to vote on every law, and for or against every agent who expounds, administers, or executes. Unstable and jealous confederacies, constantly apprehending assaults without and treason within, formidable only to each other and contemptible to all beside: how long will it be before, on the plea of public safety, they will surrender all this inestimable and unequaled liberty, and accept the hateful and intolerable espionage of military despotism?

And now, Mr. President, what is the cause for this sudden and eternal sacrifice of so much safety, greatness, happiness, and freedom? Have foreign nations combined, and are they coming in rage upon us? No. So far from being enemies, there is not a nation upon earth that is not an interested, admiring friend. Even the London Times, by no means partial to us, says:

> It is quite possible that the problem of a democratic republic may be solved by its overthrow in a few days in a spirit of folly, selfishness, and short-sightedness.

Has the Federal Government become tyrannical or oppressive, or even rigorous or unsound? Has the Constitution lost its spirit, and all at once collapsed into a lifeless letter? No; the Federal Government smiles more benignantly, and works to-day more beneficiently than ever. The Constitution is even the chosen model for the organization of the newly rising confederacies.

The occasion is the election of a President of the United States, who is unacceptable to a portion of the people. I state the case accurately. There was no movement of disunion before the ballots which expressed that choice were cast. Disunion began as soon the result was announced. The justification it assigned was that Abraham Lincoln had been elected, while the success of either one of the three other candidates would have been acquiesced in. Was the election illegal? No; it is unimpeachable. Is the candidate personally offensive? No; he is a man of unblemished virtue and amiable manners. Is an election of President an infrequent or extraordinary transaction? No; we never had a Chief Magistrate otherwise designated than by such an election, and that form of choice is renewed every four years. Does any one even propose to change the mode of appointing the Chief Magistrate? No; election by universal suffrage, as modified by the Constitution, is the one crowning franchise of the American people. To save it they would defy the world. Is it apprehended that the new President will usurp despotic powers? No; while he is of all men the most unambitious, he is, by the partial success of those who opposed his election, subjected to such restraints that he cannot, without their consent, appoint a minister or even a police agent, negotiate a treaty, or procure the passage of a law, and can hardly draw a musket from the public arsenals to defend his own person.

What, then, is the ground of discontent? It is that the disunionists did not accept as conclusive the arguments which were urged in behalf of the successful candidate in the canvass. This is all. Were their own arguments against him more satisfactory to his supporters? Of course they were not; they could not be. Does the Constitution, in letter or spirit, require or imply that the arguments of one party shall be satisfactory to the other? No; that is impossible. What is the constitutional remedy for this inevitable dissatisfaction? Renewed debate and ultimate rehearing in a subsequent election. Have the now successful majority perverted power to purposes of oppression? No; they have never before held power. Alas! how prone we are to undervalue privileges and blessings. How gladly, how proudly, would the people of any nation in Europe accept, on such terms as we enjoy it, the boon of electing a Chief Magistrate every four years by free, equal, and universal suffrage! How thankfully would they cast aside all their own systems of government, and accept this Republic of ours, with all its shortcomings and its disappointments, maintain it with their arms, and cherish it in their hearts. Is it not the very boon for which they supplicate God without ceasing, and even wage war, with intermissions only resulting from exhaustion? How strange are the times in which we live! The coming spring season, on one side of the Atlantic, will open on a general conflict, waged to obtain, through whatever indirection, just such a system as ours; and on this side of the Atlantic, within the same parallels of latitude, it will open on fraternal war, waged in a moment of frenzied discontent to overthrow and annihilate the same institutions. Do men, indeed, live only for themselves, to avenge their own wrongs, or to gratify their own ambition? Rather do not men live least of all for themselves, and chiefly for posterity and for their fellow-men? Have the American people, then, become all of a sudden unnatural, as well as unpatriotic? and [sic] will they disinherit their children of the precious estate held only in trust for them, and deprive the world of the best hopes it has enjoyed since the human race began its slow and painful, yet needful and wisely-appointed progress?

Here I might close my plea for the American Union; but it is necessary, if not to exhaust the argument, at least to exhibit the whole case. The disunionists, consciously unable to stand on their mere disappointment in the recent election, have attempted to enlarge their ground. More than thirty years there has existed a considerable—though not heretofore a formidable—mass of citizens in certain States situated near or around the delta of the Mississippi, who believe that the Union is less conducive to the welfare and greatness of those States than a smaller confederacy, embracing only slave States, would be. This class has availed itself of the discontents resulting from the election to put into operation the machinery of dissolution long ago prepared and waiting only for occasion. In other States there is a soreness because of the want of sympathy in the free States with the efforts of slaveholders for the recapture of fugitives from service. In all the slave States there is a restiveness resulting from the resistance which has been so determinedly made within the last few years, in the free States, to the extension of slavery in the common Territories of the United States. The Republican party, which cast its votes for the successful presidential candidate on the ground of that policy, has been allowed, practically, no representation, no utterance by speech or through the press, in the slave States; while its policy, principles, and sentiments, and even its temper, have been so misrepresented as to excite apprehensions that it denies important constitutional obligations, and aims even at interference with slavery and its overthrow by State authorities or intervention of the Federal Government. Considerable masses even in the free States, interested in the success of these misrepresentations as a means of partisan strategy, have lent their sympathy to the party claiming to be aggrieved. While the result of the election brings the Republican party into the foreground in resisting disunion, the prejudices against them which I have described have deprived them of the cooperation of many good and patriotic citizens. On a complex issue between the Republican party and the disunionists, although it involves the direct national calamities, the result might be doubtful; for the Republican party is weak in a large part of the Union. But on a direct issue, with all who cherish the Union on one side, and all who desire its dissolution by force on the other, the verdict would be prompt and almost unanimous. I desire thus to simplify the issue, and for that purpose to separate from it all collateral questions, and relieve it of all partisan passions and prejudices.

I consider the idea of withdrawal of the Gulf States, and their permanent reorganization with or without others in a distinct Confederacy as a means of advantage to themselves, so certainly unwise and so obviously impossible of execution, when the purpose is understood, that I dismiss it with the discussion I have already incidentally bestowed upon it.

The case is different, however, in regard to the other subjects which I have brought in this connection before the Senate.

Beyond a doubt, Union is vitally important to the Republican citizens of the United States; but it is just as important to the whole people. Republicanism and Union are, therefore, not convertible terms. Republicanism is subordinate to Union, as everything else is and ought to be—Republicanism, Democracy, and every other political name and thing; all are subordinate—and they ought to disappear in the presence of the great question of the Union. So far as I am concerned, it shall be so; it should be so if the question were sure to be tried as it ought only to be determined, by the peaceful ordeal of the ballot. It shall be so all the more since there is on one side preparedness to refer it to the arbitrament of civil war. I have such faith in this republican system of ours, that there is no political good which I desire that I am not content to seek through its peaceful forms of administration without invoking revolutionary action. If others shall invoke that form of action to oppose and overthrow Government, they shall not, so far as it depends on me, have the excuse that I obstinately left myself to be misunderstood. In such a case I can afford to meet prejudice with conciliation, exaction with concession which surrenders no principle, and violence with the right hand of peace. Therefore, sir, so far as the abstract question whether, by the Constitution of the United States, the bondsman, who is made such by the laws of a State, is still a man or only property, I answer that, within that State, its laws on that subject are supreme; that when he has escaped from that State into another, the Constitution regards him as a bondsman who may not, by any law or regulation of that State, be discharged from his service, but shall be delivered up, on claim to the party to whom his service is due. While prudence and justice would combine in persuading you to modify the acts of Congress on that subject, so as not to oblige private persons to assist in their execution, and to protect freemen from being, by abuse of the laws, carried into slavery, I agree that all laws of the States, whether free States or slave States, which relate to this class of persons, or any others recently coming from or resident in other States, and which laws contravene the Constitution of the United States, or any law of Congress passed in conformity thereto, ought to be repealed.

Secondly. Experience in public affairs has confirmed my opinion, that domestic slavery, existing in any State, is wisely left by the Constitution of the United States exclusively to the care, management, and disposition of that State; and if it were in my power, I would not alter the Constitution in that respect. If misapprehension of my position needs so strong a remedy, I am willing to vote for an amendment of the Constitution, declaring that it shall not, by any future amendment, be so altered so as to confer on Congress a power to abolish or interfere with slavery in any State.

Thirdly. While I think that Congress has exclusive and sovereign authority to legislate on all subjects whatever, in the common Territories of the United States; and while I certainly shall never, directly or indirectly, give my vote to establish or sanction slavery in such Territories, or anywhere else in the world, yet the question what constitutional laws shall at any time be passed in regard to the Territories, is, like every other question, to be determined on practical grounds. I voted for enabling acts in the cases of Oregon, Minnesota, and Kansas, without being able to secure in them such provisions as I would have preferred; and yet I voted wisely. So now, I am well satisfied that, under existing circumstances, a happy and satisfactory solution of the difficulties in the remaining Territories would be obtained by similar laws, providing for their organization, if such organization were otherwise practicable. If, therefore, Kansas were admitted as a State, under the Wyandotte constitution, as I think she ought to be, and if the organic laws of all the other Territories could be repealed, I could vote to authorize the organization and admission of two new States which should include them, reserving the right to effect subdivisions of them whenever necessary into several convenient States; but I do not find that such reservations could be constitutionally made. Without them, the ulterior embarrassments which would result from the hasty incorporation of States of such vast extent and various interests and character would outweigh all the immediate advantages of such a measure. But if the measure were practicable, I should prefer a different course, namely: when the eccentric movements of secession and disunion shall have ended, in whatever form that end may come, and the angry excitements of the hour shall have subsided, and the calmness once more shall have resumed its accustomed sway over the public mind, then, and not until then—one, two, or three years hence—I should cheerfully advise a convention of the people, to be assembled in pursuance of the Constitution, to consider and decide whether any and what amendments of the organic national law ought to be made. A Republican now—as I have heretofore been a member of other parties existing in my day—I nevertheless hold and cherish, as I have always done, the principle that this Government exists in its present form only by the consent of the governed, and that it is as necessary as it is wise, to resort to the people for revisions of the organic law when the troubles and dangers of the State certainly transcend the powers delegated by it to the public authorities. Nor ought the suggestion to excite surprise. Government in any form is a machine; this is the most complex one that the mind of man has ever invented, or the hand of man has ever framed. Perfect as it is, it ought to be expected that it will, as least as often as once in a century, require some modification to adapt it to the changes of society and alterations of empire.

Fourthly. I hold myself ready now, as always heretofore, to vote for any properly guarded laws which shall be deemed necessary to prevent mutual invasions of States by citizens of other States, and punish those who shall aid and abet them.

Fifthly. Notwithstanding the arguments of the gallant Senator from Oregon, [General LANE], I remain of the opinion that physical bonds, such as highways, railroads, rivers, and canals, are vastly more important for holding civil communities together than any mere covenants, though written on parchment or engraved upon iron. I remain, therefore, constant to my purpose to secure, if possible, the construction of two Pacific railways, one of which shall connect the ports around the mouths of the

Mississippi, and the other the towns on the Missouri and the Lakes, with harbors on our western coast.

If, in the expression of these views, I have not proposed what is desired or expected by many others, they will do me the justice to believe that I am as far from having suggested what in many respects would have been in harmony with cherished convictions of my own. I learned early from Jefferson, that in political affairs we cannot always do what seems to us absolutely best. Those with whom we must necessarily act, entertaining different views, have the power and the right of carrying them into practice. We must be content to lead when we can, and to follow when we cannot lead; and if we cannot at any time do for our country all the good that we would wish, we must be satisfied with doing for her all the good that we can.

Having submitted my own opinions on this great crisis, it remains only to say that I shall cheerfully lend to the Government my best support in whatever prudent yet energetic efforts it shall make to preserve the public peace, and to maintain and preserve the Union; advising, only, that it practices as far as possible the utmost moderation, forbearance, and conciliation.

And now, Mr. President, what are the auspices of the country? I know that we are in the midst of alarms, and somewhat exposed to accidents unavoidable in seasons of tempestuous passions. We already have disorder; and violence has begun. I know not to what extent it may go. Still my faith in the Constitution and in the Union abides, because my faith in the wisdom and virtue of the American people remains unshaken. Coolness, calmness, and resolution, are elements of their character. They have been temporarily displaced; but they are reappearing. Soon enough, I trust, for safety, it will be seen that sedition and violence are only local and temporary, and that loyalty and affection to the Union are the natural sentiments of the whole country. Whatever dangers there shall be, there will be the determination to meet them; whatever sacrifices, private or public, shall be needful for the Union, they will be made. I feel sure that the hour has not come for this great nation to fall. This people, which has been studying to become wiser and better as it has grown older, is not perverse or wicked enough to deserve so dreadful and severe a punishment as dissolution. This Union has not yet accomplished what good for mankind was manifestly designed by Him who appoints the seasons and prescribes the duties of States and empires. No, sir; if it were cast down by faction to-day, it would rise again and reappear in all its majestic proportions to-morrow. It is the only Government that can stand here.

Woe! Woe! to the man that madly lifts his hand against it. It shall continue and endure; and men, in after times, shall declare that this generation, which saved the Union from such sudden and unlooked-for dangers, surpassed in magnanimity even that one which laid its foundations in the eternal principles of liberty, justice, and humanity.

Mr. GWIN. I move that the Senate do now adjourn.

The motion was agreed to; and the Senate adjourned.

11

Senate Resignations

Senators John A. Slidell and Judah P. Benjamin, Louisiana
February 4, 1861

John A. Slidell (1793-1871) was born in New York City, graduated from Columbia College, studied law, was admitted to the New York bar, later moved to New Orleans and practiced law in New Orleans beginning in 1819. He served in the state legislature and as a U.S. district attorney. He was elected to the U.S. House of Representatives as a State Rights Democrat, and served from 1843-1845, whereupon he resigned to serve as U.S. Minister to Mexico, but that country refused to accept him. He was elected to the U.S. Senate and served from 1853 until his resignation in 1861. While on a mission for the C.S.A. to England and France, he was captured on the British steamer Trent and confined in Fort Warren, Boston Harbor. He was released in 1862 and lived in England until his death in 1871.

Judah P. Benjamin (1811-1884) was born in the Danish West Indies and immigrated with his family in 1816 to Savannah, Georgia, and later relocated to Wilmington, North Carolina. He attended Yale College, moved to New Orleans in 1831, studied law, and was admitted to the bar in 1832. He was elected as a Whig to the U.S. Senate in 1853 and served until his 1861 resignation. He served as Attorney General, Secretary of

War, and Secretary of State for the C.S.A. At the war's end he moved to England and was admitted to the London bar in 1866.

Mr. SLIDELL. I send to the Secretary a paper, which I desire to have read.

The Secretary read as follows:

> An Ordinance to dissolve the union between the State of Louisiana and other States united with her, under the compact entitled "The Constitution of the United States of America."
>
> We, the people of the State of Louisiana, in convention assembled, do declare and ordain, and it is hereby declared and ordained, that the ordinance passed by us in convention on the 22d day of November, in the year 1811, whereby the Constitution of the United States of America, and the amendments of said Constitution, were adopted, and all laws and ordinances by which the State of Louisiana became a member of the Federal Union, be, and the same are hereby, repealed and abrogated; and that the union now subsisting between Louisiana and other States, under the name of the "United States of America," is hereby dissolved.
>
> We do further declare and ordain, that the State of Louisiana hereby resumes all rights and powers heretofore delegated to the Government of the United States of America; that her citizens are absolved from all allegiance to said Government; and that she is in full possession and exercise of all those rights of sovereignty which appertain to a free and independent State.
>
> We do further declare and ordain, that all rights acquired and vested under the Constitution of the United States, or any act of Congress, or treaty, or under any law of this State and not incompatible with this ordinance, shall remain in force and have the same effect as if this ordinance had not been passed.
>
> The undersigned hereby certifies that the above ordinance is a true copy or the original ordinance adopted this day by the convention of the State of Louisiana.
>
> Given under my hand and the great seal of Louisiana, at Baton Rouge this 25th day of the month of January, in the year of our Lord, 1861.
>
> [L.S.]
>
> A. MOUTON,
>
> *President of the Convention.*
> J. Thomas Wheat, *Secretary of the Convention.*

Mr. SLIDELL. Mr. President, the document which the Secretary has just read, and which places on the files of the Senate official information that Louisiana has ceased to be a component part of these once United States, terminates the connection of my colleague and myself with this body. The occasion, however, justifies, if it does not call for, some parting words to those whom we leave behind, some forever, others we trust to meet again and to participate with them in the noble task of constructing and defending a new confederacy; which, if it may want at first the grand proportions and vast resources of the old, will still possess the essential elements of greatness, a people bold, hardy, homogenous in interests and sentiments, a fertile soil, an extensive territory, the capacity and the will to govern themselves through the forms and in the spirit of the Constitution under which they have been born and educated. Besides all these, they have an advantage which no other people seeking to change the Government under which they had before lived have ever enjoyed; they have had to pass through no intervening period of anarchy; they have in their several State governments, already shaped to their hands, everything necessary for the preservation of order, the administration of justice, and the protection of their soil and their property from foreign or domestic violence. They can consult with calmness and act with deliberation on every subject, either of immediate interest or future policy.

But, if we do not greatly mistake the prevailing sentiment of the southern mind, no attempt will be made to improve the Constitution; we shall take it such as it is; such as it has been found sufficient for our security and happiness, so long as its true intent and spirit lived in the hearts of a majority of the people of the free States, and controlled the action not only of the Federal but of the State Legislatures. We will adopt all laws not locally inapplicable or incompatible with our new relations; we will recognize the obligations of all existing treaties—those respecting the African slave trade included. We shall be prepared to assume our just proportion of the national debt; to account for the costs of all the forts and other property of the United States, which we have been compelled to seize in self-defense, if it should appear that our share of such expenditure has been greater than in other sections; and above all, we shall, as well from the dictates of natural justice and the principles of international law as of political and geographical affinities of mutual pecuniary interests, recognize the rights of the inhabitants of the valley of the Mississippi and its tributaries to its free navigation; we will guaranty to them a free interchange of all agricultural productions without impost, tax duty, or toll of any kind; the free transit from foreign countries of every species of merchandise, subject only to such regulations as may be absolutely necessary for the protection of any revenue system we may establish, and for purposes of police.

As for such States of the Union as may not choose to unite their destinies with ours, we shall consider them, as we shall all other foreign nations, "enemies in war, in peace friends." We wish and we hope to part with them amicably; and, so far as depends on us, they shall have no provocation to pursue a hostile course; but in this regard we, from the necessities of the case, can only be passive; it will be for the people of the non-slaveholding States to decide this momentous question. This declaration, however, requires some qualification. Could the issue be fairly presented to the people of those States, we should have little doubt of a peaceful separation, with the possibility of a complete, and the probability of a partial, reconstruction on a basis satisfactory to us and honorable to them; but, with the present representations in either branch of Congress, we see nothing to justify our indulging any such expectation. We must be prepared to resist coercion, whether attempted by avowed enemies, or by a hand heretofore supposed friendly, by open war, or under the more insidious, and, therefore, more dangerous pretext of enforcing laws, protecting the public property, or collecting the revenue. We shall not cavil about words, or discuss legal and technical distinctions; we shall consider the one as equivalent to the other, and shall be prepared to act accordingly. *Utroque arbitrio parati.* You will find us ready to meet you with the outstretched hand of fellowship, or in the mailed panoply of war, as you may will it; elect between these alternatives.

We have no idea that you will even attempt to invade our soil with your armies; but we acknowledge your superiority on the sea, at present, in some degree accidental, but in the main, natural, and permanent, until we shall have acquired better ports for our marine. You may, if you will it, persist in considering us bound to you during your good pleasure; you may deny the sacred and indefeasible right, we will not say of secession, but of revolution—ay, of rebellion, if you choose so to call our action— the right of every people to establish for itself that form of government which it may, even in its folly, if such you deem it, consider best calculated to secure its safety and promote its welfare. You may ignore the principles of our immortal Declaration of Independence; you may attempt to reduce us to subjection, or you may, under the color of enforcing your laws or collecting your revenue, blockade our ports. This will be war, and we shall meet it, with different but equally efficient weapons. We will not permit the consumption or introduction of any of your manufactures; every sea will swarm with our volunteer militia of the ocean, with the striped bunting floating over their heads, for we do not mean to give up that flag without a bloody struggle, it is ours as much as yours; and although for a time more stars may shine on your banner, our children, if not we, will rally under a constellation more numerous and more resplendent than yours. You may smile at this as an impotent boast, at least for the present, if not for the future; but if we need ships and men for privateering, we shall be amply supplied from the same sources as now almost exclusively furnish the means for carrying on, with such unexampled vigor, the African slave trade—New York and New England. Your mercantile marine must either sail under foreign flags or rot at your wharves.

But, pretermitting these remedies, we will pass to another equally efficacious. Every civilized nation now is governed in its foreign relations by the rule of recognizing Governments "*de facto.*" You alone invoke the doctrine of the "*de jure,*" or divine right of lording it over an unwilling people strong enough to maintain their power within their own limits. How long, think you, will the great naval Powers of Europe permit you to impede their free intercourse with their best customers for their various fabrics, and to stop the supplies of the great staple which is the most important basis of their manufacturing industry, by a mere paper blockade? You were, with all the wealth and resources of this once great Confederacy, but a fourth or fifth rate naval Power, with capacities, it is true, for large, and in a just quarrel, almost indefinite, expansion. What will you be when not merely emasculated by the withdrawal of fifteen States, but warred upon by them with active and inveterate hostility?

But enough, perhaps somewhat too much of this. We desire not to speak to you in terms of bravado or menace. Let us treat each other as men, who, determined to break off unpleasant, incompatible, and unprofitable relations, cease to bandy words, and mutually leave each other to determine whether their differences shall be decided by blows or by the code which some of us still recognize as that of honor. We shall do with you as the French guards did with the English at the battle of Fontenoy. In a preliminary skirmish, the French and English guards met face to face; the English guards courteously saluted their adversaries by taking off their hats; the French returned the salute with equal courtesy. Lord Hay, of the English guards, cried out, in a loud voice: "Gentlemen of the French guards, fire." Count D'Auteroche replied in the same tone: "Gentlemen, we never fire first." The English took them at their word, and did fire first. Being at close quarters, the effect was very destructive, and the French were, for a time, thrown into some disorder; but the fortunes of the day were soon restored by the skill and courage of Marshal

Saxe, and the English, under the Duke of Cumberland, suffered one of the most disastrous defeats which their military annals record. Gentlemen, we will not fire first.

We have often seen it charged that the present movement of the southern States is merely the consummation of a fixed purpose, long entertained by a few intriguers for the selfish object of personal aggrandizement. There never was a greater error—if we were not about to part, we should say a grosser or more atrocious calumny. Do not deceive yourselves; this is not the work of political managers, but of the people. As a general rule, the instincts of the masses, and the sagacity of those who, in private life, had larger opportunities for observation and reflection, had satisfied them of the necessity of separation long before their accustomed party leaders were prepared to avow it. We appeal to every southern Senator yet remaining here, whether such be not the case in his own State. Of its truth, we can give no stronger illustration than the vote in the Louisiana convention. Of one hundred and thirty members, every delegate being in his seat, one hundred and thirteen voted for immediate secession; and of the seventeen who voted against it, there were not more than four or five who did not admit the necessity of separation, and only differed as to the time and mode of its accomplishment.

Nor is the mere election, by the forms of the Constitution, of a President distasteful to us, the cause, as it is so often and so confidently asserted, of our action. It is this: we all consider the election of Mr. Lincoln, with his well-known antecedents and avowed principles and purposes, by a decided majority over all other candidates combined in every non-slaveholding State on this side of the Pacific slope, noble, gallant New Jersey alone excepted, as conclusive evidence of the determined hostility of the northern masses to our institutions. We believe that he conscientiously entertains the opinions which he has so often and so explicitly declared; and that, having been elected on the issues thus presented, he will honestly endeavor to carry them into execution.

While now we have no fears of servile insurrection, even of a partial character, we know that his inauguration as President of the United States, with our assent, would have been considered by many of our slaves as the day of their emancipation; and that the 4th of March would have witnessed, in various quarters, outbreaks, which, although they would have been promptly suppressed, would have carried ruin and devastation to many a southern home, and have cost the lives of hundreds of the misguided victims of northern negrophilism.

Senators, six States have now severed the links that bound them to a

Union to which we were all attached, as well by many ties of material well-being, as by the inheritance of common glories in the past, and the well-founded hopes of still more brilliant destinies in the future! Twelve seats are now vacant on this floor. The work is only yet but begun. It requires no spirit of prophecy to point to many, many chairs around us that will soon, like ours, be unfilled; and if the weird sisters of the great dramatic poet could here be conjured up, they would present to the affrighted vision of those on the other side of the Chamber, who have so largely contributed to "the deep damnation of this taking off," a "glass to show them many more." They who have so foully murdered the Constitution and the Union will find, when too late, like the Scottish Thane, that "for Banquo's issue they have filed their minds;" "they have but placed upon their heads a fruitless crown, and put a barren scepter in their grip, no son of theirs succeeding."

In taking leave of the Senate, while we shall carry with us many agreeable recollections of intercourse, social and official, with gentlemen who have differed with us on this, the great question of the age, we would that we could, in fitting language, express the mingled feelings of admiration and regret with which we look back to our associations on this floor with many of our northern colleagues. They have, one after the other, fallen in their heroic struggle against a blind fanaticism, until now but few—alas! how few—remain to fight the battle of the Constitution. Several even of these will terminate their official career in one short month, and will give place to men holding opinions diametrically opposite, which have recommended them to the suffrages of their States. Had we remained here, the same fate would have awaited, at the next election, the four or five last survivors of that gallant band; but now we shall carry with us at least this one consoling reflection, our departure realizing all their predictions of ill to the Republic, opens a new era of triumph for the Democratic party of the North, and will, we firmly believe, reestablish its lost ascendancy in most of the non-slaveholding States.

———

Mr. BENJAMIN. Mr. President, if we were engaged in the performance of our accustomed legislative duties, I might well rest content with the simple statement of my concurrence in the remarks just made by my colleague. Deeply impressed, however, with the solemnity of the occasion, I cannot remain insensible to the duty of recording, amongst the authentic reports of your proceedings, the expression of my conviction that the State of Louisiana has judged and acted well and wisely in this crisis of her destiny.

Sir, it has been urged, on more than one occasion, in the discussions here and elsewhere, that Louisiana stands on an exceptionable footing. It has been said that whatever may be the rights of the States that were original parties to the Constitution—even granting *their* right to resume, for sufficient cause, those restricted powers which they delegated to the General Government in trust for their own use and benefit—still Louisiana can have no such right, because *she* was acquired by purchase. Gentlemen have not hesitated to speak of the sovereign States formed out of the territory ceded by France as property bought with the money of the United States, belonging to them as purchasers; and, although they have not carried their doctrine to its legitimate results, I must also conclude that they also mean to assert, on the same principle, *the right of selling for a price that which for a price was bought.*

I shall not pause to comment on this repulsive dogma of a party which asserts the right of property in free-born white men, in order to reach its cherished object of destroying the right of property in slave-born black men—still less shall I detain the Senate in pointing out how shadowy the distinction between the condition of the servile African and that to which the white freemen of my State would be reduced, if it indeed be true that they are bound to this Government by ties that cannot be legitimately dissevered, without the consent of that majority which wields its powers for their oppression. I simply deny the fact on which the argument is founded. I deny that the province of Louisiana, or the people of Louisiana, were ever conveyed to the United States for a price as property that could be bought or sold at will. Without entering into the details of the negotiation, the archives of our State department show the fact to be, that although the domain, the public lands, and the other property of France in the ceded province, were conveyed by absolute title to the United States, *the sovereignty was not conveyed otherwise than in trust.*

A hundred fold, sir, has the Government of the United States been reimbursed by the sales of public property, of public lands, for the price of the acquisition; but not with the fidelity of the honest trustee has it discharged the obligations as regards the sovereignty.

I have said that the Government assumed to act as trustee or guardian of the people of the ceded province, and covenanted to transfer to them the sovereignty thus held in trust for their use and benefit, as soon as they were capable of exercising it. What is the express language of the treaty?

> The inhabitants of the ceded Territory *shall be incorporated in the Union* of the United States, and admitted *as soon as possible*, according to the principles of the Federal Constitution, to the enjoyment of *all* the rights, advantages, and immunities of citizens of the United States; and in the mean time they shall be maintained and *protected* in the enjoyment of their liberty, *property*, and the religion which they profess.

And, sir, as if to mark the true nature of the cession in a manner too significant to admit of misconstruction, the treaty stipulates no price; and the sole consideration for the conveyance, as stated on its face, is the desire to afford a strong proof of the friendship of France for the United States. By the terms of a separate convention stipulating the payment of a sum of money, the precaution is again observed of stating that the payment is to be made, not as a consideration or a price or a condition precedent of the cession, but it is carefully distinguished as being a consequence of the cession. It was by words thus studiously chosen, sir, that James Monroe and Thomas Jefferson marked their understanding of a contract now misconstrued as being a bargain and a sale of sovereignty over freemen. With what indignant scorn would those staunch advocates of the inherent right of self-government have repudiated the slavish doctrine now deduced from their action!

How were the obligations of this treaty fulfilled? That Louisiana at that date contained slaves held as property by her people through the whole length of the Mississippi valley—that those people had an unrestricted right of settlement with their slaves under legal protection throughout the entire ceded province—no man has ever yet had the hardihood to deny. Here is a treaty promise to *protect* that property, that *slave property*, in that *Territory, before* it should become a State. That this promise was openly violated, in the adjustment forced upon the South at the time of the admission of Missouri, is a matter of recorded history. The perspicuous and unanswerable exposition of Mr. Justice Catron, in the opinion delivered by him in the Dred Scott Case, will remain through all time as an ample vindication of this assertion.

If, then, sir, the people of Louisiana had a right, which Congress could not deny, of the admission into the Union with *all* the rights of *all* the citizens of the United States, it is in vain that the partisans of the right of the majority to govern the minority with despotic control, attempt to establish a distinction, to her prejudice, between her rights and those of any other State. The only distinction which really exists is this: that she can point to a breach of treaty stipulations expressly guarantying [sic] her rights, as a wrong superadded to those which have impelled a number of her sister States to the assertion of their independence.

The rights of Louisiana as a sovereign State are those of Virginia; no more, no less. Let those who deny her right to resume delegated powers, successfully refute the claim of Virginia to the same right, in spite of her express reservation made and notified to her sister States when she consented to enter the Union. And, sir, permit me to say that, of all the causes which justify the action of the southern States, I know none of greater gravity and more alarming magnitude than that now developed of the denial of the right of secession. A pretension so monstrous as that which perverts a restricted agency, constituted by sovereign States for common purposes, into the unlimited despotism of the majority, and denies all legitimate escape from such despotism, when powers not delegated are usurped, converts the whole constitutional fabric into the secure abode of lawless tyranny, and degrades sovereign States into provincial dependencies.

It is said that the right of secession, if conceded, makes our Government a mere rope of sand; that to assert its existence imputes to the framers of the Constitution the folly of planting the seeds of death in that which was designed for perpetual existence. If this imputation were true, sir, it would merely prove that their offspring was not exempt from that mortality which is the common lot of all that is not created by higher than human power. But it is not so, sir. Let facts answer theory. For two thirds of a century this right has been known by many of the States to be, at all times, within their power. Yet, up to the present period, when its exercise has become indispensable to a people menaced with absolute extermination, there have been but two instances in which it has been even threatened seriously: the first, when Massachusetts led the New England States in an attempt to escape from the dangers of our last war with Great Britain; the second, when the same State proposed to secede on account of the admission of Texas as a new State into the Union.

Sir, in the language of our declaration of secession from Great Britain it is stated, as an established truth, that "all experience has shown that mankind are more disposed to suffer while evils are sufferable, than to right themselves by abolishing the forms to which they have been accustomed." And nothing can be more obvious to the calm and candid observer of passing events than that the disruption of the Confederacy has been due, in great measure, not to the existence, but to the denial of this right. Few candid men would refuse to admit that the Republicans of the North would have been checked in their mad career, had they been convinced of the existence of this right, and the intention to assert. The very knowledge of its existence, by preventing occurrences which alone could prompt its exercise, would have rendered it a most efficient instrument in the preservation of the Union. But, sir, if the fact were otherwise—if all the teachings of experience were reversed—better, far better, a rope of sand, ay, the flimsiest gossamer that ever glistened in the morning dew, than chains of iron, and shackles of steel; better the wildest anarchy, with the hope, the chance, of one hour's inspiration of the glorious breath of freedom, than ages of the hopeless bondage and oppression to which our enemies would reduce us.

We are told that the laws must be enforced; that the revenues must be collected; that the South is in rebellion without cause, and that her citizens are traitors.

Rebellion! The very word is a confession; an avowal of tyranny, outrage, and oppression. It is taken from the despot's code, and has no terror for other than slavish souls. When, sir, did millions of people, as a single man, rise in organized, deliberate, unimpassioned rebellion against justice, truth, and honor? Well did a great Englishman exclaim on a similar occasion:

> You might as well tell me that they rebelled against the light of heaven; that they rejected the fruits of the earth. Men do not war against their benefactors; they are not mad enough to repel the instincts of self-preservation. I pronounce fearlessly that no intelligent people ever rose, or ever will rise, against a sincere, rational, and benevolent authority. No people were ever born blind. Infatuation is not a law of human nature. When there is a revolt by a free people, with the common consent of all classes of society, there must be a *criminal* against whom that revolt is aimed.

Traitors! Treason! Ay, sir, the people of the South imitate and glory in just such treason as glowed in the soul of Hampden; just such treason as leaped in living flame from the impassioned lips of Henry; just such treason as encircles with a sacred halo the undying name of Washington!

You will enforce the laws. You want to know if we have a Government; if you have any authority to collect revenue; to wring tribute from an unwilling people? Sir, humanity desponds, and all the inspiring hopes of her progressive improvement vanish into empty air at the reflections which crowd on the mind at hearing repeated, with aggravated enormity, the sentiments against which a Chatham launched his indignant thunders nearly a century ago. The very words of Lord North and his royal master are repeated here in debate, not as quotations, but as the spontaneous outpourings of a spirit the counterpart of theirs.

In Lord North's speech, on the destruction of the tea in Boston harbor, he said:

> We are no longer to dispute between legislation and taxation; *we are now only to consider whether or not we have any authority there.* It is very clear we have none, if we suffer the property of our subjects to be destroyed. We must punish, control, or yield to them.

And thereupon he proposed to close the port of Boston, just as the representatives of Massachusetts now propose to close the port of Charleston, *in order to determine whether or not you have any authority there.* It is thus that, in 1861, Boston is to pay her debt of gratitude to Charleston, which, in the days of her struggle, proclaimed the generous sentiment that "the cause of Boston was the cause of Charleston." Who, after this, will say that Republics are ungrateful? Well, sir, the statesmen of Great Britain answered to Lord North's appeal, "yield." The courtiers and the politicians said, "punish," "control." The result is known. History gives you the lesson. Profit by its teachings.

So, sir, in the address sent under the royal sign-manual to Parliament, it was invoked to take measures "for better securing the execution of the laws," and acquiesced in the suggestion. Just as now, a senile Executive, under the sinister influence of insane counsels, is proposing, with your assent, "to secure the better execution of the laws," by blockading ports and turning upon the people of the States the artillery which they provided at their own expense for their own defense, and intrusted [sic] to you and to him for that and for no other purpose. Nay, even in the States that are now exercising the undoubted and most precious rights of a free people; where there is no secession; where the citizens are assembling to hold peaceful elections for considering what course of action is demanded in this dread crisis by a due regard for their own safety and their own liberty; ay, even in Virginia herself, the people are to cast their suffrages beneath the undisguised menaces of a frowning fortress. Cannon are brought to bear on their homes, and parricidal hands are preparing weapons for rending the bosom of the mother of Washington.

Sir, when Great Britain proposed to exact tribute from your fathers against their will, Lord Chatham said:

> Whatever is a man's own is absolutely his own; no man has a right to take it from him without his consent. Whoever attempts to do it, attempts an injury. Whoever does it, commits a robbery. You have no right to tax America. I rejoice that America has resisted.

> Let the sovereign authority of this country over the colonies be asserted in

as strong terms as can be devised, and be made to extend to every point of legislation whatever, so that we may bind their trade, confine their manufactures, and exercise every power, *except that of taking money out of their own pockets without their consent.*

It was reserved for the latter half of the nineteenth century, and for the Congress of a Republic of freemen, to witness the willing abnegation of all power, save that of exacting tribute. What imperial Britain, with the haughtiest pretensions of unlimited power over dependent colonies, could not even attempt without the vehement protest of her greatest statesmen, is to be enforced in aggravated form, if you can enforce it, against independent States.

Good God! sir [sic], since when has the necessity arisen of recalling to American legislators the lessons of freedom taught in lisping childhood by loving mothers; that pervade the atmosphere we have breathed from infancy; that so form part of our very being, that in their absence we would lose the consciousness of our own identity? Heaven be praised that all have not forgotten them; that when we shall have left these familiar Halls, and when force bills, blockades, armies, navies, and all the accustomed coercive appliances of despots shall be proposed and advocated, voices shall be heard from this side of the Chamber that will make its very roof resound with the indignant clamor of outraged freedom. Methinks I still hear ringing in my ears the appeal of the eloquent Representative [Hon. GEORGE H. PENDLETON, of Ohio] whose northern home looks down on Kentucky's fertile borders: *"Armies, money, blood, cannot maintain this Union; justice, reason, peace may."*

And now to you, Mr. President, and to my brother Senators, on all sides of this Chamber, I bid a respectful farewell; with many of those from whom I have been radically separated in political sentiment, my personal relations have been kindly, and have inspired me with a respect and esteem that I shall not willingly forget; with those around me from the southern States, I part as men part from brothers on the eve of a temporary absence, with a cordial pressure of the hand and a smiling assurance of the speedy renewal of sweet intercourse around the family hearth. But to you, noble and generous friends, who, born beneath other skies, possess hearts that beat in sympathy with ours; to you, who, solicited and assailed by motives the most powerful that could appeal to selfish natures, have nobly spurned them all; to you who, in our behalf, have bared your breasts to the fierce beatings of the storm, and made willing sacrifice of life's most glittering prizes in your devotion to constitutional liberty; to you, who have made our cause your cause, and from many of whom I feel I part forever, what shall I, can I say? Nought, I know and feel, is needed for myself; but this I will say for the people in whose name I speak to-day: whether prosperous or adverse fortunes await you, one priceless treasure is yours—the assurance that an entire people honor your names, and hold them in grateful and affectionate memory. But with still sweeter and more touching return shall your unselfish devotion be rewarded. When, in after days, the story of the present shall be written; when history shall have passed her stern sentence on the erring men who have driven their unoffending brethren from the shelter of their common home, your names will derive fresh luster from the contrast; and when your children shall hear repeated the familiar tale, it will be with glowing cheek and kindling eye, their very souls will stand a-tiptoe as their sires are named, and they will glory in their lineage from men of spirit as generous and of patriotism as high-hearted as ever illustrated or adorned the American Senate.

12

The Right of Secession

Senator Joseph Lane, Oregon
March 2, 1861

Joseph Lane (1801-1881) was born in North Carolina, moved to Kentucky with his family where he attended common schools, and then moved to Indiana where from 1821-1846 he served intermittently in the Indiana state legislature. During the Mexican War he was commissioned as a colonel of the Second Indiana Volunteer Regiment and eventually promoted to the rank of brigadier general. In 1849 President Polk appointed him Governor of the Territory of Oregon; from 1850 to 1851 he served as a Democratic delegate to the Congress. Upon the admission of Oregon into the Union he served in the U.S. Senate from 1859-1861. He did not seek reelection, but was nominated for Vice President on the Democratic ticket of Breckinridge and Lane. Senator Lane pleaded to his colleagues, "in God's name, let us have peace." From the "summit of prosperity," the people are being plunged "headlong into an abyss of woe" to keep the southern States in the Union "to foot the bills, to pay the taxes, and to be governed and ruled against their will."

Mr. LANE. Mr. President, I hope I shall be permitted to proceed without interruption, and I trust not to consume much time. While I had the floor yesterday, I stated some of my objections to the proposed amendments to the Constitution which are now before us. They are: that they do not do justice to the whole country—that they do not do justice to all the States. I have always held that the territory is the common property; that it belongs to all the states; that every citizen of every State has an equal right to emigrate to, and settle in, the common Territories; and that any species of property, recognized as such in any State of the Confederacy, should have a like recognition in the Territories, and be guarantied, protected, and secured in its full integrity, to the owner thereof. That this should be so, was the intent of the revolutionary fathers who shaped and framed the Constitution; and it was this principle, more, perhaps, than any other, which called into being that noble compact, which has so long been a bound of Union and goodness between all the States. It is the very life-blood and vitality of the Constitution. It is the ligament that has held us together heretofore, and which, if now cut, will result in hopeless and immutable disruption. I have never deviated a single iota from this correct doctrine. Had we lived up to this equitable principle— the foundation upon which the Constitution rests, upon which only this Union can be maintained—we should have had no trouble in this country to-day. It is not my fault that the trouble and dissatisfaction prevail; it is not my fault that secession has taken place, and that further secession will take place, unless Congress shall recognize this great principle of justice, of right, and of equality. That is the doctrine upon which this Union rests; and it must be maintained, or the connection will be severed.

While upon this question, Mr. President, I may be permitted to allude to my course in the Senate last session, and I shall do so very briefly. Upon a series of resolutions introduced by the Senator from Mississippi [Mr. DAVIS]—a series of resolutions that were considered in this body, after having been previously maturely and deliberately adopted by a caucus composed of Democratic Senators, and agreed upon by them, as setting forth the principles necessary to be maintained in order to secure the existence and perpetuity of this Confederacy. It has been charged upon this floor that, on the 25th of May last, I voted against the right of protection to slave property in the Territories. In order that the Senate may know how I voted, and that I may show you and every other man that I stood then as I stand to-day, and as I have always stood upon this question, I will read some extracts from the discussions upon this series of resolutions. The fourth resolution was in these words:

> *Resolved,* That neither Congress, nor a Territorial Legislature, whether by direct legislation or legislation of an indirect and unfriendly nature, possess the power to annul or impair the constitutional right of any citizen of the

United States to take his slave property into the common Territories, but it is the duty of the Federal Government there to afford for that, as for other species of property, the needful protection; and if experience should at any time prove that the judiciary does not possess power to insure adequate protection, it will then become the duty of Congress to supply such deficiency.

Now mark, this resolution states that all the property of all the people of any State, whether slave or otherwise, has an equal right to protection; and if experience should at any time prove that the courts had not the power to afford that protection, *then* it was the duty of Congress to enact such laws as were necessary to protect every man in his legal and rightful property, no matter of what description or characteristic. Sir, not long since, upon this floor, a Senator was hardy enough to say that I voted against protecting property in Territories; and he desired to know what had happened that States should be concerned; what had occurred to alarm the States that were seceding from the Union? I will show you, sir, very briefly what I said upon that question then; and I will repeat it now, for I have never changed my sentiments on this subject. No living man can assert, and in doing so tell the truth, that I ever uttered a word against the equality of the States, and their equal right in the common Territory of our common country; and any charge that I voted then to refuse protection to property in the territory is *false*. I have always held that the territory belonged to all; that it was acquired, as I knew, at the expense of the southern States as well as of the northern; and upon the battlefield where I had witnessed the good conduct of northern and southern troops, I found the soldier from the southern States pouring out his blood as freely, and certainly in very much larger quantity—for there were very many more from the southern States who participated in the battles of our country in the war which resulted in the acquisition of territory, than there were from the northern States. Then, so far as the acquisition is concerned, it is joint, and it was for the joint benefit of all portions of the country. Consequently, I have held, and I hold now, that the Territories should be so appropriated. And when those resolutions were up last winter, I said what I will now read:

I only desire to say, in relation to the series of resolutions, a portion of which I have already voted in favor of, that I shall vote in favor of the rest; for the whole of them together meet with my hearty approbation. They assert the truth; they assert the great principle that the constitutional rights of the States are equal; that the States have equal rights in this country under the Constitution; and as I understand it, they must be maintained in that equality. These resolutions only assert that principle; and I say that it is a misfortune to the country, in my opinion, that the principle laid down in these resolutions had not been asserted sooner. They ought to have been asserted by the Democratic party in plain English ten years ago. If they had been, you would have no trouble in this country to-day; the Democratic party would have been united and strong, and the equality of the constitutional rights of the Sates would have been maintained in the Territory, and in all other things; squatter sovereignty would not have been heard of, and to-day we should be united. It is the fault of the Democratic party in dodging truth, in dodging principle, in dodging the Constitution itself, that has brought the trouble upon the country and the party that is experienced to-day.

I believe, if we had asserted and maintained these great truths ten years ago, and placed ourselves upon them boldly, as it was our duty to have done, we would have no trouble in this country to-day; but instead of declaring the great truths enunciated in these resolutions, we went off upon issues unbecoming the Democratic party. A portion of our leaders wandered and went astray, and asserted that the people of a Territory had the right to prohibit slavery whenever, in their judgment, it ought to be prohibited; a power which Congress does not even possess, and consequently cannot confer upon a Territorial Legislature, unless the creature becomes greater than the creator. It was this kind of trouble, and this sort of heresy introduced into the Democratic party, that have broken it up, and brought the disasters upon our country which we experience to-day. I say, then, let the blame fall upon the guilty; I am innocent of it; for I have held but one doctrine upon this question from the beginning to the present hour, and I shall hold that doctrine to the end. In the speech from which I have already read, I also used the following language:

> Sir, it appears to me to be very singular indeed, that any man can hold that the territory of this country belongs to a portion of the people, and that the people of one portion of the Union can go there and enjoy their property, when the people of another portion cannot enjoy the right of property in that territory—territory common to the whole country; territory that was earned or acquired by the common blood and common treasure of all; territory that is sustained by the common treasure of all; and to say that all shall not have an equal right there, is to deny a fact so plain, a principle so just, a right so manifest, that I can hardly see how any man who professes to be a Democrat can deny it, or how he can attempt to embarrass the adoption of the correct principles announced in these resolutions. I shall therefore vote against all the amendments, and everything that is offered to obstruct their passage, upon the ground that they assert justice, that they assert truth, that they assert the equality and the constitutional rights of all the States, which principle must be maintained, or this Union cannot be preserved.

That was my doctrine then, it is the doctrine which I have held and advocated for twenty years. It is the doctrine I hold now; and I so notified the Senator from Tennessee, who arraigned me here as voting against protecting property, and who did me willful and gross injustice in it—for I voted for it and he voted against it. That is to say, I voted against the resolution introduced by Mr. CLINGMAN declaring "that slave property did not need protection in the Territories," while the Senator from Tennessee voted for it; and when the motion was made to reconsider the vote adopting it in lieu of the fourth resolution of the Davis series, I voted to reconsider, and the Senator from Tennessee voted against it, showing clearly that he was against affording that protection to slave property which the fourth resolution provided for. Did I not maintain the truth? Was I not prophetic in the announcement that I made in this Senate Chamber then? I said, that unless this great principle of justice, of equality, of the right of every man to the common territory should be maintained, this Union would be broken up. This great principle has not been maintained, but the Union has been destroyed.

But, sir, to go to the votes. It will be borne in mind, and every Senator on this floor will bear me out in my statement, that while the Davis resolutions—the series which I speak—were up, various propositions were made to amend them, and I voted against all amendments. There are Senators here at this moment who will sustain me when I say that, when in caucus and we had under consideration this series of resolutions, I said, and said it boldly and in plain terms, that if every man from every southern State of this Union would come here and say, for the sake of peace, if you please, or any other reason, he was willing to abandon his equality, his right in the common territory, then, if alone, I would stand and protest against it; protest that he had no right to surrender a constitutional right; that none but a coward would do it; that every man had a right in the common territory; that it was his privilege, and he should never surrender it with my permission. On the other hand, I said that if every northern man in the Senate Chamber—nay, but even every northern citizen—expressed a desire to surrender his right, his equality, his privilege, to go to the common territories with his property, I should enter my solemn protest against it, and insist that he had a constitutional right to go there which he should never surrender with my consent. Then, how any man could assert that I ever entertained the opinion that slavery did not need protection from aggression, is to me the strangest, falsest thing in nature. I said, as I have shown you, that I had voted against all amendments, and would continue to vote against all amendments, or any attempt whatsoever calculated to obstruct the passage of the resolutions; for they asserted the right of the people to go to the Territories, asserted the power of the court to protect them in the possession of their property, and that if the court failed to protect them, Congress should afford the necessary authority to do so.

But, sir, allow me to observe: there was a resolution that I never voted for, and that no man can charge me with ever having voted for. Senators will recollect—and whoever has read the proceedings of the Senate will recollect—that an amendment was offered as a substitute to the fourth resolution, in these words:

> That the existing condition of the Territories does not require the intervention of Congress for the protection of property in slaves.

I did not vote for that resolution; but the Senator from Tennessee did. That amendment was adopted in lieu of the fourth resolution of the series that I have read, which insured protection to slave property in the Territories. It was adopted not entirely by Democratic votes; and that there may be no mistakes, I will read what the Senator from Massachusetts said when he moved a reconsideration:

> I wish simply to say that I voted for the resolution because I believed the condition of the Territories requires no such law now or ever, and I do not believe in the enactment of any such law; but my friends on this side of the Chamber have put that resolution in the series; and for myself, I do not want to be responsible for any portion of these resolutions; and I therefore wish the vote to be reconsidered.

This was the language of the Senator from Massachusetts, when he found that the Republicans, united with some Democrats, had stricken out the fourth resolution of the series, and inserted this as a substitute. I said to Mr. WILSON on that occasion:

> I desire merely to tender my thanks to the honorable Senator from Massachusetts. The series of resolutions, as introduced by the honorable Senator from Mississippi, are germane one to the other. They are a declaration of principles by the Democratic party. This amendment, as the Senator has said correctly, has been fastened on the Democratic resolutions by the votes of the Republican Senators. I feel grateful, indeed, to the Senator for making the motion to reconsider. I hope the vote will be reconsidered, and the resolution voted down.

The motion was put, and on the yeas and nays the vote was reconsidered, and I voted against the amendment when it was adopted as a substitute for the fourth resolution. Among those who voted in the affirmative for reconsideration were Messrs. BENJAMIN, BROWN, CHESTNUT, CLAY, DAVIS, FITZPATRICK, GREEN, GWIN, HAMMOND, HARLAN, HUNTER, IVERSON, JOHNSON of Arkansas, and LANE. Among those who voted against it, I find Johnson of Tennessee. I did not vote to continue in the series a resolution that refused protection to all the people in the common Territories. Portions of the Journal have been paraded to show the vote on Mr. BROWN'S amendment to Mr. CLINGMAN'S amendment. I said, in several speeches, that I should vote against all amendments, because the series had been considered not only here, but in a caucus composed of the Democratic Senators of this body, and we had agreed to take them as a whole, and to vote them through altogether if we had the strength to do so. I voted against every proposition to amend. I voted against Mr. BROWN'S, and I voted against Mr. CLINGMAN'S, and I voted against every other amendment that was calculated to weaken or embarrass the passage of the resolutions. Yet I am represented here as having voted against affording protection to slave property in the Territories! I ask again, if any Senator, if any man who can read, can say that the fourth resolution, for which I did vote and for which I struggled and contended, does not declare that slave property shall be protected in the common Territories of our country. I will read it again:

> *Resolved*, That neither Congress nor a Territorial Legislature, whether by direct legislation or legislation of an indirect and unfriendly nature, possess the power to annul or impair the constitutional right of any citizen of the United States to take his slave property into the common territories, but it is the duty of the Federal Government there to afford for that, as for other species of property, the needful protection; and if experience should, at any time, prove that the judiciary does not possess the power to insure adequate protection, it will then become the duty of Congress to supply such deficiency.

Could anything be stronger? Could any man desire a more direct declaration of principles than this? Upon the yeas and nays I voted for it. I voted against the amendment that was adopted, and afterwards reconsidered. How, then, can a man arraign me before the country as having said upon oath, on the 25th of May last, that slave property should not be protected in the common Territories with other property? I have always held that all property should be protected, slave as well as other property; that it should have the same protection as, and no more protection than, any other property. That they do not secure all this, is the objection I have to the amendments to the Constitution proposed by the peace conference. They are ambiguous, loose, and deceptive. I do not know that the people can comprehend them. There will be no certainty under them; and they would, if adopted, result in endless troubles and litigation. I trust no amendments will ever be made to the Constitution, unless they are made upon principles of right, justice, and equality, so that there can be no mistake in construing them hereafter. If we amend the Constitution, let us do it with a view to the peace of the country, with a view to the harmony of the country, with a view to the security of every interest, and of every State in the Union. If we could do that, and this day amend the Constitution as to provide expressly that every State should have equal rights in the Territories and elsewhere within the Union, this Confederacy would last forever, the States that have left us would come back, and we should have then a great and lasting Union indeed. Without it, we never can have a permanent Union. We must do something that is clearly right, or the States that have left us will never return. They never ought to return, unless they can have the right of equality secured to them by the Constitution. I claim for my State just that which she is entitled to, and not a particle more. I would concede to the southern States that to which they are entitled, and not a particle more. That they must have, or there can be no peace, no union; no harmony, no security, and no perpetuity of this Confederacy. Such amendments to the Constitution, securing these objects and principles, are indispensable to the maintenance of the Government as it was formed.

Then why not do right? Why not every southern man ask just that which he is entitled to and no more? He ought to be content with nothing short of what he is entitled to; and if he be [sic], he is untrue to his section and his constituents; untrue to the people whose servant he is; and untrue to the institutions of the country; for the country can exist only upon the triumph of such principles. He who is unwilling to deal fairly by the North and the South, is a man who is guilty of shattering and ruining the Confederacy; destroying the peace and harmony and success of this great experiment of ours.

The doctrine asserted in the series of resolutions offered by Mr. DAVIS have not been maintained; and, as a consequence, events have since transpired detrimental to the public peace and welfare of the country, and destructive of its unity. The Union has been in fact broken up. But, although the ship is wrecked, the principles that guided her survive— live, even in the heart of New England. The very doctrines which I have enunciated or advocated are laid down in the resolutions of the late Democratic convention of the State of Connecticut. I send them to the

Secretary, and request that they be read.

The Secretary read, as follows:

> *Resolved*, That it is the opinion of the Democracy of Connecticut, in convention assembled, that this Government is a Confederacy of sovereign and independent States, based and founded upon the equal rights of each; and any legislation trenching upon the great principle of their equality, is a wanton violation of the spirit and letter of the constitutional compact.
>
> *Resolved*, That the present lamentable condition of the country finds its origin in the unconstitutional acts and sectional spirit of a great northern party, the principles of whose organization deny to the people of one class of States the enjoyment and exercise of the same political rights claimed and demanded by another class of States; thus ignoring and destroying the great political truth which is the foundation of our Government, and the vital principle of the Constitution of the United States.
>
> *Resolved*, That the pernicious doctrine of coercion, instead of conciliation, to be applied to the seceding States, which is now advocated and urged by the leaders of the northern sectional party, is utterly at war with the exercise of right, reason, matured judgment, and the principles of the Constitution of the United States, and should be strongly resisted by every lover of our common country, by every well-wisher to the best interests of the human race, as opposed to the progress and civilization of the age, as the sure precursor of an internecine war, in which would be sacrificed the lives of hundreds of thousands of our fellow citizens, the expenditure of countless millions of treasure, the destruction of the moral and commercial interests of our people; and not only utterly fail of its avowed object, the restoration of the Union, but defeat forever its reconstruction.
>
> *Resolved*, That a restoration of good feeling between the inhabitants of our common country should be, and is, the paramount feeling in every patriotic heart; to that great object should be sacrificed sectional prejudice and the spirit of partisanship; therefore the Democracy of Connecticut earnestly commend to the attention of Congress the propositions of the venerable and distinguished Senator from Kentucky; believing that the adoption thereof, or those of a similar character, would greatly conduce to harmonize the opinions of the North and the South, stay the progress of secession, and to the reconstruction of a now dissevered Union.

Mr. LANE. Mr. President, in the State of Connecticut the Democracy assert the correct principle, and they charge the trouble in the country to the right quarter. I stated, on a former occasion, that the Democracy of old Connecticut would never join the Republican party in any attempt to coerce the southern States; and I am now authorized by their own declaration to say again, what I said before, that they, like the Democracy of Oregon and every other northern State, will never join a party that has refused justice; that has refused equality and right; that has refused to protect property in the Territories, or wherever the jurisdiction of the

United States extends, in putting down those who contended for their rights and for the equality to which they were entitled. Sir, the loyal Democracy of this country fully understand the question, and they assert the right.

Now, sir, these great principles were not carried out. The platform on which the Democracy presented their candidates for President and Vice President was not heeded, though based upon the Constitution. I will say to the Senator who has boasted of his efforts in Tennessee in behalf of the Breckinridge ticket, that I shall notice that hereafter; but I have only to say now, that, for the sake of the country, I would [sic] to God the ticket had succeeded. We should then have had those principles endorsed upon which the Government was established, and the country would have been at peace. For that alone I wished it to succeed; for, sir, I say in your presence, and in the presence of all here, and before the country, that I never saw the day when I would have tossed a copper for either the Presidency or Vice presidency, unless it could be obtained upon principles indispensable to the maintenance of this Union. For the sake of the country, then, I say I regret the ticket did not succeed; otherwise, I have no feeling about it.

I will say only a word, now, as to the amendments proposed to the Constitution. I had the pleasure of listening, yesterday, to the distinguished Senator from Kentucky. I know his patriotism and his devotion to the Union. I know his willingness to take anything, however small, however trifling, however little it might be, that would, in his opinion, give peace to the country. Sir, I am actuated by no such feeling. We should never compromise principle nor sacrifice the eternal philosophy of justice. Whenever the Democratic party compromised principle it laid the foundation of future troubles for itself and for the country. When we do, then, amend the Constitution, it ought to be in the spirit of right and justice to all men and to all sections. I voted for the Senator's propositions, and I will do so again, if we can get a vote, because there was something in them; something that I could stand by; but there is nothing in the amendments proposed by the peace conference. He proposed to establish the line of 36° 30′, and to prohibit slavery north of it and protect it south of it, in all the present territory, or of the territory to be hereafter acquired. In that proposition there was something like justice and right; but there is nothing in the amendments proposed by the peace conference that any man, north or south, ought to take. They are a cheat; they are a deception; they are a fraud; they hold out a false idea; and I think, with all due respect to the Senator—for I have the highest regard for him personally—

that he is too anxious to heal the trouble that exists in the country. He had better place himself upon the right and stand by it. Let him contend, with me, for the inalienable and constitutional rights of every American citizen. Let him beware of "compromising" away the vital rights, privileges, and immunities of one portion of the country to appease the graceless, unrelenting, and hostile fanaticism of another portion. Let him labor with me, to influence every State to mind its own affairs, and to keep the Territories entirely *free* to the enterprise of all, with equal security and protection—without invidious distinctions—to the property of every citizen. Thus, and only thus, can we have peace, happiness, and eternal Union.

Then the Senator from Oregon comes. He talked flippantly about "his" people and "his" State, and what they would do. Mr. President, I have lived a long time in Oregon—longer than that Senator—and I have never claimed that the people of Oregon belonged to me. I have never assumed to call them "my people." I am their servant, and I desire to represent them honestly and faithfully, as I have done at all times, and under all circumstances. I pledge them to nothing. "My State," "My people!" Good God, sir! has it come to this, that a Senator who has been there but a short time; who can hardly claim a residence there; who owns no house or land there; who has paid no taxes there, or even worked upon the public roads; who was simply imported like a machine, to political order; who never fought a battle to protect the emigrants and settlers, or to prevent the Indians from committing depredations and outrages there; should have the assurance to get up in his place in the Senate and claim that *his* "people" would trample upon the rights of the South, and join with the Senator and his confreres in their fanatical ranks? I pledge the people of Oregon to nothing. They are a free people; they are a gallant people; they are a sensible people; they are a patriotic people. They had the kindness to send me to Congress, and I have served them faithfully. They are my masters. I shall soon be one of them. We shall soon balance accounts, and I will return and be with them and of them—an honest, industrious farmer, as most of them are. I shall pay my taxes, and discharge all my duties, as a citizen should; and I will be with them whether I am in Congress or out of Congress.

These observations, relative to my colleague, have been a deviation from the regular of my argument; but I could not avoid noticing the anxiety of the Senator from Kentucky to accept anything, and the readiness of the Senator from Oregon to pledge his people—"my people"—to anything that he chooses. Now, I know there are many free people in the

State of Oregon. They generally do as they please. They have no master. No man owns them; and no man can claim to control them. But this I am warranted in asserting—for I know long, well, and intimately, the gallant men of Oregon—that they will not be found ready or inclined, at the Senator's and his master's beck, to imbrue their hands, for a godless cause, in fraternal gore.

Mr. President, the principles asserted in the resolutions adopted by this Senate, last winter, have not been carried out. We see the consequences. We see a dissevered country and a divided Union. A number of States have gone off, have formed an independent Government; it is in existence, and the States composing it will never come back to you, unless you say in plain English, in your amendments to the Constitution, that every State in the future Union has an equal right to the Territories and all the protection and blessings of this government— never! I tell you, sir, although some foolish men and some wicked ones may say I am a disunionist, I am for the Union upon the principles of the Constitution, and not a traitor. None but a coward will even think me a traitor; and if anybody thinks I am, let him test me. This Union could exist upon the principles that I have held and that are set forth in the Davis resolutions; but upon no other condition can it exist. Then, sir, disunion is inevitable. It is not going to stop with the seven States that are out. No, sir; my word for it, unless you do something more than is proposed in this proposition, Old Virginia will go out, too—slothful as she has been, and tardy as she seems in appreciating her own interests and her rights, and kind and generous as she has been in inviting a peace congress to agree upon measures of safety for the Union. The time will come, however, when Old Virginia will stand trifling and chicanery no longer. Neither will North Carolina suffer it. None of the slave States will endure it; for they cannot separate one from the other, and they will not. They will go out of this Union and into one of their own; forming a great, homogeneous, and glorious southern confederacy. It is and it has been, Senators, in your power to prevent this; it is and has been for you to say (you might to-day, as it is the last day, say so,) whether the Union shall be saved or not. I know that gallant Old Dominion will never put up with less than her rights; and if she should, I should entertain for her contempt. I should feel contempt for her if she were to ask for anything more than her rights; and so I would if she were to put up with anything less than her constitutional rights. Then, sir, secession has taken place, and it will go on unless we do right.

Mr. President, in the remarks which I made on the 19th of December last, in reply to the Senator from Tennessee, I took the ground that a State might rightfully secede from the Union when she could no longer remain in it on an equal footing with the other States; in other words, when her continuance as a member of the Confederacy involved the sacrifice of her constitutional rights, safety, and honor. This right I deduced from the theory of the equality of the States, upon which rests the whole fabric of our unrivaled system of government—unrivaled, as it came from the hands of its illustrious framers—a model as perfect, perhaps, as human wisdom could devise, securing to all the blessings of civil and religious liberty, when rightly understood and properly administered; but like all other Governments, and even Christianity itself, a most dangerous engine of oppression when, having fallen into the hands of persons strangers to its spirit, and unmindful of the beneficent objects for which it was framed, it is perverted from its high and noble mission to the base uses of a selfish or sectional ambition, or a blind and bigoted fanaticism. I said, on that occasion—referring to this fundamental principle of our Government, the equality of the States—that "as long as this equality be maintained the Union will endure, and no longer." I might here undertake to enforce, by argument and the authority of writers on the nature and purposes of our Government, this, to me, self-evident proposition. But I deem it unnecessary to consume the time of the Senate in discussing that branch of the subject.

A certain distinguished Senator, [Mr. TRUMBULL,] in language which, though parliamentary, was not remarkable for good taste, took me to task, a few days ago, for my frequent allusions to "State equality." I will not again, if I can help it, incur the displeasure of that Senator by referring to a principle of the Constitution which he affects to treat as unworthy of being discussed, or even alluded to in this august body. It may be quite unsenatorial for a member of this body to refer to a great principle of the Constitution. If so—and in the judgment of the Senator it seems to be so—I have committed a mistake. My excuse is, that I forgot at the moment that I was speaking *since* the adoption of the Chicago platform, which seems, in the opinion of the gentlemen on the other side, to have superceded the Constitution. I hope this will be received as a sufficient apology for violating the rules of this body, as understood on the Republican side of the Chamber.

I propose, Mr. President, to confine what I have to say in regard to the right of secession to the question: who must judge whether such a right exists, and when it should be exercised? According to theory of every despotic Government, of ancient or modern times, there is no such right. A province of an empire, how much soever oppressed, is held by the oppressor as an integral part of his dominions. The yoke, once fastened on the neck of the subject, is expected, however galling, to be worn with patience and entire submission to the tyrant's will. This is the theory of despotism. What are its fruits? We have seen, in modern times, some of the bloodiest struggles recorded in history growing out of the assertion by one party, and the denial by the other, of this very right. Hungary undertook to "secede" from the Austrian empire. Her right to do so was denied. She constituted an integral part of the empire—a great "consolidated" nation, as some consider the United States to be. Being an integral part of the empire, according to the theory of the Austrian Government, she must so remain forever. Austria not having the power to enforce an acquiescence in this doctrine, Russian legions were called to her aid; and Hungary, on whose gallant struggle for independence the liberty-loving people of this country looked with so much admiration and sympathy, soon lay prostrate and bleeding at the tyrant's feet. You may call this attempt of Hungary to regain her independence revolution. That is precisely what Austria called it. I call it an effort on her part to peaceably secede—to peaceably dissolve her connection with a Government which, in her judgment, had become intolerably unjust and oppressive. Her oppressors told her it was not her province but theirs, to judge of her alleged grievances; that to acknowledge the right of secession would strike a fatal blow at the integrity of the empire, which could be maintained only by enforcing the perfect obedience of each and every part.

We have, in the recent struggle of the Italian States, an instructive commentary on the now mooted questions of secession and coercion. Indeed, history, through all past ages, is but a record of the efforts of tyrants to prevent the recognition of the doctrine, that a people deeming themselves oppressed might peaceably absolve themselves from allegiance to their oppressors. When our Government was formed, our fathers fondly thought that they had made a great improvement on the despotic systems of modern Europe. They saw the infinite evil resulting from coercing the unwilling obedience of a subject to a Government which he abhorred and detested. They accordingly declared the great truth, never enunciated until then, that "Governments derive all their just power from the consent of the governed." A Government without such consent they held to be a tyranny.

Now, Mr. President, this brings us to the very point in issue. Who is to determine whether this consent is given or withheld? Must it be determined by the ruler? If so, the proposition just stated is an absurdity. Clearly it was the meaning of those who enunciated this great truth, that the subjects of a Government have the right to declare or withhold their consent; otherwise no such right exists. They, and they only, must judge whether their rights are protected or violated. If protected, every consideration of interest and safety impels them to consent to live under a Government which secures the blessings they desire. If, on the other hand, in their judgment their most sacred rights are violated, interest and honor, and the instinct of self-preservation, all conspire to impel them to withhold their consent; which being withheld, the Government, so far as they are concerned, ceases.

Here I would call the attention of the Senate to the first of the Kentucky resolutions of 1798-99, written by Mr. Jefferson, in which he says distinctly, that the parties to a political compact must judge for themselves of the mode and measure of redress, when they consider the compact violated and their rights invaded:

> *Resolved*, That the several States composing the United States of America, are not united on the principle of unlimited submission to their General Government; but that by compact, under the style and title of a Constitution for the United States, and of amendments thereto, they constituted a General Government for special purposes, delegated to that Government certain definite powers, reserving, each State to itself, the residuary mass of right to their own self government; and that whensoever the General Government assumes undelegated powers, its acts are unauthoritative, void, and of no force; that to this compact each State acceded as a State and is an integral party; that this Government, created by this compact, was not made the exclusive judge of the extent of the powers delegated to itself, since that would have made its discretion, and not the Constitution, the measure of its power; but that, as in all other cases of compact among parties having no common judge, each party has an equal right to judge for itself, as well of infractions as of the mode and measure of redress.

Here Mr. Jefferson asserts that a State aggrieved shall judge not only of the mode, but the measure of redress. Is this treason? If the measure of redress extends to secession, how can the Senator from Tennessee [Mr. JOHNSON] do less than denounce the great apostle of liberty—as Mr. Jefferson has been called—a traitor?

No less clear and explicit on this point, is the language of Mr. Madison. Being chairman of a committee to whom the subject was referred—the resolutions having been returned by several of the States—he says in his report:

> It appears to your committee to be a plain principle, founded in common

sense, illustrated by common practice, and essential to the nature of compacts, that where resort can be had to no tribunal superior to the authority of the parties, the parties themselves must be the rightful judges, in the last resort, whether the bargain made has been pursued or violated. The Constitution of the United States was formed by the sanction of the States, given by each in its sovereign capacity. It adds to the stability and dignity, as well as to the authority, of the Constitution, that it rests on this legitimate and solid foundation. The States, then, being parties to the constitutional compact, and in their sovereign capacity, it follows, of necessity, that there can be no tribunal above their authority, to decide, in the last resort, whether the compact made by them be violated, and consequently that, as the parties to it, they must themselves decide, in the last resort, such questions as may be of sufficient magnitude to require their interposition.

In the remarks which I made on the 19th of December last, I referred to the fact that Virginia, in accepting the Constitution, declared that the powers granted under that instrument "being derived from the people of the United States, may be resumed by them whensoever the same shall be perverted to their injury or oppression." I referred, also, to the fact that New York had adopted the Constitution upon the same condition and with the same reservation. I may here quote the language of Mr. Webster, distinctly recognizing the right of the people to change their Government whenever their interest or safety require it. He says:

We see, therefore, from the commencement of the Government under which we live, down to this late act of the State of New York—

To which he had just referred—

one uniform current of law, of precedent, and of practice, all going to establish the point that changes in Government are to be brought about by the will of the people, assembled under such legislative provisions as may be necessary to ascertain that will truly and authentically.

If the people of a State, believing themselves oppressed, undertake to establish a Government, independent of that to which they formerly owed allegiance, and the latter interferes with the movement, and employs force to prevent such a consummation, no one who acknowledges the great truth that the basis of all free government is the "consent of the governed," will deny that such interference is an act of usurpation and tyranny. Those only who borrow their ideas of political justice from the despotic codes of Europe, and are more imbued with the spirit of Metternich and Bomba than of Jefferson and Madison, will attempt to justify, palliate, or excuse such violation of the sacred rights of the people. I have observed that often the noisiest champions of popular rights are the first to trample those rights underfoot. The word "freedom" is continually on the tongues of gentlemen on the other side of the Chamber; and I believe the Senator from Tennessee has been suspected of a decided leaning to agrarianism, so zealous has he been in advocating the rights, so entirely devoted is he to the interest, of the "dear people." But now, when the *people* of the seceding States have pronounced, in tongues of thunder, the fiat which absolves them from allegiance to a Government which they no longer respect or love, these same gentlemen all lift their hands in horror, roll up the whites of their eyes, as did Lord North many years ago, and exclaim "Treason!" "Treason!" Then, boiling with patriotic rage, they rise up and declare that "this treason must be punished; the laws must be enforced." History tells us that this was the language of King George and Lord North when the colonies renounced their allegiance to the mother country. The former of these worthies, we are told, spent much of his life in a state of mental darkness—in other words, he was a lunatic. The other received from nature a narrow intellect, and inherited prejudices common to the aristocracies of that period and of all other periods of the world's history. Their errors were the natural offspring of incapacity and false teaching received in their youth. While, therefore, we cannot admire or approve their conduct, these circumstances incline us more to sorrow than to anger, disarm our resentment, and dispose us to forgive what, under other circumstances, would deserve the severest censure.

But what excuse can we find for the peculiar champions of popular rights in this Chamber; these zealous servants of the people, forever ringing in our ears "Let the voice of the people be heard; respect the will of the people; *vox populi vix Dei!* " Sir, I say, too, let the voice of the people be heard and respected. And I think, for the sake of consistency with all my past professions as a Democrat, I am bound to respect the declared will of the sovereign States which, for reasons satisfactory to themselves, have seceded from the Union and established a separate and independent government. Whatever the causes may have been which impelled them to a separation from the other States, I am bound to respect the expression of their sovereign will; and I heartily reprobate the policy of attempting to thwart that will under the pretense of "punishing treason" and "enforcing the laws." We are told that the design is to attempt nothing more than to collect the revenue in the ports of the seceded States. To say nothing of the justice or injustice of the attempt so to do, I ask Senators from the North and the Senator from Tennessee, *will it pay?* Will it not be a declaration of war against the seceding States, involving the people of all the States in a long and bloody conflict, ruinous to both sections? Are their ethics not the ethics of the school-boy pugilist, "Knock the chip off my shoulder"?

One of the framers of the Constitution, whose expositions of that instrument all classes, all parties, have heretofore received, and still receive or pretend to receive, with profound deference and respect, has left on record his views of the injustice, impracticability, and inefficiency of force as a means of coercing States into obedience to Federal authority. The subject being under consideration in the convention which framed the Constitution—

> Mr. Madison observed, that the more he reflected on the use of force, the more he doubted the practicability, the justice, and the efficiency of it, when applied to people collectively, and not individually. A Union of the States containing such an ingredient, seemed to provide for its own destruction. The use of force against a State would look more like a declaration of war than an infliction of punishment, and would probably be considered by the party attacked as a dissolution of all previous compacts by which it might be bound. He hoped that such a system would be framed as might render this resource unnecessary; and moved that the clause be postponed.—*Madison Papers, Debates in the Federal Convention*, vol. 5, p. 140.

Among the statesmen of the Revolution—those who participated in the formation of our Government—there was no one who had such exalted notions of the power and dignity of the Federal Government, as the great Hamilton. He was a consolidationist. The advocates of coercion might naturally expect to obtain "aid and comfort" from the recorded declarations of one of his peculiar political faith. But an examination of his writings will show, that instead of favoring coercion, instead of being the advocate of force, he was the advocate of leniency and conciliation towards refractory States, and deprecated a resort to force as madness and folly. He said, in a debate on this subject:

> It has been observed, to coerce the States is one of the maddest projects that was ever devised. A failure of compliance will never be confined to a single State. This being the case, can we suppose it wise to hazard a civil war? Suppose Massachusetts, or any large State, should refuse and Congress should attempt to compel them, would they not have influence to procure assistance, especially from those States which are in the same situation as themselves? What picture does this idea present to our view? A complying State at war with a non-complying State; Congress marching the troops of one State into the bosom of another; this State collecting auxiliaries, and forming, perhaps, a majority against its Federal head. Here is a nation at war with itself. Can any reasonable man be well disposed towards a Government which makes war and carnage the only means of supporting

itself—a Government which can exist only by the sword? Every such war must involve the innocent with the guilty. This single consideration should be sufficient to dispose every peaceable citizen against such a Government.—*Elliot's Debates*, vol. 2, p. 233.

I might cite other authorities on this point. But these are enough. If the great names of Madison and Hamilton have not sufficient weight to restrain the madness of those who urge a coercive policy against the seceding States, then, indeed, I see no escape from that most dreadful of all calamities which can befall a nation—civil war. If those in this Chamber who talk so flippantly of war, had seen, as it has been my lot to see, some of its actual horrors, they might, perhaps, heed the warnings and respect the counsels of the sages and patriots whose language I have quoted. They would at least refrain from ungenerous insinuations against the patriotism of those northern Democrats, who like myself, reprobate the policy of coercion as destructive of the peace, the prosperity, and happiness of every part of the country, north as well as south.

But to return to the remarks of the Senator from Tennessee. In the pamphlet report of his speech, page 7, Jefferson is quoted; but the concluding part of the quotation is repeated in the Globe report and not in that of the pamphlet. That part is:

When two parties make a compact, there results to each a power of compelling the other to execute it.

Jefferson is here quoted to show that the Confederation has a power to enforce its articles on the delinquent States. But the citation is unfortunate for the Senator from Tennessee. He had just previously asserted that Vermont and other States had, by personal liberty bills, violated the Constitution. Well, can he tell us how Virginia and South Carolina could enforce the Constitution on Vermont in that respect? It cannot be done. What follows? Why, as Mr. Webster said at Capon Springs, "a compact broken by one party is broken as to all." Hence, according to the doctrines of Jefferson and Webster as to the actual case which, according to the Senator, has occurred, the compact having been broken, the southern States have a right to retire—are absolved from further obligations under the constitutional compact.

Again at page 9 of his pamphlet, the Senator from Tennessee asserts the identity of the secession of a State with the whisky insurrection in Pennsylvania. My God! Mr. President, what can I say to a man that likens the secession of a State to the whisky insurrection? What argument can you make that would reach such a Senator as this? How can you approach his intellect? How can you get at his understanding? A Senator upon your floor likens the solemn action, the sovereign action of a State in her sovereign capacity, to the whisky insurrection that occurred in Pennsylvania in Washington's time; an insurrection against the laws of the State when it was attempted to collect revenue. The Governor called on General Washington, then President of the United States, for aid in suppressing the insurrection and enforcing the laws; and the Senator likens that to the action of a State in her sovereign capacity, withdrawing from the Union, meeting in convention and dissolving her connection with her former confederates. Having done this, having passed an ordinance of secession, her delegates go home; no Governor calls upon the President for aid to put down the insurrection or rebellion, for rebellion or insurrection there were none. It was not insurrection; it was not rebellion; it was the solemn act of sovereign States in their sovereign capacities; and the Senator gets up and likens their action to the whisky insurrection in Pennsylvania! He tells us that he thinks one ought to be put down as well as the other; but he does not call this coercion; it is only the execution of the laws. All the powers of the Government, he holds, must be used in enforcing the laws; the laws must be enforced whether the State has seceded or not; whether she is in the Union or out of the Union. Well, sir, I am not inclined to argue with a Senator confessedly incapable of discrimination between an insurrection in a State and the secession of a State. I will merely add, parenthetically, that if the new allies of the gentleman from Tennessee had, as good citizens in the past, been obedient to the laws instead of having openly violated them, there would now be no necessity of their enforcement by war and extermination against men loyal and brave as ever existed.

He then goes on to assert that the case of South Carolina nullification was identical in principle with the whisky insurrection; and as the first was quelled by General Washington, by a display of military force, so the latter was by General Jackson.

Now, sir, I will tell you what I think. Whenever it takes a man six weeks to study, and two days to disgorge, he never has a correct idea of what has been cogitating. He fails to comprehend the simplest problem.

South Carolina passed an ordinance to nullify the tariff laws on and after a certain day. Did General Jackson undertake to enforce those laws on or after that day? No; he approved and signed a bill passed by Congress *before that day arrived, repealing those laws* and adopting the very principles of revenue contended for by South Carolina. So that, as there was no resemblance in the cases, there was none in the adjustment. The

State prevailed. Coercion may have been contemplated by General Jackson at first, but his opinions afterward underwent a radical change. Every man who is well acquainted with the history of the country knows that he never would have struck a blow, he never would have fired a gun. His heart had relented after he had made his proclamation. He had approved the law, and then sent a commission, as we all know, to South Carolina, to use all possible means to avert bloodshed. If the question had to be decided by the bayonet, he never would have used it, in my judgment.

Still denying that he is for coercion, the Senator proceeds to assert that what South Carolina has done is treason; and treason, we know, is punishable with death. And yet he proposes to make us believe that to inflict death on a people is not coercing them.

As to the argument founded on the purchase of Louisiana, Florida, California, and the cession of the ground on which the Federal forts stand—that secession cannot be resorted to as applicable to them—the simple answer is, that the right of secession being fundamental and paramount, all those Territories and sites of forts have been acquired subject to that right, and must abide by it. And in buying, acquiring, or annexing Territories or people, it must always be done subject to the first principles of our Government, for they are more precious than even the golden sands of California, or the sugar islands of the West Indies.

But the Senator does not avoid the difficulties he refers to by denying the right of secession, for they would all result, and with tenfold aggravations, from his principle of the right of revolution. For, as that is a right involving force, each party would, of course, seek foreign alliances, and that would bring the armies and navies of Europe to our shores. Is that the grand result of his policy, which he says is *not* coercion, but only the execution of the laws? Why, the policy of the Senator does not rise one degree above that of the most servile and barbarous Government. The execution of the laws, as he proposes, is only the collection of tribute by force from a conquered people. That is the Turkish system.

I might say here, Mr. President—for there are gentlemen now on this floor that know it as well as myself—I have seen this policy of collecting tribute carried out on the Pacific coast. I happened once to be present when a great Indian tribe came and demanded the tribute it had received annually from the Umpqua people. I saw the process of collection. The chief went all over the country. He divided his bands and sent them to every village and forced them to pay the amount of tribute that he desired; and when they failed to pay it, he carried the delinquents away, and reduced them to slavery. I witnessed that myself. The idea of the Senator collecting tribute or taxes or revenue from the States that have seceded from this Union is not one iota above the barbarous policy of the Clickitats.

Such is the grand result at which a Senator of the United States from a southern State has arrived, backed by the anti-slavery universal-equality peace-loving and super-enlightened Republican organization!

Waving, now, Mr. President, the references made by the Senator to the extravagant and intemperate expressions of a very few persons in the seceding States, and to which I might oppose those of a multitude of presses and distinguished men in the North, I come to meet his demand to learn the wrongs inflicted on the South. He, himself, admits that the Constitution has been trampled underfoot by many of the northern States. Is not that enough? No, he says; he will approach them in a proper manner and request them to abstain. Well, sir, have they not been requested and urged for more than ten years to abstain? How have these request been treated? They have been met by further outrages. What new process of request, of persuasion, of entreaty, has the Senator discovered that is to stay the torrent and turn back the tide? Is he so profound, so conciliatory, so mighty a master of magic, as to be able to say to the advancing flood of fanaticism, "Thus far and no further shalt thou come; and here shall thy proud waves be stayed?" He has been in public life for several years. What has been his success in this undertaking? Why, the thing has been continually getting worse; and are we to infer, from his failures thus far, that he is to lead us to future success and safety?

I have had the honor of knowing the honorable Senator for ten years, and I have never known him to try to do anything but to give away the public lands, and he has not even succeeded in doing that. I recollect the impression he made on my mind when I first heard him advocate the so-called homestead bill. He will pardon me for mentioning it with all respect. I was then a Delegate. It was on a hot summer day, in the House of Representatives, and there was the distinguished Senator, with his sleeves rolled up, delivering himself a flaming and characteristic speech. "Land for the landless and homes for the homeless" was then his cry. The Senator has not succeeded in giving away all the public lands; neither has he been fortunate in staying this torrent of fanaticism that has been rolling over the country, and I am afraid he cannot. I am willing to give him the balance of his life to work in, and I hope he may succeed in rolling it back. I hope he will have better success than he has had in depriving the country of its public lands, and giving them away to those that do not deserve them. "Land for the landless, and homes for the homeless!" has been his constant cry.

But while, in one part of his speech, he distinctly charges on the North a trampling of the Constitution under foot, in another part, turning to the South, he exclaims: "Why should we go out of the Union; have we anything to fear? What are we alarmed about?" What, sir! a people like the South [sic], numerically inferior to their associate section in the same Government, have nothing to fear from trampling on the Constitution, the only defense in that Government for a minority against the majority!

But let us be more specific. Let us answer the oft-repeated question as to what the South complains of, and what she fears.

She complains, then:

1. That, having $4,000,000,000 of property in slaves, and $4,000,000,000 more of real and personal property connected with it, the right to that property, and the protection thereof, are denied by the party that now, under the forms of the Constitution, claims control of the common Government.

2. That having an immense interest in the common territory of the Union, not only as to its market value, but as to the right of occupation and settlement, that party now claiming the Government has distinctly pronounced for its confiscation, unless the southern emigration shall renounce their own institutions, and adopt those of the North—and this with the avowed design and inevitable effect of overthrowing, gradually, the entire system of southern property, prosperity, and civilization.

3. That the plainest stipulations of the Constitution for the restitution of slave property have been practically set at naught by the action of the State Legislatures, and a perverted public sentiment in the free States.

4. That, while anti-slavery new States are forming rapidly to be admitted into this Union, States like their own are to be excluded altogether hereafter; and they hold that if such States as theirs have no right to be admitted among us, there would be no honor or safety in their remaining any longer.

5. That, in consequence of the intense and fanatical hostility that prevails in the North against their institutions, many zealots from that region, abusing the freedom of intercourse which the present Union affords, have been, and are now, going among them to stir up insurrection, thus destroying their property, and endangering the safety of their homes, their families, and their firesides.

And in this place—having shown to the Senator from Tennessee what are the complaints of the South—it is proper to refer to an article of the treaty for the cession to us of Louisiana, which the Senator cites to prove that, somehow or other, the people of that State have less right than those of the original States. I have already answered that argument. But this very third article which he quotes, while it does not avail him, shows specifically that the people of Louisiana had a special treaty right, besides the constitutional one, to go with their property into the Territories; the right now denied by the Chicago platform. The article says:

> The inhabitants of the ceded territory shall be incorporated into the Union of the United States, and admitted as soon as possible, according to the principles of the Federal Constitution, to the enjoyment of the rights, advantages, and immunities of citizens of the United States; and in the mean time, they shall be maintained and protected in the free enjoyment of their liberty, property, and the religion they profess.

Now, before Arkansas was admitted, her people were, by the compromise of 1820, cut off from emigrating with their property to any of the Louisiana territory north of 36° 30′. And when the treaty of 1803 was made, all Louisiana territory was slaveholding, and the right was undisputed of migrating from one part of it to another with slaves; nor was there any pretense of right asserted in this country to exclude slavery from any part of it; so that the people of Louisiana have a peculiar right, or special provocation, to secede.

Mr. President, the Senator from Tennessee complains of my remarks in his speech. He complains of the tone and temper of what I said. He complains that I replied at all, as I was a northern Senator. Mr. President, I am a citizen of this Union, and a Senator of the United States. My residence is in the North, but I have never seen the day, and I never shall, when I will refuse justice as readily to the South as to the North. I know nothing but my country, the whole country, the Constitution, and the equality of the States—the equal right of every man in the common territory of the whole country; and by that I shall stand.

The Senator complains that I replied at all, as I was a northern Senator, and a Democrat whom he had supported at the last election for a high office. Now, I was, as I stated at the time, surprised at the Senator's speech—because I understood it to be for coercion, as I think it was by almost everybody else except, as we are now told, by the Senator himself; and I still think it amounted to a coercion speech, notwithstanding the soft and plausible phrases by which he described it—a speech for the execution of the laws and the protection of the Federal property. Sir, if there is, as I contend, the right of secession, then, whenever a State exercises that right, this Government has no laws in that State to execute, nor has it any property in any such State that can be protected by the power of this Government. In attempting, however, to substitute the smooth phrases of "executing the laws" and "protecting the public property" for coercion, for civil war, we have an important concession, i.e., that this Government dare not go before the people with a plain avowal of its real purposes, and of their consequences. No, sir, the policy is to inveigle the people of the North into civil war, by masking the design in smooth and ambiguous terms. But the Senator is surprised that I, as a northern Senator, should have replied to him at all. It was because I was astonished that he, as a southern Senator, should make the speech he did. He is surprised that I, as a Democrat, should reply to him. It was because I was mortified that he, as a Democrat, should make the speech he did.

But in the very close of his speech, he referred to the northern Democrats, of whom I am one, and complimented us on our defense of southern rights, and urged that we should not be deserted by the secession of our southern friends. But then he left the inference very clear that we were to aid this Government, soon to be Black Republican, in enforcing the laws against what I believe to be the constitutional rights of southern seceding States. Sir, I thought no time was to be lost in giving him and the country notice that we would do no such thing; that we were not going to be the tools, the hangmen, or the executioners of brethren for the gratification of fanatics; that we would not be their allies, or his allies, in the incendiary and unnatural scheme of desolating the South, our fellow-men and fellow-Democrats. As for the services which the Senator from Tennessee parades and recites, in the late presidential canvass in his State, so far as they were rendered to our party, or in any degree for my personal benefit, I am duly grateful; but I must be permitted to say, that if in his speeches in that contest he advanced such doctrines as he now proclaims, I am not so much surprised that we were defeated in that State. And as for the intimation of the Senator, that in replying to him the other day I, acted at the instance of other Senators here, or persons elsewhere, or that I had any understanding or concert with them, is utterly unfounded.

Now, sir, I want it distinctly understood, as I have already shown, that during the last session I stood firmly by the Davis resolutions. I voted against every amendment. I voted against an amendment that he voted for, because I believed it was partial, and did not do justice. That Senator, with those declarations before him, supported the ticket on which I ran in Tennessee. He ought not to have deceived the people, or himself, and it was not my fault if he did; for he saw published in every paper here a telegraphic dispatch from me to one of the delegates from Oregon at Charleston, during the sitting of the Charleston convention. He asked me what Oregon should do; and in that dispatch I told him to go with the States that stood by the Constitution; to stand by them to the last. That was the basis on which I stood. The Senator knew what I said here; he knew the nature of my votes here; he knew what I said in that dispatch; he knew what I said in my speeches, and in the letter accepting the nomination. If he told the people that I was in favor of submitting to the rule of a party that would refuse justice and equality in this country, he deceived the people. I contend for the right, and will not submit to the wrong. If the Senator, in his speeches in Tennessee, represented me as a submissionist to a wrong, to injury, to inequality, he presented me in a cowardly position, that I would not occupy for any consideration. I speak for myself. I say it is a position I would never occupy in Tennessee, Oregon, or anywhere else. I intend to stand by the right. If every man in every State should be servile enough to refuse to contend for their rights, I alone will contend for all they are entitled; nothing more and nothing less.

The Senator on that occasion looked at me, pointed in my direction, and made remarks not becoming a Senator—remarks that have been too often made on this floor, and that no gentleman ever would make. He said he had struck treason a blow. The mighty Senator from Tennessee struck treason a blow! To whom did he allude? He said he saw the commotion on this side of the House; he saw the books being brought in; he saw that I was to reply to him. Sir, if the word "treason" was to be applied by him or any other man to me, I would say, you are a coward that cannot maintain it. Sir, I cannot express my contempt of the man who would so insinuate, even in thought. A drop of treason never ran in my veins. At an hour's notice, when working in a cornfield for the support of my family, when I heard that Indiana had been called on for troops, I offered my services; and I did not look upon my family from ten minutes after I had received the notice until I had gone through the bloody battles; until I had carried home with me evidence of my devotion to the Union. Does the Senator dare to charge treason upon me? I think not; for no gentleman would have the temerity to do it. I might go on and say that I entered that service as a private, with my knapsack on my back, and I came home out of the service with the rank of Major General in the Army. I earned it on the battle field [sic]. On the battle field I lost almost the last drop of my blood without a murmur, in the service of my country. Who, then, is he that would dare have the brazen effrontery to charge me with treason to my country—a country which I have loved from my infancy, which my father fought for, and which I never failed to fight for myself? I never will fail to meet the foe of my country, or to bleed in her cause, while I am able. Though my arm is not as strong as it once was, though my limbs may not be now supple or elastic as in youth, I am yet able, when my country shall need my services, to offer them; and I shall be the first to do it on any just occasion; but never against one of the States of this Union who has left it because justice has been denied to her. No, sir; never!

Then, sir, whom could the Senator from Tennessee refer to [sic]? Could he allude to my friend DAVIS? Sir, I saw *him* on the battle field. I was looking right in his face when he was wounded. I saw a shudder pass over him as the bullet struck him, precisely at the side-end of his spur, and passed through the center of his heel. There was perceptible simply a shudder [sic]; but not a murmur; just a shudder for the instant, when struck by the bullet; but never, for a moment, did he lose sight of the enemy or the flag, but struggled on through the battle to the end, following the glorious stars and stripes, that emblem of the Union, that emblem of the Constitution, that emblem of protection to every State of the Confederacy under the Constitution, as gallantly as ever did mortal man; and yet upon this floor there are some base enough to allude to him as a traitor. Mr. President, I have not words to express my contempt for any man that can apply such a term to such a man as JEFFERSON DAVIS. JEFFERSON DAVIS a traitor! Treason applied to him! He, the purest and bravest of patriots! He fought for his flag and country when the cowards and poltroons that now dare vilify him were supine at home. He will live glorious in history when they are earth and forgotten. Sir, this "treason" of our seceding brethren does not fall within the definition given by Hudibras to that crime; for the South *flourishes* and prospers. The people who have seceded from the Union, and have formed a government of their own, are charged with treason. I will tell gentlemen they will have more than ordinary difficulty to contend with when they invade the rights of that government. But to proceed with my argument.

Now, sir, in reference to that speech of the Senator, it was, as I regard it, an unnatural speech. It was a bad speech; and did more to strengthen the Black Republican party than all the speeches of all the Senators on the other side of the Chamber during this session. But for that speech, we should have had a settlement of the difficulty before this. It went to the country, and made the people believe that the "giant" Senator from

Tennessee was for coercion. It was complimented and eulogized by the Republican press, and in pamphlet form circulated by hundreds of thousands throughout the North. And the distinguished Senator from New York speaks of him as the "noble" Senator from Tennessee. Noble for what? Noble for his abandonment of the rights of the States; noble for the abandonment of the rights of his section; noble for aiding and assisting a party who refuses justice to the citizens of the South?

But the Senator from Tennessee proceeded with an air and tone of great triumph to bring my vote on the amendments proposed to the Davis resolutions. I think I have said all that it is necessary for me to say upon that subject. I have shown that I voted for them under all circumstances, and against every amendment. Those resolutions assert the right of property in the Territories, and that when the courts fail to afford protection, then it is the duty of the Congress to come forward and provide that protection. I wished to put the slave property upon the same footing as other property. That is where I then stood, where I now stand, and where I intend to stand. The Senator asks, with a kind of triumphant air, what has happened since that day? Mr. President, I have said that I have done all in my power, by standing firm to the resolutions agreed to by the Democratic party, to afford protection. The Senator misrepresented my vote on those resolutions. I never voted against the Davis resolutions, nor did their substitute ever come up as a separate proposition. It was an amendment to one of that series of resolutions I voted against; and I would vote against anything and everything that would embarrass their passage, for they contained just what I thought was right, and just what he did not vote for; but, as I have already shown, he voted to substitute instead thereof a proposition which was unsatisfactory and inadequate— neither satisfactory to me, to the Democratic masses and Representatives, nor to the South.

The Senator from Tennessee, with great exultation, asks, if protection was not necessary then, what has happened since to make it so, and to break up the Union for the want of it? What has happened since? Why, a thing has happened that never happened before. The denial of any and all protection to slave property in any and in all the territory; the denial of the right to take slave property to any of them has been proclaimed and affirmed at the ballot-box by a majority of the States and a majority of the electoral votes of this Union. And yet the Senator has the coolness to ask what has happened, and to make merry with the question, and have the sympathetic merriment of the Republican Senators. What has happened? Why, the thing has happened that has been three times before attempted, and three times before failed; the first attempt having endangered the formation of the Union, and the second and third its continuance. The first attempt was made in 1784; to exclude slavery from all the Territories. It was abandoned in 1787 by excluding it only from the territory northwest of the Ohio, leaving it to colonize that portion southwest of that river. The same thing was again attempted in 1820, as to the territory acquired from Louisiana; and after a terrible agitation, was abandoned by adopting the Missouri line. The third attempt was made in 1850, as to the territory acquired from Mexico; and then also the Union narrowly escaped destruction; but the compromise measures were adopted. And now it comes again, but in a more formidable way than ever. A President has been elected on that issue; for the first time the people of the North, after all previous compromises and warnings, have voted on the question, and every northern State has pronounced for the spoliation; and there stood the Senator from Tennessee and asked, with an air of triumphant ignorance and exulting stupidity, what has happened?

Oh! but [sic] we are told that although the people of the North have so voted, and so elected, and thereby are about to seize the gigantic power of this Government to accomplish the flagitious design, they have not accomplished it yet. We must wait for the overt act!

What! if [sic] a man proclaims his intention to burn my barn, and I see him approach it with a lighted torch, am I to wait for the overt act? If some military chieftain was about to bombard this splendid edifice, and had drawn out his artillery to lay these marble columns in ruins, and level yon proud dome with the ground, must we wait for the thing to be done? But if there are some people not quite so blind as not to see what has happened, and not quite so servile or so base as to wait until that still more splendid fabric, the Constitution, is falling in ruins around them, from the torches of frenzied fanatics, and amid their exultant shouts, but conclude to separate themselves from such brethren, they show that they at least know not only what has happened, but what would be likely to happen next, if they had no more perception nor foresight than the Senator from Tennessee.

But we have been told by the Senator, as we have often been told by others, that the secession movement is a sudden and violent excitement, caused by the plans and harangues of artful and ambitious leaders; and that it must soon subside. A sudden and precipitate movement! Why, it is now more than twelve years since all the southern States, Tennessee included, decided by the almost unanimous vote of both parties in their Legislatures, that they would at all hazards, and to the last extremity, resist the adoption of the Wilmot proviso. Now, the North has resolved upon it by the unanimous votes of all her States, and has the power, according to the forms of the Constitution, to execute that resolve; and yet, for preparing at once to resist this aggression, three times solemnly attempted before, and three times before repulsed by the South, we are now told that the South is precipitate—is mad.

I know it is said that there are still some Senators and Representatives from the North in Congress who will oppose this Republican design, and that it may be ultimately defeated by their votes in connection with that of the South. But, in the mean time [sic], the Chicago convention, with consummate cunning, declares that there is no right for slavery to go into the Territories; and hence, if it does go, the new Executive will afford it no protection if assailed; and it is well known that many of the supporters for the Presidency of the Senator from Illinois, [Mr. DOUGLAS,] who, together with the Republicans, make up a large portion of the North, also deny that slavery has any right to protection in the Territories; the decision of the Supreme Court, that it has the right to go there, to the contrary notwithstanding.

For the South, then, to wait would be to submit until her forts were armed and garrisoned against her, and the guns turned landward; to wait until her share of the public arms were placed in possession of her enemies; to wait until the Federal Army is stationed to act with promptitude to subdue her; to wait until Republican postmasters are stationed throughout her villages and cross-roads, to circulate the works of Greely and of Helper; to wait until servile insurrection is organized, and all these things the President alone can do. The South is to wait for all this; while southern Senators sit, blind as moles and deaf as adders, or, having eyes, see not, and having ears, hear not the things that pertain to her temporal salvation.

Mr. President, perhaps the most signal instance of the evils of compulsory union between dissimilar people, is that of Ireland and England. The people of Ireland—the home and heritage of my ancestors—have, as the South has, a representation in the national Legislature; but being also, as the South is, in a minority in that body, have no power to protect themselves from the aggressions of England. The consequence is, that they have been excluded from the common benefits of British legislation, commercially, and even religiously, to say nothing of their exclusion from official station in the Empire. And, accordingly, Ireland has been impoverished, degraded, and discontented. She has been trampled upon, outraged, insulted, treated like Cinderella. The people of this country have always sympathized with the wrongs of Ireland, and her struggles for independence. Yet there is now a greater difference between the people of the South and of the North than between those of England and Ireland, and greater antagonism of opinion and feeling. Nevertheless, it is proposed to hold the South in political subjection to the North, and for that purpose to employ naval and military force.

Sir, I might mention many other cases: the subjection of Greece to Turkey; of Poland to Russia; of the Netherlands to Spain; Italy to Austria. In all these cases we have sympathized with, and, in many of them aided, the secession from the common government, by contributions and individual service. Yet those Governments were not founded on consent, and there was no compact conceding the right of secession.

And now, after I have shown that modern history abounds in such cases, and after proving that our opinions and sympathies have invariably been with the seceding parties, it is deliberately proposed and proclaimed that the northern section of this Union, so devoted to liberty, so exalted in civilization, so pure in morals, and devout in religion, shall imitate the most despotic policy of England, Austria, Turkey, Spain, and Russia? Is it reserved for this enlightened age and this land of the free, for that section which arrogates to itself preeminence in piety and civilization, to show itself capable of imitating the worst crimes of the Governments of the Old World, to emulate the most atrocious examples of the very worst Governments, whether civilized or semi-barbarous. But, sir, while I have referred to the several cases of people heretofore undertaking to secede from oppressive Unions, I do not for a moment compare the ability of the South, or the probable issue of the impending struggle, to the cases cited. Not at all, sir. The southern States will not be conquered. They may be destroyed, but never subjugated. Let me beg the party who are soon to take charge of this Government to let the seceded States alone, and by no means to attempt to collect revenue in their ports; that would result in a bloody, terrible war: but, on the contrary, acknowledge the independence of the Confederate States of America, and treat with them as an ally and friendly nation.

Sir, in conclusion, whether the course the seceding States have seen fit to take be right or not, is a question we must leave to posterity, and the verdict of impartial history. Our time will probably be more profitably employed in considering how we shall deal with secession than in discussing the causes which have produced it. Secession, right or wrong, justifiable or unjustifiable, is an accomplished fact; and it presents to us no less an alternative than that of peace or war. Sir, I believe that, in the general ruin which would follow coercive measures against the seceding States, all sections, all classes, all the great interests of the country, without any exception, would be involved. How much better, Mr. President, that, in so fearful a crisis as the present, instead of passing "force bills," and preparing for war, instead of "breathing threatenings and slaughter," and preparing implements of destruction to be used against our brethren of the South, how much better, I say, for ourselves, for posterity, for the cause of civil liberty throughout the world, that our thoughts should be turned on peace? Peace, not war, has brought our country to the high degree of prosperity it now enjoys. The energies of the people up to this time have been directed to the development of our boundless resources, to the mechanic arts, to agriculture, mining, trade, and commerce with foreign nations. Banish peace, turn these mighty energies of the people to the prosecution of the dreadful work of mutual destruction, and soon cities in ruins, fields desolate, the deserted marts of trade, the silent workshops, gaunt famine stalking through the land, the earth cumbered with the bodies of the dying and the dead, will bear awful testimony to the madness and wickedness which, from the very summit of prosperity and happiness, are plunging us headlong into an abyss of woe.

Sir, in God's name, let us have peace. If we cannot have it in the Union, as it existed prior to November last, let us have it by cultivating friendly relations with those States which have dissolved their connection with that Union, and established a separate government. Though we and they may not, and, perhaps, in the nature of things, cannot live harmoniously under the same Government, it is our interest, no less than theirs, that we should at once endeavor to establish between our Government and theirs those amicable relations which should ever exist between two neighboring Republics. War, with its attendant horrors being thus happily averted, the people of each Republic will be left at liberty to pursue, undisturbed, their several vocations. A mutually advantageous commerce will grow up between the two nations; treaties, such as regulate our intercourse with the Canadas, will be formed; confidence in all branches of business will be restored; a new impetus given to every variety of industry; the march of improvement accelerated, and the cause of humanity, of civilization, and of Christianity, advanced throughout the world. The people of Europe accustomed to refer the settlement of the slightest differences to the bloody arbitrament of the sword, will behold with silent wonder and amazement the spectacle of a great people unable to agree in reference to one of their peculiar domestic institutions, peacefully separating, as did the patriarchs of old; resolving themselves into two distinct political communities, not hostile, discordant, belligerent; but each, animated with a spirit of generous rivalry towards the other, pursuing a more successful and prosperous career in its own chosen path, than when, united under the same Federal head, they painfully sought together the same common destiny.

Mr. President, we are living at a day and at a time when a northern sectional party have obtained possession of the power of this great Government, who have declared in their platform, in their speeches everywhere, and in their press, that slavery shall never go into another foot of territory; that no other slave State shall ever be admitted into this Union; that slavery shall be put in the course of ultimate extinction. We have the announcement of the party that the foot of a slave shall never press the soil of one of the Territories; that no new slave State shall be admitted; and, in addition to that, that no slave State shall go out of the Union. Who ever saw such a party as that? Who ever knew anything like it in the world before? They will not let slavery go into the Territories; they will not let a slave State come in; and they will not let one go out! They will not let them go out because they could not carry out their programme of placing slavery in the course of ultimate extinction. They want to keep the slave States in for their benefit—to foot the bills, to pay the taxes—that they may govern them as they see fit, and rule them against their will. Well, sir, I wish to say one word to that party, in all kindness; for I shall not trouble them again on this subject. I shall be a private, independent citizen before long. But I will say to that party, they had better change their tactics; they had better change front, and do it speedily. Let them place themselves upon the high ground of right and justice, and adopt such amendments to the Constitution as will not only hold old Kentucky, which has produced the greatest "compromiser" of us all— that good old State where I was raised, and that I am proud of—but the other southern States also. I am afraid that Republicanism will not do this. I know those old Kentucky people from terrace to foundation. They will endure much—very much—peaceably and quietly; but if they are goaded too far; if, by repeated wrongs, they are compelled to fight, then I would say to their enemy "beware!" There are chivalry and patriotism in Kentucky which is neither in the power of accident nor nature to subdue. You should better not press them too far. Do not drive them to the goal of last resort. Give them justice while you have it in your power to do so. Satisfy them that ultimately they shall have equality in this broken Government, or Union, if you will. But, sir, I leave the patching up of the

Constitution to the distinguished Senator from Kentucky and other gentlemen, especially my friend from Pennsylvania, [Mr. BIGLER,] who has labored harder to patch up the Constitution than any man I ever knew, except my friend from Kentucky, and I wish him God speed in the work. Let it be upon just principles; let it be right; let us have justice; and I shall be content.

Now, Mr. President, I owe it to myself to say a few words upon another subject. I am sorry it is necessary; but the superciliousness of the honorable Senator from Tennessee in taking me to task the other day in a manner that I thought was unparliamentary, to say the least, on the subject of the navigation of the Mississippi river [sic], renders it indispensable that I should do so. I desire to say but a few words relative that point, and leave the Senate to decide between us. By the way, before I commence, I will say that I have been borne out in all I have said in relation to that matter by the action of Louisiana, and by the action of the confederated States. I look upon that government as one of the finest experiments on the face of the earth, or in the history of mankind, embodying the purest patriotism, the highest order of statesmanship, and the greatest amount of talent and administrative capacity that can be found among the same number of people in any Government on the face of the globe. They, by their action, have endorsed all that I said upon the subject of the navigation of the Mississippi river. The Governor of the State of Louisiana had the kindness, seeing what I said, and that the Senator from Tennessee had doubted the chivalry, the general honesty, and patriotism of the people of Louisiana, to send me—and I have had it here for the last two weeks, but have not had the opportunity of presenting it before—the ordinance of secession and accompanying it a resolution on the subject of the navigation of the Mississippi river, which is in these words:

> *Resolved,* That we, the people of Louisiana—

in their sovereign capacity, mark you; not a little whisky insurrection, but the people in their sovereign capacity, as a State in convention assembled:

> *Resolved,* That we, the people of Louisiana, recognize the right of the free navigation of the Mississippi river and its tributaries by all friendly States bordering thereon. And we also recognize the right of ingress and egress of the mouths of the Mississippi by all friendly States and Powers; and we do hereby declare our willingness to enter into any stipulations to guaranty the exercise of said rights.

Since Louisiana has passed this resolution, the government of the confederate States, by its congress, has passed a similar resolution, resolving, as they ought to do, and as I said they would do, that the navigation of the Mississippi river should be free to all friendly States, and free to all States bordering on it or its tributaries. But I will go into a little history of the Senator's remarks on the occasion of his last two days' speech: God save the country from such speeches!

Mr. President, the Senator from Tennessee expressed his disapprobation at what I said as to the navigation of the Mississippi, and misrepresented me, when he said that I spoke of the right to navigate the Mississippi, as if I had great familiarity with international law. I affected no such familiarity. What I did say, I spoke rather doubtingly, and I cannot understand how a mind not inclined to perversion could give such an interpretation to my words. His words I will read. Referring to me, with a marked manner, he said:

"He seemed to show great familiarity with international law."

In the next sentence he repeated this, and said:

"He spoke about it with great familiarity, as if he understood it well."

Now, sir, this is not the truth. I will here repeat the words which I used, that elicited the criticism of this new expander of international law. I said:

> I believed it is recognized as the law of nations, as the law of civilized nations, that a great inland sea, running through several Governments, shall be open equally to all of them.

I did not speak like a lawyer, confident in his knowledge, but I spoke rather doubtingly, and without assurance or pretense, and just as I felt became one who was not professionally informed. In relation to what I said as to the rule of national law, as applied to the Mississippi, I used the phrase "I believe," certainly not a presumptuous term. The Senator goes to work and ponders for several weeks over my speech, made without premeditation, and the speeches of other Senators, scrapes up as many fragments as possible for the manufacture of his own, and then comes into the Senate with what he thinks, no doubt, is a very learned display. With the air of a learned giant, burdened with wisdom and knowledge, he undertakes to rebuke me by a supercilious sneer at my alleged familiarity with international law. He assumes to rebuke me, also, for not knowing what he knew; which was, that the navigation of the Mississippi river had been the subject of negotiation for "years and years," as well as other rivers throughout the world. This was all very wise and very triumphant, if there were not two sides to the question. He quoted from Mr. Wheaton's Elements, in order to show, as I suppose, his own deep research in the matters of international law. As usual, the Senator understood very little of what he quoted. He utterly missed the true point, and, of course, failed to state the case as it really stood.

Now, mark you, sir, I say, "I believe," I am right. I will state it, and I do so believing it will be understood, as I have heretofore represented it, and would be endorsed by professional men of eminence. As to the Mississippi having been the subject, for years, of negotiation, is a fact I was aware of. But, sir, notwithstanding the Senator's lengthy quotations, I think I can demonstrate to the satisfaction of others, if not to him, that my view of the question is correct. He has made a quotation at great length from Mr. Wheaton, which has no special application to this case, like most of the law quotations he selects.

I spoke of the law of nations, of course, as relative to the incidents of the subject-matter adverted to—an inland sea, (or great river,) under the circumstances of the Mississippi; of course, not under adverse circumstances. Rome once claimed the right to shut up the navigation of the entire Mediterranean; but such cases decide nothing. She held control of its entrance. So, at one time, in a less enlightened day, Russia claimed despotic mastery over the mouth of the Danube. The other great river of western Europe, the Rhine, rising in Switzerland, passing France and Baden, Prussia, Belgium, and the Netherlands, was, under a less liberal policy of national law than now prevails, subject to tolls.

But, sir, what are the facts. Austria, and other Powers, never conceded that Russia had the right of controlling the mouth of the Danube. In 1814, as I understand it—I may be wrong—the navigation was settled to be free. The demonstration of Russia afterwards, to change this, was resisted by Austria; and the other Powers of Europe interposed and prevented its disturbance, upon the ground that it was the true rule of national law, as between their Governments, that the river should remain free to its mouth. The same western Powers, as I believe, further enforced that principle in the treaty which followed the capture of Sebastopol. The navigation of the Rhine was finally adjusted upon the same basis, as the true rule of national law under the circumstances, and as between the parties. When I say, therefore, an inland sea—or river, if you please—passing through several nations, is open to the navigation of all, it is not meant that any fixed and acknowledged right is to be violated. What is meant is simply that which is correspondent with the circumstances and the history of the case. If all the parties had claims, no greater nation possessing the mouth of the river, is at liberty, by a mere exercise of power, to violate those rights because of that power. In this sense has been established, and now exists, the rules of national law which govern the Danube and the Rhine. No tolls, I believe, are collected on either. A state of war, for the time being suspends those rights, but does not abolish them.

Now, sir, as to the principles laid down among the highly civilized nations of Europe, at this day, as applicable to the Mississippi, I am right, and he is wrong. He has no principles about it. He goes back to an old fogy land for his precedent. He is a long way behind the times, in my opinion, just as he was in relation to the rights of the southern States, and as he will be in relation to the action of his own. Now, sir, bear in mind this diagram of national principles, as I have tried to state it, and as now adjusted among the great Powers of Western Europe, which is the great source of ascertaining national law, and it necessarily follows, that the States of this Confederacy—I believe I am right in that—having been equally interested with Louisiana in the navigation of the Mississippi, by the law of nations, they retain that equal right, and are not affected by a change of Government. It is such a right, as having been always equally enjoyed, it cannot be disturbed except in two ways: first, by treaty; and second, by war. The latter only suspends it. This, sir, is the explanation as I understand it, and as I believe it to be right. I hope the reporter will put down the words "I believe;" that is the word I intend to use on this subject. What a pageant—what a ridiculous pageant—has the Senator made by stuffing himself (it only took six weeks) with inapplicable scraps of law of learned length, as if specially to be exhibited before this Senate, to prove nothing, and to fit nothing. I, sir, will not deal in either innuendoes or irony; but will plainly say that, if the Senator would quote only a little law, and understand all that little well, it would be better, than to quote so much, and comprehend so very small a portion of what he does quote.

Now, Mr. President, I have paid all the attention to the attempt that was made to place me in the wrong that I deem necessary. I can only now repeat, in the conclusion of my speech, that neither the Senator from Tennessee, nor any other Senator, nor can any man, tell the truth and say that I have, by any vote, word, or act of mine, at any time or on any occasion, refused protection to all property alike in the Territories. I have made it a point always. Indeed, the doctrine of the equal right of property, whether slave or any other, in the Territories, and its equal right to protection, is as strong in me as life itself. I have never uttered a word against that principle; but I have said, upon all occasions, that that doctrine must be maintained, or this Union could not stand. I have fought for it; but as I said in the outset, while I deeply deplore the condition of the country, it has been caused by no act of mine. And with this remark, I part with him, who, in imitation of Esau, seeks to sell his birthright. I would, if there was time, give a little advise to all sides, to every Senator on this floor. I would say: Senators, come up to the great importance of this question; meet it; adopt, by a two thirds vote—as we could do if Senators would deal rightly—amendments to the Constitution, placing all the States upon an equality in the Territories, and on every other question; submit them to the people; and by such amendments I believe we could prevent, or stop, a further rupture of this Union.

13

The Momentous Issue of Civil War

President Abraham Lincoln's Inaugural Address
March 4, 1861

When Mr. Lincoln delivered his inaugural address on March 4 to a joint session of Congress, South Carolina (December 20), Mississippi (January 9), Florida (January 10), Alabama (January 11), Georgia (January 19), Louisiana (January 26), and Texas (February 1) had by that date passed ordinances of secession. Virginia (April 17), Arkansas (May 6), Tennessee (May 6), North Carolina (May 20), Missouri (October 31), and Kentucky (November 20) followed suit.

President LINCOLN. Fellow-citizens of the United States:

In compliance with a custom as old as the Government itself, I appear before you to address you briefly, and to take in your presence, the oath prescribed by the Constitution of the United States, to be taken by the President "before he enters on the execution of his office."

I do not consider it necessary, at present, for me to discuss those matters of administration about which there is no special anxiety or excitement.

Apprehension seems to exist among the people of the southern States, that by the accession of a Republican Administration their property and their peace and personal security are to be endangered. There has never been any reasonable cause for such apprehension. Indeed, the most ample evidence to the contrary has all the while existed, and has been open to their inspection. It is found in nearly all the public speeches of him who now addresses you. I do but quote from one of those speeches, when I declare that—

> I have no purpose, directly or indirectly, to interfere with the institution of slavery in the States where it exists. I believe I have no lawful right to do so, and I have no inclination to do so.

Those who nominated and elected me did so with full knowledge that I had made this, and many similar declarations, and have never recanted them. And more than this: they placed in the platform for my acceptance, and as law to themselves and to me, the clear and emphatic resolution which I now read:

> *Resolved*, That the maintenance inviolate of the rights of the States, and especially the right of each State to order and control its own domestic institutions according to its own judgment exclusively, is essential to the balance of power on which the perfection and endurance of our political fabric depend; and we denounce the lawless invasion by armed force of the soil of any State or Territory, no matter under what pretext, as among the gravest of crimes.

I now reiterate these sentiments; and in doing so, I only press upon the public attention the most conclusive evidence of which the case is susceptible, that the property, peace, and security of no section are to be anywise endangered by the now incoming Administration. I add, too, that all the protection which, consistently with the Constitution and the laws, can be given, will be cheerfully given to all the States when lawfully demanded, for whatever cause—as cheerfully to one section as to another.

There is much controversy about the delivering up of fugitives from service or labor. The clause I now read is as plainly written in the Constitution as any other of its provisions:

> No person held to service or labor in one State, under the laws thereof, escaping into another, shall, in consequence of any law or regulation therein, be discharged from such service or labor, but shall be delivered up on claim of the party to whom such service or labor may be due.

It is scarcely questioned that this provision was intended by those who made it for the reclaiming of what we call fugitive slaves; and the intention of the lawgiver is the law. All members of Congress swear their support to the whole Constitution; to this provision as well as any other. To the proposition, then, that slaves whose cases come within the terms of this clause "shall be delivered up," their oaths are unanimous. Now, if they would make the effort in good temper, could they not, with nearly equal unanimity, frame and pass a law by means of which to keep good that unanimous oath? There is some difference of opinion whether this clause should be enforced by national or by State authority; but surely that difference is not a very material one. If the slave is to be surrendered, it can be of little consequence to him, or to others, by which authority it is done. And should any one [sic], in any case, be content that his oath should go unkept on a merely unsubstantial controversy as to *how* it shall be kept? Again: in any law upon this subject, ought not all the safeguards of liberty known in civilized and humane jurisprudence to be introduced, so that a free man be not, in any case, surrendered as a slave? And might it not be well, at the same time, to provide by law for the enforcement of that clause in the Constitution which guaranties that "the citizens of each State shall be entitled to all the privileges and immunities of citizens in the several States?"

I take the official oath to-day with no mental reservations, and with no purpose to construe the Constitution or laws by any hypocritical rules. And while I do not now choose to specify particular acts of Congress as proper to be enforced, I do suggest that it will be much safer for all, both in official and private stations, to conform to, and abide by, all those acts which stand unrepealed, than to violate any of them, trusting to find impunity in having them held to be unconstitutional.

It is seventy-five years since the first inauguration of a President under our national Constitution. During that period, fifteen different and greatly distinguished citizens, have, in succession, administered the executive branch of the Government. They have conducted it through many perils; and, generally, with great success. Yet, with all this scope for precedent, I now enter upon the same task for the brief constitutional term of four years, under great and peculiar difficulty. A disruption of the Federal Union, heretofore only menaced, is now formidably attempted.

I hold that, in contemplation of universal law, and of the Constitution, the Union of these States is perpetual. Perpetuity is implied, if not expressed, in the fundamental law of all national Governments. It is safe to assert that no Government proper ever had a provision in its organic law for its own termination. Continue to execute all the express provisions of our national Constitution, and the Union will endure forever—it being impossible to destroy it, except by some action not provided for in the instrument itself.

Again: if the United States be not a Government proper, but an association of States in the nature of contract merely, can it, as a contract, be peaceably unmade by less than all the parties who made it? One party to a contract may violate it—break it, so to speak; but does it not require all to lawfully rescind it?

Descending from these general principles, we find the proposition that, in legal contemplation, the Union is perpetual, confirmed by the history of the Union itself. The Union is much older than the Constitution. It was formed, in fact, by the Articles of Association, in 1774. It was matured and continued, by the Declaration of Independence, in 1776. It was further matured, and the faith of all the then thirteen States expressly plighted and engaged that it should be perpetual, by the Articles of Confederation, in 1778. And, finally, in 1787, one of the declared objects for ordaining and establishing the Constitution was "*to form a more perfect Union.*" But if destruction of the Union, by one, or by a part only, of the States, be lawfully possible, the Union is *less* perfect than before; the Constitution having lost the vital element of perpetuity.

It follows from these views that no State, upon its own mere motion, can lawfully get out of the Union; that *resolves* and *ordinances* to that effect are legally void; and that acts of violence, within any State or States, against the authority of the United States, are insurrectionary or revolutionary, according to circumstances.

I therefore consider that, in view of the Constitution and the laws, the Union is unbroken; and, to the extent of my ability, I shall take care, as the Constitution itself expressly enjoins upon me, that the laws of the Union be faithfully executed in all the States. Doing this I deem to be only a simple duty on my part; and I shall perform it, so far as practicable, unless my rightful masters, the American people, shall withhold the requisite means, or, in some authoritative manner, direct the contrary. I trust this will not be regarded as a menace, but only as the declared purpose of the Union that it *will* constitutionally defend and maintain itself.

In doing this there needs to be no bloodshed or violence; and there shall be none unless it be forced upon the national authority. The power confided to me will be used to hold, occupy, and possess the property and places belonging to the Government, and to collect the duties and imposts; but beyond what may be necessary for these objects, there will be no invasion, no using of force against or among the people anywhere.

Where hostility to the United States, in any interior locality, shall be so great and so universal as to prevent competent resident citizens from holding the Federal offices, there will be no attempt to force obnoxious strangers among the people for that object. While strict legal right may exist in the Government to enforce the exercise of these offices, the attempt to do so would be so irritating and so nearly impracticable withal, I deem it better to forego, for the time, the uses of such offices. The mails, unless repelled, will continue to be furnished in all parts of the Union. So far as possible, the people everywhere shall have that sense of perfect security which is most favorable to calm thought and reflection. The course here indicated will be followed, unless current events and experience shall show a modification or change to be proper, and, in every case and exigency, my best discretion will be exercised, according to circumstances actually existing, and with a view and hope of a peaceful solution of the national troubles, and the restoration of fraternal sympathies and affections.

That there are persons in one section or another who seek to destroy the Union at all events, and are glad of any pretext to do it, I will neither affirm nor deny; but, if there be such, I need address no word to them. To those, however, who really love the Union, may I not speak?

Before entering upon so grave a matter as the destruction of our national fabric, with all its benefits, its memories, and its hopes, would it not be wise to ascertain precisely why we do it? Will you hazard so desperate a step while there is any possibility that any portion of the ills you fly from have no real existence? Will you, while the certain ills you fly to are greater than all the real ones you fly from? Will you risk the commission of so fearful a mistake? All profess to be content in the Union, if all constitutional rights can be maintained. Is it true, then, that any right, plainly written in the Constitution, has been denied? I think not. Happily the human mind is so constituted that no party can reach to the audacity of doing this. Think, if you can, of a single instance, in which a plainly-written provision of the Constitution has ever been denied?

If, by the mere force of numbers, a majority should deprive a minority of any clearly-written constitutional right, it might, in moral point of view, justify revolution—certainly would if such right were a vital one. But such is not our case. All the vital rights of minorities and of individuals are so plainly assured to them, by affirmation and negotiation, guarantees and provisions, in the Constitution, that controversies never arise concerning them. But no organic law can ever be framed with a provision specifically applicable to every question which may occur in practical administration. No foresight can anticipate, nor any document of reasonable length contain, express provisions for all possible questions. Shall fugitives from labor be surrendered by national or by State authority? The Constitution does not expressly say. *May* Congress prohibit slavery in the Territories? The Constitution does not expressly say. *Must* Congress protect slavery in the Territories? The Constitution does not expressly say.

From questions of this class spring all our controversies, as we divide upon them into majorities and minorities. If the minority will not acquiesce, the majority must, or the Government must cease. There is no other alternative; for continuing the Government is acquiescence on one side or the other. If a minority, in such case, will secede rather than acquiesce, they make a precedent which, in turn, will divide and ruin them; for a minority of their own will secede from them whenever a majority refuses to be controlled by such minority. For instance: why may not any portion of a new confederacy, a year or two hence, arbitrarily secede again, precisely as portions of the present Union now claim to secede from it? All who cherish disunion sentiments are now being educated to the exact temper of doing this. Is there such a perfect identity of interests among the Sates to compose a new Union as to produce harmony only, and prevent renewed secession? Plainly, the central idea of secession is the essence of anarchy. A majority held in restraint by constitutional checks and limitations, and always changing easily with deliberate changes of popular opinions and sentiments, is the only true sovereign of a free people. Whoever rejects it, does, of necessity, fly to anarchy or to despotism. Unanimity is impossible; the rule of a minority, as a permanent arrangement, is wholly inadmissible; so that, rejecting the majority principle, anarchy or despotism, in some form, is all that is left.

I do not forget the position assumed by some, that constitutional questions are to be decided by the Supreme Court; nor do I deny that such decisions must be binding in any case, upon the parties to a suit, as to the object of that suit, while they are also entitled to very high respect and consideration in all parallel cases by all other departments of the Government. And while it is obviously possible that such decision may be erroneous in any given case, still the evil effect following it being limited to that particular case, with the chance that it may be overruled, and never become a precedent for other cases, can better be borne than could the evils of a different practice. At the same time, the candid citizen must confess that if the policy of the Government upon vital questions effecting the whole people is to be irrevocably fixed by the decision of the Supreme Court, the instant they are made in ordinary litigation between parties in personal actions, the people will have ceased to be their own rulers, having, to that extent, practically resigned their Government into the hands of that eminent tribunal.

Nor is there in this view any assault upon the court or judges. It is a duty from which they may not shrink, to decide cases properly brought before them, and it is no fault of theirs if others seek to turn their decisions to political purposes. One section of the country believes slavery is *right*, and ought to be extended; while the other believes it is *wrong*, and ought not to be extended. This is the only substantial dispute. The fugitive slave clause of the Constitution and the law for the suppression of the foreign slave trade are each as well enforced, perhaps, as any law can be in a community where the moral sense of the people imperfectly supports the law itself. The great body of the people abide by the dry legal obligation in other cases, and a few break over in each. This, I think, cannot be perfectly cured; and it would be worse in both cases *after* the separation of the sections than before. The foreign slave trade, now imperfectly suppressed, would be ultimately revived without restriction, in one section; while fugitive slaves, now only partially surrendered, would not be surrendered at all by the other.

Physically speaking, we can not separate. We cannot remove our respective claims from each other, nor build an impassable wall between them. A husband and wife may be divorced, and go out of the presence and beyond the reach of each other; but the different parts of our country cannot do this. They cannot but remain face to face, and intercourse, either amicable or hostile, must continue between them. Is it possible, then, to make that intercourse more satisfactory, *after* separation than *before*? Can aliens make treaties easier than friends can make laws? Can treaties be more faithfully enforced between aliens than laws can among friends? Suppose you go to war: you cannot fight always; and when, after much loss on both sides, and no gain on either, you cease fighting, the identical old questions, as to terms of intercourse, are again upon you.

This country, with its institutions, belongs to the people who inhabit it. Whenever they shall grow weary of the existing Government, they can exercise their *constitutional* right of amending it, or their *revolutionary* right to dismember or overthrow it.

I cannot be ignorant of the fact that many worthy and patriotic citizens are desirous of having the national Constitution amended. While I make no recommendation of amendments, I fully recognize the rightful authority of the people over the whole subject, to be exercised in either of the modes prescribed in the instrument itself; and I should, under existing circumstances, favor, rather than oppose, a fair opportunity being afforded the people to act upon it.

I will venture to add, that to me the convention mode seems preferable, in that it allows amendments to originate with the people themselves, instead of only permitting them to take or reject propositions originated by others, not especially chosen for the purpose, and which might not be precisely such as they would wish to either accept or approve. I understand a proposed amendment to the Constitution, which amendment, however, I have not seen, has passed Congress, to the effect that the Federal Government shall never interfere with the domestic institutions of the States, including that of persons held to service.

To avoid misconstruction of what I have said, I depart from my purpose not to speak of particular amendments, so far as to say that, holding such a provision to now be implied constitutional law, I have no objection to its being made express and irrevocable. The Chief Magistrate derives all his authority from the people; and they have conferred none upon him to fix terms for the separation of the States. The people themselves can do this, also, if they choose; but the Executive, as such, has nothing to do with it. His duty is to administer the present Government, as it came to his hands, and to transmit it, unimpaired by him, to his successor. Why should there not be a patient confidence in the ultimate justice of the people? Is there any better or equal hope in the world? In our present difficulties, is either party without faith of being in the right? If the Almighty Ruler of nations, with His eternal truth and justice, be on your side of the North, or on your side of the South, that truth and that justice will surely prevail, by the judgment of this great tribunal—the American people.

By the frame of the Government under which we live, this same people have wisely given their public servants but little power to do mischief; and have, with equal wisdom, provided for the return of that little to their own hands at very short intervals. While the people retain their virtue and vigilance, no Administration, by any extreme of wickedness or folly, can very seriously injure the Government in the short space of four years.

My countrymen, one and all, think calmly and *well* upon this whole subject. Nothing valuable can be lost by taking time. If there be an object to hurry any of you, in hot haste, to a step which you will never take deliberately, that object will be frustrated by taking time; but no good object can be frustrated by it. Such of you as are now dissatisfied still have the old Constitution unimpaired; and, on the sensitive point, the laws of your own framing under it; while the new Administration will have no immediate power, if it would, to change either. If it were admitted that you, who are dissatisfied, hold the right side in dispute, there is still no single good reason for precipitate action. Intelligence, patriotism, Christianity, and a firm reliance on Him who has never yet forsaken this favored land, are still competent to adjust, in the best way, all our present difficulty. In your hands, my dissatisfied fellow-countrymen, and not in mine, is the momentous issue of civil war. The Government will not assail you. You can have no conflict without being yourselves the aggressors. You have no oath registered in Heaven to destroy the Government, while I shall have the most solemn one to "preserve, protect, and defend" it.

I am loath to close. We are not enemies, but friends. We must not be enemies. Though passion may have strained, it must not break, our bonds of affection. The mystic chords of memory, stretching from every battle-field and patriot grave to every living heart and hearthstone all over this broad land, will yet swell the chorus of Union, when again touched, as surely they will be, by the better angels of their nature.

[The oath of office was then administered to him by the Chief Justice of the Supreme Court, Roger Taney.]

Index